RESEARCH IN MARKETING

Volume 2 • 1979

RESEARCH IN MARKETING

A Research Annual

Editor: JAGDISH N. SHETH
Department of Business
Administration
University of Illinois

VOLUME 2 • 1979

 JAI PRESS INC.
Greenwich, Connecticut

CONTENTS

PREFACE

The research papers included in the second volume can be classified into four categories: social marketing, consumer behavior, marketing theory, and research methods.

Social Marketing. There are three contributors in this area. The research paper by Michael Belch and Robert Perloff is essentially a conceptual and methodological approach to promoting anticonsuming of certain products which the policy maker deems socially undesirable or personally harmful to the consumer. The basic proposition in their paper is that one must identify substitute products or behaviors so that the underlying need (biological or psychological) can be channeled toward socially more desirable alternatives. The emphasis in the paper is the development of a Products-Needs Matrix to obtain a better understanding of perceived substitutes for undesirable consumption objects. The procedure resembles to a considerable degree the earlier pioneering work of Volne Stefflre in the more traditional areas of market research.

Paul Bloom presents a very interesting and thoughtful analysis of the antitrust suit filed by the Federal Trade Commission against the big four cereal manufacturers in the United States. In many ways, the bases for the FTC's antitrust case seem to be the indictment of the marketing practices and syndicated market research. The implicit assumption is that the very large market share concen-

Research in Marketing—Volume 2, 1979, pages vii–x.
Copyright © 1979 by JAI Press Inc.
ISBN 0-89232-059-1

trated among these four cereals manufacturers is due to a tacit conspiracy and collusion which effectively blocks out competition from other smaller suppliers in the market place, rather than due to the exercise of free choice by consumers in the market place. Bloom critically examines many assumptions that FTC has made about the psychology of consumers in arriving at their conclusion. It is an extremely readable paper on a very important issue faced by the marketing practice.

The third research paper, by Thaddeus Spratlen, addresses the current issue of "redlining" in moneylending and insurance business especially related to mortagages on residential properties. After a thorough review of different perspectives on the redlining issue as well as examining its social and marketing welfare implications, Spratlen proposes a two-stage multivariate statistical research procedure. The first stage requires clustering of all census tracts into several clusters based on median income and house value criteria. Then, a search is made *within* a cluster to isolate those areas which have one third or more nonwhite population versus those which are predominantly white. Then, a discriminant analysis is performed using the standard loan application variables. The results are then compared with the actual decision by the loan company to either accept or reject the application.

It is concluded that many loan applications are turned down from the nonwhite neighborhoods even though the discriminant model based on standard financial application variables suggest that the mortgage loan be granted to the residential unit.

Consumer Behavior. There are four research papers in the consumer behavior area. The first paper is by Stephen Arnold and James Barnes. Utilizing the popular life-style battery (AIO scale) developed by Douglas Tigert and William Wells, they demonstrate similarities and differences between the American and Canadian people. In general, they find that Canadians are more permissive, less religious, less self-confident, less involved in interpersonal communication, less community-oriented, less convenience-oriented, and believe less in advertising. On the other hand, they are more inclined to city living, to traveling and flying, to buying private brand names and more home cleanliness. The authors then attempt to explain these differences in terms of environmental and cultural differences between the two countries.

Russell Belk presents an interesting research paper on gift-giving behavior which has not received as much attention in the marketing area. After identifying various functions performed by gift-giving behavior (social exchange, economic exchange, socializing, etc.), Belk utilizes the principles of balance theory from cognitive consistency area by identifying the gift giver, the gift receiver, and the gift itself as the tripod which must be consistent and congruent to provide stable balance over time.

John McElwee and Leonard Parsons present yet another refinement of the expectancy-value (or adequacy-importance) models of attitudes in consumer behavior. Their model, called the Parametric Marginal Desirability (PMD) model, differs from other varieties of attitude models with respect to three things: a curvilinear facing of the belief scale allowing for a nonmonotonic scale, dual ideal points on the belief scale (least and most desirable) and a purchase importance parameter. In a comparative analysis on the same data the PMD model performed much better than three alternative common formulations. This is attributed to the development of more realistic assumptions in the PMD model.

The last research paper in the consumer behavior area by William Wells and Fred Reynolds demonstrates the application of the popular life-style battery (AIO scale) in pinpointing the regional differences within the United States. The authors found some regional differences in activities, attitudes, interests and opinions. As expected, the South was more traditional, the West relatively more liberal, and the East more cosmopolitan and innovative. The expected characterizations of the Southwest and Midwest, however, were not supported by the analysis.

Marketing Theory. This area has three rather diverse research papers. Ernest Cadotte and Louis Stern propose a new model of interorganizational relations in marketing channels based on the processes of conflict and power management. They identify five stages of the process of interaction among channel members (manufacturers, wholesalers, retailers): conflict potential, dependence, conflict perception, resultant force, and conflict aftermath. The conceptual model is then transformed into a mathematical model which should enable other researchers to test it at least on a simulation basis. Their approach is uniquely behavioral and mathematically formal, which is a refreshing change from the traditional descriptive, anecdotal, and case history approaches to theorizing about channel relations.

A second research paper by Merle Crawford narrates the still evolving area of product audit system for corporate marketing planning. Basically, it is a planned approach to comparing the company's products with those of its competitors on a set of predefined criteria such as product attributes, market shares and profit margins. As Crawford points out, we need to know more about which companies are actually using a product audit system, what is the variety of methods adopted by these companies, where should it be housed in the organization and what role outside market research companies can play in standardizing and streamlining a general approach to product audit system. Furthermore, it seems interesting to speculate whether the public accounting companies will take the leadership in this area as they broaden their horizons from auditing strictly the financial and accounting aspects.

The last paper in the marketing theory area is by Alan Sawyer and Scott Ward on the age-old question of carry-over effects of advertising. After a thorough review of the area, especially from a behavioral viewpoint, they offer a number of propositions for marketing policy implications with respect to persistence of attitude change, attitude decay over time, and the specific marketing factors which are likely to be most effective in generating desired communication effects.

Research Methods and Models. This final category consists of two very different papers. The first paper, by Andrew Ehrenberg, is mostly a primer in a number of simple but highly useful rules of thumb for reorganization, rearrangement, and transformation of data to produce some meaningful inductive insights into the market realities. He proposes a total of six rules: rounding to two digits, row and and column averaging, column arrangements for comparative purposes, ordering rows or columns by size, spacing and layout aspects, and presentation of data in graphical forms as opposed to tables. While these rules may seem quite obvious, it is surprising that very few researchers and practitioners actually make use of them in their own work.

The second methodological paper, by Arun Jain and Vijaya Mahajan, is the application of multiplicative competitive interaction (MCI) model to understanding and evaluating retail competition. Based on the law of gravitation in physics, the model is an attempt to structure the relative attraction of each retail store to a block of residents as a function of such factors as distance (location), image, appearance, service, sales area within the store, and employee impressions. The model is tested using least squares procedures on a sample of data related to retail food store competition. As a further test of the model, the authors bring about a set of hypothetical changes in the relative competitive situation and measure their effects on a simulation basis. The MCI model is an attractive macro approach to understanding retail competition which has been otherwise dominated by micro-level consumer surveys.

In Conclusion. Volume 2 of *Research in Marketing* is an extension of the trend noticed in the first volume: marketing scholars are simultaneously researching across a very broad spectrum of problems and issues. The diversity of research efforts can be mapped by a three-dimensional space consisting of a micro-macro dimension, a behavioral-quantitative dimension, and a theoretical-empirical dimension.

The twelve research papers are once again presented in alphabetical order of first author names.

CANADIAN AND AMERICAN NATIONAL CHARACTER AS A BASIS FOR MARKET SEGMENTATION*

Stephen J. Arnold, QUEEN'S UNIVERSITY

James G. Barnes, MEMORIAL UNIVERSITY OF

NEWFOUNDLAND

I. INTRODUCTION

The problem motivating the program of research (Arnold and Tigert, 1974; Arnold and Barnes, 1976, 1977; Barnes and Arnold, 1975) which resulted in this particular paper was one of market segmentation. Several multinational firms

*This paper would not have been possible without the cooperation of Douglas J. Tigert, Faculty of Management Studies, University of Toronto, and the support and encouragement of Baker Lovick Limited, and in particular Wilf LaVigne, Senior Vice-President and Manager Toronto Operations; and Bob McAlear, Executive Vice-President and Creative Director.

Research in Marketing—Volume 2, 1979, pages 1–35.
ISBN 0-89232-059-1

1

straddle an essentially open border between Canada and the United States. In addition to considering nationalistic concerns, environmental differences related to relative market sizes, and length of distribution channels, management in these firms might wish to know if there are differences in Canadian and American national character that should be accounted for in marketing decisions. Are differences so great as to justify differentiation and a subsequent excess of marginal benefits over marginal costs? Or, are the differences in national character so slight, or even nonexistent, that the same marketing strategy can be efficiently followed in both countries?

Some examples illustrate these questions and the basic problem. Warner-Lambert experienced a successful introduction of throat lozenges in the United States with a specific product, price, distribution and promotion package (Von Lanzenauer, 1975). The Canadian management team had to determine whether they should adopt the successful U.S. decision package or whether they should make changes to reflect a different country and people.

Another example occurred when Kodak introduced its instant photography cameras and films to the North American market (Dunlop, 1976). For this introduction, Kodak's Canadian regular advertising agency was replaced by J. Walter Thompson, the U.S. agency, for what appeared to be a coordinated North American introduction. Did the advertising produced by the U.S. agency for Canada perform as well as advertising that might have been created by the regular Canadian agency?

Two points of view characterize answers to the questions posed in these examples. On the one hand, there are those who argue that evidence of differences implies different marketing strategies. In a comparison of Canada, the United States, Australia and Britain, Sommers and Kernan (1967), for example, identified differences in the value orientations of the four countries. They then argued that these dissimilarities cause differences in the activities that people perform, including product evaluation and purchase. Such differences, therefore, should be taken into account in formulating a marketing strategy. To the extent that the differences are recognized or ignored, the products will flourish or fail. A similar position was taken by Arnold and Barnes (1977) and Beckman (1977).

The other point of view is expressed by those who argue that a focus upon differences tends to deemphasize the similarities that exist between countries as well as minimize the differences that exist within a country. Douglas (1976, p. 12), for example, argued that multinational firms look for opportunities where "production skills or marketing expertise developed in one country can be exploited on a wider scale, by marketing similar products or to similar market segments in other countries." Furthermore, she argued, studies indicate considerable heterogeneity within a country and consequently, " 'national' consumer stereotypes are unlikely to be particularly meaningful or useful."

In considering both points of view, it is not clear that either one can be adopted without further evidence. In principle, the firm should continue to differentiate its marketing strategy until the marginal benefits of the segmentation equal the marginal costs (Frank et al., 1972, pp. 190, 203). Any planning, therefore, must include not only identification and consideration of any differences but also estimates of the expected costs and revenues of such differentiation.

One step taken in order to help solve this problem of Canada/U.S. market segmentation is the subject of this paper. Within a deterministic framework, origins of and differences in Canadian and American national characters as described in the comparative literature are first reviewed. Data from comparable surveys conducted in Canada and the United States are then examined for differences and similarities. Various difficulties with the comparison are also discussed.

II. RESEARCH FRAMEWORK

The perspective for the research program undertaken in order to consider this problem in market segmentation has been an extension of what LeVine (1973) classified as the anticulture-personality model. This model is essentially a rationalist point of view where the normal individual, motivated to maximize his rewards and minimize his risks, first appraises and then adapts to his environment as he believes is necessary. Differences between individuals of different environments are thus interpreted as not due to differences in individual psyches but instead traced to differences in the ecological, institutional, and ideological conditions to which the individual must adapt in order to survive. Survival here does not only mean escape from starvation or death but also "social survival" which refers to the maintenance and enhancement of career, reputation, status, and the esteem of others.

The adaptation of individuals to an environment may be further described. For example, it is possible to identify the emergence of "national character" which Inkeles and Levinson (1968, p. 482) defined as "enduring personality characteristics and patterns that are modal among the adult members of the society." From a trait-theoretic perspective, these "characteristics and patterns" appear to be continuums over which individuals are distributed. For individuals of one nation, national character is then their average or mean position.

National character also is actual or descriptive behavior. It can be contrasted to the collection of prescriptive or normative beliefs which collectively are referred to as "culture."

III. OBSERVATIONS FROM THE COMPARATIVE LITERATURE

A review of the comparative literature (Barnes and Arnold, 1975) identified differences between Canadians and Americans in their environments and national character that appear to have implications for market segmentation.

A. Environment

The two environments of Canada and the United States are first differentiated by the population distributions. In Canada, there is a sparse population spread over a long east-west corridor north of the U.S./Canada border. The U.S. population, in contrast, is densely spread over the continental United States and is ten times larger than that of Canada.

Different historical developments, such as the evolutionary nature of Canada and the revolutionary nature of the United States, also characterize the two countries. Lipset (1963), for example, identified the "frontier development" which in the United States was completed by individuals and private enterprise. In Canada, the west was opened by the government in the form of the North-West Mounted Police and the military. Thus, the United States is said to be characterized by the "cowboy" and Canada by the "Mountie."

Other differences in development are described in the comparative literature. A primarily British immigration brought to Canada Tory values as well as inclinations toward particular forms of the church, government and educational institutions. Clark (1950, p. 385) also noted that British colonial status led to land grants and political preferments and a subsequent strong aristocracy. A privileged and hence loyal and conservative elite was further enhanced by appointments in government and the military.

In contrast, the United States was said to have experienced a more heterogeneous immigration. A greater sense of experimentation and a more democratic movement also allowed emancipation from traditional values. A higher proportion of students in educational institutions in the United States experienced a more vocational, technical and professional emphasis. In comparison, the smaller proportion in Canada training for political leadership experienced a greater emphasis on scholarship (Vallee and Whyte, 1968, p. 837).

Still another difference noted by the same authors (ibid., p. 840) was the earlier and greater industrialization in the United States. The result was greater role specialization and hence a stronger need to find common criteria by which to judge other people. The "American way" and "melting pot" could be consequently contrasted to the Canadian "mosaic."

B. National Character

1. Collectivist-individualist. The comparative literature suggests that these differences in environment are antecedent to and consequences of several differences in national character. First, Canadians are said to be more collectivist and to conform more to the defined interests of the larger group. Wrong (1955, p. 29), for example, noted that the frontier experience in Canada meant little opposition to growing involvement such as evidenced today by a stronger control of social welfare programs and economic and cultural affairs. In contrast, Americans are said to be more individualistic and place greater value on the right of each individual to define his own destiny.

2. Elitist-egalitarian. It has also been suggested that the frontier experience and British immigration have led to Canadians being more elitist and Americans more egalitarian. According to Lipset (1963), Vallee and Whyte (1968, p. 386), Wrong (1955, pp. 24, 25), Naegele (1961, p. 27) and Clark (1950, p. 385), Canadians are more prepared to defer to formally constituted authority such as the Crown and government as well as the higher echelons of social class, family and established leadership. Americans, on the other hand, are said to believe more in the equality of all men and to be more resistant to hereditary class differences. Americans are more rebellious and show more animosity toward authority.

3. Ascriptive/achievement-oriented. A third national character difference also related to the frontier experience is that Canadians are said to be more ascriptive and Americans more achievement-oriented. Lipset (1963, p. 38), for example, noted that Canadians accept sex, family background, race, age and ethnic background as placing limitations upon success. Americans, in contrast, accept individual performance and believe more that hard work, frugality, self-discipline and individual initiative are the only limitations upon achievement.

4. Particularistic-universalistic. A related national character trait is the particularistic-universalistic continuum. Ethnic background, social class and other unique characteristics to Canadians not only limit success but are also indicative of it (Lipset, 1965, p. 55). Americans, on the other hand, look for a general or universal standard to apply to all (Vallee and Whyte, 1968, p. 840).

5. Non-American/ethnocentric. A fifth national character trait arises, at least for Canadians, out of early concerns for U.S. expansion, and inherent diversity which made self-definition difficult, and a relative geographic proximity to the United States (Porter, 1971, pp. 2, 3). Canadians are said to be non- or anti-American. They tend to be defensive against American things, are ready to find fault, and gloat over American failures. If it can be considered a contrast, it is suggested that Americans are more ethnocentric.

6. Conservative/risk-taker. The church, elite, Tory values and frontier experience are linked to another national character trait. Canadians are said to be more conservative while Americans are greater risk-takers. Canadians are more cautious, restrained, reserved, sober and unimaginative according to Dhalla (1966, p. 308), Hutchinson (1954, p. 43), Goodis (1972, pp. 50, 51) and Naegele (1961, pp. 27, 29). Americans, it is suggested, hesitate less to take risks and are more impulsive and self-confident. Other differences characterized by their frequency of observation are that Canadians are also said to be more morally conservative (Lipset, 1965, p. 64) and financially conservative (Wrong, 1955, p. 209).

C. Validity

If these differences between Canadians and Americans as described in the comparative literature are in fact valid, they may have several implications for the market segmentation problem such as suggested by Sommers and Kernan (1967) and others. On the other hand, if the differences do not exist, segmentation based upon these observations may be both unnecessary and unwise. The method of derivation of these differences suggests at least consideration of this latter possibility.

According to Vallee and Whyte (1968, p. 836), "sociologists who have written on national character and values in Canada have based their conclusions on impressions, introspection, and on inferences from such disparate sources as literature, historical developments and statistics on a variety of subjects." However, the difficulty with this approach, according to Truman (1971) and Romalis (1966) is that the observer has a wide variety of evidence from which to pick and choose and that even the same evidence can lead to different conclusions. For example, Truman (1971) suggested that greater government influence in Canada was not so much the result of deference to an elite but simply the consequence of a desire on the part of Canadians for a better life. As a consequence, further evidence is needed.

According to Inkeles and Levinson (1968, p. 425), a valid study of national character requires an empirical base which means "the psychological investigation of adequately large and representative samples of persons studied individually." A further characteristic of the comparative literature, however, is a dearth of empirical survey-type studies upon which to base the observations. Naegele (1961), for example, in discussing conservatism did not examine per capita stock holdings or venture capital investment. Neither did Horne (1961) compare credit purchasing statistics. Lipset (1963, p. 521) recognized the lack of data but he too depended upon "impressionistic evidence" to support his thesis. "To demonstrate that such differences really exist would involve considerable research."

In those instances where survey research was in fact done, it appears to have involved comparisons between groups of students. Rokeach (1974), for example, compared students at the University of Western Ontario with students at Michigan State University in order to make observations about Canadian-American differences. Similarly, Williams (1975) compared alumae from the University of British Columbia and the University of Washington.

The conclusion is that empirical studies based upon survey data from national samples are necessary in order to produce valid comparative evidence about Canadian and American national character. The method of assessment, according to Inkeles and Levinson (1968, pp. 452, 456) includes the "personality assessment of individuals'' which they further subdivided to include measurement of the ''attitude-value complex.''

Arnold and Barnes (1976) have consequently proposed a comparative study of Canadians and Americans based upon surveys of attitudes and values. As a preliminary step to this study, however, a reanalysis of some available survey data was conducted in order to test aspects of the survey method as well as some of the observations from the comparative literature. The remainder of this paper describes this analysis and the results.

IV. METHODOLOGY

A. U.S. Sample

In Fall 1968, questionnaires were mailed to two panels of the Market Facts, Inc. Consumer Mail Panel. One panel was composed of 1,000 female homemakers who were asked in the questionnaire to indicate their level of disagreement or agreement over a six-point scale to 300 items concerned with activities, interests and opinions (the attitude-value complex). In addition, each panel member was asked to respond to approximately 170 questions concerning product usage, 55 questions concerning magazine readership, and 45 questions concerning occupational choice. A variety of socioeconomic and demographic information had already been provided by each member when she joined the panel.

A postage-paid return envelope and promise of a ''nice gift'' was included with each questionnaire. Of the 1,000 female panel members, 857 returned usable questionnaires. This group of respondents formed the American female sample for the analysis.

A similar questionnaire was sent to another panel composed of 1,200 male heads of households. As in the female questionnaire, each respondent was asked to express his level of agreement with 300 items. Approximately one quarter of the items in the male questionnaire, however, were different from those in the female questionnaire. In addition, 130 questions were concerned with product usage and 55 questions with magazine readership.

With the same incentives as the female questionnaire, 986 males returned usable questionnaires. This group formed the American male sample for the analysis.

The method of constructing and maintaining a mail panel has been described elsewhere (Boyd and Westfall, 1970). Although random sampling is the basis for selection in the initial stages of panel construction, a claim for representation is based upon selective sampling in the later stages. The objective is to match the panel's socioeconomic, demographic and regional characteristics with those of census data. For example, in describing the Consumer Mail Panel as of January 1973, a Market Facts, Inc. (1973) brochure demonstrated that the 45,000 panel households matched the U.S. Census and a "Sales Management Survey of Buying Power" on geographic division, total annual household income, population density, degree of urbanization, and age of panel member. Comparisons, however, were made in this study between the sample and equivalent census data on their age, income, education and geographic distributions.

B. Canada Sample

One and one-half years after data collection in the United States, a similar questionnaire was administered in Canada. Instead of data collection with a mail panel, however, the data were collected in a two-stage survey known as Trendtape 3, administered by Research Interviewing Services of Toronto.

The first stage of this survey was completed via personal, in-home interviews conducted among 6,100 respondents. The data collected during this first stage were related to product and brand usage.

The sampling plan used to select the Canadian respondents was designed by Marketmath, Inc., New York. The population was defined to be all persons aged 18 years and older in Canadian urban centers excluding those in the Yukon and Northwest territories. In the design, "primary sampling units" (Kish, 1965, p. 155) were assigned a fixed number of starting points with cluster sizes fixed at ten. Starting points were selected from telephone directories and the clusters developed using the method of "half-open intervals from random starts" (ibid., p. 56). No callbacks were made.

The second stage of the survey was accomplished with a second questionnaire that was left with each respondent for later completion and return by mail. In this questionnaire, each respondent was asked to indicate level of agreement with 300 statements of which approximately 250 were common to the U.S. questionnaires. In addition, each male respondent was asked to complete 30 product usage and 80 television program questions. The female questionnaire was similar except that there were 60 product usage questions and a slightly different set of 300 items.

Completion of the second questionnaire was encouraged through the use of a prepaid self-addressed envelope and a gift wallet worth $5. Under these incentives, approximately 4,100 respondents returned the questionnaire.

Of the 4,100 respondents cooperating in the second stage of the survey, approximately 24 percent completed the French-language version. Because Tigert (1973) found that French and English Canadians differed significantly in their responses to the 300 items, the French-language questionnaires were not further considered. The questionnaires from respondents who were not heads of households were also not considered in order to make the American and Canadian samples more directly comparable. Of the English-speaking respondents, 1,859 females and 816 males were identified as being either the male or female head of household. These respondents formed the Canadian male and female samples for the comparative analysis. These samples were also compared with census data on the age, income, education and geographic distributions.

C. Separate Male and Female Analyses

The 4,518 respondents in the two surveys were first divided on the basis of sex into a male sample (N = 1,802) and a female sample (N = 2,716). Subsequent steps in this comparative analysis were conducted separately on each sample.

Three reasons dictated the parallel analyses. One reason was that Tyler (1965, pp. 273–298) described sex differences in several of the areas being considered in the questionnaires used in this study. In that the Canadian sample had more than twice as many females as males, an analysis conducted on a combined male and female file would tend to identify differences between Canadians and Americans that were due to sex rather than national character.

A second reason for the separate analyses of the male and female samples is that a number of the items were not common to both the male and female questionnaires. Conducting a combined analysis would tend to result in lower reliability coefficients in scale construction because of the smaller number of common items available for each scale.

A third reason for the separate analyses is that the separation effectively permits a split-half test for reliability. In other words, nearly all scales are common to both sexes. While the absolute level of agreement might differ in the male and female samples, the relative position of Canadians and Americans on any item or scale should remain the same in both the male and female samples if, in fact, there are major differences in national character.

D. Robustness of the *t*-test

The basis for the Canadian and American comparison was the differences in agreement exhibited by each sample on each one of the 330 items. Each item was a simple statement to which each respondent either definitely disagreed ("1"), generally disagreed ("2"), moderately disagreed ("3"), moderately agreed ("4"), generally agreed ("5"), or definitely agreed ("6").

Statistical comparisons on data of this nature would probably best be made with nonparametric procedures such as the Kolmogorov-Smirnov test for differences (Siegel, 1956). However, a Kolmogorov-Smirnov test of all items in both files was found impractical because of the available computer technology. The nature of the test, such as its need to contain all data for an item in core, meant impossibly high processing costs. As a result, the *t*-test was considered as a possible alternative.

In order to use the parametric *t*-test, it is necessary to assume that the data are interval as opposed to ordinal in nature. The *t*-test also assumes normality in the underlying distributions as well as common variance. In that Winer (1971, p. 38) suggested that the *t*-test is robust under departures from some of the assumptions, an analysis was completed in order to determine the performance of the test on the data used in this study.

More specifically, the first ten items in the female file as well as the six items that comprised the "weight conscious" scale were first identified as items where the Canadian and American samples showed a wide range of similarities and differences in response patterns. A Kolmogorov-Smirnov statistic was computed for each item and used to test the null hypothesis of no difference. A two-tailed *t*-test was then made of the difference between sample means on each item. The null hypothesis that the two samples were drawn from the same population was rejected if the *t*-statistic was significant at the 0.001 level. A comparison was then made of the two sets of results.

E. Scaling of Items

One feature of the data analyzed in this study is the large sample size. As described earlier, 1,838 respondents were from the United States and 2,675 respondents were from Canada.

One characteristic of a large sample is that any standard error is extremely small, as can be determined by looking at any formulae. The effect is that even a small difference between the mean levels of agreement in two samples over- whelms the standard error of this difference and causes the investigator to con- clude that the two samples are from different populations.

It was observed in this study that differences significant at the 0.001 level are observed in over one-half of the items. Are Canadians and Americans indeed different in many ways or is this result some statistical artifact that results from the large sample size and the large number of items?

As is well known, "significant" differences due only to sampling error can be accounted for by considering "consistency." By consistency, it is meant that items indicative of the same construct are examined simultaneously before any conclusion is reached about a difference. If indeed there is a difference, then most if not all items applicable to the construct should reflect the difference.

The approach taken to test for consistency was to "scale" the items, whereby scores on items common to the same construct were first combined into an aggregate score.

The allocation of each of several hundred items to a scale was based upon several sources of information. One source was Wells and Tigert (1971) who factor-analyzed a large proportion of the items used in this study and indicated how they could be combined into scales. Other sources were unpublished studies which used the items and indicated how they could be sorted into areas of similar content. In fact, "similar content" was the primary criterion in the initial stages of scale construction in this study.

The other criterion for scale construction in this study was the internal consistency of the items. Items were deleted where the average correlation with the other items tended to fall below 0.15. Where doubt remained, the reliability coefficient, r_{kk} (Nunnally, 1967, p. 194) was calculated both with and without the item. The scale with the higher reliability coefficient was selected.

The scale score for each respondent was calculated by simple addition or subtraction of each item score depending upon whether the item positively or negatively reflected the trait title.

F. Sample Comparisons

The two samples were compared on the scale scores as well as on the individual item scores. It was concluded that Canadians and Americans differed if the computed two-tailed t-statistic was significant at the 0.001 level.

In order to meet the assumption of the t-test of common variance, the null hypothesis of $\sigma_1^2 = \sigma_2^2$ was tested by performing an F-test on the sample variances. When the F-statistic was significant at the 0.001 level, the hypothesis was rejected and an approximation to the t-statistic was calculated using a separate variance estimate as described by Nie et al. (1975). Otherwise the t-statistic was calculated using the standard pooled variance estimate procedure. The latter procedure was applicable in about 95 percent of the tests.

G. Age Difference

The Canadian female sample was younger on average than the U.S. sample. If this age difference between samples was significant, it is likely that it would create differences between the samples' responses to the items. As observed by Tyler (1965), advancing age may be associated with more conservatism in attitudes and behavior. Many of the items used in the study reflected facets of conservatism and other traits that apparently correlate with age. As a consequence, it was necesssary to determine if the differences between Canadians and Americans observed in this study were a result of this age difference rather than inherent differences in national character.

The approach taken in this study to check for the age effect was to conduct a series of multiple regressions. In each regression, the scale variable was regressed against the age variable as well as a nationality variable coded "1" if the respondent was Canadian or "0" otherwise. It was concluded that Canadians and Americans differed if the F-statistic for the nationality regression coefficient was significant at the 0.005 level.

H. Intranational vs. International Differences

Another problem considered in this analysis was the notion suggested by Douglas (1976) that marketers should be more concerned with regional differences *within* each of these countries than with differences *between* the two national markets. The suggestion is that consumers in British Columbia are probably quite different from those in Ontario and, in fact, probably more similar to consumers in Oregon and Washington. Similarly, consumers in the Atlantic provinces probably bear greater similarity to New Englanders than they do to consumers in other parts of Canada. If there is any attempt at geographical segmentation of English-speaking North America, a scheme more appropriate than one based on nationality would be to construct North-South segments.

It would certainly appear possible that segments constructed from states and provinces on the Atlantic seaboard, in the Midwest, or on the Pacific coast might each demonstrate greater homogeneity than a segment made up of all American states or another segment made up of all Canadian provinces. Geography is a well-recognized determinant of culture and national character. The suggestion here, however, is that the most efficient method of grouping all Canadian provinces and continental American states whenever there are only two segments is by following national boundaries. In other words, it is not believed possible to group the states and provinces into any two segments where the ratio of between-group over within-group differences is better maximized than in the two segments based upon nationality.

A partial test of this hypothesis was made by first constructing East and West groupings of all 4,518 respondents in the sample. In the test, the East segment included the respondents in and east of the province or states of Ontario, Wisconsin, Illinois, Kentucky, Tennessee, and Mississippi.[1] These two groups would then be compared on the basis of their scale scores and the results compared with the groupings based on national boundaries. The more efficient segmentation would be the scheme with the greater number of t-statistics significant at the 0.001 level.

I. National Versus Regional Differences

The notion that there is probably more within-country variance than between-country variance was also explored in this study. In other words, Douglas (1976) and others might argue that even if significant differences are identified between Canada and the United States, the variations within each country are far greater. As a result, any differentiation in marketing or communications must either reflect this reality or no difference at all. A compromise two-segment Canadian-American differentiation would simply not reflect this variation and would be an inefficient use of resources.

At least a partial test of this notion was made by answering the following question. On those scales with significant national differences, are there also significant regional variations? This question was answered as follows. Respondents in the Canadian sample were divided into five groups according to whether the individual resided in the Atlantic provinces (Newfoundland, Nova Scotia,

Prince Edward Island, New Brunswick), Quebec, Ontario, the Prairie provinces (Alberta, Saskatchewan, Manitoba), or British Columbia. Similarly, the Americans were divided into nine groups according to whether the respondent was from the New England states (Connecticut, Maine, Massachusetts, New Hampshire, Rhode Island, Vermont), Middle Atlantic (New Jersey, New York, Pennsylvania), East North Central (Illinois, Indiana, Michigan, Ohio, Wisconsin), West North Central (Iowa, Kansas, Minnesota, Mississippi, Nebraska, South Dakota, North Dakota), South Atlantic (Delaware, District of Columbia, Florida, Georgia, Maryland, South Carolina, North Carolina, Virginia, West Virginia), East South Central (Alabama, Kentucky, Mississippi, Tennessee), West South Central (Arkansas, Louisiana, Oklahoma, Texas), Mountain (Arizona, Colorado, Idaho, Montana, Nevada, New Mexico, Utah, Wyoming) or Pacific states (California, Oregon, Washington).

In each national sample, an analysis of variance was conducted and the regional variations declared important if the F-statistic was significant at the 0.001 level. Thus, if regional variation was more important than the national variation, the analysis should indicate at least as many significant statistics over regions as there are between the two countries.

V. RESULTS AND DISCUSSION

A. Sample-Census Comparisons

The correspondence between the U.S. samples and their respective populations on age, income, education and geography can be observed in Tables 1 through 4. There do not appear to be any consistent differences between the samples and the population with respect to age. The U.S. samples, however, appear to overrepresent the middle-income group and appear to underrepresent the lowest educational category. The geographical distributions appear representative, but the American sample under-represents the black population.[2]

A comparison of the Canadian male and female sample distributions with that of the census can also be observed in Tables 1 through 4. No pattern of difference with respect to age is evident although the sample does appear to underrepresent the lower income group. The lower educational segments are underrepresented and there is evidence of overrepresentation of the populations of the Prairie provinces.

Overall, then, the Canadian and American comparative analysis described here is in fact a comparison of the English-speaking, white, adult middle class of Canada and the United States.

In comparing the demographic/socioeconomic distributions of the two samples, it is observed that the Canadian female sample is younger than the U.S. female sample and that the American samples exhibit a higher education level

Table 1. Age Distribution of Samples and Populations

	Males				Females			
	Canada		U.S.A.		Canada		U.S.A.	
Age	Sample	Census[1]	Sample	Census[2]	Sample	Census	Sample	Census
20–24	9.5%	14.6%	14.0%	12.5%	13.5%	14.2%	10.9%	12.2%
25–34	26.2	22.6	20.3	20.0	27.3	21.6	19.6	18.8
35–44	22.8	19.9	22.7	19.8	25.3	18.8	22.6	18.8
45–54	16.3	17.5	21.3	19.0	17.5	17.5	20.3	18.5
55+	25.2	25.4	21.7	28.7	16.4	27.9	26.6	31.7
	100.0%	100.0%	100.0%	100.0%	100.0%	100.0%	100.0%	100.0%
	(N = 816)	6,457,430	984	58,056,000	1859	6,615,605	854	64,049,000

[1]Canadian census percentages adapted from *Population: Age Groups 1971 Census of Canada*, 92–715 (Ottawa: Statistics Canada, April 1973), pp. 7-1, 7-2.

[2]U.S. census percentages adapted from *Statistical Abstract of the U.S.*: 1969, 90th ed.. (Washington, D.C.: U.S. Bureau of the Census, 1969), p. 10, "All Classes."

Table 2.   Household Income Distribution of Samples and Populations[1]

Household Income	Males				Females			
	Canada		U.S.A.		Canada		U.S.A.	
	Sample	Census[2]	Sample	Census[3]	Sample	Census	Sample	Census
Less than $5,000	16.6%	24.8%	16.2%	20%	17.0%	24.8%	22.7%	20%
$5,000–$9,999	46.4	41.8	44.5	34	47.8	41.8	41.1	34
$10,000 or more	37.0	33.4	39.3	46	35.2	33.4	36.2	46
	100.0%	100.0%	100.0%	100.0%	100.0%	100.0%	100.0%	100.0%
	(N = 730)	8,085,000	984	51,237,000	1,528	8,085,000	854	51,237,000)

[1]Census data not distinguished by sex of respondent.
[2]Canadian census percentages from *Income Distributions by Size in Canada: 1969, 13–544* (Ottawa: Statistics Canada, April 1972), p. 25, Table 3. "Percentage Distribution of Families by Income Groups, Employment Status and Sex of Head, 1969," "Total."
[3]U.S. census percentages from *Statistical Abstract of the U.S.: 1971*, 92nd edition (Washington, D.C.: U.S. Bureau of the Census, 1971), p. 316, Table No. 500, "All Families 1969."

Table 3. Education Distribution of Samples and Populations

	Males				Females			
	Canada		U.S.A		Canada		U.S.A.	
Education	Sample	Census[1]	Sample[2]	Census[3]	Sample	Census	Sample	Census
Grade school or less	18.8%	39.5%	5.6%	31.1%	14.7%	36.2%	7.3%	28.6%
Some high school	29.2	44.0	15.8	17.0	33.1	51.2	14.5	18.2
High school graduate	15.1	4.1	42.1	28.9	21.1	4.7	40.1	35.7
Some college	23.6	5.7	23.8	9.8	24.0	4.9	23.8	9.5
College graduate	13.3	6.8	12.7	13.3	7.1	3.0	14.3	8.0
	100.0%	100.0%	100.0%	100.0%	100.0%	100.0%	100.0%	100.0%
	(N = 815)	6,161,340	981	50,510,000	1,859	6,426,855	853	55,959,000)

[1]Adapted from Population: The Out-of-School Population, 1971 Census of Canada pamphlet, 92–743 (Ottawa: Statistics Canada, July 1974), pp. 4-1, 4-2, Table 4. "Population 15 years and over, not attending school full-time by level of Schooling, Showing Age Groups and Sex, Canada, 1971, categories "20–24" to "65+" only. The census descriptors "Less than Grade 5," and "Grades 5–8" were equated to the category "Grade School or less"; "Grades 9-10," "Grade 11" and "Grade 12" to "Some high school"; "Grade 13" to "High School Graduates"; "University without degree" to "Some College" and "University with degree" to "college graduate."

[2]The educational categories used in the U.S. questionnaire were "Went to elementary or grammar school only," "Went to vocational or trade school or went to high school for less than four years," "Graduated from high school but did not go on with additional schooling," "Completed less than four years of college," and "Completed four or more years of college."

[3]Adapted from Statistical Abstract of the United States: 1969 (Washington, D.C.: U.S. Bureau of the Census, 1969), p. 106, Table No. 152, "Persons 25 years and over, 1968."

Table 4.   Geographical Distribution of Samples and Populations

Region	Males		Females	
	Sample	Census[1]	Sample	Census
Canada (English Speaking)				
Atlantic provinces	9.7%	13.6%	6.9%	13.6%
Quebec	4.8	6.1	4.6	6.1
Ontario	40.6	46.1	39.8	46.1
Prairie provinces	32.3	20.2	34.0	20.2
British Columbia	12.6	14.0	14.7	14.0
	100.0%	100.0%	100.0%	100.0%
	(N = 816	12,942,157	1,859	12,942,157)
United States				
New England	5.4%	5.5%	6.3%	5.9%
Middle Atlantic	19.5	16.0	19.2	17.2
East North Central	19.4	17.8	20.2	18.6
West North Central	9.5	7.6	8.6	8.0
South Atlantic	14.4	11.9	13.7	12.4
East South Central	6.0	5.0	5.7	5.2
West South Central	9.2	8.0	9.5	8.3
Mountain	3.7	4.0	3.9	4.1
Pacific	12.9	12.4	12.9	12.7
	100.0%	100.0%	100.0%	100.0%
	(N = 984)		(N = 854)	

[1]Canadian Census percentages adopted from *Canada Year Book 1973* (Ottawa: Information Canada, 1973), p. 214, Table 5.17, "1971," "English" (data is for both sexes). American census percentages from *Statistical Abstract of the U.S.: 1971,* (Washington, D.C.: U.S. Bureau of the Census, 1971), p. 28, Table 28.

than the Canadian samples. The male samples, however, are comparable in age as are both male and female samples on household income.

These sample demographic and socioeconomic differences are probably not sources of bias to the extent they parallel census differences as is evident in the age distributions. In such cases, differences observed in national character may partially be a result of this demographic difference as well as the environmental differences earlier described. Nonetheless, they are still "real" differences.

To the extent that the sample distributions on education do not parallel the census distributions, the observed differences in national character may in fact reflect some complicated interaction between "real" differences, differences due to the socioeconomic factor, and differences due to different methods of data collection. Some degree of caution is consequently in order in interpreting the remainder of the results.

B. Robustness of the *t*-Test

Table 5 lists the *t* and Kolmogorov-Smirnov statistics for each of the test items as well as the associated significance levels. As can be observed in Table 5, there

Table 5.   Comparison of *t* and Kolmogorov–Smirnov Tests
for Sample Differences

Item	*t* Statistic	Kolmogorov–Smirnov Statistic
1. I like gardening	−1.85	.90
2. I spend a lot of time with my children talking about their activities, friends and problems	−.48	.26
3. I would rather listen to classical music than popular music.	.21	.70
4. A house should be dusted and polished at least 3 times a week.	−7.08***	3.74***
6.† I am or have been active in the PTA.	12.84***	5.71***
7. I do not get enough sleep.	2.33*	.95
8. I enjoy going to concerts.	−.57	.92
9. Before going shopping, I sit down and prepare a complete shopping list.	3.79***	1.92***
10. A woman's place is in the home.	−1.18	.97
59. I am careful what I eat in order to keep my weight under control.	1.80	.80
111. I eat more than I should.	5.77***	2.53***
149. I am too heavy.	4.46***	2.00***
160. During the warm weather, I drink low-calorie soft drinks several times a week.	14.49***	6.72***
232. I have used Metrecal or other diet foods at least one meal a day.	10.00***	4.98***
258. I buy more low-calorie foods than the average housewife.	7.29***	4.18***

***Significant at the 0.001 level.
** Significant at the 0.01 level.
* Signficant at the 0.05 level.
† Item 5 not included in American questionnaire.

is a direct, monotonic relationship between the *t* and Kolmogorov-Smirnov statistics. In addition, the null hypothesis of no difference between the populations is rejected at the 0.001 level using the *t*-test on the same items which resulted in the null being rejected using the Kolmogorov-Smirnov test. It was concluded that the *t*-test would be suitable for the comparative analysis.

C. Scaling Results

Nunnally (1967) suggests that scales comprising agree-disagree type of items will normally contain at least 15 items in order to attain reasonable reliability. As indicated in Tables 6 through 10, however, approximately 75 percent of the scales contained five or fewer items. No scale contained more than twelve items.

Table 6. Generalized Attitudes

Scale	Sex of Sample	Number of Items in Scale	r_{kk}	t Statistic	National Sample Significantly Characterized on Scale
Nonpermissive	F	5	.5	9.4***	U.S.
Nonpermissive	M	12	.7	12.6***	U.S.
Oriented toward women's liberation	M	4	.5	6.3***	C
Religious	M	4	.7	14.0***	U.S.
Oriented toward unaffected women	F	3	.5	7.0***	U.S.
Routine-oriented	F	2	.5	3.0**	—
Security-oriented	F	4	.4	2.1*	—
Security-oriented	M	5	.5	0.2	—
Skeptical	M	4	.5	4.2***	U.S.
Worrier	F	9	.7	2.6**	—
Worrier	M	9	.6	1.4	—
Optimistic about the future	F	3	.6	0.1	—
Optimistic about the future	M	4	.6	0.1	—
Self-confident	F	4	.6	4.4***	U.S.
Self-confident	M	6	.6	2.5*	—
Opinion leader	F	4	.6	11.4***	U.S.
Opinion leader	M	6	.7	6.3***	U.S.
Interpersonal communicator	F	7	.8	9.0***	U.S.
Interpersonal communicator	M	3	.5	4.2***	U.S.
Socializer-cosmopolitan	F	10	.7	6.8***	C
Socializer-cosmopolitan	M	8	.7	8.4***	C
Liquor user	F	2	.6	2.7**	—
Liquor user	M	6	.7	7.3***	C
Community-oriented	F	6	.7	12.5***	U.S.
Community-oriented	M	5	.7	3.5***	U.S.
City-oriented	F	2	.7	7.3***	C
City-oriented	M	2	.7	7.4***	C
Mobile	F	2	.5	2.9**	—
Mobile	M	2	.4	2.4*	—
Judges by appearance	M	2	.4	0.6	—
Oriented toward more education	M	2	.3	12.2***	U.S.

Note: ***significant at the 0.001 level
  **significant at the 0.01 level
   *significant at the 0.05 level

Table 7. Generalized Activities

Scale	Sex of Sample	Number of Items in Scale	r_{kk}	t Statistic	National Sample Significantly Characterized on Scale
Enjoys fine arts	F	5	.8	1.0	—
Enjoys fine arts	M	4	.7	2.4*	—
Sports observer	F	4	.8	4.7***	U.S.
Sports observer	M	3	.7	4.2***	U.S.
Oriented toward the outdoors	M	6	.7	1.2	—
Oriented toward flying	M	3	.6	2.1*	—
A craftsman	M	4	.6	5.0***	U.S.
Follows the news	M	2	.4	1.1	—
T.V. viewer	F	4	.5	1.7	—
Prefers T.V. over reading	M	3	.5	5.3***	U.S.
Reader	F	2	.4	4.4***	U.S.

Note: ***significant at the 0.001 level
      **significant at the 0.01 level
      *significant at the 0.05 level

Table 8. Purchasing Activities

Scale	Sex of Sample	Number of Items in Scale	r_{kk}	t Statistic	National Sample Significantly Characterized on Scale
New brand trier	F	4	.4	4.6***	U.S.
New brand trier	M	4	.5	0.2	—
Oriented toward private brands	F	3	.6	7.6***	C
Oriented toward private brands	M	3	.6	4.6***	C
Sale and bargain-oriented	F	7	.7	7.2***	—
Sale and bargain-oriented	M	4	.6	4.6***	C
Credit-oriented	F	4	.7	12.8***	U.S.
Credit-oriented	M	4	.7	10.0***	U.S.
Receptive to advertising	F	7	.5	11.9***	U.S.
Receptive to advertising	M	7	.6	5.0***	U.S.

Note: ***significant at the 0.001 level
      **significant at the 0.01 level
      *significant at the 0.05 level

Table 9.   Housewife Activities

Scale	Sex of Sample	Number of Items in Scale	r_{kk}	t Statistic	National Sample Significantly Characterized on Scale
Convenience-food user	F	3	.4	11.1***	U.S.
Convenience-food user	M	2	.4	5.2***	U.S.
Canned food user	F	4	.6	11.5***	U.S.
Cook	F	6	.7	4.9***	U.S.
Sewing	F	2	.8	0.4	—
Does what mother did	F	2	.5	0.7	—
Believes leftovers should be wrapped	M	2	.7	1.12	—
Compulsive homemaker	F	12	.8	2.9**	—
Disinfectant user	F	2	.5	8.1***	U.S.
Concerned about home cleanliness	M	5	.6	2.3*	—
Family is close knit	M	5	.7	0.9	—
Family is close knit	F	2	.8	2.3*	—
Children oriented	F	5	.7	1.8	—

Note: ***significant at the 0.001 level
     **significant at the 0.01 level
      *significant at the 0.05 level

The reliability coefficients for the 74 scales constructed in this study ranged from 0.27 to 0.83. Approximately 80 percent of these scales had reliability coefficients of 0.5 or greater. In each of the male and female data files, it was found that approximately one-third of the items could not be allocated to any scale. In the male file, 83 out of 257 items remained unused, and in the female file, 90 out of 245.

D. Sample Comparisons

Tables 6 through 10 indicate the results of the comparative analysis on each scale as well as the sex of the sample to which each scale is applicable, the number of items of each scale, the reliability coefficient r_{kk}, the t-statistic and the national character most described by the trait when the scale t-statistic is significant at the 0.001 level. The following sections summarize these results, in addition to indicating individual items where the difference is significant at the 0.001 level.

Table 10.   Personal Activities

Scale	Sex of Sample	Number of Items in Scale	r_{kk}	t Statistic	National Sample Significantly Characterized on Scale
In good health	M	2	.5	0.4	—
Enjoys eating	M	3	.5	6.1***	U.S.
Weight-conscious	F	6	.7	12.8***	U.S.
Weight-conscious	M	3	.4	6.4***	U.S.
Concerned about personal cleanliness	F	5	.5	9.0***	U.S.
Concerned about personal cleanliness	M	5	.6	8.3***	U.S.
Appearance-conscious	F	5	.4	3.8***	U.S.
Clothes-conscious	M	6	.6	2.7**	—
Fashion-conscious	F	7	.7	3.6***	C

Note: ***significant at the 0.001 level
      **significant at the 0.01 level
       *significant at the 0.05 level

1. Nonpermissive.   Americans were observed to be more nonpermissive than Canadians. They tended to agree more with statements which said that there was not enough discipline or that there was "too much emphasis on sex," "too much makeup," "too many privileges" and "too much violence." In addition, Americans believed more that "hippies should be drafted" and that "movies should be censored." They also agreed more that a "woman's place is in the home" and that "the man should be boss in the house." Contrary to the comparative literature, Americans appear more morally conservative.

2. Religious.   Americans were more religious than Canadians, both in terms of church attendence and emphasis upon spiritual values. They agreed more that if everyone was more religious "it would be a better country."

3. Security-oriented.   Canadians and Americans demonstrated no difference in their desire for security. Similar levels of agreement were observed in their responses to statements concerning job security, taking chances and enjoying danger. In contrast, the literature had suggested that Americans were greater risk-takers.

4. Skeptical.   American males were more skeptical than Canadians about such individuals as car salesmen and politicians.

5. Worrier-optimist.   Canadians and Americans generally exhibited the same level of optimism about the past, present and future. They wished for "the good old days" or would "do things differently" to the same degree. They were the same on believing they were "too heavily in debt" and wishing they "had a lot more money." Levels of agreement about obtaining in the future their "greatest achievement," "more money" and a "top executive position" were also the same.

6. Self-confident.   There was some evidence, particularly among the females, that Americans were more self-confident than Canadians. Americans agreed more that they "have more self-confidence than most people," "have a lot of personal ability" and are "more independent than most people." This result and that of the next scale could be interpreted as supporting the hypothesis that Americans are more individualistic.

7. Opinion leader.   There was evidence that Americans believed more than Canadians that they were opinion leaders. They agreed more that people came to them for "advice" or "information" about brands. They also agreed more with the statements that they "sometimes influence what my friend buys" and that they "like to be considered a leader."

8. Interpersonal communicator.   Americans not only exhibited greater opinion leadership than Canadians, but also appeared more involved in interpersonal communications. They received as well as transmitted more information than Canadians. For example, Americans agreed more with the statements that they "spend a lot of time talking with my friends" and that "my neighbors or friends usually give me pretty good advice," as well as with the statement "when I find a brand I like, I usually tell my friends about it."

9. Socializer-cosmopolitan.   Although Americans tended to be greater interpersonal communicators, Canadians were the greater socializers. Canadians agreed more that they were "a bit of a swinger," that they "like parties where there is lots of music and talk" and that they "would like to take a trip around the world" or "spend a year in London or Paris." In contrast, Americans agreed more that they "would rather spend a quiet evening at home than go to a party" and that "they stay home most evenings."

10. Alcohol user.   While the evidence among the females is not clear, it is evident that Canadian males were greater alcohol users than American males. Canadians agreed more that they "serve wine at dinner," that "a party wouldn't be a party without liquor," and that "beer is a real man's drink." In contrast, Americans agreed more with the statement that "liquor is a curse on American life'' than did Canadians agree with the statement ''liquor is a curse on Canadian life.''

11. Community-oriented. The greater community orientation of Americans was quite evident. Compared to Canadians, Americans agreed more that they worked ''on community projects,'' were ''active in the PTA,'' ''belonged to one or more clubs'' or were ''an active member of more than one service organization.'' These differences might suggest that Americans are more collectively oriented, which is contrary to the observations of the comparative literature.

12. City-oriented. Canadians, more than did Americans, preferred the city. Canadians agreed more that they ''would rather live in or near the big city than in or near a small town'' or ''live in the city rather than the suburbs.''

13. Judges by appearance. Canadians and Americans were equally ascriptive in their national character. Each sample provided similar levels of agreement to statements about judging a man by ''the car he drives'' or the ''clothes he wears.'' The comparative literature had suggested that Canadians would be more ascriptive.

14. Oriented toward more education. Americans exhibited a stronger orientation toward more education than did Canadians. Americans were more ''willing to pay higher taxes to get better schools'' and agreed more that their children should get ''a college education.'' The comparative literature predicted that Americans were more oriented to education.

15. Enjoys fine arts. Canadians and Americans did not differ in their orientation toward the fine arts. Similar levels of agreement were recorded on questions concerning ''classical records,'' ''classical music,'' ''concerts,'' ''art galleries,'' and ''ballet.''

16. Sports observer. In contrast to similarities on the more aesthetic activities, Americans, more than did Canadians, enjoyed sports. Americans agreed more that they would ''rather go to a sporting event than a dance.'' Americans also agreed more with statements about watching or listening to ''baseball or football games,'' enjoying ''conversations about sport,'' and reading ''the sports page in the daily paper.''

17. Oriented toward the outdoors. Canadians and Americans did not differ in their orientation toward the outdoors. Both samples provided similar levels of agreement on statements about enjoyment of the outdoors, fishing, camping and a ''cabin by a quiet lake.''

18. Oriented toward flying.   The greater adventuresome spirit exhibited by Canadians with respect to socializing and travelling did not apply toward flying activities. Males in both countries indicated similar levels of agreement on statements about flying and feeling "safer in an airplane than in a car."

19. Craftsman.   American males appeared more oriented toward being a handyman than were the Canadian males. Americans agreed more that they owned "many power tools," did "repair work on their car" and were "good at fixing mechanical things."

20. Follows the news.   Canadians and Americans did not differ in their receptiveness to news. The two male samples did not differ in their levels of agreement about "news magazines" and "television news programs."

21. Oriented toward the television and print media.   Americans demonstrated a stronger orientation toward both the television and print media. While Americans agreed more than did Canadians that "magazines are more interesting than television" and that they "like to read," they also agreed more that "television is our primary source of entertainment" and that they "watch more TV" than they should.

22. Oriented toward private brands.   Canadians showed a greater preference than did Americans for private as opposed to nationally advertised brands. Canadians agreed more that "a store's own private brand is usually just as good as a nationally advertised brand" and that "a store's own brand usually gives you good value for your money." In contrast, Americans agreed more with the statement that "nationally advertised brands are usually worth a few pennies more than a store's own brand."

23. Credit-oriented.   Americans exhibited a much stronger receptiveness to credit than did Canadians. They agree more with such statements as "I buy many things with a credit card or charge card" and "it is good to have charge accounts." In contrast, Canadians agreed more that they "liked to pay cash" and that "to buy anything other than a car on credit is unwise."

24. Receptive to advertising.   Americans were also much more receptive to advertising than were Canadians. For example, they agreed more strongly that their "choice of brands for many products is influenced by advertising" and that they "look at advertising in magazines almost as much" as they look at pictures or read the stories. In contrast to Americans, Canadians believed more that there is "too much advertising on television," that "advertising leads to wasteful buying," that "national advertising of most products has little or no benefit to the average consumer'' and that "advertising cannot sell me anything I don't want.''

25. Convenience and canned food user. Americans appeared much more receptive to the use of convenience and canned foods. They believed more, for example, that they "depend on canned food for at least one meal a day,'' they "couldn't get along without canned foods,'' and that "canned foods usually give you good value for the money.'' In contrast, Canadians agreed more that "things just don't taste right if they come out of a can.'' Canadians also agreed more that a "good mother will not serve her family TV dinners'' and that "a lot of convenience foods on the market today just aren't very tasty.'' In addition, Canadian females agreed more that they "always make my cakes from scratch.''

26. Oriented to cooking. The greater American orientation toward the home extended to cooking activities. More so than did Canadians, American females agreed that they "loved to bake,'' were "a good cook,'' that the kitchen was their favorite room'' and that they saved "recipes from newspapers and magazines.''

27. Oriented toward sewing. Canadians and Americans did not differ in their orientation toward sewing or making their "own or my children's clothes.''

28. Compulsive homemaker. Canadians appeared more concerned than Americans about cleanliness of the home. Canadians, for example, were more uncomfortable when the house was not completely clean, felt that "dirty dishes should be washed promptly after each meal,'' that a "house should be dusted and polished at least three times a week'' and that they "enjoyed most forms of housework.'' In contrast, Americans agreed more that they found "cleaning my house an unpleasant task'' and that they would "like to have a maid to do the housework.''

29. Disinfectant user. Despite the consistent greater agreement with statements about home cleanliness, it was the Americans who were more convinced about the power of disinfectants. They agreed more that "you have to use disinfectants to get your house really clean'' and that they "use one or more household disinfectants.''

30. Oriented toward family and children. Canadians and Americans did not appear to differ in their orientation toward their family and the importance that they placed on their children. Similar levels of agreement were recorded on statements dealing with love in the family and how close-knit the family was. No differences were observed in statements describing the time they spend with their "children talking about their activities, friends and problems,'' the importance of their children in their life and consideration of children when they were ill or when important family decisions were being made.

31. In good health.   American and Canadian males provided equal levels of agreement with the statements "I am in good physical condition" and "my family's health is excellent."

32. Weight-conscious.   Americans more than Canadians indicated that they enjoy eating. They tended to agree more that they "love to eat," "eat more than they should," and that they were "too fat."

Their greater concern about their weight possibily explains the fact that Americans tended to be greater users of low-calorie food products. They agreed more than did Canadians that they drank "low-calorie soft drinks several times a week" or that they "used Metrecal or other diet foods at least one meal a day."

33. Concerned about personal cleanliness.   Whereas Canadians were more concerned about home cleanliness, Americans were more concerned about their personal cleanliness. They agreed more that everyone should use "mouthwash," "a deodorant," and "wash their hands before eating each meal." They also agreed more that they did not "feel clean without a daily bath." The females agreed more that they felt more alive when their "hair is clean and combed" while the males agreed more that "every man should use an aftershave cologne."

34. Appearance and fashion-conscious.   There was no consistent evidence to indicate that Canadians and Americans differed on their concern about their appearance, their clothes or adherence to fashion. They tended to provide similar levels of agreement on statements concerning "looking through fashion magazines," dressing "for fashion, not for comfort," shopping "for clothes," and having "one or more outfits of the very latest style." While some differences were originally apparent on some items of this trait, they disappeared when age differences between the samples were taken into account.

E. Indeterminate Scales

Certain scales did not permit a final judgment on whether Canadians and Americans were similar or different. These scales were "mobile," "new brand trier," "did what mother did," "wraps leftovers," and "sale and bargain oriented."

F. Single Item Differences

Certain items, with differences between Canadian and American mean scores exceeding 1.0 on the 6-point scale, but which did not fit into any scale, deserve mention. The probability of the difference occurring because of sampling error is so low that they can be given recognition. For example, Americans agreed much more with the statements "there should be a gun in every home" (individualist and egalitarian) and "when I think of bad health I think of doctor bills." American females also agreed more that they "like to save and redeem trading stamps" while the males agreed more with the statement "I usually work more than forty-five hours a week" (individualist). Canadian females, on the other hand, felt more that "most big companies are just out for themselves." Canadian males agreed more that "it is hard to get a good job these days" while both males and females agreed more that "the government should guarantee everyone at least $3,000 a year whether he works or not" (collectivist).

G. Absolute Versus Relative Level of Agreement

A relevant consideration when significant but absolutely small differences are observed is the recognition of relative versus absolute level of agreement. Although Canadians and Americans provide significantly different mean levels of agreement on many items, both samples in such cases almost always are found to either agree or disagree with the statement. For example, in response to the statement, "I like to try new and different things," the mean level of agreement for Americans is 5.0 whereas for Canadians it is 4.6. Although the difference is statistically significant at the 0.001 level, both groups on average generally agree with the statement. Should Canadian and American consumers be treated differently? In other words, just because the sample data permit rejection of the null hypothesis that there are no differences between Canadians and Americans, do they necessarily imply a conclusion about the operational significance of the differences?

In general, the answer is "no," but there nonetheless are three relevant points for consideration. The first point is that a distinction must be made between the range of agreement over which individuals can lie and the range over which national characters can lie. Individuals may differ in their responses over the entire range of the scale. It might be the case, however, that samples could be taken from all countries of the world, and that on the item quoted above, the range of the mean levels of agreement for all the samples *might* be found to be only 4.5 to 5.0. In other words, there may be general agreement with the statement and all national characters may fall within a fairly narrow range. In the context then of a 4.5 to 5.0 range, the difference between the Canadian and American respective means of 4.6 and 5.0 is impressive.

This point is not unrelated to the Bass, Tigert and Lonsdale (1968) argument that market segmentation deals with groups and not individuals. Thus, while a proportionate difference of 5 to 10 percentage points may appear relatively small, it absolutely translates into millions of dollars of extra sales.

The other relevant point concerning small but significant differences is that importance of the difference for application will probably only be determined by a market test or other form of experimentation. For example, advertising reflecting the relative orientations of Canadians and Americans could be designed and, on a test basis, applied in both countries. If the difference is meaningful, the advertising appropriate to a country should achieve a higher degree of believability, memorability or other measure of effectiveness than advertising that is not appropriate. This approach has been proposed for the next step of the research program as described in Arnold and Barnes (1976).

H. Mail Panel vs. One-Time Survey

One possible source of bias in this comparative analysis arises out of the fact that the American data were gathered from a mail panel whereas the Canadian data were gathered in a one-time survey. Is it possible that the observed differences in national character are in fact due to the differences in data collection?

The characteristics and limitations of mail panels have been described by Boyd and Westfall (1960). For example, they observed that the sampling unit in the initial stages of panel construction usually consists of households which are, by definition, occupied dwelling units. The mail panel would then tend to include homes with common housekeeping facilities as well as exclude individuals residing in institutions, boardinghouses, transient residences, and other places with no housekeeping facilities. The sampling would also tend to exclude illiterates, heavy travelers, and housewives with newborn babies or other constraints. By its nature, the sampling would tend to include the more stable and better-organized households.

The Canadian sampling technique and restriction of the sample to heads of households probably compensates to some degree for any mail panel characteristics in the U.S. data. As noted earlier, the Canadian sample was limited to urban centres where it would be expected that the literacy rate would be higher than in rural or isolated regions. Furthermore, the absence of callbacks in the Canadian sampling would tend to result in the exclusion of transients and other mobile individuals. Overall, these sample characteristics would probably tend to make the two samples more different from their parent populations and more similar to each other.

Two other sources of bias were described by Boyd and Westfall (1960) which would tend to differentiate the American and Canadian samples. In a mail panel, there is continual attrition and those sampled at any one point in time tend more to be the cooperators or more stable households. These more cooperative respondents would tend to be different from those in the Canadian sample who perhaps were prepared to cooperate on a one-time basis but would not do so again.

One result of this attrition might be a bias variously labeled as "politeness bias," "yea-saying" or "acquiescence." To the extent that the American sample is subject to this bias, the American respondents should show greater agreement on a majority of statements. To the extent that this bias does not exist, Americans should show greater agreement on about one half of the items and Canadians greater agreement on the other half.

Items in both files showing significantly different levels of agreement at the 0.001 significance level were reviewed in order to identify the sample showing stronger agreement. It was found that the American sample agreed more on 155 of the items while the Canadian sample agreed more on 88. This ratio of nearly 2 to 1 suggests the possibility that the observed differences are due to sampling procedure rather than inherent differences in national character.

Nonetheless, it must be recognized that other factors can explain these results. For example, one possibility for this disproportionate American agreement is that Americans by nature are greater yea-sayers. As a consequence, the next stage of the research program (Arnold and Barnes, 1976) will include application of Jackson's (1968) "acquiescence" scale.

Another explanation for the results is that there was undue sampling of items from the trait domain on which Americans by nature agree more. Application of scales with equal numbers of positive and negative loading items in the next comparative study should remove this possibility.

A second source of bias that might arise because the American sample was drawn from a mail panel is that the panel members are influenced in response and behavior by the very fact that they are panel members. They become sensitized in certain areas due to repeated questioning.

While such a bias might affect product and brand purchases, it would appear inapplicable to items considered here. Correspondence with a senior executive at Market Facts, Inc., revealed that the questionnaire used had been the first of its kind seen by the U.S. respondents.

I. Time Period Between Surveys

Another source of bias in this comparative analysis might arise out of the fact that the U.S. data were gathered in Fall 1968, whereas the Canadian data were gathered in Spring 1970. The time period between surveys might mean that the apparent differences in national character were in fact a result of maturation in the Canadian sample.

It is clear that the questionnaires probed areas apparently experiencing change. For example, the questionnaire contained items reflecting permissiveness and the role of women. It would consequently be expected that a later sample would tend to reflect greater permissiveness or to be more positive about women's liberation.

Whether or not the later Canadian sample in this study was subject to bias in a year and a half is an empirical question. Repeated surveys would be required before the extent of change was ascertained and the question could be answered.

Perhaps a more relevant question concerns the possibility of change between the time of the two surveys and the present. Are the apparent differences between Canadians and Americans during 1968–1970 still evident today?

Again, the answer to the question apparently lies in a future study. It would appear, however, that a major social upheaval would be required in one country and not in the other before the relative position of the two peoples would change. In any other circumstances, the more permissive group would remain more permissive over five years even though the people in both countries might become more absolutely permissive.

J. Age Differences

As described earlier, each scale variable was regressed against age and a dummy nationality variable in order to see if the age difference between samples was the reason for the observed differences between Canadians and Americans. Of the 74 scales, there were only the female "appearance-conscious" and "fashion-conscious" scales where the F-statistic for the nationality regression coefficient was not significant at the 0.001 level even though the t-statistic was significant on the previous trait comparisons. By observing the very large F-statistics for the age regression coefficients and manner in which the correlation between the scale and nationality variables fell when age was held constant, it was concluded that the null hypothesis that there were no differences between Canadians and Americans on these two scales could not be rejected. On all other scales, however, the conclusions about differences remained unchanged.

K. East-West vs. U.S.-Canada Segmentation

Whereas 44 scales in the U.S.-Canada comparisons demonstrated significant North-South differences, only six scales showed significant East-West differences. Western United States and Canada had higher scores on the "mobile," "oriented toward the outdoors," a "craftsman," and "sewing" scales than the Eastern segment. In contrast, Eastern United States and Canada appeared to be greater "convenience-food users" (females) and more "concerned about personal cleanliness" (females).

The relatively few significant differences between east and west helped allay another concern. Were the many differences between Americans and Canadians in trait scores again an artifact of the large sample sizes and consequent small standard errors or were they, in fact, valid reflections of differences in national character? The relatively few significant differences between east and west with the same large sample sizes answers this question. The sample differences appear to reflect real differences in national character.

L. International vs. Regional Differences

Of the 44 scales with significant national differences, only three also reflected significant *regional* differences within both Canada and the United States. These scales were "religious," "liquor user," and "sports observer" (female).

An additional five scales yielded significant differences among regions of Canada. These scales were "opinion leader," "city-oriented" (males and females), "convenience-food user" (female), and "fashion-conscious."

Another eight scales yielded significant differences among regions of the United States. These scales were "socializer" (male and female), "education oriented," "T.V. over reading," "canned-food user," "disinfectant user," and "concern about personal cleanliness" (male and female).

Twenty-eight scales did not reflect significant regional differences in either Canada or the United States.

A difficulty in interpreting these results is related to the lack of a decision rule. Is the fact that of the 44 scales showing significant U.S.-Canada differences, only 16 also show regional differences enough for Douglas (1976) to conclude there is "considerable heterogeneity" within the countries and that "national consumer stereotypes are unlikely to be particularly meaningful or useful?"

The suggestion here is that there is not enough evidence to support such an agreement. The marketer would want to consider the relevance of each scale to his particular product. Furthermore, and as discussed earlier, he would want to compare the marginal costs and benefits of national segmentation and regional segmentation against the alternative of no segmentation at all. Again, a market test would appear appropriate.

VI. SUMMARY AND CONCLUSION

The differences summarized and further analyzed in the preceding pages can probably be best related to one of the national character traits that was said to differentiate Canadians from Americans. Americans were found to be individualistic, whereas Canadians were more collectively oriented. Americans in the results were observed to be more self-confident, greater opinion leaders and stronger interpersonal communicators. Having a gun gives the individual his power but means that he, rather than government, has to look after his community. Without socialized medicine, the American will also be more concerned about medical bills when he suffers from illness. In contrast, the Canadians, because of their greater collective orientation, would more likely support a guaranteed minimum income.

The Canadians' greater orientation toward government and a communitarian ideology appears to leave them less positively inclined toward private firms and companies. To the Canadian, the private firm perhaps represents the individual emphasis which he does not desire as much as does the American. Thus the Canadian is more oriented toward private brands and feels more that "big companies are just out for themselves." In contrast, Americans were found to be much more receptive to the machinations of business—trading stamps, advertising, credit, and the print and television media.

Americans and Canadians were found to be different in other areas as well. For example, Americans appeared much more nonpermissive, traditional, skeptical and even more religious than Canadians. These differences suggest that Americans are *more* and not less morally conservative as has been suggested in the comparative literature.

In their interests, Americans tended to be greater sports observers or handymen, or more involved in cooking, depending on their sex. Americans also appeared much more concerned about their weight and personal cleanliness. While Canadians appeared to be more concerned about home cleanliness, they nonetheless appeared more sociable, greater liquor users, more city-orientated and, in general, more cosmopolitan.

There were areas in which Canadians and Americans were quite similar. For example, no one sample was more pessimistic or optimistic or more security or routine oriented than the other. This was a finding also opposite to the comparative literature. The two samples were similar in their attitudes about the family, children and homemaking and exhibited no differences in their orientation toward the fine arts, the outdoors, flying, sewing or fashions.

Returning to the questions posed at the beginning of this paper, it is concluded that there is considerable evidence that there are differences in the national characters of Canadians and Americans and that a differentiated marketing approach could be undertaken to reflect these differences such as discussed by Arnold and Barnes (1977). Consistent observations of differences were noted in the comparative literature on certain traits and these and other differences were respectively either confirmed or discovered in the data analysis described in this paper. While reservations about the other differences are in order because of the secondary nature of the data, every attempt was made in the analyses to explore sources of bias and to control them where possible.

Whether or not these national character differences are great enough to result in a successful U.S.-Canada advertising differentiation was a question not completely resolved. The analysis at least suggested that a U.S.-Canada segmentation scheme is better than an East-West two-segment scheme. It was also determined that there are a significant number of differentiating national character traits where there is little or no evidence of regional heterogeneity. However, whether or not Canadians and Americans would respond appropriately to a differentiated advertising approach was not resolved but will be treated in the next stage of research (Arnold and Barnes, 1976). Whether or not the benefits of a U.S.-Canada differentiation would justify the costs was also not resolved and will be the problem for still another study.

FOOTNOTES

1. The rationalization for this division is that the center of population for contiguous United States in 1970 is near St. Louis on the Illinois–Missouri state border. See *Statistical Abstract of the U.S.: 1969,* 90th ed. (Washington, D.C.: U.S. Bureau of the Census, 1969), p. 10, Figure No. 9.

2. The black proportion in the panel was 1.0 percent, which can be compared to the U.S. census figures of 11.2 percent (U.S. Bureau of the Census, 1971, 24, Table No. 22, "1970 (prel.)").

REFERENCES

Arnold, S. J. and Tigert, D. J. (1974), "Canadians and Americans: A Comparative Analysis," *International Journal of Comparative Sociology* XV: 68–83.

_____ and Barnes, J. G. (1976), "A Proposal for Testing Canadian and American Response to Appropriate Advertising Copy," *Rapport-Proceedings,* Fourth Annual Conference, Canadian Association of Administrative Sciences: 5–10 to 5–19.

_____ and _____ (1977), "Canadians and Americans: Implications for Marketing," in *Problems in Canadian Marketing* (D. N. Thompson, ed.), Chicago: American Marketing Association, pp. 3–27.

Barnes, J. G. and Arnold, S. J. (1975), "Modal Personality, Institutional and Sociocultural Manifestations of Canadian-American Differences," unpublished working paper, Queen's University (December).

Bass, F. M., Tigert, D. J. and Lonsdale, D. T. (1968), "Market Segmentation: Group Versus Individual Behavior," *Journal of Marketing Research* 5: 264–270 (August).

Beckman, M. D. (1977), "Long-Term Values and Attributes of the Canadian Consumer: Some Aspects of Canadian Life Style," in *Problems in Canadian Marketing* (D. N. Thompson, ed.), Chicago: American Marketing Association, pp. 29–53.

Boyd, H. W. Jr. and Westfall, R. L. (1960), *An Evaluation of Continuous Consumer Panels as a Source of Marketing Information,* Chicago: American Marketing Association.

Clark, S. D. (1950), "The Canadian Community," in *Canada* (G. W. Brown, ed.), Berkeley: University of California Press, pp. 375–389.

Dhalla, N. K. (1966), *These Canadians,* Toronto: McGraw-Hill Ryerson.

Douglas, S. P. (1976), "Cross-National Comparisons and Consumer Stereotypes: A Case Study of Working and Non-Working Wives in the U.S. and France," *Journal of Consumer Research* 3: 12–20 (June).

Dunlop, J. (1976), "Kodak Poised to Move in on Polaroid Territory," *Marketing:* 1 (April 26).

Frank, R. E., Massey, W. F., and Wind, Y. (1972), *Market Segmentation,* Englewood Cliffs, N.J.: Prentice-Hall.

Goodis, J. (1972), *Have I Ever Lied to You Before:* Toronto: McClelland and Stewart.

Horne, A. (1961), *Canada and the Canadians,* London: Macmillan.

Hutchison, B. (1954), "The Canadian Personality," in *Our Sense of Identity,* Toronto: Ryerson Press, pp. 39–48.

Inkeles A. and Levinson, D. J. (1968), "National Character: The study of Modal Personality and Sociocultural Systems," in *The Handbook of Social Psychology,* 2nd ed., (G. Lindzey and E. Aronson, eds.), Addison-Wesley, Vol. 4, pp. 418–506.

Jackson, D. N. (1968), *Jackson Personality Research Form,* Goshen, N.Y.: Research Psychologists Press, Inc.

Kish, L. (1965), *Survey Sampling,* New York: John Wiley & Sons.

LeVine, R. A. (1973), *Culture, Behavior and Personality,* Chicago: Aldine.

Lipset, S. M. (1963), "The Value Patterns of Democracy: A Case Study in Comparative Analysis," *American Sociological Review:* 515–531 (August).

_____ (1965), "Revolution and Counterrevolution: The United States and Canada," in *The Revolutional Theme in Contemporary America* (T. Ford, ed.), Lexington: University of Kentucky Press, pp. 21–64.

Market Facts, Inc. (1973), *Consumer Mail Panels Data Book Rebalanced Sample as of January 1973,* Chicago: Market Facts, Inc.

Naegele, K. D. (1961), "Canadian Society: Some Reflections," in *Canadian Society: Sociological Perspectives* (B. Blishen et al., eds.), pp. 1–53.

Nie, N. H., Hull, C. H., Jenkins, J. G., Steinbrenner, K., and Bent, D. H. (1975), *SPSS Statistical Package for the Social Sciences,* 2nd ed., New York: McGraw-Hill.

Nunnally, J. C. (1967), *Psychometric Theory,* New York: McGraw-Hill.

Porter, J. (1971), "Canadian Character in the Twentieth Century," in *Canada: A Sociological Profile* (W. E. Mann, ed.), Toronto: Copp Clark.

Rokeach, M. (1974), "Some Reflections About the Place of Values in Canadian Social Science," in *Perspectives on the Social Sciences in Canada* (T. N. Guinsburg and G. L. Rueber, eds.), Toronto: University of Toronto Press.

Romalis, C. (1966), "A Man of His Time and Place: A Selective Appraisal of S. M. Lipset's Comparative Sociology," *Sociological Inquiry* 42: 211–231.

Siegel, S. (1956), *Non-Parametric Statistics for the Behavioral Sciences,* New York: McGraw-Hill.

Sommers, M. S. and Kernan, J. B. (1967), "Why Products Flourish Here, Fizzle There," *Columbia Journal of World Business* 2: 89–97 (March–April).

Tigert, D. J. (1973), "Can a Separate Marketing Strategy for French Canada Be Justified: Profiling English-French Markets through Life Style Analysis," in *Canadian Marketing: Problems and Prospects* (D. N. Thompson and D. Leighton, eds.), Toronto: John Wiley and Sons Canada, pp. 113–142.

Truman, T. (1971), "A Critique of Seymour M. Lipset's Article, Value Differences Absolute or Relative: The English-Speaking Democracies," *Canadian Journal of Political Science* 14: 497–525.

Tyler, L. E. (1965), *The Psychology of Human Differences,* New York: Appleton-Century-Crofts.

U.S. Bureau of the Census (1971), *Statistical Abstract of the United States: 1971* (92d edition), Washington, D.C.: U.S. Bureau of the Census.

Vallee, F. G. and Whyte, D. R. (1968), "Canadian Society: Trends and Perspectives," in *Canadian Society: Sociological Perspectives,* 3rd edition (B. Blishen et al., eds.), pp. 833–852.

Von Lanzenauer, C. H. (1975), *Cases in Operations Research.* London, Ont.: The University of Western Ontario, pp. 172–182.

Wells, W. D. and Tigert, D. J. (1971), "Activities, Interests and Opinions," *Journal of Advertising Research* 11: 27–35.

Williams, T. M. (1975), "Canadian Childrearing Patterns and the Response of Canadian Universities to Woman as Childbearers and Childrearers," *Canada's Mental Health:* 6–9 (September).

Winer, B. J. (1971), *Statistical Principles in Experimental Design,* 2nd ed., New York: McGraw-Hill.

Wrong, D. H. (1955), *American and Canadian Viewpoints.* Washington, D.C.: American Council on Education.

THE PRODUCTS-NEEDS MATRIX AS A METHODOLOGY FOR PROMOTING ANTI-CONSUMING

Michael A. Belch, SAN DIEGO STATE UNIVERSITY

Robert Perloff, UNIVERSITY OF PITTSBURGH

INTRODUCTION

Since the period of abundance that existed during the decades of the 1950s and 1960s now seems to have ended, it appears that the role of the marketer will be forced to undergo significant changes. No longer will the marketer's prime function be to promote the sale of products and satisfy profits with little or no regard for the environment in which he operates. Rather, the marketing manager may find himself devoting more of his time toward "Demarketing" (Kotler, 1976) and "Anti-consuming" (Perloff and Belch, 1974).

Owing in part to the lack of foresight and in part to the suddenness with which the "era of shortages" arose, marketers have devoted little attention to the

Research in Marketing—Volume 2, 1979, pages 37–64.
ISBN 0-89232-059-1

concept of decreasing or terminating consumption of products or services. However, with the coming of the energy shortage during 1973–1974, a number of proposals designed to suggest possible solutions to product shortages and environmental problems appeared in the marketing literature. These proposals can be classified as belonging to either of two categories:

1. Firm or corporate level proposals—i.e., those designed to stress the role of the firm as regards specific actions to be pursued so as to minimize negative consequences or increase benefits that might result from the less than favorable environments; and

2. Individual or consumer level proposals—those stressing the individual's responsibilities during these changing environmental conditions.

A brief summary of the proposals in each of these areas follows:

FIRM/CORPORATE LEVEL PROPOSALS

Kotler and Levy (1971) propose a concept of "demarketing." While the article was actually written prior to the shortage crisis that surfaced in 1973–1974, it does show foresight by presenting alternatives to deal with an excess demand over supply situation. According to Kotler and Levy, "Demarketing is that aspect of marketing that deals with discouraging customers in general, or a certain class of customers in particular on either a temporary or permanent basis" (p. 75). The basis of the "demarketing" concept concerns the role of the firm that finds itself with an oversupply of customers relative to its resources, and thus, strategies for discouraging potential consumers are offered.

In a later proposal, Kotler (1974) reviews the role of the firm during periods of shortages. As in the earlier work, Kotler presents marketing mix strategies to be utilized to better the position of the firm. He presents three schools of thought on shortages, and specific strategies are provided for dealing with each. These strategies involve three areas of reprogramming of marketing efforts including 1) altering the product mix; 2) altering the customer mix; and 3) altering the total marketing mix.

Weiss (1974) similarly presents strategies for the firm dealing with shortages. In his initial article, Weiss presents twenty-nine ways for the firm to deal with shortages while increasing benefits to itself. The later article (Weiss, 1974) adds thirty-four more "check points" to the list. Hanna (1975), Weiss (1974), and McGuire (1974) follow the same general approach as presented, and thus will not be discussed.

Also written prior to the energy crisis and also dealing at the level of the firm, but displaying more consideration for the welfare of the environment and society, are proposals by Gelb and Brien (1971) and Feldman (1971) which both present marketing's role in social responsibility. The former of these refers to a "survival university" while the latter suggests switching from a product to a service orientation and placing more emphasis upon societal criteria.

Cullwick (1975) and Levitt (1974) also offer proposals, both of which consider the possibility of offering substitutes.

In summary, these reviews tend to concentrate at the *level of the firm* for dealing with product shortages, environmental problems, and societal threats. Most of the articles present opportunities for the firm in periods of shortages, while none actually deals with individual consumption patterns. As a result, such proposals are limited in their capabilities to provide the necessary solutions.

INDIVIDUAL LEVEL PROPOSALS

A fewer number of articles have been presented dealing with shortages, pollution, and other environmental problems at the level of individual consumption responsibilities.

Kelley and Schwee (1974) stress the need for dealing with problems in a "stagflation/shortages" economy using a micro rather than macro approach to buyer behavior. Rothe and Benson (1974) offer an alternative to the existing marketing concept which they refer to as "Intelligent Consumption." Intelligent consumption would require that consumers be aware of social and environmental problems when making purchases, so they might select products or services that are less harmful to the environment and to society. The authors stress that it is necessary to provide the consumer with attractive choice alternatives if such a concept is to work.

In dealing with the problems of consumers and the need for energy conservation, Hannon (1974) examined the relationship between consumer activities, the energy created by these activities, and consumer options for energy conservation. He proposes a number of solutions designed to conserve energy use, including: 1) an energy resource tax; 2) energy rationing through the use of coupons; and 3) adopting energy as a standard of value, and perhaps affording it legal rights.

Each of the proposals considered in this segment emphasizes the need for dealing at the level of the individual for the purpose of changing consumption habits. Each proposes ideas and concepts of the possibilities involved in changing individual consuming behavior, but offer little evidence of success of the methods for implementing consumption reducing strategies. The research to be presented later in this report emphasizes the investigation of a methodology for substituting products for the express purpose of promoting "anti-consuming." Prior to discussing the methodology, it is necessary to first examine the meaning and purpose of "anti-consuming," and to demonstrate the relevance of the concept to marketing research.

ANTI-CONSUMING

Perloff and Belch (1974) present a proposal that incorporates a number of these earlier suggestions for dealing with social and environmental problems. Such a plan calls for the joint efforts of both the individual and the business community, and considers the need to decrease consumption as well as shifting the same to those products having a less scarce supply or that are less detrimental to the environment. While most strategies have emphasized the former approach—i.e., decreasing consumption—most of the research that has been conducted in the area of learning theory would suggest a greater likelihood of switching behavior to a new product as opposed to extinguishing the desire for that currently being consumed. The approach of anti-consuming does, in fact, stress the importance of providing viable alternatives to which the consumer might switch.

Anti-consuming is defined as "the process whereby one reduces or substitutes consumption of a product or service for the express purpose of increasing benefits—i.e., health or well-being as opposed to those of a hedonic nature—to himself or to society." Anti-consuming efforts need not be limited to the specific act of consuming. It is generally accepted that most behavior follows from a prior belief or attitude toward the act (this is not to say that attitudes necessarily precede behavior in every instance, or are the causes of behavior). Anti-consuming conceptualizing, then, can be extended to include the process of changing attitudes in an attempt to achieve the desired results.

Further, an understanding of why one does *not* consume may well enhance the probability of increasing our understanding of why one *does* consume, with the logical extension being an increased ability to decrease this level of consumption. If one exhausts the reasons why an individual avoids a particular product, it is not unreasonable to infer, then, that other imaginable incentives for consuming are thereby plausible. For example, understanding why consumers do not take advantage of mass transit, car-pooling or other cost and energy-saving alternatives may lead to an increased probability of determining why consumers prefer to continue using their automobiles despite increased costs and public policy recommendations.

WHO SHOULD ANTI-CONSUME?

An ethic of anti-consuming would not necessarily apply to all consumers, although it does include all classes, or segments of the consuming public.

At first glance, one might assume that only those who now consume more than is necessary should be included in the group who should cut back on their rates of consumption. This would encompass, by way of illustration, the obese, the indigent, and the excessive consumer (for example, alcoholics) whose physical or mental states are potentially unhealthy as the direct result of overconsumption. While these groups are certainly to be included, they do not comprise the totality of the targets of anti-consuming efforts. One must not limit such efforts to a narrow segment comprising merely those who "have." While this segment might be one of the prime targets of such efforts, the benefits might also be extended to:

Minorities—in this sense minorities include all those who may have less than equal opportunity, possibly blacks, Puerto Ricans, Chicanos, individuals existing on fixed annuities or incomes, and virtually all others who might more effectively utilize their limited resources by consuming less, or by improving current consumption patterns.

Young marrieds—newlyweds, students, and others still striving for firm foundations can certainly benefit from a program designed to improve or discipline existing consumption habits.

Retirees—upon retiring from the labor force, individuals find it necessary to adjust to a lower level of income. A re-evaluation of consumption habits is in such a case not only desirable but mandatory.

Disabled and retarded—better education in ways to consume can certainly benefit these segments of society in many ways; for example, in structuring products or environments congruent with the individual's limitations.

By providing assistance and education on more prudent consumption patterns to the aforementioned groups, a step is taken toward the frustrating, but no less desirable goal of more equal (read less unequal) income distribution. While it is obvious that one's gross income will not be increased, wiser utilization of that income will result in net gains in real or usable financial resources, with a possible narrowing of the gap.

These economically pinched groups are not the only segments that stand to benefit by anti-consuming. Middle- and upper-class strata likewise can benefit by more Spartan consumption habits, as can all who consume in a limited resources environment.

THE ROLE OF THE FIRM

The initial reaction to a program for anti-consuming is quite likely to be an expression of alarm or disbelief, or at best a feeling that it is a concept relevant only to the academia. What manager would even consider advocating to management the concept of reducing sales of his product? What is to be gained by such a radical departure from all that has ever been taught in the business environment? To see one's superior on such a notion—and still be employed the next day—the manager must stress the benefits to be derived from such an action by the firm. These possible benefits follow:

Increased Longevity

The decrease of levels of consumption—especially in a time of shortages—might help to increase the firm's life span. Increased demand for products requires increased demand for the materials available to produce that product. Should such materials be in limited supply, rapid exhaustion could terminate the firm's ability to continue production and seriously diminish the public's trust in the organization. A borrowing of time could, perhaps, allow for the development of substitutes or replacement of existing materials, and thus insure a longer life span for the firm. Situations such as the closing of plants in the Midwest as a result of the shortage of fuel, and the closing of lumber companies in the West due to the too rapid consumption of trees, could be avoided.

Customer Satisfaction

As most marketers are aware, one of the quickest ways to lose accounts is to be short of supply. Such a situation precipitates a search for new products or new providers—both detrimental for the current supplier. Many firms already are considering orders for no earlier than 1978, while others are refusing to accept new orders from all those other than their most loyal customers. A reduction of levels of consumption initiated earlier would have made such an embarrassing situation unnecessary and less harmful to the firm's image.

Improved Forecasting

By promoting anti-consumption it would be easier to anticipate future demands and thereby gear production to meet those demands. Currently, firms are stockpiling supplies when possible, in anticipation of future shortages—a state of affairs serving only to worsen the existing situation. A workable program to reduce consumption could result in an improved prediction in the levels of demand as a result of more stable purchasing patterns to the benefit of both producer and consumer.

Social Responsibilities

Not to be ignored is the ever increasing public demand for social responsibility by the firm. As this demand is likely to increase in the future, it is in the best interest of the business community to take positive action in this regard. To support a program that will result in less consumption, and thereby less waste of our resources, the firm not only satisfies public clamor, but does so in a manner beneficial to itself as well as to society as a whole.

Government Intervention

Government strategies to decrease the rate of inflation have had far-reaching effects on industry. Price and wage controls and profit ceilings are just a few of the actions that have been implemented. A plan of anti-consumption in which demand is brought more into line with supply could have desirable effects on reducing inflation and, at the same time, help eliminate the need for government controls. Reduced consumption through self-regulation would reduce the necessity of government interventions.

IMPLEMENTATION OF ANTI-CONSUMING

To initiate a program for anti-consuming, empirical investigation of those attitudes, motivations, and behaviors inherent in the buying processes of the individual is necessary. With this information it will become possible to formulate strategies designed to implement a program of anti-consuming. These strategies can be utilized in a manner similar to those used to promote consumption, as well as some of those used previously to deter product use. A presentation of a few of these tactics follows, as an example, and to help in the generation of additional strategies.

Advertising

Reinstatement of campaigns similar to the anti-smoking campaign of the late 1960s and 1970s is one possible vehicle for achieving an anti-consuming objective. Hamilton (1972) found such persuasive messages to be effective in changing attitudes toward smoking to a more unfavorable position. While no evidence is offered that such ads were effective in reducing actual consumption, evidence of cigarette sales during the years of the anti-smoking campaign tend to support this conclusion. Hamilton provides evidence through his research "that the health scare as a consumption deterrent was several times more powerful than was advertising as a stimulant." Further, "Since the health scare was a several-fold more potent determinant of per capita consumption than was promotional cigarette advertising, and since anti-smoking advertising simply promulgated and intensified the health scare, findings that anti-smoking ads were more potent than promotional ads does not seem surprising."

Education

The introduction of courses at all levels of education designed to instill better buying habits is desirable. Such courses would emphasize instruction on how to buy, which products to buy (for example, low-income families should purchase nourishing foods as opposed to sweets), and from whom to buy. Such a course might demonstrate cost savings by purchasing returnable bottles vs. cans, or possible alternative products or services available to satisfy the same generic need.

Group Influence

The conformity studies conducted by Asch (1951) among others, demonstrates the potential of using groups to apply pressure aimed at enhancing anti-consuming efforts. Social group influence exerted by civic clubs, church groups, and peers should support actions for anti-consuming. By offering their support for such a program, large numbers of consumers could be reached. By organizing such actions as boycotts against firms guilty of waste pollution, etc., the positive effects of anti-consumption could be experienced.

Role of the Firm

For their involvement, firms should (a) support local programs aimed at anti-consuming, (b) emphasize service of existing products vs. replacement of the same, (c) retrain their sales force to instruct customers on how to anti-consume, and (d) undertake a program of "demarketing."

Marketing Academicians

The marketing educator must lend support through the development of courses in such areas as consumer education, social responsibility, and anti-consuming. In addition, more research efforts focusing on the problems of switching or reducing consumption of scarce or socially detrimental products is necessary.

The remainder of this report will focus on one such empirical study. The study involves the exploration of a methodology for the determination of product substitutes. While the results of the study do not necessarily reflect the discovery of more viable alternatives per se, they do demonstrate the feasibility of a methodology that can be useful in the promotion of anti-consuming efforts. Thus, while the research will not specifically demonstrate products that should serve as substitutes, its value lies in the determination of a methodology by which such alternatives could in fact be discovered.

METHODOLOGY

Theoretical Basis

The theoretical basis upon which the methodology for determining product substitutes has been established has been derived from the disciplines of consumer behavior and psychology. More specifically, contributions from research studies concerning brand loyalty and brand switching, needs satisfaction, and substitution, have been synthesized into the framework supporting the methodology under consideration. Without reviewing each of these areas in detail, the relative contributions of each will be examined briefly:

Product/Brand Switching. While the research conducted on product and brand switching has emphasized the overt actions of the consumer and thus can contribute little in the way of understanding consumer motivations per se, the area does provide information useful for the purposes of this research. For example, Comish's (1953) determination that consumers switch brands due to dissatisfaction supports the contentions made by Kotler and others who note that the basis of the marketing concept is need satisfaction. It becomes obvious, then, that in order to switch consumption from one product or service to another, a number of conditions are essential:

1) the alternative offered as the substitute must satisfy basically the same need as the target product;
2) this product/service/activity must be perceived as being need satisfying by the *consumer* at whom product-switching efforts are targeted; and
3) from Howard and Sheth (1969) the alternatives under consideration need not belong to the product set as defined by the industry. For example: "A person may see Sanka coffee, Ovaltine, and Tetley's tea as three alternatives to satisfy his motives related to beverage consumption."

Needs/Need Satisfaction.   Although neither marketers nor psychologists can agree upon an acceptable definition of need—witness the various definitions provided by Murray, (1938) Tolman, (1959) and Maslow (1954)—it is nevertheless necessary to establish an operational definition of need for purposes of this study. Based in part on the inability to effectively measure subconscious needs, and in part on the assumption that the majority of marketers are referring to needs of a cognitive nature in regards to consumer desires, wants or drives, the following definition of need shall serve as the basis for this study: *Need*—"a conscious, cognitive, and articulable want, preference, or desire possessing motivational properties so long as it is unfulfilled." As a result of this definition, to be considered a need for the purposes of this study, the following minimum conditions must be met:

1. It must be conscious—i.e., the individual must be aware of its existence and have thoughts, sensations, and feelings about it. So used herein, a need cannot be unconscious. Should the individual not be aware of the need, then it cannot, in fact, exist.
2. It must be cognitive—i.e., known to the individual, said knowledge or awareness having been acquired through experience.
3. It can be articulated—i.e., the individual can express the need clearly and effectively. Needs in this study are represented only by those that can be stated by the individual; and
4. It must be wanted—i.e., from Webster's definition, the need must not be possessed (not fulfilled, not satisfied), and it must be desired. A need is then somewhat similar to a preference in that it is liked by the individual, and the individual has some choice regarding its existence.

While one might legitimately argue that the definition suggested is more narrow than one would prefer to adequately represent a need, it is sufficient for the purposes of determining substitutes due to its obvious ability to be imparted by the consumer, and, therefore, represents the consumer's own *felt* reasons for using the product. If the determination can be made as to why the consumer *feels* he or she is consuming, the probability that one can determine a substitute based on satisfying that same *felt need* is enhanced.

SUBSTITUTION

Beyond the work of Stefflre (1972), little has been done in marketing regarding the determination of product substitutes. Stefflre's basis of considering products as substitutable based on their perceived ability to satisfy the same *use* requirements—while proving to be somewhat effective—does not extend far enough into actual *need-satisfying* capabilities. As a result, it was considered necessary to view the literature in economics and psychology to search for possible bases of substitution. A review of this literature demonstrates that psychologists have given surprisingly little attention to the process of substitution. Freud's (1948) referral to sublimation as an ego defense constitutes his extent of involvement in the subject, while most others have seemingly ignored the process completely.

The most extensive work in this area has been conducted by students of the Lewinian school, including Lissner (1933), Ovsiankina (1928) and Zeigarnik (1927). The theoretical basis for determination of substitutes in this study is based on the work of Ovsiankina. While considering substitute activities (as opposed to products), Ovsiankina demonstrated that the substitute value of an activity was dependent upon its similarity to the original activity, in respect to goal attainment. The logical extension of marketing would seem to be the determination of substitute products based on perceived similarities. Specific to this research, this similarity is predicated upon the consumers' perception of products as being similar in respect to their abilities to satisfy given needs. Based on the work of Ovsiankina, and marketing theory, the following definition of a substitute is offered:

"The substitute value of product or activity 'A' for product or activity 'B' is determined by the extent to which 'A' satisfies the same need(s) as 'B'. Substituting 'A' for 'B' at time 't' (the time of the felt need) should result in a significant reduction in the intensity of the need at time 't + 1.' "

This definition of substitution emphasizes the psychological meaning, with little or no economic considerations. For the purpose of this study we are concerned only with psychological determinants. Future studies might be expanded to include economic considerations.

The cumulative contributions of studies in each of these respective disciplines leads to the conclusion that one effective way to discover product substitutes would be to determine the following:

1. The consumer's felt need(s) (as defined above) for consuming the product;
2. Alternative products perceived by the consumer as being possible alternatives for satisfying the same needs; and

3. The most likely substitutable alternative based on the ability to reflect similar need satisfactions as the target product.

A products/needs (p/n) matrix has been developed in an attempt to make these determinations. The description of this instrument, as well as the methodology employed to establish the most likely substitute will be described next.

THE METHODOLOGY EMPLOYED IN THE DETERMINATION OF PRODUCT SUBSTITUTES

A brief review of the previous attempts of marketers to determine substitutes first provided for review purposes.

At the time of this research only two known methods for establishing substitutes based on similarities had appeared in the marketing literature. Bass, Pessemier, and Tigert (1969) used factor analysis to explore complementary and substitute relations between purchase and usage rates. The authors defined substitutes as those products satisfying the same needs but consumed separately. While the authors conclude that variations in usage rates could be explained somewhat by attitudinal and interest values, the results must be considered tentative due to the evolving of particular factors that intuitively do not appear valid.

Stefflre used multidimensional scaling to determine similarities, arguing that products are substitutable to the extent that they are perceived as similar. A similarity index was established based on three dimensions: (1) items having similar uses; (2) items having the same patterns of preference; and (3) a combination of (1) and (2) in which substitutes were defined as products having the same uses and liked by the respondent.

The methodology presented in this research is similar to that used by Stefflre in that it recognizes the need to have consumers themselves generate both needs and alternatives. A number of changes have been implemented in this methodology that the authors feel will add to and improve upon Stefflre's design. For example:

(1) Stefflre considered products as substitutes if they were perceived as similar. Similarity alone may not be sufficient for substitution, as substitution as shown seems to indicate reduction of a drive or need.

(2) The establishing of similarities is based on the clustering of 1's or x's (same uses and preferences respectively) rather than degrees of similarity. The use of a seven-point scale designed to determine the *relative* similarities is necessary.

(3) Determining *uses* (i.e., in the winter, in the summer—in the case of medicines; with tea, with coffee, with milk—in the case of snacks) may not be effective as establishing the *goals* to be accomplished, or the *needs* to be satisfied through consumption of the product.

(4) Combining (1) and (2) above would lead to a determination of how well each product serves as a substitute for another based on its ability to satisfy

particular needs, as opposed to the frequencies with which they were considered similar as employed in Stefflre's research.

The research proposed here is similar to that conducted by Stefflre in that consumers themselves define the sets of products and/or activities to be considered. In this study, however, degrees of similarity will be shown, based upon the relative ability of each of these products or activities to satisfy (on a 7-point scale) the stated needs or goals of the consumption. Further, the ability of a product/activity will be represented by the distance (in geometric space) between the two. This author suggests that the determination of substitutes derived in this manner will result in an indication of the degree to which such products can be considered substitutable rather than just an indication of their similarities.

Figure 1 represents a flow diagram of the procedures followed, as well as the number of respondents, constituting the sample at each step of the process. A description of each phase follows:

Figure 1. Flow Diagram of Procedures.

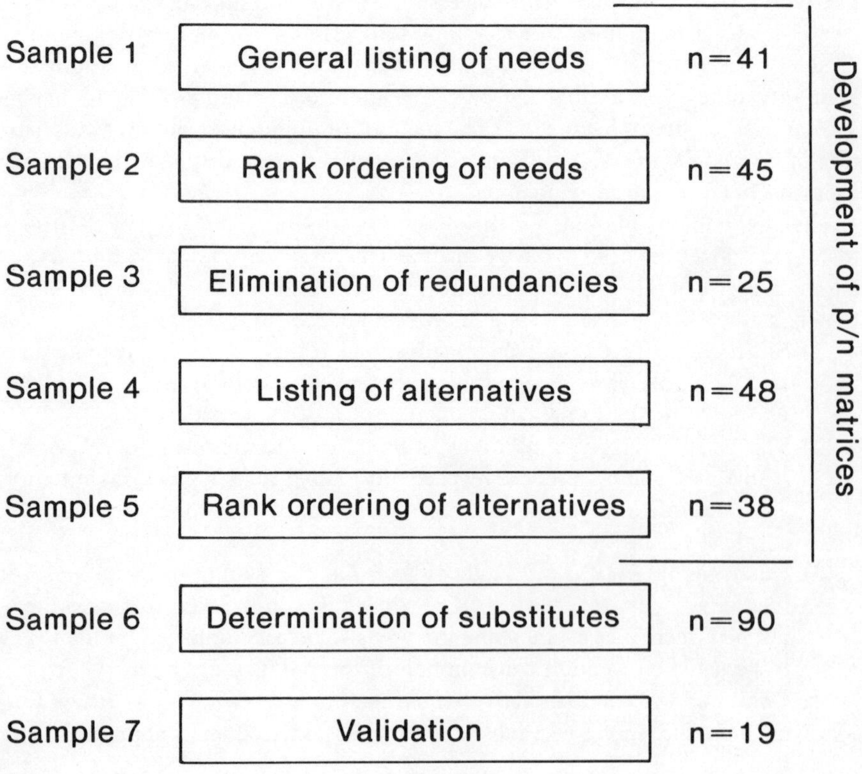

Sample 1	General listing of needs	n = 41	
Sample 2	Rank ordering of needs	n = 45	Development of p/n matrices
Sample 3	Elimination of redundancies	n = 25	
Sample 4	Listing of alternatives	n = 48	
Sample 5	Rank ordering of alternatives	n = 38	
Sample 6	Determination of substitutes	n = 90	
Sample 7	Validation	n = 19	

POPULATION

A convenience sample of 306 respondents were used for the gathering of the data. Of these, 197 were employed in samples 1 through 5 (each sample 1–7 was independently drawn) for the purpose of developing the data collection instrument—the products/needs matrices. The remaining 100 constituted the final two samples. The purpose of these were to actually derive the product substitutes and to provide a measure of validity for the same. The respondents were undergraduate students of various colleges in the Pittsburgh, Pennsylvania, area. The total sample included approximately 60 percent men and 40 percent women with a mean age of 24 years. In an attempt to include a representative sampling, the students were selected from various disciplines, in three different universities, and from day and evening courses.

PRODUCT SELECTION

The products considered as targets for which substitutes would be derived were selected on the basis of:

1. products or activities that might be considered as candidates for "anti-consuming" efforts by particular segments of the population based on societal or health reasons, as opposed to religious or special interest group causes.
2. products or activities that might have a number of viable alternatives as regards costs or efforts to be expanded for purposes of consumption.
3. As a result of certain constraints (for example, the need for a large number of respondents of relatively homogeneous age, sex, or social class, and/or education), students were used as respondents. The validity of using students is enhanced by proper selection of products/activities consumed by this population and by a previously reported study by Sheth (1970), among others. (In fact, the use of products commonly used by students was more easily identifiable than would be products consumed by the population at large.)

The establishment of these selection criteria resulted in the use of beer, cigarettes, and candy as target products, and television watching as the target activity for which substitutes would be generated. While it is obvious that some may argue that such products may not be those deserving of prime consideration for anti-consuming purposes, their selection can be defended on two accounts:

1. The products have been shown to be detrimental to some consumers; and
2. the purpose of this research is to examine a methodology for the determination of substitutes. For that reason products are relevant only to the extent that they are useful for the validation of the method under consideration. Specific products of interest can be examined after the methodology itself has been shown to be effective.

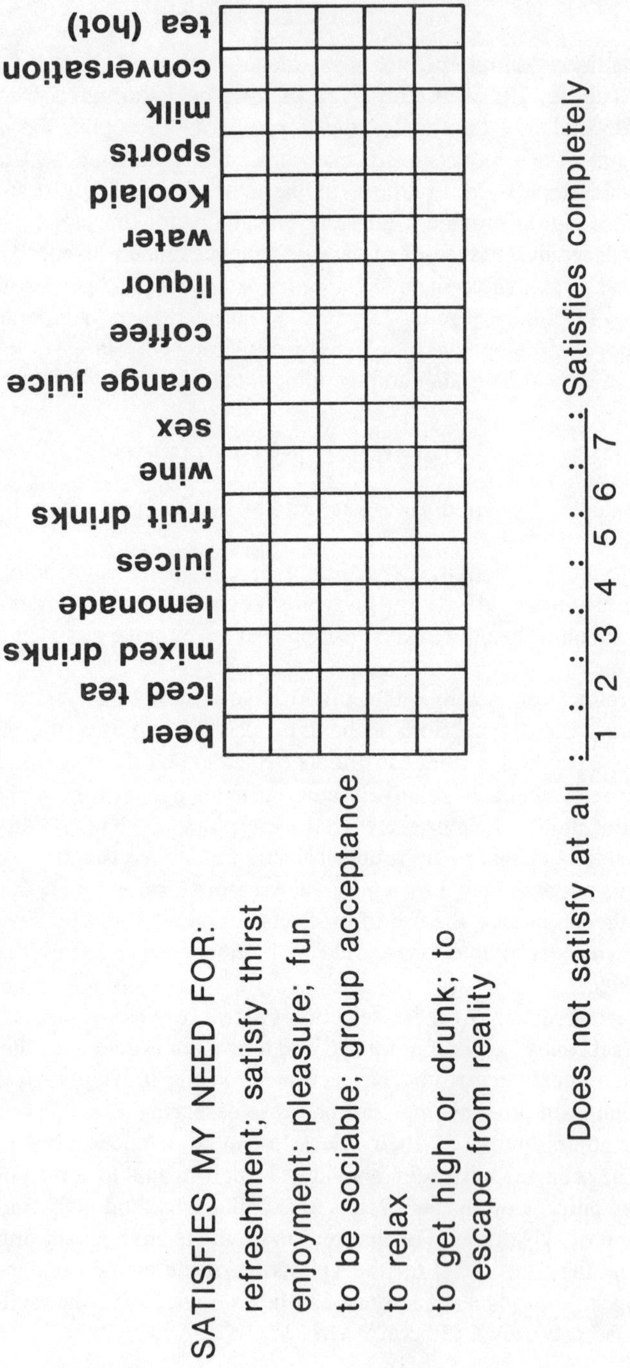

MICHAEL A. BELCH and ROBERT PERLOFF

Figure 2. p/n Matrix for Beer.

Column labels (rotated): beer, iced tea, mixed drinks, lemonade, juices, fruit drinks, wine, sex, orange juice, coffee, liquor, water, Koolaid, sports, milk, conversation, tea (hot)

SATISFIES MY NEED FOR:

refreshment; satisfy thirst

enjoyment; pleasure; fun

to be sociable; group acceptance

to relax

to get high or drunk; to escape from reality

Does not satisfy at all _: _: _: _: _: _: _: Satisfies completely
                          1   2   3   4   5   6   7

INSTRUMENTATION

The instrument used in this investigation—the p/n matrix—was designed specifically for this research based on the contributions of the specific disciplines discussed earlier. Figure 2 is a reproduction of one of the matrices used in the actual study. As will be noted, the matrix is designed to determine substitutes for beer based on six needs considered salient by the respondents in samples 1 through 5.

The procedure followed for determination of alternatives and needs included in the matrices will be presented in the subsequent section of this report.

DEVELOPMENT OF THE P/N MATRICES

Based on the review of the various literatures (as noted earlier), it was determined that to serve as a product/activity substitute, the alternative would have to be perceived as satisfying the same needs as the target product. The more the product was perceived as being capable of satisfying these same needs, the more likely it would be to serve as a substitute. Thus it was deemed necessary to:

1) allow the consumer to elaborate the needs she/he felt were being satisfied by the consumption of the target product/activities;
2) have the consumers list the alternatives that *they* felt would be used to satisfy these same needs; and
3) assign a score to each product based on its perceived ability to satisfy the listed needs.

Referring to Figure 1, the reader can examine the process involved in arriving at the final matrices. The specific function performed by each sample follows: (This discussion will be limited to the development of the p/n matrix for beer only. As the exact procedures were followed for each matrix, it is not considered necessary to elaborate on each. Generalizations to the other p/n matrices should be obvious.)

Sample 1

Respondents were asked to generate as many *reasons* as they felt important for *drinking,* and were asked to garner such reasons from their friends, relatives or self. To eliminate biases caused by the semantics attributed to the word need, and so as to generate as extensive a list as possible, the word "reasons" was used. This list of reasons was to be returned to the administrator two days later (to allow for an extensive list generation). The specific product *beer* was not used so that a variety of reasons for drinking would be considered, involving a wide range of products and situations. A list of 31 reasons resulted from this procedure.

Sample 2

As many of the reasons were cited with a frequency of one and were thus considered as contributing to a too extensive listing, only those reasons cited with a frequency of five times or greater were included in the list to be administered to Sample 2. This list of 16 reasons was then given to the second group, who were instructed to rank each of the *needs* according to its importance to the individual for consuming beer. It was considered as appropriate to use *needs* in this instance, as the purpose was to get a more specific indication as to why one drinks *beer*. Further, the attributed meaning of *need* at this point becomes salient as (1) the list generated in Sample 1 was to be general and not specific to drinking beer; and (2) the consumer's perception of needs satisfied is of concern. As a result of their process, ten needs evolved. (The cut-off point was established by noting significant differences between subsequent needs.)

Sample 3

To eliminate apparent redundancies in the ten remaining needs, a third sample was obtained. Following a procedure suggested by Burton (1972), the respondents were given a stack of 3 × 5 index cards and asked to sort the needs into piles such that *those needs that seem the same are in the same piles*. The resulting list of six needs constituted the list to be used in the final p/n matrix. (See Figure 2.)

Sample 4

Following the same procedure as established for Sample 1, this sample was assigned the task of generating alternatives for drinking beer. A list of 61 alternatives resulted, with those cited with a frequency of five or greater constituting the list to be presented to Sample 5.

Sample 5

The list of 21 products from Sample 4 was presented for the purpose of rank ordering so that only those products most likely to serve as viable alternatives would be considered. Following the same procedure for establishing the cut-off point as was used in Sample 2, a final list of 17 products was to constitute the p/n matrix for beer.

In summary, the development of the p/n matrices for each of the products under consideration followed the sequence of procedures outlined above. The resulting matrices for each included:

Beer = 17 products/activities × 6 needs

Watching Television = 11 products/activities × 7 needs

Candy = 20 products/activities × 9 needs
Smoking Cigarettes = 18 product/activities × 10 needs

DETERMINATION OF PRODUCT SUBSTITUTES

The final p/n matrices as derived in Samples 1 through 5 were administered to a sixth sample. The respondents in Sample 6 were to rate on a 7-point scale, ranging from Does Not Satisfy At All to Satisfies Completely, *each* products/ activities ability to satisfy *each* need by placing the appropriate number in the boxes provided by the p/n matrices. Thus those alternatives most likely to serve as product substitutes would be determined by similar response profiles on abilities to satisfy the listed needs.

Analysis of the Data

A cluster analysis was performed for analyzing the data. The objective of cluster analysis is to form groups or similarity clusters so that the elements within a cluster have a high degree of "natural association" among themselves, while the clusters are "relatively distinct" from one another (Anderberg, 1973). Products/activities falling *within* a cluster are, therefore, more likely to be substitutable than all those falling outside the cluster.

A variety of alternative methods for clustering are available. For the most part these can be classified as hierarchal or centroid sorting methods. The selection of the method to be used is, in essence, dependent upon the particular research being conducted. The method used in this study—an hierarchal method proposed by Sokal and Sneath (1973)—has as its basis the formation of clusters through the average linkage method. In this method two entities are grouped as a new cluster is formed based on the formula $(1/N)\ S_{ij}$ over all i in 1 and all j in J where N is the product of the number of variables in 1 and the number of variables in J. That is, when clusters i and j merge, the sum of the pairwise similarities is used to form a new cluster. This updated cluster is then compared to other clusters by averaging the links of all entities within the cluster and the subsequent merging results based on establishing the shortest difference between clusters until all of the objects are assembled into one group. The value of the average linkage method follows from the fact that the cluster is characterized by the *average* of all the links within it, as opposed to relying on (maximum or minimum) extreme values for the cluster formation. While a number of proximity measures are available for clustering purposes, this analysis made use of one of the more common of these, Euclidean Distance. Squared, the distance between two products i and j in Euclidean space is given by:

$$D_{ij}^2 = (X_{1i} - X_{1j})^2 + (X2i - X2j)^2 = \Sigma(X_{ki} - X_{kj})^2$$
$$k = 1$$

where x . . . represents the respective coordinates for objects i and j. The most likely product substitute would be determined by the shortest distance (in geometric space) between the target product and the alternative.

In addition to the cluster analysis, a second test was used a posteriori to determine if there existed significant differences between the clusters: Duncan's New Multiple Range Test is used to carry out all pairwise comparisons between means, and while for cluster analysis this procedure cannot be considered a true test for providing validity for the clusters, it will lend further (or less) support for the classification scheme.

RESULTS

Identification of Substitutes

Figure 3 through 6 represent the results of the clustering program for beer, television, candy, and cigarettes, respectively. A brief analysis follows:

Beer

Four clusters can be identified for those products under consideration as substitutes for beer. Not unexpectedly the cluster of products that represents the closest grouping includes the alcoholic-content beverages of mixed drinks, wine, and liquor, while soft drinks and activities are less likely to serve as substitutes. Perhaps the only surprising result is that beer was perceived as standing alone rather than grouping with the other alcohol content beverages.

Thus, while beer is considered similar to the other alcohol-based products, it is

Figure 3. Cluster Diagram for Beer.

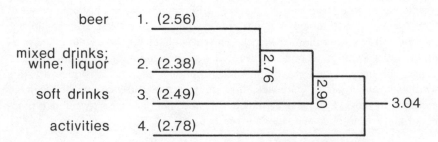

Cluster:

beer 1. (2.56)
mixed drinks; wine; liquor 2. (2.38)
soft drinks 3. (2.49)
activities 4. (2.78)

1. numbers in ( ) represent within cluster average distance
numbers not in ( ) represent between cluster average distance

Figure 4.   Cluster Diagram for Television.

Cluster:

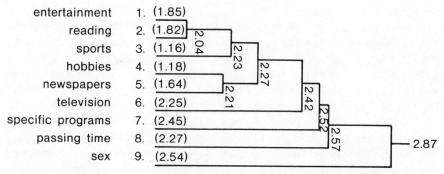

entertainment	1.	(1.85)
reading	2.	(1.82)
sports	3.	(1.16)
hobbies	4.	(1.18)
newspapers	5.	(1.64)
television	6.	(2.25)
specific programs	7.	(2.45)
passing time	8.	(2.27)
sex	9.	(2.54)

1. numbers in ( ) represent within cluster average distance
numbers not in ( ) represent between cluster average distance

also perceived as differing somewhat in respect to the needs under consideration in this study. Therefore, while mixed drinks, liquor, and wine are more likely to be substitutable than the other products under consideration, their degree of similarity is not as high as one might intuitively expect them to be.

Television

Unlike the cluster diagram for beer, that representing television is not as discriminant. Referring to Figure 4, the reader will note that the distances between clusters increases at a very slow pace, as one proceeds from the first cluster formation (entertainment). Based on these results, it appears as though any of the products or activities contained in clusters 1 through 5 might be an acceptable alternative to watching television, though it also appears that television stands alone so far as its ability to satisfy all of the needs listed. The closest substitute (averaging over all needs) would merely be reading magazines (approximately 2.33) or listening to the radio (approximately 2.34). In essence, the change agent might successfully switch the consumer to virtually any of the products under consideration. (Perusal of the mean scores supports this contention, as there seems to be a preponderance of means in the 5 to 6 range, thereby signifying a strong satisfaction with all of the products under consideration.

Candy

Figure 5 represents the clustering process for 144 variables (9 needs × 16 products) that made up the third p/n matrix—the matrix containing alternatives for candy. It was necessary to drop five of the products from the list provided in the questionnaire due to the inability of the computer program to consider such a large number of variables. The decision was made to omit those products that had the lowest rank ordering.

Referring to the cluster diagram in Figure 5, one notes that the first amalgamation of candy with other alternatives involves the cluster containing ice cream, baked goods, cookies, cakes, and pies. The average distance at this juncture is 2.48, which reflects somewhat less than a high probability for substitution than was seen in the television matrix. Perusal of the diagram does demonstrate that the highest likelihood of substitution is likely to come from other sweets—an intuitively logical consideration. By examining the distances between each product on each need, and then averaging the same across products, it would appear that the most likely substitute for candy would be cookies, as the distance of approximately 2.30 is the lowest of the five products. Since all products under consideration are sweets, one might speculate that the lack of preparation, convenience, size, or other factors involving a similarity not contained in the others results in the closeness of these products. The marketer attempting to substitute a product for candy then would be best advised to emphasize switching to cookies.

Cigarettes

Earlier it was noted that a number of drugs have been used as attempted substitutes for cigarettes—the results of their relative effectiveness being incon-

Figure 5.   Cluster Diagram for Candy.

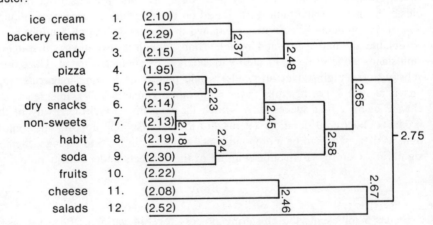

1. numbers in ( ) represent within cluster average distance
numbers not in ( ) represent between cluster average distance

Figure 6.   Cluster Diagram for Cigarettes.

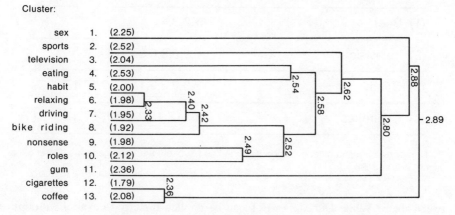

1. numbers in ( ) represent within cluster average distance
numbers not in ( ) represent between cluster average distance

clusive. The fourth p/n matrix under consideration attempts to establish non-drug substitutes for cigarettes.

By referring to Figure 6, it is obvious that of all of those products and activities under consideration in matrix 4, there appears to be only one viable substitute for cigarettes, and that is coffee. Over all the needs tested, there remains a cluster for these two products that is separate from all others. In reality, it appears from the distance measures that none of the products/activities are obvious substitutes based on the needs under consideration. Rather, the results such as those of clusters 5, 6, 10, show that based on specific needs, some products are more substitutable than others, thereby allowing for no clear consensus as to which is most substitutable overall.

SUMMARY OF THE CLUSTERING PROCESS

The results of the clustering process reveal little in the way of unexpected results, or rare insights. The cluster formations appear to follow an intuitively logical pattern and appear to reflect careful consideration of each of the needs. While such results suggest evidence of the success of the methodology employed to determine substitutes, further verification is necessary.

DUNCAN'S NEW MULTIPLE RANGE TEST

As noted previously, Duncan's New Multiple Range Test is used a posteriori to test the resulting clusters to determine whether significant differences exist be-

Figure 7.   Results of Significance Tests for Cluster Analyses of p/n Matrices.

(1) Beer	1,2,3,4
(2) Television	7,9,5,8,6,3,2,4,1
(3) Candy	7,8,2,3,9,11,6,10,12,1,5,4
(4) Cigarettes	10,12,13,9,6,8,1,2,7,4,3,5,11

1. Numbers represent cluster numbers. Underlined subsets are homogeneous. Other pairs significant at p .05.

tween them. While Duncan's MRT can be applied directly to examine groups with equal or nearly equal n's, an extension of the test is needed should largely unequal (as defined by an n of one group exceeding the other by 3 times the original) group memberships occur. Kramer (1956) provides a methodology for making this extension. In essence, Kramer explains that for grouping means of unequal numbers, a table of factors should be established, resulting in making the test for each individual case. According to Kramer, this test then becomes identical to a t-test when comparing only two means. Figure 7 represents the results of comparing each of the sets of means at 95 percent confidence level.

MRT FOR PRODUCT CLUSTERS FOR BEER

Figure 7 (Part 1) reflects the results of testing for significance among the 4 clusters derived from the first p/n matrix.

One will note that clusters 1 and 2 (beer and wine, liquor, and mixed drinks, respectively) are significantly different from those clusters containing soft drinks and activities (clusters 3 and 4, respectively). One might conclude that the clusters are seen as two distinct classes, so far as the needs under consideration. Relative to this study, corroborative evidence of the greater substitutability of those products in cluster 2—as opposed to those in clusters 3 or 4—is offered.

MRT FOR PRODUCT CLUSTERS FOR TELEVISION

No distinct subsets of the clusters resulting from the p/n matrix containing alternatives to watching television are shown in Figure 7 (Part 2). As a result, this test supports the earlier contention that all of the products/activities appear to be viable candidates for substitution, with the lack of significant differences between the clusters bearing out this contention. Thus, none of the alternatives appears to be unacceptable, nor do any appear to differ significantly in their perceived ability to serve as substitutes. Referring to Figure 4, one notes that the clustering process reflects the amalgamation of various product clusters at increasing distance levels. The results of the significance test do not necessarily refute the validity of the methods employed, but rather show that even though sex may be the last to enter the clustering process—and therefore is likely to be the least likely substitute—it is not necessarily a poor substitute.

MRT FOR PRODUCT CLUSTERS FOR CANDY

Three distinct homogeneous subsets can be seen for the clusters resulting from the matrix containing needs for consuming, and alternative products for candy. Figure 7 (Part 3) shows that candy can be considered a member of two of these subsets, both of which when combined contain all of the alternative products under consideration. While the results of this test do seem to substantiate the clustering classification represented in Figure 5, they do not lend to as succinct an interpretation of substitutability as was seen in the p/n matrix for beer. In essence, it appears that all of the products under consideration are likely to be substitutable, and thus one must rely on the clustering procedure as presented for determination of the most probable alternative.

MRT FOR PRODUCT CLUSTERS FOR CIGARETTES

Figure 7 (Part 4) identifies three subsets differing significantly at .05 for those clusters which contain substitute products and activities for cigarettes. As seen in the conclusions, there are a number of alternatives that are not close substitutes for cigarettes. The larger number of members of the homogeneous subset containing cigarettes seems to indicate, however, that a number of the alternatives are likely to be more acceptable than one might expect from Figure 6. (The inclusion of sex as a member of the subset containing cigarettes was a borderline grouping.) The likelihood of any of these alternatives to be a viable substitute appears somewhat less likely than one might have hoped for, however.

SUMMARY OF TESTS OF SIGNIFICANCE FOR CLUSTER ANALYSIS

In summary, the significance tests of the clusters showed few heterogeneous subsets, lending support to the clustering process employed. Such results are not to be considered as surprising, however, in that the selection of the alternatives was conducted in a manner such that only likely candidates would be included. In those particular instances where homogeneous subsets were defined, one can still conclude that all of the alternatives are to some degree substitutable, however, some are significantly more so than are others. The implications of these conclusions will be discussed in greater detail later in this report.

VALIDATING THE METHODOLOGY

While a number of tests of validity are available, including measures of content, construct, and predictive validity, the latter was deemed most appropriate for this study, due to its ability to employ actual behavior as a criterion. In order to provide as authentic a test as possible, and therefore an effective measure of validity, a behavioral measure of product substitution was employed. More specifically, the investigator conducted a "product substitute experiment" in his home with an assortment of friends and neighbors. None of the respondents were informed of the test. (Respondents included ten males, nine females.) Various persons, limited to two per session, were invited to the investigator's apartment for various reasons ranging from a mere social visit to dinner invitations. Upon entry, each was asked what he/she would like to drink and was given the following choices: beer, wine, a mixed drink, soda, iced tea or coffee. Thus, at least two choices from each product cluster were represented in the experiment. When the participant "guests" responded with their choices, they were told that the product selected was unavailable. Each was then asked what his/her second choice would be. Table 1 represents the choices of the "guests" as well as their substitute selections. Additionally, the frequency with which each occurred is represented.

The ages of the participants ranged from 22 through 27 with a mean of slightly over 24 years. The occupations represented in the sample included college students, businessmen, housewives and businesswomen, and a professional football player.

According to the results obtained in the clustering process, one should expect the greater frequency of second choices among those whose first choice was beer to be either wine or mixed drinks with a much lower frequency of second choices from those products from other clusters. The results reported do support this conclusion and show that there is a high degree of predictive validity. Of the twelve "guests" who selected beer as a first choice, eleven (91 percent) selected wine or mixed drinks as a second choice. In addition, three of the four, or 75

Table 1.　Initial Product Selection and Substituted Alternatives
n=19

Initial Selection		Substitute	
Product	Frequency	Product	Frequency
Beer	12	Wine	10
Wine	4	Mixed Drink	1
Mixed Drink	1	Soda	1
Soda	2	Beer	3
Iced Tea	0	Soda	1
Coffee	0	Beer	1
		Coffee	1
		Wine	1

percent of those who requested wine as a first choice, subsequently selected a beer substitute. In addition to this, there is evidence of external validity as the respondents, while in the same age range as those from Samples 1-6 of the study, were not college undergraduate students, but instead were degree holders or noncollege persons. The results of this study, therefore, show at least some ability to generalize to the population at large and offer direct validation of the methodology which has been employed to determine product substitutes.

CONCLUSIONS AND IMPLICATIONS

Four product/needs matrices based on consumers' own perceptions of their needs satisfied by consuming particular products and alternative products that might also satisfy these needs were developed. A cluster analysis technique along with Duncan's New Multiple Range Test was used as corroborative evidence for the various clusters. A behavioral test was also used in order to demonstrate the predictive validity of the results and of the specific methodology employed. Based on the results of these analyses, a number of conclusions were drawn:

1. The proposed methodology appears to have merit so far as its ability to determine product substitutes. The results of the cluster analysis reflect intuitively logical clusters of substitutes lending evidence of face validity. The behavioral measure of predictive validity shows additional evidence in support of the methodology since actual substitute selections followed those which were predicted by the study. The resulting clusters reflect a consideration of each product's perceived ability to satisfy each need—as opposed to merely a rank ordering based on likeability, etc.—as seen by the respondent.

2. The designated substitutes for the "undesirable" products under consideration in this study can be viewed as: beer substitute = wine; candy substitute = cookies; television substitute = reading magazines or listening to the radio; cigarette substitute = coffee.

While the second listing of the results may appear to offer nothing extraordinary so far as the unexpected relationships or rare insights are concerned—or for that matter, improved substitutes from an anti-consuming perspective—the implications to the change agent concerned with promoting anti-consumption are indeed important. First of all, it has been established that a viable methodology for determining product substitutes has been developed. The implication for the change agent is that it is now possible to determine consumers' needs for consuming, the specific products which they consider as potential alternatives to satisfying these needs, and the most likely substitutes from the list of alternatives. Second, by examining the basis of the cluster formations, it is possible to determine the *specific* needs being satisfied by the alternatives. As a result, the change agent may extend the methodology employed in the research to additional areas utilizing different sets of needs and different sets of products as determined by the target group at which anti-consuming is aimed. Finally, the substitutes determined for the products/activities under consideration—i.e., beer, candy, cigarettes, and watching television—may now serve as the basis for building campaigns which are designed to promote product-switching behavior in consumers, at least within the specific population which this study involved. In summary, it has been established that the methodology proposed to determine product substitutes is, in fact, successful in accomplishing its stated objectives.

DIRECTING FOR FUTURE RESEARCH

While it has been demonstrated that the proposed methodology for determining substitutes does, in fact, have merit, there are a few improvements which are worthy of consideration:

1. The sample used in this study was deliberately kept homogeneous for control purposes. Thus, although the results have been shown to be generalizable to a less homogeneous group—subjects of the same age range with various educational levels—it may not always be possible to generalize, for example, to older or younger groups. Future research which is designed to include a much wider range in regard to socioeconomic and demographic variables would further enhance the generalizability of the results.

2. While no *one* particular theory could serve as a basis upon which this study could be built, the establishment of such a theoretical basis would enhance the interpretation of the results. Theory-guided conclusions would permit a further understanding as to why such products were chosen—e.g., beyond the potential to satisfy the stated needs—based upon expectancies derived from earlier studies. Future studies should, therefore, attempt to incorporate more theoretical considerations.

3. Having now derived the clusters, additional insights would be gained by using multidimensional scaling to determine how the products *within* each cluster are perceived relative to the product under consideration. Pairwise comparisons and/or rank-orderings would allow for the presentation of a "map" in which a product-space would be derived, displaying each product's position, as well as the relevant dimensions under consideration. Such information would be useful for deriving marketing strategies aimed at promoting switching.

4. The information provided by the results of this research should be tested in a behavioral setting designed to promote substitution, with actual product switching being the goal. The most likely substitutes—as derived—could be used as an offered alternative to which the consumer could/should switch through:
   a. advertising campaigns designed to promote the substitute based on the particular needs satisfied; or
   b. campaigns (by social groups, organizations, etc.) conducted in which the substitute is considered as a viable alternative to which to switch. Such campaigns might involve group discussions, films, or other methods previously reviewed.

In conclusion, it is now necessary to examine prospective product substitutes through the use of a much larger and broader sample of the population, and with an increased number of products for consideration for anti-consuming purposes. This study has shown that the proposed methodology is efficacious. A longitudinal study designed to institute phase 11 of this plan—e.g., using the information obtained in the study to promote product switching behavior—would logically be in order.

REFERENCES

Anderberg, Michael R. (1973), *Cluster Analysis for Applications,* New York: Academic Press.
Asch, S. E. (1951), "Effects of Group Pressure upon the Modification and Distortion of Judgment," in H. Guetzkow (ed.), *Groups, Leadership and Men,* Pittsburgh: Carnegie Press, pp. 177–190.
Bass, Frank, M., Pessemier, Edgar A., and Tigert, Douglas T. (1969), "Complimentary and Substitute Patterns of Purchasing and Use," *Journal of Advertising Research* 9 (2): 19–29.
Burton, Mike (1972), "Semantic Dimunitives of Occupation Names," in Roger N. Shepard, A. K. Romney, and Sarah Nerlove (eds.), *Multidimensional Scaling: Theory and Application in the Behavioral Sciences,* New York: Seminar Press, pp. 55–71.
Comish, N. H. (1953), "Why Customers Change Brands," *Journal of Marketing* 18: 66.
Cullwick, D. (1975), "Positioning Demarketing Strategy," *Journal of Marketing,* 39: 51–57.
Feldman, L. P. (1971), "Societal Adaption: A New Challenge for Marketing," *Journal of Marketing* 35: 54–60.
Freud, Sigmund (1948), "Instincts and Their Vicissitudes," *Collected Papers,* Vol. 4, London: Hogarth Press and the Institute of Psychoanalysis.
Gelb, Betsy D., and Brien, Richard H. (1971), "Survival and Social Responsibility: Themes for Marketing Education and Management," *Journal of Marketing,* 35: 3–9.
Hamilton, James R. (1972), "Demand for Cigarettes: Advertising, the Health Scare, and the Cigarette Advertising Ban," *Review of Economics and Statistics* 54: 406.
Hanna, N. (1975), "Marketing Strategy Under Conditions of Economic Scarcity," *Journal of Marketing,* 39: 63–67.
Hannon, Bruce (1974), "Energy Conservation and the Consumer," *Science* 29–34.
Howard, John A., and Sheth, Jagdish N. (1969), *The Theory of Buyer Behavior.* New York: John Wiley, p. 520.
Kelley, Eugene J., and Scheewe, Rusty (1975), "Buyer Behavior in a Stagflation/Shortage Economy," *Journal of Marketing* 39: 44–50.
Kotler, Philip (1974), "Marketing During Periods of Shortages," *Journal of Marketing* 38: 20–29.
———, and Levy, Sidney (1971), "Demarketing, Yes, Demarketing." *Harvard Business Review* 49: 74–80.
———, and Zaltman, Gerald (1976), "Targeting Prospects for a New Product," *Journal of Advertising Research* 16: 7–18.
Kramer, C. J. (1956), "Extension of Multiple Range Tests to Group Means with Unequal Numbers of Replications," *Biometrics:* 307–310.
Levitt, T. (1974), "Marketing Tactics in a Time of Shortages," *Harvard Business Review* 52: 6–7.
Lissner, K. (1933), "Die Entspannung von Bedurfnissen durch Erstazhandlungen," *Psychologische Forschung* 18: 218–250.
Maslow, A. H. *Motivation and Personality* (1954), New York: Harper.
McGuire, E. P. (1974), "Marketing in a Shortage Economy," *Conference Board Record* 11: 25–27.
Murray, H. A. (1938), *Explorations in Personality,* Cambridge, Mass.: Harvard University Press.
Ovsiankina, M. (1928), "The Resumption of Interrupted Activities," *Psychologische Forschung* 2: 302–379.

Perloff, R., and Belch, M. (1974), "Toward an Anti-Consuming Ethic," paper presented at the APA symposium, New Orleans, La.

Rothe, James T., and Benson, Lissa (1974), "Intelligent Consumption: An Attractive Alternative to the Marketing Concept," *MSU Business Topics* (Winter): 29–34.

Sheth, Jagdish N. (1970), "Are There Differences in Dissonance Reduction Behavior Between Students and Housewives?" *Journal of Marketing Research* 8: 243–245.

Sokal, R. R., and Sneath, P. H. A. (1973), *Numerical Taxonomy: The Principles and Practices of Numerical Classification,* San Francisco: Witt-Freeman and Co.

Stefflre, Volney J. (1972), "Some Applications of Multidimensional Scaling to Social Science Problems," in Roger N. Shepard, A. K. Romney and Sarah Nerlove (eds.), *Multidimensional Scaling: Theory and Application in the Behavioral Sciences,* New York: Seminar Press, pp. 211–243.

Tolman, Edward C. (1959), "Principles of Purposive Behavior," in Sigmund Koch (ed.), *Psychology: A Study of a Science,* Vol. 2, New York: McGraw Hill.

Weiss, E. B. (1974), "Here Are 29 Checkpoints for Market Planners in an Era of Shortages," *Advertising Age,* (April 15): 19–21.

———— (1974), "New Era of Shortages Complicates Marketing," *Advertising Age* (July 22): 46.

———— (1974), "Shortage Era Affects Marketing Planning, Control," *Advertising Age* (July 22): 46.

Zeigarnik, B. (1927), "On the Retention of Completed and Uncompleted Activities," *Psychologische Forschung* 9:1–25.

THE CEREAL ANTITRUST CASE: AN ANALYSIS OF SELECTED ISSUES[1]

Paul N. Bloom, UNIVERSITY OF MARYLAND

I. INTRODUCTION

The Federal Trade Commission's antitrust case against the four largest manufacturers of ready-to-eat breakfast cereal has produced a great deal of controversy and discussion (Root, 1972; Huth, 1973, 1974; Stern and Dunfee, 1973; Brozen, 1974). Regardless of the final outcome, the case promises to go down in history as one of the most important antitrust initiatives ever taken by the FTC. Moreover, the case has probably raised a larger number of fundamental questions about the social welfare effects of large-firm marketing practices than any prior antitrust proceedings. Clearly, there is much about the cereal case that should be of interest to the members of the marketing profession.

The primary goal of this paper is to provide a preliminary evaluation of several of the key charges made by the FTC in the cereal case.[2] A secondary goal is to stimulate more research by marketing scholars into the types of issues raised in the case. Three major sections are presented in an effort to accomplish these

Research in Marketing—Volume 2, 1979, pages 65–93.

goals. The first section consists of a summary of the major FTC charges and
arguments. An attempt has been made to, in effect, translate the cumbersome,
complicated, legal language of the first two volumes of the FTC's pretrial brief
(524 pages) into a more concise, readable statement of the FTC's case. The
second section contains a detailed analysis of the FTC's charges about the
exclusionary effects of the marketing practices of intensive advertising, product
differentiation, brand proliferation, and shelf-space allocation. Theoretical arguments and empirical findings from both the economics and marketing literature
are drawn upon to raise numerous questions about the appropriateness of these
charges. Finally, the third section contains a short listing of research projects that
could help to resolve some of the issues in the cereal case and similar future
antitrust cases. These projects generally involve the testing of some of the
theoretical arguments discussed in the second section.

SUMMARY OF THE FTC CHARGES

The FTC originally filed a formal complaint against Kellogg, General Mills,
General Foods, and Quaker Oats in 1972, following several years of speculation
that such a case was forthcoming (Wilson, 1971; Cohen, 1972). The complaint
charged the four firms with violating Section 5 of the FTC Act, and it emphasized how the ready-to-eat breakfast cereal industry's "noncompetitive"
market structure and intensive use of advertising had produced numerous undesirable outcomes. The notion that the four companies had achieved their alleged
"shared-monopoly" position through some form of conspiracy or collusion was
conspicuously absent from the original complaint—something which seemed to
make the case a significant departure from previous antitrust initiatives against
oligopolies (Morris, 1972; Lazarus, 1972).[3]

By the time the case came to trial before an FTC Administrative Law Judge in
April, 1976, however, several adjustments had been made in the FTC charges.
The pretrial brief submitted by the FTC Complaint Counsel (1976)[4] identified the
most basic offense of the four respondents as the maintenance of a "tacit conspiracy" to (1) keep prices high, (2) avoid certain forms of behavior that might
foster price competition, and (3) encourage forms of behavior that exclude entry
to the industry. In addition to raising the issue of conspiracy or collusion for the
first time, the pre-trial brief also placed relatively less emphasis on the harmful
effects of intensive advertising than the original complaint had done.[5]

Conspiracy Charges

To be more specific, the FTC[6] is first arguing that an elaborate set of competitive monitoring procedures has been used by the four companies to "police"
compliance with the "tacit conspiracy." Competitive monitoring allegedly
facilitates parallel behavior on the part of the four respondents by discouraging

deviations from the accepted "code" of conduct of the industry described below. Deviations are avoided since they will tend to be spotted rapidly and draw harsh retaliatory actions. According to the FTC, the procedures used by the firms to monitor one another include:

1. Having salespersons collect information on the prices, shelf locations, new product introductions, and promotions of rivals. Some of this information is obtained during conversations which rival salespersons have with one another.
2. Using standard reports on industry marketing activities obtained from Nielsen, SAMI, and other data-reporting services. Reports on competitor behavior have also been obtained from advertising agencies and marketing research firms.
3. Exchanging information on advertising expenditures, using the A.C. Nielsen Co. as a clearinghouse. Each company has submitted data on their advertising expenditures to Nielsen and then received back from Nielsen a supplemental report on advertising expenditures in each media for every brand in the industry. There are no other industries for which Nielsen performs such a service.
4. Participating in the activities, meetings, and programs of the Cereal Institute (a trade association).

The FTC believes that the "tacit conspiracy" or "code" of conduct that is policed using the above monitoring procedures is one that has several dimensions. First, the conspiracy or code allegedly discourages the use of any pricing policies that could produce price competition in the industry. Instead, pricing decisions are formulated to encourage interdependence and the orderly following of one another's price increases, with Kellogg generally serving as the price leader. The FTC claims that a desire for interdependence has been demonstrated in the following pricing actions by the respondents:

1. The announcing of price increases to the public well before they are to take effect.
2. The use of delivered pricing systems which charge all customers the same price for a given shipment, regardless of location.
3. The offering of "price protection" to retailers. This protects retailers by giving them an immediate credit if a price reduction occurs on goods that are in transit to them or are sitting in their warehouses.
4. The suggesting of retail prices to retailers, accompanied by considerable sales efforts to get retailers to follow these prices.
5. The changing of prices in a timing pattern inconsistent with (and more spaced out than) the incidence of cost changes.
6. The charging of high prices for failing brands (a "milking" strategy), rather than using price cuts to stimulate sales of these brands.

By (1) reducing uncertainty about the pricing decisions of rivals and retailers, (2) by allowing immediate reaction to rival price changes (through "price protection''), (3) cutting the frequency of price changes, and (4) signaling an unwillingness to lower price, the above actions have allegedly helped the four respondents overcharge consumers by $128,800,000 in 1970 alone.

The FTC is also charging that the conspiracy or code has discouraged the use of any promotion tactics or product modifications that might possibly stimulate price competition. The respondents have allegedly avoided the use of trade deals and ''cents off'' promotions, refused to produce or sell private labels (even when asked to do so by the major supermarket chains), held back on the vitamin fortification of their products until pressured by the government to do so, and maintained a ''gentlemen's agreement'' for over ten years (1957 to 1968) to limit the use of in-pack premiums. In short, the FTC feels that the respondents have all gone along with a policy enunciated by a Kellogg marketing executive in a quote repeated in the pretrial brief: ''Kellogg has a long history of consistently resisting price cutting and gimmicks and withstanding competitive pressure in these areas with notable restraint—up to the point where it was necessary to participate, overwhelmingly, in order to put an end to destructive prices'' (FTC Complaint Counsel, 1976, p. 204).

Finally, the FTC is claiming that the conspiracy or code tends to restrict competitive behavior to actions that have the effect of excluding new firms from the industry. Four exclusionary practices that are allegedly being used are: *shelf-space allocation, brand proliferation, product differentiation,* and *intensive advertising.* The FTC arguments about the effects of each of these practices are presented in separate sections below.

Shelf-Space Allocation Charges.   The FTC claims that the four respondents have promoted an exclusionary shelf-space allocation plan that has received widespread acceptance by retailers. The plan is one that is promoted by Kellogg and it gives each brand a share of the available shelf space in proportion to its share of the market. Although the other respondents offer shelf-space plans to retailers, the FTC says that these plans have been promoted very lightly and that there generally has been acquiescence to the Kellogg plan. The other respondents have allegedly seen no need to challenge the Kellogg plan as long as they have gotten their ''fair share'' of the space, especially since Kellogg has a larger and more experienced sales force.

The Kellogg's plan has, according to the FTC, managed to exclude entrants and discourage competition in several ways. First, the plan gives the brands of the four respondents ''better'' locations at the center of the aisles while relegating other brands to ''poorer'' locations at the ends of the aisles. Second, the plan has the brands of each manufacturer displayed in a different grouping, making it more difficult for consumers to compare similar brands (e.g., branded and private-label corn flakes) of different manufacturers, and also making it more likely that consumers will select second brands made by the same company which manufactured their first selection. Third, the plan displays the respondents' brands in a "billboarded" fashion (several facings are put next to one another), getting them more attention and impulse purchases. Last, the plan's "fair share" concept of allocating space based on market share has the tendency to stabilize market shares, since a brand's share depends to some extent on the amount of shelf space it receives.

Brand Proliferation Charges. The respondents' practice of continually bringing out new cereal brands is the second major activity that has been labeled as exclusionary by the FTC. Brand proliferation allegedly excludes entrants in the following basic way:

1. Virtually every single profitable "position" in the "product space" of the ready-to-eat breakfast cereal industry is occupied by several brands belonging to the four respondents.
2. With so many brands competing to let consumers know where they stand in the space, the costs of getting the attention of consumers and establishing just one new brand in a profitable position in the space are very high.
3. With so many brands already established in each profitable position in the space, it is extremely difficult for one brand (such as a private label) to create enough preference for itself to obtain a share of the total cereal market large enough to take advantage of economies of scale in production (approximately a 4 to 6 percent share).
4. Even if a new firm manages to establish a brand in some unoccupied, profitable position, it will not be able to maintain a high share for this brand for a long period of time. The respondents can be expected to immediately bring out new brands to compete in this location—as they did with natural cereals.
5. Thus, in order for a new firm to attain competitive production costs, it will need to establish several successful brands (a 1.0 percent brand share is considered good) in multiple positions across the product space. The promotional costs needed to establish several brands in profitable positions, and to obtain adequate market shares for each, serve to deter entry.

In addition to the above argument, the FTC is also claiming that brand proliferation discourages entry by making less shelf space available to new firms.

Product Differentiation Charges. The FTC's criticism of the respondents' product differentiation practices is tied very closely to its argument about brand proliferation. The FTC essentially sees product differentiation, supported by intensive advertising, as the means by which the respondents are able to place brands in profitable positions all across the product space. As discussed above, this spread-out positioning allegedly helps to insulate the respondents from competition from newcomers to the industry—especially from private labels. In addition, the FTC argues that this spread-out positioning also helps to insulate the respondents from competition from each other—since a brand only has to compete with the few other brands that are positioned near it.

The FTC defines product differentiation as "conduct which draws the consumer's attention to minor variations between products, thereby diverting his attention from a comparison of the basic similarities between them" (FTC Complaint Counsel, 1976, p. 325). Practices identified in the pretrial brief as constituting this form of conduct include the use of: product spokesmen (e.g., "Cap'n Crunch" or "Tony the Tiger"), unique package designs, trademarks, nutritional claims, premiums, and changes in the shapes, colors, textures, flavors, additives, or sugar content of old brands in order to create new brands. In essence, the FTC is arguing that these practices make it more difficult and time-consuming for consumers (particularly children) to make value comparisons between brands to discover their true similarities, and therefore consumers start to prefer brands that are perceived to exist all across the product space.

Intensive Advertising Charges. The FTC is charging that the respondents use intensive advertising not only to support their brand proliferation and product differentiation activities, but also to help them discourage new entrants in other ways. Intensive advertising is allegedly used to create consumer brand loyalties for the respondents' products, making it more difficult for new firms to acquire customers. The FTC also claims that intensive advertising gives the respondents an advantage with retailers in getting shelf locations for their products. In addition, it is argued that intensive advertising allows the respondents to obtain quantity discounts from the media, putting small firms that cannot obtain such discounts at a cost disadvantage. Finally, intensive advertising has allegedly allowed the respondents to obtain "product protection" from the television media—making their advertisements isolated in time (for a substantial period both before and after) from ads for other cereal brands. In sum, the FTC feels that newcomers to the cereal industry simply could not afford the advertising campaigns needed to overcome the advantages the respondents have obtained through intensive advertising.

Additional Charges

While the charge of "tacit conspiracy" tends to dominate the FTC arguments, there are several other charges that deserve mention. The FTC claims that the respondents should still be ruled in violation of Section 5 of the FTC Act even if a "tacit conspiracy" is not found to exist. The noncompetitive market structure, exclusionary conduct, and poor performance of the industry are alleged to provide evidence, by themselves, of a need for remedial action. In addition, the FTC is raising objections to the use of heavy advertising directed at children.

A significant portion of the pretrial brief is devoted to arguing that the cereal industry's noncompetitive market structure provides evidence, by itself, of monopoly power. The industry's high concentration, high entry barriers, stable *firm* market shares, and high product differentiation all allegedly provide signs that competition has been lacking. It is also argued that this structure has not come about because of the existence of scale economies or patents, but has resulted solely from the exclusionary behavior of the respondents (whether intentional or not) and two corporate acquisitions that took place in the 1940s. In other words, the FTC is saying that the present structure of the industry cannot be defended on efficiency grounds.

The results produced by the structure and conduct of the cereal industry are considered socially undesirable by the FTC (i.e., performance has been poor). The profits of the four respondents have allegedly been very high relative to other food manufacturers, and the FTC considers this a sign that too many of society's scarce resources have been directed toward the cereal industry. The FTC also feels that the industry has wasted huge sums of money on advertising and that the industry has not been particularly innovative. Finally, the FTC claims that the industry has confused and misled children (and adults too) about the characteristics of ready-to-eat cereals.

Proposed Remedies

The FTC is trying to do more than just stop the "tacit conspiracy" in seeking its proposed remedies. It is trying to restructure the entire industry so as to prevent the re-emergence of such a conspiracy in the future. This means that in addition to prohibiting the respondents from allocating shelf space or exchanging advertising data, the FTC would like to create a total of nine cereal firms out of the four respondents plus require Kellogg, General Mills, and General Foods to license most of their trademarks on a royalty-free basis to any firm willing to maintain the necessary quality control standards (except for Quaker Oats).

The divestiture plan of the FTC would break three new firms away from Kellogg and one firm apiece from General Mills and General Foods. Each new firm would be given the exclusive rights to the trademark of at least one major brand (e.g., Special K, Rice Krispies, Wheaties) in order to give them a sound basis upon which to expand their operations. Royalty-free licensing of trademarks would be required for a twenty-year period for all the remaining brands of Kellogg, General Mills, and General Foods. In addition, for a twenty-year period these three firms would (1) have to license the trademarks of any new brands they develop on a royalty-free basis after a period of five years, (2) have to provide licensees with formulas and methods of production, including quality control standards, (3) have to license "trade dress" (e.g., package design) as part of the trademark licenses, and (4) have to avoid acquiring any cereal firms (Quaker also faces this prohibition). The FTC feels that these remedies will restore workable competition to the ready-to-eat breakfast cereal industry by discouraging brand proliferation, product differentiation, and intensive advertising and by encouraging new firms to enter the industry with low-price strategies.

AN EVALUATION OF SELECTED CHARGES

To say that there are numerous issues that must be resolved in the cereal case is an understatement. The initial trial of the case is taking several years to complete just to give each issue a reasonable airing, and it will probably take until the mid-1980s before the entire case is settled. Of the many issues being considered, it is difficult to determine which ones will emerge as the most pivotal or crucial. The final verdict in the case may very well depend on the resolution of certain legal questions concerned with whether the language in Section 5 of the FTC Act can be interpreted to prohibit "tacit conspiracies" or "shared monopolies." Or the verdict could depend on the answers to questions concerned with whether one can infer an intent to collude from actions such as exchanging advertising data, refraining from using premiums, or acquiescing to one firm's shelf-space plan. The case could also hinge on whether the ready-to-eat breakfast cereal industry is found to be a distinct market and not just a portion of a larger breakfast foods market.

A large proportion of the issues in the case clearly have enormous relevance for marketers. The FTC has raised questions about the legitimacy of using a wide range of common marketing practices, including ones like having salespeople file reports on competitor activities or having reports on industry marketing activities purchased from Nielsen or SAMI. However, in raising questions about the effects of shelf-space allocation, brand proliferation, product differentiation, and intensive advertising, the FTC is bringing to the forefront some fundamental issues that should be of particular concern to marketers. In fact, it could be argued that by criticizing these practices the FTC is questioning the very essence of modern marketing. If these practices are found to be exclusionary or anticompetitive, then a substantial number of well-known marketers may have to make dramatic changes in their marketing programs.

The remainder of this paper is therefore primarily devoted to an evaluation of the FTC charges about intensive advertising, product differentiation, brand proliferation, and shelf-space allocation. The charges are evaluated in reverse order from the way they are presented above (and in the pretrial brief) in order to show how the brand proliferation and shelf-space allocation charges appear to try to remedy the weaknesses of the intensive advertising charge.[7]

Is Intensive Advertising Exclusionary?

The cereal case is raising several questions about the economic effects of advertising that have been hotly debated in the economics literature in recent years. The FTC has essentially adopted an argument that has been developed by Kaldor (1949–1950), Bain (1956), Comanor and Wilson (1974), and others (Porter, 1976a, 1976b; Mueller, 1973) which states that intensive advertising creates entry barriers by (1) producing consumer loyalty for established brands and/or (2) allowing established firms to take advantage of economies of scale in advertising. The following two sections contain discussions of the theoretical and empirical support for both elements of this anti-advertising argument. In addition, a third section is devoted to an evaluation of a competing, pro-advertising argument—Nelson's (1974, 1975) claim that advertising stimulates competition by providing inexpensive, but valuable, information to consumers.

The Brand Loyalty Argument. The typical charge about advertising, brand loyalty, and entry barriers (Bain, 1956; Comanor and Wilson, 1974) can be summarized as follows:

1. Intensive advertising is used by established firms in some industries to persuade consumers to become loyal to certain brands.
2. Intensive advertising must therefore be used by newcomers to an advertising-intensive industry in order to overcome consumer brand loyalty.
3. Many potential entrants cannot afford the cost of the advertising needed to overcome brand loyalties in advertising-intensive industries, especially since the capital markets are reluctant to provide funds to invest in advertising. An investor cannot recover any tangible assets from an unprofitable investment in advertising.
4. Even those potential entrants who can afford the advertising needed to enter an advertising-intensive industry are reluctant to do so, since investments in advertising tend to be much more risky than many other investment opportunities.

In other words, it is argued that by persuading consumers to become brand loyal, intensive advertising creates high "entry fees" to certain industries.

The most basic weakness of the above argument is that it relies on the debatable premise that intensive advertising is a necessary condition for creating consumer brand loyalty. The argument implies that newcomers to an advertising-intensive industry must bombard consumers with repeated advertising messages in order to, in a sense, make up for all the messages consumers have received about existing brands over the years. The argument seems to overlook the possibility that one highly creative advertisement for a superior new brand with a low price could get consumers to switch loyalties at a very reasonable entry fee. Likewise, the possibility that existing brands obtained consumer loyalties by being superior products or by merely being *first* in the market seems to be overlooked. History is filled with examples of brands that have been successful with little or no advertising—such as Hershey's chocolate bars, Rolls Royce automobiles, and, recently, Jewel Food Stores' "no name" groceries (*Time,* 1977).

A second weakness of the above argument is the failure of existing empirical evidence to provide it with support. While no attempts have been made to perform the difficult task of conducting a *direct* test, through experimental methods, of the proposition that advertising *causes* brand loyalty, several prior indirect tests have not given the proposition much support. For instance, studies reported in the marketing literature have found that repeated exposure to an advertising message will not make an individual like a product more than he did after a first exposure (Ray and Sawyer, 1971; Mitchell and Olson, 1977). This tends to refute the notion that a newcomer to an industry must bombard consumers with advertisements to overcome old loyalties. It seems that if the first message fails to win the consumer over, then repetition may not accomplish anything. In addition, interindustry empirical studies that have been done in economics have not found a relationship between market share stability and advertising intensity (Telser 1964; Gort, 1963; Schneider, 1966; Mann and Walgreen, 1970), suggesting that intense advertising may not even be capable of producing enough loyalty to keep market shares from fluctuating widely.

A third weakness of the above argument, as it applies specifically to the cereal industry, is that there is no evidence that strong brand loyalties exist for cereal brands. The instability of brand shares in the industry (see Table 1) provides some evidence of a lack of brand loyalty (Stern and Dunfee, 1973). Further evidence concerning brand loyalty to cereals comes from data reported by the National Commission on Food Marketing (1966). These data, which were obtained from the advertising agency Benton and Bowles, are reprinted here as Figure 1. The National Commission gave the following interpretation to these data:

> The low-level of brand loyalty to cold cereals is shown in figures 13-1 and 13-2. Although a large proportion of consumers exhibited strong loyalties to brands of coffee (70 percent) and detergents (88 percent), only 6 percent of cereal-consuming families were strongly "brand loyal." Sixty percent of cereal-consuming families bought the most popular cereal less than 4 out of 10 times. In figure 13-2, the lightest cereal consuming families (group I) bought an average of eight packages of cereal a year and spread these purchases among four brands. Among the heaviest consumers (group VI), an average of 96 purchases was spread among 15 different brands [National Commission on Food Marketing, 1966, p. 197].

The weaknesses in the typical argument about advertising, brand loyalty, and entry barriers were probably recognized by the FTC staff. This would account for the secondary emphasis given to this argument and for the greater emphasis given to the modifications of this argument that are discussed in the remainder of this paper. One modified argument that the FTC has adopted claims that intensive advertising produces consumer brand loyalty in an indirect way through its effect

Table 1.   Market Shares of Leading Cereal Brands[a]

	1963	1966	1969	1972	1975
Corn Flakes (K)[b]	13.0[c]	11.5	10.0	8.1	8.3
Cherrios (GM)	7.0	8.5	7.3	6.7	6.6
Sugar Frosted Flakes (K)	5.5	6.0	6.0	6.1	5.8
Rice Krispies (K)	6.0	6.5	7.0	6.1	5.1
Raisin Bran (K)	2.0	2.0	3.1	3.6	4.0
Wheaties (GM)	6.0	6.5	4.7	3.8	3.6
Raisin Bran (GF)	2.0	N.A.	3.0	3.0	3.6
Grape-Nuts (GF)	1.7	1.0	2.8	2.5	3.0
Special K (K)	4.0	4.0	4.0	4.0	2.8
Cap'n Crunch (Q)	—	2.5	2.5	2.8	2.5
Sugar Crisps (GF)	N.A.	N.A.	2.3	2.2	2.5
Froot Loops (K)	N.A.	N.A.	1.6	2.2	2.3
100% Natural (Q)	—	—	—	.5	2.3
Life (Q)	1.7	2.0	1.9	1.9	2.2
Post Toasties (GF)	4.5	4.0	2.4	2.5	1.9
Trix (GM)	N.A.	2.0	1.5	1.3	1.7
Total (GM)	—	2.5	2.5	2.6	1.6
Sugar Smacks (K)	N.A.	N.A.	1.5	1.6	1.6
Honeycombs (GF)	—	1.5	1.2	.9	1.6
Sugar Pops (K)	N.A.	N.A.	1.5	1.8	1.5
Lucky Charms (GM)	—	.5	1.5	1.3	1.5
Monsters, etc. (GM)	—	—	—	1.9	1.3
Nature Valley (GM)	—	—	—	—	1.3
Alpha-Bits (GF)	2.0	1.5	1.2	1.1	1.3

[a]*Sources: Advertising Age,* March 24, 1975 and March 29, 1976; *Marketing/Communications,* March, 1970; and *Printer's Ink,* June 23, 1967.
[b]K = Kellogg, GM = General Mills, GF = General Foods, and Q = Quaker Oats.
[c]Figures indicate share of total pounds of ready-to-eat cereal sold in the United States during year.

on retailer buying decisions. It is contended that retailers of convenience goods will not stock a brand or give it adequate shelf displays unless it is supported by substantial amounts of consumer-directed advertising. Retailers want the products they carry to sell themselves and not require additional advertising or sales support. Intensive advertising therefore becomes a necessary ingredient or an entry fee for creating consumer brand loyalty, since without it a brand will not even be put on the shelves (Porter, 1976b).

The validity of this argument depends on whether or not retailer decisions about which brands to stock and display are, in fact, influenced by the amount of consumer-directed advertising a manufacturer does. Although little empirical evidence is available on this issue, what exists indicates that the amount of consumer-directed manufacturer advertising is probably a secondary consideration in retailer buying decisions. For example, an exploratory study by Montgomery (1975) on the decisions made by three supermarket buyers about 24 new

Figure 1[a]. Brand loyalty.

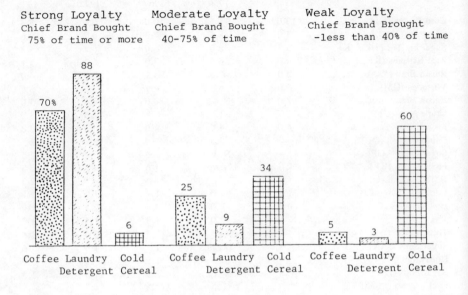

Strong Loyalty   Moderate Loyalty   Weak Loyalty
Chief Brand Bought   Chief Brand Bought   Chief Brand Brought
75% of time or more   40-75% of time   -less than 40% of time

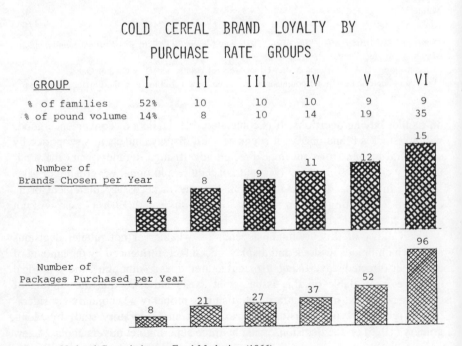

COLD CEREAL BRAND LOYALTY BY
PURCHASE RATE GROUPS

GROUP	I	II	III	IV	V	VI
% of families	52%	10	10	10	9	9
% of pound volume	14%	8	10	14	19	35

[a]*Source:* National Commission on Food Marketing (1966).

products found that "company reputation" and "perceived newness" seemed to have a much larger influence on adoption decisions than the amount of consumer-directed advertising behind a new product (brand). Similarly, Haines and Silk (1967) found no strong evidence of a direct relationship between advertising expenditures and retail availability in a time-series analysis of a single product.

On the other hand, Parsons (1974), in a study that was apparently done with data on the cereal industry, found a strong positive association between advertising expenditures in one period and retail availability. However, his study was done using data on twenty-two brands introduced in the industry between 1950 and 1966 by the *major* manufacturers. Thus, his findings do not necessarily lend support to the contention that intensive advertising is needed to obtain retail availability, since the results could *at most* be interpreted to say that advertising determines the availability of the brands of *established* firms. Moreover, the association found between advertising and availability could have come about because both availability and advertising in a given period are determined by market share or sales in the previous period (as a result of the Kellogg's shelf-space program and decision rules that make advertising a function of past sales).

In sum, the evidence and logic supporting the argument that intensive advertising has either directly or indirectly produced consumer brand loyalties, and thereby a high entry fee to the cereal industry, seems weak. Intensive advertising does not seem capable of having played a major role in creating any consumer or retailer loyalties that exist for established cereal brands, and intensive advertising does not seem to be necessary for a new brand to obtain a loyal following. It would seem that, in the absence of other factors that might push up the entry fee to the cereal industry, a reputable firm with a sufficiently unusual product and some creative advertising could place a brand on the supermarket shelves and obtain enough loyal customers for it without spending a substantial sum of money for advertising. However, there are other factors that *might* push up the entry fee to the industry, and these are discussed further below.

The Economies of Scale Argument. The second way that intensive advertising has typically been viewed as creating entry barriers is by allowing established, large firms to take advantage of economies of scale in advertising that smaller newcomers to an industry cannot hope to obtain (Kaldor, 1949; Bain, 1956; Comanor and Wilson, 1974). These economies supposedly develop because (1) large advertisers can obtain quantity discounts from the media and (2) large advertisers can take advantage of increasing returns to advertising. With economies of scale in advertising, small advertisers (firms) must spend a larger amount on advertising per unit sold than larger advertisers, and this serves to deter entry. A potential entrant will presumably not want to come into an industry where it faces a cost disadvantage for as long as it operates at a relatively small scale.[8]

Both of the conventional explanations for the emergence of economies of scale in advertising can be challenged on empirical and theoretical grounds. The assertion that quantity discounts from the media lead to such economies can be countered with the following arguments:

1. Studies of television rate structures have shown that small advertisers do not incur a larger cost, per thousand homes reached, than large advertisers (Peterman, 1968; Blank, 1968).
2. Even if quantity discounts did favor large advertisers, it would not be difficult for most firms to take advantage of them. Larger, multiproduct firms could purchase advertising time or space for all their products together, while smaller firms could have their advertising agencies purchase time and space for several firms together (Ferguson, 1974).

Similarly, the following arguments can be used to counter the assertion that increasing returns to advertising lead to economies of scale:

1. Empirical studies of the relationship between advertising and sales have consistently shown that there are diminishing returns to advertising. Reviews of this research have been done by Simon (1970), Schmalensee (1972), and Ferguson (1974).
2. If an individual is exposed to an advertisement more than once, the additional amount he will purchase after receiving each successive message will decline—i.e., there are decreasing returns to frequency of exposure. This outcome has been found to occur in several studies (see Benjamin et al., 1969; Simon, 1965). Diminishing returns to frequency of exposure must inevitably lead to diminishing returns to advertising, since one cannot hope to increase advertising expenditures and only increase the reach of an advertisement. There are bound to be some messages designed to reach new prospects that will end up, instead, reaching people who have been exposed to the message before (Schmalensee, 1972).
3. Even if additional advertising expenditures only increase reach (and not frequency), diminishing returns to advertising will still occur. The rational firm will first attempt to reach the best prospects (through its media selection) and then reach successively worse prospects. The result is bound to be diminishing returns (Schmalensee, 1972).

The FTC staff apparently recognized the weaknesses of the typical arguments about the exclusionary effects of economies of scale in advertising.[9] The quantity discounts argument is given minor emphasis in the pretrial brief and the increasing returns argument is presented in a modified form. First, it is contended that intensive advertising has allowed the respondents to gain the advantage of receiving "product protection" from the television media. Second, it is contended, in conjunction with the brand proliferation charge, that intensive advertising and brand proliferation have helped to create a "noise" level that a newcomer must penetrate with numerous advertising messages in order to gain consumer awareness for his brand. Both of these arguments are basically saying that there are certain threshold levels of advertising expenditure that must be reached, at which point the marginal returns to advertising suddenly take an increase. In other words, the FTC seems to be arguing that increasing returns *do* exist, but only as the result of a few upward bends in the sales-response function (to advertising) facing the potential entrant, and not because this function tends to increase at an increasing rate for any wide range of advertising expenditures.

The ability of increasing returns of the type described above to effectively blockade entry depends upon the size and location of the upward bends in the sales-response function (to advertising) facing the potential entrant. If these bends are small and/or at low levels of advertising expenditure, then entry should not be deterred too much. Small upward bends will produce only slight cost advantages over narrow ranges of output, and bends at low levels of expenditure can be reached without large cash outlays.

Since the bend in the cereal sales-response function caused by "product protection" is likely to be small, and the bend caused by the need to overcome a "noise" level is not likely to be at a very high expenditure level, a single brand should be able to pay an entry fee and enter the cereal industry without facing a significant cost disadvantage. Product protection probably does not produce a major bend (if it produces any) in the potential entrant's sales-response function because its effects are more than likely counteracted by the forces leading to diminishing returns to advertising that are discussed above. In addition, while the existence of a "noise" barrier might produce a significant upward bend in the function—especially since there is probably a need to use national television advertising to gain enough awareness to compete effectively (Porter, 1976a)—this bend should occur at an advertising expenditure level that can be reached by many firms. With a product like ready-to-eat cereal, which is likely to be a "low-involvement" item for most consumers, it might only take a few exposures to a television advertisement to stimulate a "learning without involvement" effect (Krugman, 1965, 1977) that would get consumers to pick a new brand off the supermarket shelves after having given only minimal attention and thought to the message and brand. Interindustry studies conducted by Lambin (1976, p. 129) tend to support the contention that the bend in the sales-response function occurs at fairly low levels of advertising expenditure.

It should be noted that any small "noise" barrier that has arisen can be blamed, to some extent, on the fact that cereal is probably a low-involvement product for most consumers. Although it may take only a few messages to stimulate a "learning without involvement" effect with a given person, these messages probably have to be delivered using television in order to reach an adequate number of people—since one cannot expect very much word-of-mouth advertising to take place for a low involvement product. These messages probably also have to be repeated fairly frequently, since forgetting of messages about low-involvement products probably occurs rather rapidly (Robertson, 1976).

In sum, economies of scale in advertising do not seem capable of having produced, by themselves, a major barrier to the entry of a new brand to the cereal industry. At most, such economies have probably made it necessary for a new brand to pay an entry fee in the form of a national television advertising campaign to avoid spending more on advertising per unit sold than heavily advertised, established brands. Once this entry fee has been paid, however, a new brand will probably find itself in a situation where all competing brands face diminishing returns to advertising, and therefore cost advantages for the large advertisers will no longer be present.

An Alternative View: Advertising as Information.   In a series of recent articles in the economics literature, Nelson (1974, 1975) has articulated a viewpoint about advertising that differs somewhat from the one the FTC has tended to adopt in the cereal case. Rather than seeing advertising as a force which raises entry barriers and hurts competition, Nelson argues that by providing useful information advertising makes markets more competitive. His thinking has received considerable acceptance among conservative (i.e., "Chicago-school") economists (Brozen, 1974; Ferguson, 1974; Ornstein, 1977), and it would not be surprising to see some of his arguments appear in the defenses presented by the four respondents in the cereal case.

Nelson basically argues that advertising is pro-competitive because it makes demand curves more elastic. It does this, in the case of goods which *can* be evaluated without actually trying them ("search" goods), by providing inexpensive information to consumers about product attributes and thereby making it cheaper for them to comparison shop. With more comparison shopping being done as a result of advertising, consumers will react more sharply to price changes and thus encourage more price competitiveness on the part of sellers.

In the case of goods which *cannot* be evaluated without actually trying them ("experience" goods), Nelson argues that advertising still makes demand curves more elastic, but for somewhat different reasons. Advertising informs consumers about which brands are the "best buys" (i.e., the lowest price per unit of utility). It does this because the best buys will be the most heavily advertised brands. Heavier advertising would be done for the best buys essentially because it pays to advertise a good buy (and not to advertise a bad one) and because most firms set their advertising budgets on a percentage of sales basis. With consumers knowing which brands are best, they can limit their sampling or trial of brands to a relatively small, homogeneous group and not be forced to consider a broad range of heterogeneous brands. Consumers will therefore react more sharply to price changes of brands in their "evoked set" when advertising exists than they would without advertising—since they will be more likely to notice price changes when less brands are considered for trial. Thus, advertising should produce more price competitiveness among sellers of both search and convenience goods.

Nelson also argues that the availability of advertising will tend to make entry to most industries easier than it would be otherwise. He claims that without advertising, consumers of most goods would tend to rely on information such as the recommendations of friends or the amount of shelf space a brand has to make a brand choice. Information of this type would tend to put established brands in a more favorable light than new brands that may have not been either tried by friends or shelved by retailers. By providing a mechanism for letting consumers know about the existence and qualities of a new brand, advertising increases the likelihood that the new brand will be tried or sampled by consumers who have just begun to shop in the brand's market. Nelson believes that this entry-assisting effect of advertising will overshadow any entry-inhibiting effects advertising might produce.

Although Nelson has made several highly debatable assertions—particularly the claim that the most heavily advertised brands are the best buys—the central core of his argument seems reasonably sound. He is implicitly arguing—as Rosen (1978) has recently done in a more explicit fashion—that advertising allows a seller to let consumers know where his product is positioned in the product space of a market. By doing this, advertising makes it easier for consumers to restrict their search to the brands that possess the characteristics or attributes they desire most. With consumers able to readily compare the prices and other attributes of a relatively small, homogeneous group of advertised brands, competition among the brands within the group becomes greater than it would be without advertising. Moreover, advertising can help create several competitive groupings of brands to serve several segments of consumers possessing divergent tastes.

The FTC does not seem to be completely rejecting the Nelson-Rosen line of reasoning. However, the FTC seems to be arguing that a very high entry fee must be paid in the form of advertising to both obtain a position in the cereal industry's product space and attract consumers away from other brands in nearby positions in the space. But this entry fee for a single brand is not likely to be as large as the FTC claims. As discussed above, the cost of getting consumer awareness for a brand (i.e., obtaining a position in the space) is not likely to be overwhelming, and the cost in advertising of obtaining an adequate number of loyal customers does not have to be substantial.

Conclusions About Intensive Advertising. The intensive advertising that has been done by the four respondents does not seem capable of having produced, *by itself,* a substantial barrier to entry to the cereal industry. In the absence of other barrier-producing forces, a new brand should be able to attract enough customers to survive in this industry by paying an entry fee in the form of a national advertising campaign to gain the attention of consumers and, perhaps, to convince retailers that the new brand will have adequate advertising support. Moreover, once this fee has been paid, a new brand should not face a significant cost disadvantage as a result of economies of scale in advertising.

Intensive advertising may, in fact, be responsible for making the cereal indus-

Intensive advertising may, in fact, be responsible for making the cereal industry more competitive than it might be otherwise. As Sheth (1974) has pointed out, advertising can have an extremely wide variety of effects; it can do more than just persuade consumers to choose one brand of a product over another. Among other things, advertising can trigger what Sheth calls (1) *precipitation mechanisms,* i.e., inducing consumers to buy a product they never purchased previously by arousing their curiosity and/or intensifying their motivations, and (2) *reminder mechanisms,* i.e., inducing consumers to buy more of a product they purchased previously by reminding them of its existence and/or identifying new use situations. Thus, heavy advertising has probably helped new brands to enter the cereal market to apply some form of competitive pressure on established brands. Moreover, advertising has probably contributed to the growth of the overall ready-to-eat cereal market, making entry appear more desirable. Empirical studies by Comanor and Wilson (1974) have found industry sales of cereal to be related to industry advertising expenditures. Without intensive advertising, potential entrants might find the growth rate of the industry too low to make entry attractive, and established firms could have a greater opportunity to exercise monopoly power.[10]

Are Product Differentiation and Brand Proliferation Exclusionary?

The preceding lengthy discussion of the intensive advertising charge has laid the groundwork necessary for evaluating the charges about product differentiation, brand proliferation, and shelf-space allocation in a much more compact manner. Since the product differentiation and brand proliferation charges are closely intertwined with one another, they are evaluated jointly in this section. As the discussion shows, these charges strengthen the FTC's case considerably. However, there are still several weaknesses in the FTC's position that should not be overlooked.

The FTC staff presumably recognized that reasoning similar to what is found in the preceding section might lead a judge to conclude that advertising has produced only a moderate entry fee for a new brand to the cereal industry. Thus, in addition to adopting some of the widely known anti-advertising arguments to attack the cereal oligopoly, the FTC staff has also adopted and refined several less-known arguments about the anticompetitive effects of introducing multiple brands in differentiated markets.[11] In essence, the FTC is arguing that the entry fee for a single brand—whether it is pushed to very high levels by intensive advertising or not—must be paid several times by an incoming firm in order to take advantages of economies of scale in production. This *multi-brand* entry fee will allegedly serve to deter entry even if a single-brand entry fee cannot. The FTC feels that the respondents' use of product differentiation and brand proliferation, supported by intensive advertising, forces the entering firm to pay a multi-brand rather than a single-brand entry fee.

In evaluating the product differentiation and brand proliferation charges, it will be assumed that the FTC is correct in claiming that approximately a 5 percent share of the total ready-to-eat cereal market is needed to achieve economies of scale in production. If the FTC is wrong and economies of scale in production could be achieved without having a 5 percent share—say by using a large-scale plant to produce *both* cereal and other food products—then the two charges would lose credibility. A new firm that was capable of achieving scale economies in production with only a 1 or 2 percent market share would probably have to pay only a single-brand entry fee. Moreover, this fee could possibly be reduced by introducing the product on a regional basis to avoid the expense of national television advertising.

Assuming that the FTC is correct about the industry's economies of scale in production, the first question that must be addressed in evaluating the charges about product differentiation and brand proliferation becomes: Must a new firm introduce several successful brands in order to obtain a 5 percent share of the ready-to-eat breakfast cereal market? Put differently, this question reads: Are consumer tastes so diverse that a single brand cannot hope to obtain a 5 percent market share? If an affirmative answer must be given to this question, then it becomes necessary to consider whether the four respondents are responsible for creating these diverse tastes by using product differentiation, brand proliferation, and intensive advertising.

The inability of any cereal brand introduced over the last dozen years to capture at least a 5 percent market share provides convincing evidence that consumers possess extremely diverse tastes for ready-to-eat cereal (see Table 2). It appears that consumers exhibit great diversity in terms of what they perceive as an "ideal" configuration of cereal attributes. The multi-attribute product space for cereals must therefore have the "ideal points" of consumers scattered widely across it. Those few regions of the product space that are densely populated by consumer ideal points probably represent relatively profitable locations for only a few brands—since even the densely populated regions are likely to represent configurations of attributes that are desired by only a small proportion of consumers. Thus, a new brand which would capture all of the consumers whose ideal points lie in a particular region might still not obtain a 5 percent market share. Moreover, this new brand would face the prospect of having new brands introduced by other firms to compete in the same region.

Two possible explanations can be given for the diversity of tastes which exists among cereal consumers. First, it is possible that consumers have developed these diverse tastes on their own. Second, it is possible that the diverse tastes have been produced by the product differentiation, brand proliferation, and intensive advertising done by the four respondents. The latter explanation is the one implicitly being supported by the FTC. However, the former explanation seems much more plausible.

The FTC is implicitly arguing that techniques such as changing the color or

Table 2.   Market Shares of Selected Brands Introduced Since 1965[a]

	1966	1969	1972	1975
100% Natural (Q)[b]	—	—	.5[c]	2.3
Honeycombs (GF)	1.5	1.2	.9	1.6
Monsters, etc. (GM)	—	—	1.9	1.3
Nature Valley (GM)	—	—	—	1.3
Frosted Mini Wheats (K)	—	—	1.5	1.1
Product 19 (K)	—	1.3	1.6	1.0
Apple Jacks (K)	—	—	1.1	1.0
Buc-Wheats (GM)	—	—	1.5	1.0
Pebbles (GM)	—	—	.7	1.0
Heartland (Pet)	—	—	—	1.0
Quisp and Quake (Q)	—	1.1	1.0	N.A.
Pink Panther (GF)	—	—	.8	—
King Vitamin (Q)	—	—	.9	N.A.
Country Morning (K)	—	—	—	.6
Golden Grahams (GM)	—	—	—	.6

[a]*Sources: Advertising Age,* March 24, 1975 and March 29, 1976; *Marketing/Communications,* March, 1970; and *Printer's Ink,* June 23, 1967.
[b]K = Kellogg, GM = General Mills, GF = General Foods, and Q = Quaker Oats.
[c]Figures indicate share of total pounds of ready-to-eat cereal sold in the United States during year.

shape of a cereal morsel (and advertising this new creation) are capable of deceiving many consumers into thinking that a recently adapted morsel has more desirable attributes for them than any other older morsels. In other words, the FTC is claiming that product differentiation techniques and intensive advertising are used by the respondents to change the location of ideal points in the product space to where new brands are located; that these strategies do more than just help the firms position new brands close to previously existing ideal points. Unfortunately, very little empirical evidence is available to provide insights into the accuracy of the FTC's contention. Marketers have only recently begun to study whether it is easier to (1) change people's perceptions of the attributes of an object or (2) change how important each attribute is to them (i.e, change their ideal points) (Lutz, 1975; Moinpoir et al., 1976). Future research may find, for example, that a *family's* ideal points can be changed with only moderate difficulty by directing advertising and product differentiation at children.

Until empirical evidence emerges to support the FTC's explanation for why consumers exhibit such diverse tastes for cereal, the alternative explanation seems to be more acceptable. Consumers probably developed their diverse tastes for cereal on their own, or at least as a result of more global influences than the actions of four companies. For example, a desire or taste for "natural" cereals probably came about primarily because of the growth of interest in the United States in natural foods, and secondarily because of the advertising and promotion done by the cereal companies. Moreover, the diverse tastes exhibited in the cereal market could be the result of consumers having a preference for trying out or using several different cereal brands over a period of time rather than staying loyal to a single brand (i.e., a consumer may have several ideal points). With a frequently purchased, inexpensive, convenience good like breakfast cereal, consumers may like to purchase many different brands to either satisfy their curiosity, eliminate boredom, or allow them to invent a new cereal by combining several brands at once. Recent research has shown that consumers exhibit a definite variety-seeking tendency (Raju, 1977), and this tendency may be operating in a very significant way in the cereal market.

In sum, it appears that the diverse tastes of consumers have made it necessary for any firm that wants to enter the cereal industry to pay the entry fees needed to introduce several successful brands. However, it does not seem likely that the four respondents hold the primary responsibility for this situation as a result of their use of brand proliferation, product differentiation, and intensive advertising. Instead, it seems more likely that the causality runs in the other direction; that the diverse tastes of consumers have led to the use of brand proliferation, product differentiation, and intensive advertising to try to satisfy these tastes.

In addition, the four respondents may have been encouraged to proliferate brands by the existence of diminishing returns to advertising. The marginal return to these firms of investing funds in old brands (which probably face sharply diminishing returns by advertising) may be exceeded by the marginal return that can be obtained by investing in new brands. In fact, by proliferating brands and catering to diverse tastes, the cereal companies may be acting in a "socially optimal" manner. As Lancaster (1975) and Rosen (1978) have pointed out, differentiating products to satisfy diverse tastes tends to be socially optimal *unless* there are increasing returns to scale for some inputs. Since substantial increasing returns of any type seem to be absent in the cereal industry— something with which even the FTC tends to agree (FTC Complaint Counsel, 1976, p. 149)—and some diminishing returns may even exist, the actions of the four respondents may be producing higher consumer utility levels and more efficient use of scarce resources.[12]

Is Shelf-Space Allocation Exclusionary?

It is not surprising that the FTC placed greater emphasis in the pretrial brief on shelf-space allocation than it did on the other three alleged exclusionary practices. As discussed above, there are severe weaknesses in the charges about intensive advertising, product differentiation, and brand proliferation. However, under careful examination, the shelf-space allocation charge does not hold up much better than the other three charges.

The FTC is essentially saying that the four respondents, with the cooperation of the supermarket chains, have conspired to create a "bottleneck" to the retail selling of ready-to-eat cereal. A new firm will allegedly find it extremely difficult to even get its brands on the supermarket shelves, let alone get these brands ample shelf space and eye-catching locations. With adequate shelf space hard to obtain, entry to the cereal industry is discouraged.

The first question that must be addressed in evaluating this charge is: Do the respondents have the market power necessary to make the supermarket chains follow the Kellogg's shelf-space allocation plan? Unfortunately, the answer to this question is difficult to provide at this time. To arrive at a firm conclusion about this issue, trial testimony provided by supermarket buyers would have to be considered carefully, and this testimony had not been completed at the time this paper was written.[13] Regardless of what this testimony says, however, it seems reasonably clear that the respondents do not have enough power over the supermarkets to prevent the shelving of *all* new brands of new cereal companies. Large companies such as Colgate-Palmolive and Pet should be able (and have been able in the past with Alpen and Heartland natural cereals) to obtain shelf space for at least a trial period.

Assuming for the moment that the four respondents *do* have the power to make the supermarket chains follow the Kellogg's plan, but do not have enough power to completely exclude large companies from a chance on the shelves, the next question becomes: Does the Kellogg's plan make it virtually impossible for the brands of new firms to survive? This is a question that can only be answered by looking at empirical evidence, and the empirical evidence that is available in the public domain suggests a negative answer. Although conventional wisdom (which the FTC seems to be subscribing to) states that a brand will do better if it gets more facings, middle-of-the-aisle locations, and eye-level shelvings, there simply is no strong, published evidence to support this point of view. On the contrary, the available evidence indicates that the type and number of shelf locations a brand receives has relatively little influence on its performance. A review of this shelf-space research can be found in Curhan (1973).

To summarize, it appears that even if the four respondents are succeeding in forcing the supermarket chains to follow a particular shelf-space allocation plan, entry to the cereal industry should not be severely impeded. Large entering firms still should be able to obtain some space on the shelves, and the exact location of this space should not have a substantial effect on the performance of their brands. Moreover, if the respondents do not have the ability to dictate shelf-space plans to the supermarket chains—which seems possible for many chains—then any entry barriers that exist because of a scarcity of shelf space could not be blamed on the actions of the respondents. The retailers would have to be blamed for this situation.

Conclusions About the Alleged Exclusionary Practices

The preceding discussion should not be interpreted as saying that there are no barriers to entry to the ready-to-eat breakfast cereal industry. Nor should it be interpreted as saying that the four respondents in the cereal case are innocent of all charges that have been levied against them. What has been argued is that (1) the entry barriers to the industry are probably not quite as high as the FTC claims and (2) the responsibility for these barriers probably lies more in the hands of consumers and retailers than in the hands of the respondents. No attempt has been made to evaluate whether the respondents are guilty of violating the anti-trust laws for engaging in price fixing or other forms of collusion. Furthermore, no attempt has been made to evaluate, from a legal point of view, whether the behavior of the respondents can be ruled exclusionary merely because (1) very few new firms have been able to enter the industry and/or (2) the respondents have exploited every possible new opportunity (without necessarily intending to exclude new firms). The FTC seems to feel that there are legal precedents in the *Alcoa* and other decisions that would allow this type of reasoning to apply (FTC Complaint Counsel, 1976).

It must therefore be concluded that, for a new firm to enter the cereal industry successfully, an entry fee would probably have to be paid that would be large enough to cover both the cost of national advertising campaigns for three or four new brands plus the cost of the plant and equipment needed to produce an ample supply of these brands. This fee would be needed to gain consumer awareness of the brands and, perhaps, to obtain shelf space for them. Once this fee were paid for a set of brands and consumers began to exhibit a preference for them, a new firm would be able to compete in the industry at no cost disadvantage to older, larger firms.

Although a fee of this magnitude could probably not be paid by any newly formed companies or smaller food manufacturers, there are certainly many large, multiproduct grocery manufacturing concerns that would have little difficulty affording such a charge. Since very few large concerns have attempted to enter the cereal industry, however, most larger firms apparently see the entry fee to the industry as a risky investment which cannot be expected to provide as large a rate of return as alternative investment opportunities.

Why is the entry fee to the industry as high as it is? And why do potential entrants probably see this fee as a relatively risky, low-yield, investment opportunity? In other words, who or what is to be blamed for the lack of entry into the cereal industry? The discussion in this paper has identified several possible culprits other than the four respondents. These include:

1. A tendency for supermarket chains to shelve only heavily advertised brands belonging to firms that have long-standing, favorable reputations.
2. A tendency for consumers to view ready-to-eat cereal as a low-involvement product.
3. The existence of diverse and changing consumer tastes for ready-to-eat cereal.

Thus, the blame for the lack of entry to the cereal industry should probably be directed more toward supermarket buyers and consumers than toward the four respondents. Intensive advertising, product differentiation, brand proliferation, and even shelf-space allocation are techniques that have more than likely been used by the respondents to help them cope effectively with the realities of consumer and retailer buying habits. Moreover, if the respondents had been advertising less, introducing less brands, or providing less resistance to the efforts of private labels to expand their shelf space, then the results produced by the industry might have been less desirable for society. There could have been even less firms competing in the industry and fewer desired varieties for consumers to choose from.

FUTURE RESEARCH DIRECTIONS

Much more empirical evidence is needed before accurate answers can be obtained to many of the questions addressed above. This is why the conclusions to the previous section are stated in a tentative manner. In this short concluding section, several marketing research projects are suggested that might provide the kind of empirical evidence needed to resolve some of the crucial issues in the cereal case or similar future antitrust cases.[14] Many of these projects would involve extensions or refinements of the marketing studies cited above. A lengthier discussion of how marketing or consumer research could contribute to the resolution of antitrust issues can be found in a recent paper by the author (Bloom, 1978).

Members of the marketing profession would appear to be particularly well-suited for conducting research projects such as the following:

1. Efforts to determine whether intensive advertising tends to create consumer or retailer loyalties to certain brands or companies and thereby barriers to entry.
2. Studies to determine whether entry to various industries is inhibited by the existence of large, upward "bends" in the sales response functions to advertising (produced, for example, by a need to exceed a threshold "noise" level).
3. Investigations to determine whether increasing the number and diversity of the brands in a market can increase the difficulty of communicating a new brand's position in the market's product space.
4. Tests of Nelson's (1974) and Rosen's (forthcoming) arguments about the ability of advertising to stimulate competition by providing valuable information about product attributes.
5. Attempts to determine whether diverse tastes or spread-out "ideal points" in certain markets (and any problems this phenomenon creates for entering brands) tend to be caused by the advertising and product differentiation strategies of business firms or, alternatively, by the variety-seeking traits of consumers.
6. Inquiries into whether shelf-space plans can be forced upon a large cross-section of supermarkets by powerful grocery manufacturers.

7. Examinations of whether brands of grocery products incur a significant disadvantage when they receive small amounts of shelf space, are placed at the end of an aisle, or are located apart from brands to which they are similar.

8. Pretests of how consumers will react to the proposed remedy of having several manufacturers market versions of a popular brand (all with the same trademark).

Carefully designed experiments and precise data-collection procedures would be needed to carry out these suggested research projects. However, by conducting research along these lines, marketers could begin to address antitrust issues that could never really be resolved using the economist's typical approach of analyzing aggregate, archival data. The skills that many marketers have acquired in designing experiments, conducting surveys, measuring perceptions and preferences, and analyzing data using multivariate methods—skills which are alien to most antitrust economists and lawyers—could be put to good use in settling antitrust debates.

CONCLUSION

No matter what final verdict is reached in the antitrust case involving the four largest manufacturers of ready-to-eat breakfast cereal, the case promises to stand out as one of the most important proceedings in the history of U.S. marketing. In a sense, marketing *itself* is on trial, as practices that have received widespread use by large, progressive marketing organizations have been accused of being anticompetitive and unfair.

The analysis presented in this paper suggests that there are some serious weaknesses in the FTC's case against the cereal companies. In particular, it is argued that certain practices the FTC labels as "exclusionary" are probably used legitimately by the companies in an effort to cope successfully with the realities of the marketplace. However, this paper does not pretend to contain the final word about this extraordinarily complicated case. Only a portion of the FTC's many charges are considered, and even these few evaluated charges can only be tentatively dismissed based on existing empirical evidence. Additional research on a wide variety of issues (see the previous section) is clearly needed to help one reach a firm conclusion about this case. Such research would also probably be relevant to future antitrust cases involving major consumer products marketers.

FOOTNOTES

1. The author would like to thank Jagdish Sheth, David Gardner, and Keith Hunt for their helpful comments. Financial support for this research was provided in part by a grant from the Bureau of Business and Economic Research of the University of Maryland.

2. Since the trial of the case before an FTC Administrative Law Judge was taking place at the time this was written, it was not possible to prepare a final, comprehensive evaluation of the case.

3. If the courts were to hold that merely the existence of a noncompetitive market structure accompanied by certain noncollusive forms of anticompetitive conduct made an oligopoly in violation of the antitrust laws (i.e., that collusion need not be present), then the antitrust enforcement agencies would have a much easier time penalizing or restructuring oligopolies.

4. Since the descriptions of the FTC arguments found in this paper are based on the contents of the pretrial brief, the reader should recognize that some modifications of these arguments may have occurred during the trial itself.

5. There has been some tendency for people to view the cereal case as being primarily concerned with the anticompetitive effects of advertising (Brozen, 1974; Huth, 1974). This view clearly is no longer accurate.

6. For simplicity, FTC Complaint Counsel (1976) arguments are labeled as FTC arguments in this paper.

7. Discussing the charges in this order should show some of the logic the FTC probably used when it decided to place less emphasis on the intensive advertising charge than had been expected (Brozen, 1974; Huth, 1974).

8. Attempts by a small newcomer to overcome this cost disadvantage rapidly by either lowering price or raising advertising expenditures, in order to operate at a larger scale, would be extremely costly and would risk retaliatory actions by established firms.

9. Since Richard Schmalensee, the developer of the cited counterarguments, has been a prime consultant to the FTC in the cereal case, the de-emphasis of the economies of scale argument is not surprising.

10. The author (Bloom, 1976) has examined the effect on entry of limiting the volume of advertising expenditures in a hypothetical oligopolistic industry where industry sales are influenced by industry advertising expenditures. The results indicated that entry became less desirable when total industry advertising was reduced, primarily because the growth rate of the industry diminished.

11. The brand proliferation charge is drawn essentially from the literature on spatial competition (Hotelling, 1929; Eaton and Lipsey, 1975; Hay, 1976), and the product differentiation charge is drawn, to a certain extent, from some recent writing on competition in markets characterized by imperfect information (Salop, 1976). Both charges also seem to incorporate the less abstract thinking found in essays on entry barriers written by people like Lanzillotti (1954) and Caves and Porter (1977).

12. Of course, it could be argued that the diverse tastes being catered to by the cereal companies are "bad" tastes, and that society would be better off if consumers developed less diverse, "good" tastes for the companies to serve. But the determination of what is a "good" taste and what is a "bad" taste for cereal is a "values" question that the FTC or any other party would have great difficulty resolving.

13. *Advertising Age* (1976) has reported that several supermarket executives testified in the trial that cereal shelving decisions are made solely by their firms and are not dictated by Kellogg or any of the other manufacturers. These executives also pointed out that it has long been common practice for supermarkets to allocate shelf space to brands in a product category according to market share.

14. *Business Week* (1977) recently published an article speculating that more antitrust actions against oligopolistic industries were forthcoming.

REFERENCES

Advertising Age (1976), "Grocers Deny Outside Shelf Control," 47: 2. (November 1).

Bain, Joe S. (1956), *Barriers to New Competition*, Cambridge, Mass.: Harvard University Press.

Benjamin, B., W. P. Jolly, and J. Maitland (1960), "Operational Research and Advertising: Theories of Response," *Operations Research Quarterly* 11: 205–218 (December).

Blank, David M. (1968), "Television Advertising: The Great Discount Illusion, or Tonypandy Revisited," *Journal of Business* 41: 10–38 (January).

Bloom, Paul N. (1976), *Advertising, Competition, and Public Policy: A Simulation Study*, Cambridge, Mass.: Ballinger Publishing Co.

―――― (1978), "Potential Contributions of Consumer Research to Antitrust Decision Making," in H. Keith Hunt (ed.), *Advances in Consumer Research*. Vol. 5, Chicago: Association for Consumer Research.

Brozen, Yale (1974), "Is Advertising a Barrier to Entry?" in Yale Brozen (ed.), *Advertising and Society*, New York: New York University Press, 79–110.

Business Week (1977), "Another Swipe at the Oligopolies," 127 (May 23).

Caves, R. E., and Porter, M. E. (1977), "From Entry Barriers to Mobility Barriers: Conjectural Decisions and Contrived Deterrents to New Competition," *Quarterly Journal of Economics* 91: 241–261 (May).

Cohen, Stanley E. (1972), "Cereal Industry's History Helps Explain FTC's New Anti-trust Probe," *Advertising* Age 43: 10 (January 31).

Comanor, William S., and Wilson, Thomas (1974), *Advertising and Market Power*, Cambridge, Mass.: Harvard University Press.

Curhan, Ronald C. (1973), "Shelf Space Allocation and Profit Maximization in Mass Retailing," *Journal of Marketing* 37: 54–60 (July).

Eaton, B. C., and Lipsey, R. G. (1975), "The Principle of Minimum Differentiation Reconsidered: Some New Developments in the Theory of Spatial Competition," *Review of Economic Studies* 42: 27–50 (January).

Ferguson, James M. (1974), *Advertising and Competition: Theory, Measurement, Fact*, Cambridge, Mass.: Ballinger Publishing Company.

FTC Complaint Counsel (1976), *Trial Brief—In the Matter of Kellogg Company et al.*, Docket No. 8883, Federal Trade Commission, Vols. I and II.

Gort, Michael (1963), "Analysis of Stability and Change in Market Shares," *Journal of Political Economy* 71: 51–63 (February).

Haines, George H., and Silk, A. J. (1962), "Does Consumer Advertising Increase Retail Availability of a New Product?" *Journal of Advertising Research* 2: 2–10 (March).

Hay, D. A. (1976), "Sequential Entry and Entry-Deterring in Spatial Competition," *Oxford Economic Papers* 28: 240–257 (July).

Hotelling, H. (1929), "Stability in Competition," *Economic Journal* 39: 41–57 (March).

Huth, William E. (1974), "The Advertising Industry—An Unlikely Monopolizer," *Antitrust Bulletin* 14: 653–679 (Winter).

―――― (1973), "An Ominous Storm in a Cereal Bowl," *Fortune* 88: 148–150 (July).

Kaldor, Nicholas (1949–1950), "The Economic Aspects of Advertising," *Review of Economic Studies* 18 (No. 1): 1–27.

Krugman, Herbert E. (1965), "The Impact of Television Advertising: Learning Without Involvement," *Public Opinion Quarterly* 29: 349–356 (Fall).

―――― (1977), "Memory Without Recall, Exposure Without Perception," *Journal of Advertising Research* 17: 7–12 (August).

Lambin, Jean Jacques (1976), *Advertising, Competition and Market Conduct in Oligopoly Over Time*, Amsterdam: North-Holland Publishing Co.

Lancaster, Kelvin (1975), "Socially Optimal Product Differentiation," *American Economic Review* 65: 567–585 (September).

Lanzillotti, Robert F. (1954), "Multiple Products and Oligopoly Strategy: A Development of Chamberlin's Theory of Products," *Quarterly Journal of Economics* 68: 461–474 (August).

Lazarus, Simon (1972), "Vs. the Aristocrats of the Breakfast Table," *The New York Times* (January 30).

Lutz, Richard J. (1975), "Changing Brand Attitudes Through Modification of Cognitive Structure," *Journal of Consumer Research* 1: 49–59 (March).

Mann, H. Michael, and Walgreen, J. A. (1970), "Product Differentiation and Market-Share Stability," in *Proceedings of the Fall Conference*, Chicago: American Marketing Association.

Mitchell, Andrew A., and Olson, Jerry C. (1977), "Cognitive Effects of Advertising Repetition," in William D. Perreault, Jr. (ed.), *Advances in Consumer Research,* Vol. 4, Chicago: Association for Consumer Research, pp. 213–220.

Moinpoir, Reza, McCullough, James M. and MacLachlan, Douglas (1976), "Time Changes in Perception: A Longitudinal Application of Multidimensional Scaling," *Journal of Marketing Research* 13: 245–253 (August).

Montgomery, David B. (1975), "New Product Distribution—An Analysis of Supermarket Buyer Decisions," *Journal of Marketing Research* 12: 255–264 (August).

Morris, John D. (1972), "Cereal Monopoly by 4 Top Makers Charged by FTC," *The New York Times,* p. 1 (January 25).

Mueller, Willard F. (1973), "Marketing Competition in Oligopolistic Industries: The Attack on Advertising," in Fred C. Allvine (ed.), *Public Policy and Marketing Practices,* Chicago: American Marketing Association.

National Commission on Food Marketing (1966), *Studies of Organization and Competition in Grocery Manufacturing: Technical Study No. 6,* Washington, D.C.: Government Printing Office.

Nelson, Phillip (1974), "Advertising as Information," *Journal of Political Economy* 81: 729–754 (July/August).

_____ (1975), "The Economic Consequences of Advertising," *Journal of Business* 48: 213–241 (April).

Parsons, Leonard J. (1974), "An Econometric Analysis of Advertising, Retail Availability, and Sales of a New Brand," *Management Science* 20: 938–947 (February).

Peterman, John L. (1968), "The Clorox Case and the Television Rate Structures," *Journal of Law and Economics* 11: 321–422 (October).

Porter, Michael E. (1976a), "Interbrand Choice, Media Mix and Market Performance," *American Economic Review: Papers and Proceedings* 66: 398–406 (May).

_____ (1976b), *Interbrand Choice, Strategy, and Bilateral Market Power.* Cambridge, Mass.: Harvard University Press.

Raju, P. S. (1977), "A Study of Exploratory Behavior in the Consumer Context," unpublished Ph.D. Dissertation, University of Illinois at Urbana-Champaign.

Ray, Michael L., and Sawyer, Alan G. (1971), "A Laboratory Technique for Estimating the Repetition Function for Advertising Media Models," *Journal of Marketing Research* 8: 20–29 (February).

Robertson, Thomas S. (1976), "Low-Commitment Consumer Behavior," *Journal of Advertising Research* 16: 19–24 (April).

Root, H. Paul (1972), "Should Product Differentiation be Restricted?" *Journal of Marketing* 36: 3–9 (July).

Rosen, Sherwin (forthcoming), "Advertising, Information and Product Differentiation," in *Issues in Advertising: The Economics of Persuasion,* Washington, D.C.: American Enterprise Institute.

Salop, Steve (1976), "Monopolistic Competition Reconstituted or Circular Fashions in Economic Thought," presented at the North American Meeting of the Econometric Society, Atlantic City (September).

Schmalensee, Richard (1972), *The Economics of Advertising,* Amsterdam: North-Holland Publishing Co.

Schneider, N. (1966), "Product Differentiation, Oligopoly, and the Stability of Market Shares," *Western Economic Journal* 5: 58–63 (December).

Sheth, Jagdish, N. (1974), "Measurement of Advertising Effectiveness: Some Theoretical Considerations," *Journal of Advertising* 3(1): 6–11.

Simon, Julian L. (1965), "Are There Economies of Scale in Advertising?" *Journal of Advertising Research* 5: 15–20 (June).

_____ (1970), *Issues in the Economics of Advertising,* Urbana: University of Illinois Press.

Stern, Louis W., and Dunfee, Thomas W. (1973), "Public Policy Implications of Non-Price Marketing and De-Oligopolization in the Cereal Industry,'' in Fred C. Allvine (ed.), *Public Policy and Marketing Practices,* Chicago: American Marketing Association.

Telser, Lester G. (1964), ''Advertising and Competition,'' *Journal of Political Economy* 72: 537–562 (December).

Time (1977), ''No Brand Groceries,'' 110: 80 (November 21).

Wilson, Rufus E. (1971), ''The FTC's Deconcentration Case Against the Breakfast-Cereal Industry: A New 'Ballgame' in Antitrust?'' *Antitrust Law and Economics Review* 4: 57–76 (Summer).

GIFT-GIVING BEHAVIOR[1]

Russell W. Belk, UNIVERSITY OF UTAH

I. INTRODUCTION

Gift-giving is a largely unexplored context of consumer behavior. This is rather surprising in light of the prominence of gifts in the purchases of many products such as clothing and accessories, small appliances, dinnerware, colognes, and toys. It has been conservatively estimated that gifts account for 10 percent of retail sales in North America (Belshaw, 1965, p. 50). In modern U.S. society the process of exchanging gifts often begins with prenatal "baby shower" gifts and continues through life and even beyond with gifts of money and flowers to memorialize the dead. In between, the array of ritualized gift-giving occasions includes birthdays, bar/bath mitzvahs, graduations, weddings, wedding anniversaries, Christmases, Valentine's Days, Mother's Days, Father's Days, and others.

As the nature of such occasions suggests, gifts are generally given to others in order to symbolize and celebrate important life events, religious history, and family relationships. It also appears that by means of the selection and transference of gifts on these occasions, important symbolic messages are conveyed

Research in Marketing—Volume 2, 1979, pages 95–126.
Copyright © 1979 by JAI Press Inc.
All rights of reproduction in any form reserved.
ISBN 0-89232-059-1

between the giver and recipient. But while anthropologists have examined the functions and determinants of gift-giving in primative societies (e.g., Benedict, 1960; Mauss, 1954; Malinowski, 1932), there is little published consumer research about gift-giving in modern society. As one small step toward improving our present knowledge of gift-giving and encouraging further research in this area, this paper outlines several concepts and issues relevant to the study of gift-giving and presents results from two exploratory pieces of field research focused on certain aspects of gift-giving.

A. Dimensions of Gift-Giving

Although gift-giving is a universal and ancient phenomenon, several variations of gift-giving exist, dependent upon the types of: *givers, gifts, recipients,* and *conditions* involved. The givers may be individuals, families, or organizations (e.g., corporate charitable donations). Recipients may also be individuals, families, or organizations, including organizations such as the Salvation Army which redistribute gifts to other recipients. The gifts may be monetary, purchased products and services (including greeting cards and accompanying wrappings), personally crafted objects, personal services, previously owned products and property, or even body organs and blood. And the situational conditions of gift-giving may differ according to characteristics of the gift-giving occasion, whether the presentation of the gift is public, private, or anonymous, and whether the gift is conveyed directly or contingent upon some event such as the death of the giver or performance of agreed-upon activities by the recipient. Because of their unique character, the present discussion will exclude gifts to and from organizations, gifts of body organs and blood, and gifts which are not conveyed directly to the recipient. In order to further specify the scope of the present inquiry, it is useful to consider the different functions which the process of gift-giving may serve. These functions and our present theoretical and empirical knowledge of them are considered briefly below.

B. Functions of Gift-Giving

1. Gift-Giving as Communication. Perhaps the most general function which gift-giving serves is to act as a form of symbolic communication between the giver and recipient. As Figure 1 illustrates, gift-giving can be viewed in terms of the traditional models of communication by simply replacing the message and channel with the gift. Since the gift is able to act as both message and channel for delivering the message to the recipient, there is less opportunity for distortion and slippage in this part of the paradigm. However, because meaning must be conveyed through the composite features of the gift object rather than through the more flexible features of words, there is an increased opportunity for encoding

Figure 1. Gift-giving as Communication.*

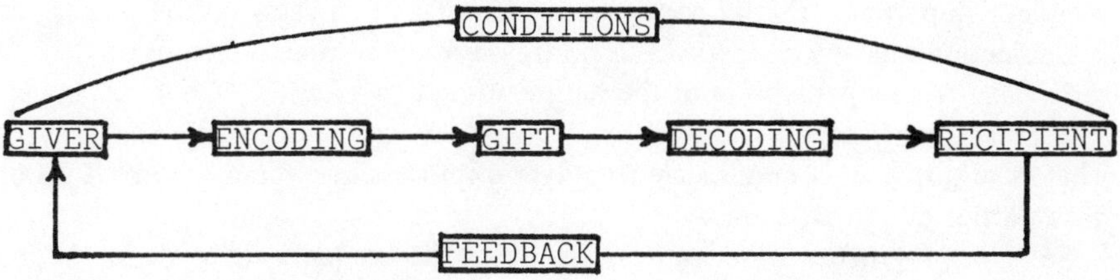

*This paradigm parallels many models of the communication process, such as those by DeFleur (1970), Cherry (1966), and Laswell (1948).

and decoding errors.[2] That is, the giver may have difficulty finding a gift selection which adequately expresses an intended message, and the recipient may misinterpret messages presumably conveyed by the gift. It is because of the indirect nature of the messages conveyed by gifts that the communication function of gift-giving may be regarded as symbolic. The feedback loop of the paradigm is somewhat more direct in that it usually involves immediate verbal expressions of thanks by the recipient, and may also involve the selection of reciprocal gifts by the present recipient for the present giver. However, even though this feedback is often immediate and concrete, it only indirectly indicates how the recipient decoded the meaning of the gift.

In seeking to understand what messages gifts *are* normally intended to convey, Mauss concluded from his studies of gifts in archaic societies that gift-giving is often a means of showing honor and respect for the recipient (Mauss, 1954). Whether the honor and respect is due to affection, admiration, deference, or appreciation, the importance of the recipient to the giver is established and confirmed through the presentation of the gift. The recipient of a gift undoubtedly recognizes this basic meaning of gifts as well. In fact, Levi-Strauss (1965) has noted that an individual who displays Christmas cards on a fireplace mantel may be saying in effect, "See how important I am." And where anticipated gifts supporting self-worth are not forthcoming, the would-be recipient is likely to be understandably upset. Anyone who has failed to note the passage of a spouse's birthday or wedding anniversary has doubtless heard some echo of these sentiments.

Goffman (1961) theorized that the fact that a gift is given is sufficient to convey the importance message, and that therefore the particular gift selected is irrelevant. While the cliché that "It's the thought that counts" is common, in the United States it tends to be offered more as a rationalization of an inappropriate gift than as an accurate statement of social values. It would be highly misleading in most cultures to assume that gift selections have no bearing on the meaning of the gift transaction. Not only can gift selection further define the *degree* of recipient importance that is communicated, but as Schwartz (1967) noted, the gift selection characteristics help to portray a more complete picture of:

1. The giver's perception of the recipient; and
2. The giver's self-perception.

That is, a gift may communicate the giver's impressions about the identities of *both* parties to the exchange.

Selecting a gift based on impressions about the recipient involves more than simply seeking a gift which the recipient will like. A person might very well like a cordless power drill and a mystery novel equally well, but would still assume that the givers of each of these gifts have very different impressions of the recipient. Although there are selections of gifts which have become traditionally acceptable and are therefore relatively "safe" gifts (e.g., an innocuous birthday card or a conservative tie), there are probably no gifts which are completely devoid of any message about the recipient. And to the extent that the giver and recipient are thought by the giver to be dissimilar, the choice of gifts cannot merely be an extension of the giver's tastes.

In one earlier study examining the process of gift selection (Belk, 1976), data were presented supporting the balance theory model shown in Figure 2. All relationships in the model were measured and coded as either positive or negative (reflecting the words in parentheses). One case of a "balanced" structure would be where all five of these relationships are positive. In this case the giver likes his or her present self-concept, perceives the recipient as similar, likes the recipient, likes the gift selected, and also perceives that the recipient likes the gift selected. Such balanced states were predicted to be preferred over less balanced states, and balance was defined to occur when the products of the signs of the top (P-P'-O) triangle, the bottom (P-O-G) triangle, and the outer (P-P'-O-G) diamond are all positive. Such complete balance would therefore occur when each of these loops has 0, 2, or 4 negative relationships. While in the example above this was achieved by choosing a gift which the giver liked and perceived the recipient to like, there are other balanced examples in which a gift which is disliked by one or both parties is predicted to be chosen. The results generally confirmed these predictions, but suggested also that many instances of "imbalanced " gift-giving exist. These instances of imbalance were found to be most common when no prior mutual gift-giving between the parties had taken place and when the recipient was not a close relative of the gift-giver. The fact that balanced cognitions about gift-giving were also found to be associated with greater satisfaction concerning the gift exchange is compatible with the cognitive consistency principle.

Although these findings may provide some insight into the conditions under which gifts that are pleasing to either the giver, the recipient, or both are chosen, they do nothing to indicate which of the possible gifts fulfilling these criteria are selected. These findings also provide no insight into what particular message

Figure 2.   Gift-Giving Diagraph.*

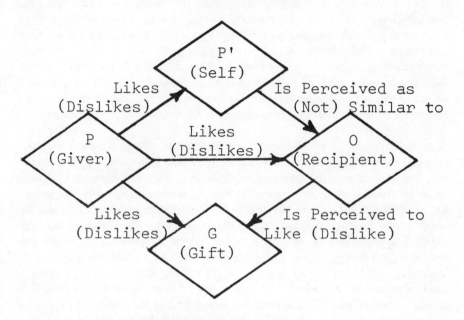

*Modified from Belk (1976).

about the giver and the giver's impressions of the recipient are conveyed. The data to be presented in the empirical portion of this paper are partially directed toward answering these questions.

Whereas the message which a gift communicates about the recipient is often, "This is the type of person you are" (or possibly "should be"), the message which the gift communicates about the giver may be either assertive or inquiring. In the more active assertive form, the giver is attempting to demonstrate a particular self-trait to the recipient (e.g., "I am generous," or "I am artistic"). This would be done by selecting a gift which is clearly expensive or artistic, respectively. In the more passive inquiring form of self-presentation in gift-giving, the giver seeks to obtain consensual validation of personal tastes and traits as reflected in the gift. This validation is hopefully obtained through the recipient's approval of the gift. The feedback sought in such cases might be, "You certainly are clever," or "My, what remarkable taste you have." In many respects this active assertion or passive affirmation of the giver's self-concept is similar to the messages conveyed and feedback sought from visible or conspicuous personal consumption, except that objects which are not normally conspicuous may become so by choosing them as gifts. Grubb and Grathwohl (1967) have presented a parallel model of visible personal consumption. In both cases the success of the communication depends upon the similarity of symbolic interpretations of a consumption object by two parties. In the case of visible personal consumption the two parties are the consumer and another to whom this person's consumption is apparent. In the case of gift-giving the two parties are the giver and receiver. Thus the one advantage that a gift-giver may have in successfully communicating is that the other party to the transaction is fixed and known. Because the perceptions of a single known individual may be anticipated much more accurately than the perceptions of people in general, there is in fact a great opportunity for successful communication in the process of gift exchange.

2. Gift-Giving as Social Exchange. In addition to gift-giving's role in interpersonal communication, the exchange of gifts also aids in establishing, defining, and maintaining interpersonal relationships. This is a somewhat broader symbolic function than communication because it involves not only interpreting the meaning of gift-giving, but also predicating future behaviors on these interpretations. From the point of view of the recipient this often requires interpreting the gift-giving motives of the giver. For instance, suppose a college instructor receives a gift from a student of the opposite sex. One motive might be that the student is merely expressing courtesy, appreciation, or respect. This practice is more common in the Orient, but runs a risk of being misinterpreted in U.S. culture. Another possible interpretation would be that the student is expressing attraction and affection. And a third motive might be that the student is attempting to bribe in return for subsequent favors in grading or student evaluation. Obviously the interpretation of the gift-giver's motives in this instance might make the difference between condemning and graciously accepting the gift.

After a relationship between two persons has been established, by gifts or other means, the mutual exchange of gifts can help to perpetuate and clarify the relationship between them. It is normally important that this gift exchange is reciprocal rather than only one-sided. In established gift-giving relationships and for gift exchange on occasions such as birthdays which do not occur for giver and receiver simultaneously, this mutuality is fairly easily achieved if both parties are interested in maintaining the relationship. But where the relationship is in its earlier stages and where the gift-giving occasion occurs simultaneously for both parties, such as Saint Valentine's Day, the risk of one-sided exchanges is greater. One-sided exchanges are probably less consequential for relationships which are strongly defined by other means, such as employment or family ties, or where the recipient is exempted from reciprocating by virtue of age, health, or resources, but normally one-sided "exchanges" create tension and are not continued.

The ability of a gift to clarify the nature of a relationship depends upon the particular gifts selected. One apparent relationship defining property of gifts is their cost to the giver. Generally, the dearer the cost, the dearer the relationship desired. However, a gift may be inappropriately or embarrassingly expensive as well. In their work with latitudes of acceptance in social judgment theory, the

Sherifs (1963) found evidence supporting the existence of both upper and lower limits on acceptable gift prices in a gift of wearing apparel for a loved one. They also found that these ranges differed between the whites, blacks, Navajo Indians, and Oklahoma Indians tested. Another characteristic of gifts which may help to define the nature of a relationship is the degree to which the gift is intimate. As used here, an intimate gift is one that is appropriate to the needs and tastes of the recipient rather than being suitable for virtually anyone. Again, the more intimate the gift, the more intimate the desired relationship. It may also be that the closer the gift is to the recipient's body (e.g., perfume, undergarments), the more intimate it is judged to be. Such intimate gifts would be inappropriate for a casual acquaintance, just as an overly functional gift like a new mop bucket would be inappropriate as a gift for an occasion such as a wedding anniversary which institutionalizes intimacy. The present data provide some evidence of such relationships.

The relationship-defining function of gift selection is modified to a degree by the nature of the occasion. For instance, a less frequent gift-giving occasion such as a high school graduation usually makes more expensive gifts acceptable. The direct relationship between cost and affection is still present, but the range of acceptance has shifted upward. Similarly, a gift which is suitably personal to describe a relationship as a Christmas gift may be inadequate to represent affection as a Valentine's Day gift. Also, while the general appropriateness of gifts may be predicted from the absolute levels of cost and intimacy of the gift, the specific appropriateness of a gift between two particular persons also depends upon the cost and intimacy of the gift relative to the prior history of gift-giving between them. Homans's (1961) "distributive justice theory" and Adams's (1963) "equity theory" also suggest that the cost of a gift should be interpreted relative to the resources of the giver. There is also likely to be less doubt over the meaning and sincerity of the giver where the gift represents an obvious sacrifice relative to the giver's available time and money.

A related social purpose in gift-giving is the ceremonial recognition of social linkages. Gift-giving, or more accurately, gift-receiving, provides tangible proof of being an integral part of others' lives or society. It may also be true that gift-giving aids in defining status within the society, but again it is the reception of gifts (e.g., bar mitzvah presents, Father's Day presents, graduation presents) which most helps to confer status. Inasmuch as gift rejection is generally unthinkable, it is the receipt of such gifts rather than the presentation of them which affirms status, roles, and achievement in society. This differs from the potlatch custom of the Kwakiutl Indians of British Columbia (Benedict, 1960), which involved gaining status by giving away or even destroying one's possessions. Although Mauss (1954) has referred to modern Christmases as "a Giant Potlatch," Veblen (1934) and Schwartz (1967) suggest that we have turned to a more hedonistic means of achieving social status by outconsuming others rather than by outgiving them.

Another extended ceremonial function of gift-giving may be to serve as symbols of social support in various rites of passage from one life stage to another. Gift-giving occasions such as graduations, engagements, religious confirmations, and weddings are among those for which such support is customarily offered. As might be suspected given the supportive intent of such gift-giving, the gifts given are frequently those needed for the new life stage which is being entered. Lowes et al. (1971) find, for instance, that household goods are the predominant wedding gift. However, generally little is known about the correspondence between gifts, occasions, and recipients. The data to be presented provide tentative comment on such patterns.

The preceding discussion of the social exchange function of gift-giving has assumed that gifts essentially *facilitate* the expression of sentiments about a relationship. Jones (1964) has presented a theory of ingratiation in which gifts may play a more strategic role in modifying at least the apparent sentiments of recipients. Where the recipient of gifts is able to respond in kind or with reasonably comparable gifts, no change in attitude toward the giver is required. But when the recipient is unable to reciprocate in kind, Jones (1964, pp. 43–44) specifies that the recipient's attraction toward the giver will increase provided that this is a result apparently valued by the giver. If gratitude may be taken as a surrogate for attraction, Tesser et al. (1968) have found evidence to support this hypothesis in subjects' estimates of gratutude in scenarios of various favors performed by another. They also found support for Jones's prediction that ingratiation increases with the cost of the gift and its value to the recipient. Dillon (1968), however, has argued that foreign aid between nations may fail to successfully ingratiate the giving action because the benefits sought are perceived to be too costly to the receiving nation's autonomy.

3. Gift-Giving as Economic Exchange.   Typical definitions of the term "gift" stress that (a) it is something voluntarily given, and that (b) there is no expectation of compensation. Thus, it may seem strange to consider gift-giving a medium of economic exchange. However, because of the previously noted tendency of most gift-giving to be reciprocal, it is not difficult to conceive of one gift being exchanged for another gift. This interpretation is central to Mauss's (1954) thesis that gift-giving is a series of obligatory reciprocal exchanges which have become institutionalized as gift-giving occasions which further enforce and reinforce the tradition of exchange.

This is not to say that the economic exchange function alone is enough to sustain gift-giving. Since gifts may recognize recipient needs and desires imperfectly at best, it would be more economically rational to agree to stop exchanging gifts and to instead devote the liberated time, effort, and funds to the direct satisfaction of personal needs. However, the other functions of gift-giving together with possible added benefits from anticipation and surprise, allow an expanded view of the rewards of gift-giving which better balance its costs. This is the basis for Kerton's view that a gift-giver''... makes transfers to another so long as the reward for so doing is greater than the costs, adjusted for the cost of social disapproval'' (Kerton, 1971). The sources of giver utility are four, according to Kerton:

1. The "social security benefit" of being able to expect return gifts from others (e.g., children) when they are needed (e.g., in old age);
2. The "humanitarian utility" of helping the gift recipient or giving them pleasure through the gift;
3. The "donor's utility" deriving from fulfilling the socially desirable role of giver; and
4. The "prestige utility" accruing from the display of wealth and power inherent in a costly gift which the recipient is obliged to accept.

The list is probably not exhaustive, but it illustrates some of the added satisfactions in gift exchange which can make the exchange compelling even though the "pure" economic satisfaction from *quid pro quo* is probably less than that which could be provided by applying gift funds to personal consumption.

Despite the strengths of the last three added benefits of gift-giving in the list above, we note again that gift-giving must generally be reciprocal. Furthermore, the exchange must be "fair." As Belshaw (1965) points out, the norm of fair exchange inspires recollections of what the other party last gave as a gift, evaluations of whether a contemplated gift would be too lavish or meager by comparison, and even considerations of whether or not a greeting card should be sent to an individual dependent upon whether or not one was received from this person. Ryan's (1977) findings that those buying small appliances as gifts were more likely to begin shopping with a prespecified price range than were those buying small appliances for personal use also supports the notion that gift-giving participants seek fair exchange. However, as noted earlier in examining the messages conveyed by gifts, the principle of fair exchange may be tempered by the reciprocating person's ability and resources so that the value of a particular gift from someone with small resources may be greater than the value of the same gift from someone with large resources.

The principle of fair exchange may also be applied to seemingly one-sided gift-giving instances. In fact, when a gift of money is offered with the expectation of favors from the recipient, this is very close to a normal purchase transaction, even though the expectation of the return favor may not be made explicit. When the gift is instead a bottle of liquor to a purchasing agent or free merchandise to a consumer (e.g., Seipel, 1971), the transaction is still less direct, but the assumption that the gift will somehow be reciprocated still weighs on the recipient unless the gift can be construed as being given in return for *prior* favors of fair value. Because the data to be presented in Study 1 was obtained from givers and not recipients, the economic function and fair exchange principle in giving is not directly considered in this paper.

A principle somewhat related to fair exchange which might be termed "fair distribution'' has been suggested by various authors (e.g., Andrews, 1953) as a basis for another economic function of gift-giving: the redistribution of wealth. According to such authors, the recognition of uneven and perhaps inequitable resource ownership creates feelings of guilt among those possessing greater assets. Gift-giving is then seen as a way to assuage this guilt to some degree. While such an expiation of wealth is probably more symbolic than real, it does result in some redistribution of resources and is commonly recognized as a motive which might be tapped in appeals for charitable contributions. Levi-Strauss (1959) has even speculated that the need to alleviate guilt is a master motive behind all giving.

4. Gift-Giving as Socializer.   Although the nature of gifts received may have little lasting effect on the self-concept and behavioral patterns of an adult, children are likely to be much more susceptible to this sort of influence. Gifts from respected adults who know the child well are potentially very powerful in helping the child to interpret who he or she is as well as what they should be like.

Besides its effect on children's identities, the selection of gifts to children may affect the formation of values regarding materialism, personal property, giving, receiving, aggression, competitiveness, education, and aesthetics. Gifts are not the sole determinants of these values, but they are a powerful means of communication at ages when the child is likely to be highly suggestible. The presentation of gifts is also a means of rewarding children for "good" behavior. For instance, Santa Claus is endowed, according to song and story, with the ability to monitor the child's behavior and to give or withhold gifts dependent upon behavioral propriety. Schwartz (1967) notes that the Jewish Hanukkah *gelt* typically exercises less control over a child than does the Christian Christmas present, because the former is usually a cash gift which the child can spend as desires warrant. But in all cases the socializing function of gifts is potentially very strong and only vaguely understood or appreciated.

The present data will present some evidence of the sex-role socialization function of gifts of toys to preschool children. Toys gain their power in the sex-role socialization process not only because they are visible symbols which may communicate adult views of "appropriate" sex-role identity, but also because toys often provide the scaled-down implements with which to practice adult sex-associated role behaviors such as house care, child care, and various career possibilities. While toys are not the sole component of sex-role training in U.S. culture, their use is an integral part of the learning process as well as testing device which reflects what has been learned. Children's choices of and preferences for various toys have been found to be highly related to both biological sex (e.g., Ross and Ross, 1972; Fagot and Paterson, 1969), and to sex-role preferences (e.g., Fling and Manosevitz, 1972; Green et al., 1972). Preferences for playing with stereotypically "male toys" (e.g., hammer, truck, gun) or "female toys" (e.g., bracelet, iron, doll) have been found to be aligned with biological sex in children as young as 20 months (Fein et al., 1975). In fact, toy preferences are the basis for measuring children's sex-role concepts in several popular tests (Brown, 1956; DeLucia, 1963; Rabin, 1950).

Because of the obvious involvement of toys in sex-role socialization, and because of the dependence of preschool children on their immediate families to provide them with toys, it is surprising that there has been almost no investigation of parental evaluations and selections of toys for their children. If we assume that parents either give or approve the gifts of toys to their children, the toys which children possess provide some clue to their parents' expectations. One study of the contents of the rooms of affluent children found that males were more likely than girls to have toy vehicles, military toys, sports equipment, and educational toys (Rheingold and Cook, 1975). Girls were found to be more likely than boys to have dolls, doll houses, and domestic toys. Girls were also found to have fewer toys than boys, especially at the younger age levels. In a study with upper- and middle-class children in Montreal, girls were found to be more likely than boys to receive clothing, musical instruments and jewelry for Christmas and boys were more likely than girls to receive noninteractive toys and competitive toys and games (Caron and Ward, 1975). However, because older children tend to have more of a voice in the items purchased for them (Ward and Wackman, 1972), and because peer pressure increases when a child enters school, the susceptible preschool years are probably when parents have the greatest opportunity to influence children's sex-role definitions through gift-giving.

II. RESULTS FROM TWO STUDIES

A. Study One

While the preceding comments have attempted to be comprehensive in their selection of gift-giving functions for review, the research undertaken was exploratory and considered only selected aspects of the functions. The first study was primarily concerned with the communication and social exchange functions of gift-giving and presents some evidence of the effects of giver, recipient, and occasion characteristics on the nature of the gifts selected. The second study focused on the socialization function of gift-giving in exploring the association between parent and child sex-role concepts and their preferences and choices among toys with sex-role connotations. Thus, the first study examines potential determinants of gift selection, while the second begins to consider the consequences of gift-receiving in a particularly significant context.

The first study was an intensive study of 219 gift-giving instances by 73 Philadelphia area residents, designed to gain some descriptive understanding of the process of gift selection and to test some of the tentative hypotheses noted in the foregoing discussion of gift-giving functions. The respondents were recruited from several community organizations during May and June of 1973. Participants provided detailed accounts of three gift-giving instances in the past year, completed an inventory of responses to hypothetical gift-giving situations, described themselves, evaluated the outcomes of the gift-giving instances reported, and characterized the gifts given—in that order. The questionnaire booklet was returned by mail and a 64 percent response rate netted 73 usable questionnaires.

Respondents were 41 percent males, 56 percent married, and ranged in age from 14 to 65. They were both urban and suburban residents and the income distribution was bimodal with 29 percent each in the $0–$5,000 and $15,000–$25,000 categories. This represents some oversampling of both groups. This sample estimated having given an average of between 26 and 27 gifts in the previous year, with a total average annual expenditure of $280.43. The data reported in the remainder of this discussion, however, concerns only the three gift-giving instances the respondents chose to describe in detail.

Since there is no assurance that the gift-giving occasions which respondents chose to report were a random sample of those for which they gave gifts, it is informative to consider the array of occasions reported. As Table 1 indicates, birthdays and Christmas were clearly the favorite occasions reported.[3] Bussey (1967) reports the same finding for a British sample which was asked about specific gift-giving occasions, except that in that study Christmas gifts were slightly more prevalent than birthday gifts, while here the opposite is true. After these first two occasions, however, probable cultural differences begin to emerge. In Bussey's study, for instance, the third most prevalent gift-giving occasion was holidays (trips), whereas in the current study there were only two reported gifts of this type.

A second major descriptive index of gift-giving is the relationship between the

Table 1.   Frequency of Gift-Giving Occasions Reported

Occasion	Number of Reports	Percent
Birthday	76	34.70
Christmas	61	27.85
Wedding/Wedding shower	15	6.85
Anniversary (Wedding)	11	5.02
Graduation	10	4.57
No occasion	8	3.66
Mother's Day	7	3.20
Father's Day	6	2.74
Valentine's Day	5	2.28
Hanukkah	3	1.37
Housewarming	3	1.37
Thank-you gift	3	1.37
Other	11	5.01
Total	219	100.0%

giver and the recipient. As shown in Table 2, the four most popular gift recipients were friends, parents (and parents-in-law), children (and sons- and daughters-in-law), and siblings (and brothers- and sisters-in-law). These findings also are paralleled by Bussey's (1967) British sample, although the order of prevalence of these groups of gift recipients is slightly different. Nevertheless, in both samples approximately one-third of the reported gift recipients were unrelated to the gift-giver. This percentage was slightly higher in the present sample than in the British sample.

A third major index of gift-giving behavior is the type of gift selected. These results are presented in Table 3. The clear favorite among these gifts is clothing, which constituted over one-fourth of the gifts selected (when accessories are included). Of these items of clothing, just under one-half were casual or sportswear. No comparable data are available in the Bussey study, but Lowes et al. (1971) report results from three years of British Gallup Poll surveys of Christmas gifts in which clothing was also found to be the most popular gift. After clothing, the results differ substantially between the two studies, but it is unclear how much of this is due to the fact that the Gallup studies only looked at Christmas gifts, how much is due to the different cultures and times involved, and the nonrepresentativeness of the present sample.

Before examining relationships between giver, gift, and recipient characteristics, several other descriptive findings should be noted. First, gift-giving appears to be pleasurable. Only 19 percent of the gift-giving instances reported were rated as less than very enjoyable, and less than 2 percent were actually rated as disliked activities. It also was found that gift selection was often aided by others. In 38 percent of the gift selections either the recipient provided hints or requests or else the giver was previously aware of the recipient's desire for a specific gift. In terms of gift-giving functions, these aids, which were more common among closer relatives, may help to improve the economic efficiency of gift exchange at the expense of the pleasure derived from the element of surprise. In about one-third of the gift-giving instances reported, the giver received other sugges-

Table 2. Frequency of Gift Recipients Reported

Recipient	Number of Reports	Percent
Friend	73	33.33
Parent/Parent-in-law	43	19.63
Child/Child-in-law	27	12.33
Sibling/Sibling-in-law	27	12.33
Spouse	17	7.76
Nephew/Niece	12	5.48
Grandparent	5	2.29
Miscellaneous relative	5	2.28
Other	10	4.67
Total	219	100.0%

Table 3.   Frequency of Gifts Reported

Gift	Number of Reports	Percent
Clothing	54	24.66
Jewelry	23	10.50
Sporting good	13	5.94
Personally made item	12	5.48
Phonograph record/tape	10	4.57
Home furnishing accessory	9	4.11
Appliance (minor)	7	3.20
Cologne/perfume	6	2.74
Dinnerware/houseware	6	2.74
Electronic entertainment equipment	6	2.74
Book	5	2.28
Cash/stock/bond/gift certificate	7	2.28
Craft kits/equipment	5	2.28
Flowers	5	2.28
Home maintenance equipment	5	2.28
Keepsake (e.g., music box)	5	2.28
Plant	5	2.28
Alcohol	4	1.83
Clothing accessory	4	1.83
Game or toy	4	1.83
Linen	4	1.83
Novelty (e.g., poster)	4	1.83
Luggage	3	1.37
Personal care product	3	1.37
Other	12	5.48
Total	219	100.0%

tions about appropriate gift selections, most commonly from a mutual friend or relative. These suggestions frequently overlapped with hints or requests by the recipient, so that only 40 percent of the givers had made up their minds about a particular gift before shopping. Nevertheless, nearly two-thirds of the gift selection decisions were described as "very easy" or "fairly easy." And less than one-third of the gift selections required more than one hour of shopping time. This time may also have been shortened by the fact that over three-fourths of the gift-giving instances involved a recipient with whom the giver had exchanged gifts previously. This also provides support for the reciprocity principle in gift-giving. Finally it should be noted that while the term giver will continue to be used to describe the gift purchaser, in just under one-half of the reported instances of giving, the gifts were given jointly, usually with other members of the purchaser's family. (However, respondents reported only instances in which they *personally selected* the gift.)

1. Gift/Recipient and Gift/Occasion Relationships.   In describing the interaction facilitating function of gift-giving, it was hypothesized that more costly and more personal gifts would be given to those toward whom the giver has the greatest affection. As a surrogate for affection, gift recipients were divided into those who could be regarded as close family members of the giver, and more distant family members or nonfamily. As Table 4 indicates, more expensive gifts were given to closer family members, although the relationship is not as strong as anticipated. A clearer determinant of the cost of the gift appears to be the nature of the occasion. As shown in Table 4, the occasions for which gifts were the most expensive were weddings, anniversaries, and Christmases. The fact that the two occasions celebrating marriage are those associated with the most expensive gifts may also lend support to the notion that gift prices are greater when the interpersonal affection being recognized is greater. Table 5 compares the frequencies of several common personal gifts (clothes, personally made items, and jewelry) and impersonal gifts (sporting goods and phonograph records or tapes) selected as Christmas or birthday presents. Opposing patterns of gift selections appear between recipients of the same sex as the giver and those of the opposite sex. For recipients of the same sex, Christmas gifts were more personal than birthday gifts, whereas for recipients of the opposite sex, birthday gifts were more personal than Christmas gifts. The apparent explanation is that it is normally more socially acceptable to display affection toward those of the opposite sex, especially when this person is an unrelated friend. If this is true, a gift of affection given to a person of the same sex is easier for a Christmas occasion since it does not single out the gift to a lone recipient, does not involve the conspicuous risk of a one-sided exchange, and provides a generally affectionate mood which encourages personal gifts.

2. Gift Characteristics by Occasion. Table 6 compares the giver's perceptions of the attributes of the items selected as Christmas, birthday, and wedding gifts.

Table 4. Gift Price Categories by Types of Recipients and Occasions

Relationship With Recipient	Price of Gift Selected		
	Under $10	$10 or More	Total
Close*	57 (39%)	88 (61%)	145 (100%)
Distant	38 (51%)	36 (49%)	74 (100%)
Occasion			
Christmas/Hanukkah	25 (39%)	39 (61%)	64 (100%)
Birthday	39 (51%)	37 (49%)	76 (100%)
Graduation	4 (40%)	6 (60%)	10 (100%)
Anniversary	3 (27%)	8 (73%)	11 (100%)
Wedding	1 (7%)	14 (93%)	15 (100%)
Mother's/Father's Day	7 (54%)	6 (46%)	13 (100%)
Other	16 (53%)	14 (47%)	30 (100%)

*Giver's Child, parent, spouse or intended spouse, sibling, grandparent, or grandchild.

Table 5. Frequency of Certain Personal and Impersonal Birthday and Christmas Gifts to Same Sex and Opposite Sex Recipients

		Recipient			
		Opposite Sex		Same Sex	
Gift Type	Occasion:	Christmas/ Hanukkah	Birthday	Christmas/ Hanukkah	Birthday
Personal*		13 (39%)	20 (59%)	16 (52%)	11 (26%)
Impersonal**		5 (15%)	4 (12%)	3 (10%)	12 (29%)
Other		15 (46%)	10 (29%)	12 (38%)	19 (45%)
Total		33 (100%)	34 (100%)	31 (100%)	42 (100%)

*Clothing, personally made items, or jewelry.
**Records or tapes, sporting goods.

Birthday gifts were uniquely personal and fun compared to Christmas and wedding gifts, and were also judged to be lower quality, less expensive, less prestigious, and less lasting. It is clear that practical wedding gifts were chosen and that these items were virtually devoid of intellectual, sporting, or entertainment appeal. Christmas gifts shared high ratings on "high quality" and "lasting" dimensions with wedding gifts, but were more likely to be seen as "fashionable."

3. A Joint Typology of Gifts, Givers, and Occasions/Recipients. In order to gain some additional insight into the characteristics of gifts selected for different respondents on different occasions, respondents rated the desireability of these

Table 6. Mean Characteristics of Gifts for Three Different Occasions

				Significant Differences		
	Mean Rating*			Christmas vs.	Christmas vs.	Birthday vs.
Characteristic	Christmas	Birthday	Wedding	Birthday	Wedding	Wedding
Practical	3.33	2.74	4.14	**	**	**
Entertaining	2.78	2.47	1.57		**	**
Prestigious	2.06	1.77	2.07	**		**
High quality	3.61	3.25	3.93	**	**	**
Unusual	2.18	2.24	2.36			
Intellectual	1.56	1.39	1.07		**	**
Inexpensive	2.06	2.33	2.07	**		
Sporting	1.98	1.64	1.07	**	**	**
Personal	3.06	3.44	1.50	**	**	**
Fashionable	3.48	2.80	2.29	**	**	**
Fun	2.35	2.51	1.50		**	**
Lasting	3.81	3.49	3.93	**		**

*5-point scale; 5 = applies very highly ... 1 = does not apply at all.
**Means differ at $p \leq .05$ via Sheffé's tests on pairwise differences.

same 12 characteristics in each of 15 gift-giving scenarios involving different occasions and recipients. These ratings were then analyzed using three-mode factor analysis in order to simultaneously classify types of givers, types of recipients/occasions, and types of gift characteristics, as well as show the interrelationships among the factors of these three modes of response.[4] These interrelationships may then be interpreted as the characteristics of gifts chosen for different types of occasions and recipients by different types of givers. The 15 occasions (each of which specified a recipient) yielded five factors which accounted for 28 percent, 15 percent, 11 percent, 9 percent, and 8 percent of the total variance. The first factor is represented by wedding, anniversary, and housewarming gift-giving occasions to someone other than a spouse. These might be described as occasions of special social significance. The second factor has high positive loadings for graduation occasions and negative loadings for birthdays, and might be termed nonrecurring achievement occasions. The third factor seemed to be characterized by recurring gift-giving occasions in which the giver's children are the recipients. Factor 4 seemed to represent gifts to recipients with whom the giver has only a nonparental and platonic relationship (e.g., brothers, sisters, same-sex friends). And factor 5 was clearly gifts to a spouse. Thus, the first two factors were characterized by the nature of the occasion and the last two factors focused on the type of recipient, while the third factor reflected the nature of both the occasion and the recipient. The factor analysis of the second mode found four gift characteristic factors. These factors were able to account for 43 percent, 10 percent, 7 percent, and 6 percent of the total variance and were labeled "unique" (e.g., unusual, personal), "imposing" (e.g., prestigious, intellectual), "useful" (e.g. practical, lasting), and "fun" (e.g., entertaining, sporting).

The three-mode factor analysis also obtained factors describing two types of gift-givers based on the similarities in their response profiles on the inventory. The best way to interpret these factors as well as obtain an impression of the relationships between types of givers, occasion/recipients, and gift characteristics, is to examine the core matrix in Table 7. This matrix may be thought of in an approximate way as the factor scores of the two types of givers for each combination of a type of gift characteristic and a type of occasion. The higher the positive entries in the core matrix, the more likely it is that a gift chosen by the corresponding type of person on the corresponding type of occasion will possess the type of characteristic indicated for that column. The higher the negative entries, the more likely it is that such a person will choose a gift for this situation which *lacks* that characteristic. Overall, the pattern of gift characteristics preferred for different gift-giving situations are quite similar between the two types of individuals, but type two persons are more inclined to give useful gifts on all occasions. Both types of givers judged that "fun" gifts were most appropriate for child recipients and on achievement occasions, and that gifts for spouses should be truly unique. Neither type of giver found "imposing" to be a very desirable gift characteristic.

Table 7.   Gift-Giving Inventory Core Matrix
(Varimax Rotations)

Person and Situation Factors	Gift Characteristic Factors			
	Unique	Imposing	Useful	Fun
Person Type I				
Socially significant occasion	6.1	−12.4	16.4	−20.0
Achievement occasion	.8	−2.0	2.4	−2.5
Recurring occasion/child				
recipient	2.7	−14.0	1.4	3.0
Friends/sibling recipient	−2.7	−14.4	1.3	−7.4
Spouse recipient	10.9	−9.9	8.3	−7.5
Person Type II				
Socially significant occasion	8.2	−3.1	28.0	−3.8
Achievement occasion	−.2	1.2	5.3	.5
Recurring occasion/child				
recipient	6.8	−6.9	13.7	12.4
Friends/sibling recipient	4.1	−3.9	16.9	6.8
Spouse recipient	13.6	−4.4	15.2	3.5

The pattern of *specific* gift suggestions made to each scenerio by the respondents who were closest to being type I or type II givers generally supported the implications of this core matrix. These suggestions are likely to be highly correlated with core matrix patterns since the ratings and suggestions were collected almost simultaneously. More rigorous validation of differences in gift-giving patterns requires more extensive data on actual gift-giving patterns for different occasions and recipients. The data presented earlier in Tables 4 and 5 is a step in this direction, but cell sizes become too small for analysis when a breakdown comparable to the core matrix is attempted.

4. Relative Strengths of Associations Between Gift Characteristics and Person Characteristics.   The final analysis from Study One to be reported is a comparison of the similarities between the giver's perceptions of the characteristics possessed by the gift and:

1. The giver's self-concept;
2. The giver's ideal self-concept; and
3. The giver's perception of the recipient.

The intent of this analysis was to provide an exploratory assessment of *which* symbolic messages appear to dominate gift selections. If the giver's self-concept is most similar to the gift characteristics (as the giver perceives them), the more passive form of self presentation and approval-seeking through gift-giving would seem most plausible. If instead the giver's ideal self-concept appears to be most reflected in gift selection, the more assertive form of symbolic self-presentation through gift-giving would appear more likely. And if the giver's perception of the recipient is found to be most closely related to the giver's impression of the gift, then the explanation of gift selection based on communicating impressions of the recipient would appear most plausible.

In order to test these hypotheses, the giver's perception of gifts given were measured on the same twelve adjectives discussed previously and on three more objective ratings of:

1. The amount of time spent shopping for the gift;
2. The amount of time spent making, assembling, or wrapping the gift; and
3. The cost of the gift.

Giver self-concept and ideal self-concept data were collected using a modified version of the Bills et al. (1951) Index of Adjustment and Values. Subjects rated themselves on a series of 40 adjectives (see Belk, 1976) using 5-point scales ranging from *"seldom* is this like me" to *"most of the time* this is like me" (self-concept), and from *"seldom* would I like this to be me" to *"most of the time* I would like this to be me" (ideal self-concept). Giver perceptions of the recipients were obtained by applying the same 40 adjectives to gift recipients using scales similar to those for measuring self-concept. In addition to the 40 adjective ratings included in these three data sets, five more objective ratings have been used in the present analysis: Sex, years of education, occupation (2-digit census categories), age, and income. While these five characteristic measures do not differ between the actual and ideal self-concept sets, they have been included in order to maintain comparability in the number of variables in each data set.

From the data just described, the gift characteristic measures consisting of 15 variables may be thought of as a criterion set of data; and each of the three groups of personal characteristic measures consisting of 45 variables each may be thought of as predictor sets of data corresponding to the three hypotheses under investigation. Because of the multivariate criterion, canonical correlation was chosen as the method of analysis. But the scores in the predictor sets involving self-concept and ideal self-concept, are invariant across three different gift-giving instances in the criterion set, which causes a heightened multicollinearity problem (see, for instance, Lambert and Durand, 1975). That is, because of the artifically high correlations of variables within each of these two predictor sets due to "triple counting" the same giver characteristics for three different gift-giving occasions, unstable variable weights would be the likely result. In order to avoid this problem, the two analyses involving actual and ideal self-concepts were preceded by separate correlations of all variables in the predictor and criterion sets for the first, second, and third gift-giving instances reported by the subject. The means of these three sets of correlation coefficients were then used for the canonical analysis, thus avoiding the correlation-inflating feature of "triple counting."

Table 8 presents the canonical analysis results testing hypothesis 1, that giver perceptions of recipient characteristics are related to the perceived characteristics

	Variable	Canonical Weights by Function				
		1	2	3	4	5
Recipient Characteristics	Sex (male = 0)	−.03	.11	.18	.62	−.21
	Age	−.39	−.18	−.22	.15	−.18
	Income	−.18	−.17	.01	.08	−.36
	Occupation	−.02	.05	.37	−.15	.19
	Appreciative	.35	.20	.00	.22	−.03
	Artistic	−.35	−.05	−.01	−.18	−.10
	Attractive	−.07	.10	−.49	.12	−.12
	Broad-minded	.23	.27	−.39	.06	.20
	Busy	−.25	−.02	−.27	−.19	.46
	Calm	−.02	.19	−.51	−.10	−.04
	Competitive	.13	.06	−.03	.31	−.33
	Confident	−.14	−.02	−.32	−.21	−.08
	Considerate	−.16	.09	.61	−.42	−.30
	Cruel	.25	−.18	.06	−.17	.39
	Emotional	.04	−.16	−.80	−.49	.24
	Energetic	.21	−.17	.37	−.07	−.23
	Fault-finding	.10	.34	−.14	−.11	−.05
	Fun-loving	−.10	−.33	−.41	−.26	.13
	Generous	.38	.06	−.28	−.03	−.27
	Informal	−.14	−.12	.17	.43	−.03
	Interesting	.28	−.20	.16	.36	−.21
	Kind	−.03	.00	−.10	−.05	.31
	Merry	−.63	.32	.25	−.22	−.10
	Outgoing	.31	.18	−.32	.24	.08
	Poised	.28	−.16	.19	−.48	.14
	Reckless	−.08	.15	.05	.39	.14
	Sarcastic	.04	−.09	.19	.08	−.30
	Selfish	−.18	.18	−.08	−.11	−.10
	Stubborn	−.53	−.07	−.22	.14	−.52
	Successful	−.17	−.25	.37	−.16	−.17
	Thrifty	.05	.53	.02	.00	.05
Gift Characteristics	Shopping time	−.35	−.10	.21	.08	.00
	Making time	−.13	−.14	−.78	.32	.22
	Price	.24	.65	−.01	.50	.12
	Practical	−.59	−.09	−.06	−.48	.32
	Entertaining	−.01	−.53	−.29	−.49	.11
	Prestigious	.12	.12	−.13	−.50	−.32
	High quality	−.51	−.16	−.02	.05	−.43
	Unusual	−.35	−.22	.26	−.09	−.06
	Intellectual	−.10	.19	.19	−.30	−.03
	Inexpensive	−.29	.14	.50	.16	.22
	Sporting	.25	−.14	−.14	−.36	.05
	Personal	.05	−.06	−.53	−.09	−.21
	Fun	.08	−.21	.37	.53	−.05
	Lasting	.37	.10	.02	−.25	.74
	Canonical R	.75	.60	.57	.53	.52
	Significance	.002	.035	.006	.001	.001
	Redundancy	.038	.023	.035	.034	.024

Total redundancy: .154

of the gift chosen for this recipient. Altogether five canonical functions were extracted which had probabilities of .05 or less of occurring by chance according to a Chi-squared test approximation for the Wilks's lambda ratios. Both this fact and the canonical correlation coefficients of from .50 to .75 are sufficient to establish that there are significant relationships between recipient characteristics and gift characteristics.

While the squared canonical correlation coefficients show the proportion of variance of one variate (weighted linear composite) which can be explained by the other variate, they do not reveal the amount of shared variance in the two raw data sets. For this purpose the Stewart and Love redundancy index has been calculated at the bottom of the table (Stewart and Love, 1968; see also Alpert and Peterson, 1972, and Lambert and Durand, 1975, for a discussion). This index reveals that only 15 to 16 percent of the variance in the raw data sets can be accounted for jointly without the benefit of the canonical functions. This is still a meaningful relationship, but it leaves open the possibility that one of the remaining hypothesized relationships may dominate perceptions of recipient characteristics as a determinant of the perceived characteristics of the gift selected.

The results presented in Table 9 test the hypothesis that the giver's actual self concept is related to the perceived characteristics of gifts chosen. Again five canonical roots were extracted, and based on their size and significance levels, hypothesis two is supported. Furthermore the sizes of canonical correlation coefficients as well as significance levels and redundancy reveal that giver self concept is *more* related to the perceived gift characteristics examined than is the giver's impression of the recipient. If this relationship is generally true it would mean that an individual selecting a gift is more concerned with whether the gift is personally appropriate to give than whether it is an appropriate gift for the recipient.

The third hypothesis, that the giver's ideal self-concept is related to the perceived characteristics of the gift chosen, is tested in the results presented in Table 10. Again five roots were extracted and again the hypothesis was supported. It may be seen from the sizes of the canonical correlation coefficients, their significance levels, and the total amount of redundancy, that this hypothesis is the strongest of those tested. Thus, it appears that while the giver's actual self-concept and perceptions of the recipient are both important to gift selection and the characteristics which the giver believes that the gift conveys, the strongest determinant of this message is the self-concept the giver would ideally like to project.

B. Study 2

The second study was an examination of the possession and perception of various sex-role related toys by preschool children and their parents. The study began by selecting a sample of $6.00 to $13.00 toys recommended for three- to

Table 9. Canonical Analysis for Gift Characteristics vs.
Giver's Actual Self-Concept

		Canonical Weights by Function				
	Variable	1	2	3	4	5
Giver's Actual	Sex (male = 0)	.06	−.41	−.61	−.26	−.58
Self-Concept	Age	.77	.53	.70	.24	−.73
	Income	−.43	.03	−.74	.15	−.58
	Education	.25	.33	.14	−.46	.58
	Appreciative	.15	−.07	.35	.14	−.15
	Attractive	−.52	−.20	.12	−.01	−.56
	Broad-minded	.64	.32	−.19	.46	.69
	Busy	−.11	.39	−.42	.31	.04
	Calm	−.11	−.50	.58	−.22	.18
	Clever	−.41	−.03	.01	.08	.01
	Competitive	−.34	.15	−.61	.13	−.41
	Considerate	−.78	.05	.38	−.02	.11
	Dependable	.59	.10	−.24	.06	.48
	Emotional	.19	.02	.11	−.67	.27
	Fashionable	−.08	.10	.38	.20	.51
	Friendly	.42	−.14	.02	.37	−.33
	Fun-loving	−.50	.01	.36	−.49	−.28
	Helpful	−.84	.08	−.24	−.18	−.29
	Imaginative	.31	−.66	.12	.54	.48
	Informal	.48	.08	−.16	−.12	.10
	Intelligent	−.66	.04	.25	.03	−.16
	Interesting	−.60	.50	−.26	−.16	−.58
	Mature	.17	−.52	−.25	−.27	.14
	Merry	−.34	.51	.18	−.42	.06
	Outgoing	−.17	−.57	−.50	.03	.65
	Orderly	−.78	.09	−.46	.20	−.17
	Poised	.49	−.21	−.22	.34	.37
	Sarcastic	−.45	.36	−.06	.49	−.04
	Selfish	−.44	.41	−.19	.13	.15
	Sincere	−.06	.31	.28	.39	−.76
	Thrifty	−.60	−.08	.08	.54	−.60
	Unconventional	.08	−.23	−.08	.25	−.43
Gift	Shopping time	.15	.48	−.54	−.26	.11
Characteristics	Making time	−.04	−.01	−.05	.32	−.32
	Price	−.02	.28	.82	.45	.30
	Practical	.00	−.22	−.27	.43	−.12
	Entertaining	−.14	.14	−.43	.04	−.10
	Prestigious	−.41	−.63	.07	−.55	−.18
	High quality	.62	−.22	−.08	−.02	−.15
	Unusual	.60	−.48	−.17	.25	.12
	Intellectual	.51	.39	.38	−.38	.25
	Inexpensive	.06	−.31	−.11	−.11	.48
	Sporting	.15	.22	.43	−.26	−.43
	Personal	−.01	.22	−.07	.40	.55
	Fun	.26	−.04	.23	.35	−.32
	Lasting	−.13	.25	.00	−.43	.28
	Canonical R	.82	.72	.71	.56	.52
	Significance	.001	.001	.006	.009	.001
	Redundancy	.061	.051	.057	.035	.023

Total Redundancy: .228

Table 10. Canonical Analysis for Gift Characteristics vs. Giver's Ideal Self-Concept

			Canonical Weights by Function			
	Variable	1	2	3	4	5
Giver's Ideal Self-Concept	Sex (male = 0)	.07	.12	−.24	−.45	−.43
	Age	.71	.04	−.26	−.47	−.70
	Income	.21	.12	−.79	−.41	.42
	Occupation	−.13	.17	.51	−.12	−.41
	Appreciative	−.81	.44	.28	.04	.12
	Artistic	.24	−.09	−.41	−.60	−.37
	Broad-minded	−.62	−.44	−.60	.12	.38
	Busy	−.29	.80	−.13	−.44	.02
	Calm	−.17	−.23	−.13	.54	.76
	Competitive	.05	−.33	.65	−.26	.17
	Confident	.50	.10	−.19	−.46	.23
	Cruel	−.10	.28	.79	−.13	.24
	Dependable	−.16	.48	.41	.27	.26
	Energetic	.61	.61	−.34	−.39	.04
	Fashionable	−.19	.64	−.16	.18	.23
	Fun-loving	.23	.15	.01	.41	−.50
	Imaginative	.39	.32	−.61	−.44	.04
	Informal	.50	.70	−.19	−.81	−.03
	Intelligent	−.66	−.08	−.82	−.47	−.08
	Interesting	.29	−.04	.11	.50	.05
	Kind	−.78	.16	.37	.05	.48
	Mature	.07	−.37	−.20	.88	−.11
	Merry	.57	.40	.78	−.55	.88
	Outgoing	.11	.05	.89	−.29	−.58
	Orderly	−.24	−.77	−.09	.64	.82
	Poised	.73	.41	−.72	−.75	.30
	Reckless	−.11	−.51	.38	−.03	.22
	Sarcastic	−.57	−.36	.04	−.50	.23
	Sincere	.58	−.48	.44	−.25	−.63
	Tactful	.62	−.25	−.31	.19	.27
	Thrifty	.43	.12	−.71	−.11	.44
	Unconventional	−.70	−.28	−.60	.46	−.40
Gift Characteristics	Shopping time	.12	−.14	−.53	.19	.32
	Making time	.14	−.07	−.31	−.07	−.51
	Price	.00	.55	.30	−.29	−.12
	Practical	.29	−.30	−.27	−.33	.02
	Entertaining	.00	.04	−.12	.96	−.11
	Prestigious	.11	−.95	.37	.07	−.03
	High quality	−.32	−.00	−.12	.13	.18
	Unusual	.16	−.07	−.20	−.62	.41
	Intellectual	−.19	.36	−.26	−.32	.12
	Inexpensive	−.49	−.06	−.14	.12	.49
	Sporting	.33	.04	.12	−.17	.66
	Personal	−.49	−.22	.04	−.23	−.17
	Fashionable	.08	.50	.09	.33	.29
	Fun	−.35	.17	−.11	−.42	−.10
	Canonical R	.86	.81	.81	.77	.74
	Significance	.001	.001	.001	.001	.001
	Redundancy	.051	.079	.039	.082	.053

Total Redundancy: .303

six-year-old children, from the 1975 Christmas catalogs of two major national retail chains. These toys were represented by mounted pictures, prices, and short descriptions taken from the catalogs. Care was taken to balance use of color and illustration size, and store names were masked. Approximately 50 such toys were pretested with parents of preschool children who rated the toys for familiarity, ownership, appropriateness for a boy, and appropriateness for a girl. A total of nine of these toys were chosen for further testing; three toys (toy workbench, toy basketball game, and toy police-car console) viewed as "boys' toys," three toys (toy iron, toy dish set, toy knitting machine) viewed as "girls' toys," and three toys ("Legos," "Viewmaster," and toy desk) for which there was no significant difference in ratings as boys' toys and girls' toys. Cooperation for the main study was obtained from 22 families having children in one of several area nursery school classes. The children were eleven boys and eleven girls between the ages of 52 months and 64 months. The father, mother, and child of each family were interviewed simultaneously in different rooms of their houses by interviewers who alternated within-household interviewing assignments. Each respondent was asked whether the child owned the toy, who gave the toy to the child, whether the parent would buy the toy for the child, and how well the toy was (or would be) liked by the child and by the parent (children responded using "smiling face" scales rather than verbal scales). Parents also completed the Bem (1974) Psychological Androgyny scale, and children completed the Brown (1956) It Scale, both of which measure sex-role concept. In addition, children were given their choice of inexpensive toy rewards which had been shown by pretest to be perceived as either boys' toys (toy cars) or girls' toys (toy animals).

The sample obtained had a median age of 33 for both male and female adults. The median family income category was $15,000 to $19,999, and the majority of both males and females were college-educated. While this represents an up-scale bias in the social class of respondents, the sample was not homogeneous in this regard.

1. Patterns of Present Toy Ownership Via Parental and Nonparental Givers. One reflection of the sex-appropriateness of the toys in this study is the pattern of toy ownership by boys and by girls. Table 11 shows that children own more same-sex toys than cross-sex toys, as expected. However, as Table 12 indicates, this pattern is substantially weaker for toys given by the child's parents. This would suggest that parents, while still bound by tradition in choosing toys, are less prone to perpetuate sex-role stereotypes than are other relatives and friends. It might then also seem that children are less *affected by* the same-sex toy gifts from givers outside of the immediate family, because of the parents' closer contact and mediating influence with the child. However, comparing the child's recollection of who gave them the various toys to the parents' recollections showed only moderate correspondence. This suggests that these four- to five-year-old children are not yet able to clearly differentiate the sources of gifts of toys presented to them.

Table 11. Number of "Boys' Toys," "Girls' Toys," and "Neutral Toys" Owned by Boys and Girls*

	Toy Gender			
Child Gender	"Boys' Toys"	"Neutral Toys"	"Girls' Toys"	Total
Boy	13	16	5	34
Girl	5	22	12	39
Total	18	38	17	73

*33 possible per cell.

2. Effects of Parental Sex-Role Preferences on Evaluations of Toys for Son or Daughter. In order to more closely examine the role of parents as the primary sources of toy gifts to children, parents' evaluations of how desirable they found each of the test toys for their preschool child were averaged separately for toys which matched the child's gender and which did not match the child's gender. Each parent was then classified by the Bem (1974) Psychological Androgyny scale as either masculine, feminine, or psychologically androgynous. The instrument involves having respondents endorse various self-descriptive adjectives which are stereotypically masculine (e.g. athletic, self-reliant, analytical) or feminine (e.g. affectionate, cheerful, yielding). Masculine individuals are judged to be those who endorse significantly more masculine items, and feminine individuals are judged to be those who endorse significantly more feminine items. All those whose endorsements of masculine and feminine traits did not differ are classed as psychologically androgynous. Bem proposed that this ability to describe oneself in terms of positive male *and* female traits is most healthy and provides a more diverse repertoire of skills than those of a person who is more strongly sex-typed. The present interest was in seeing how psychologically androgynous parents compared with more strongly sex-typed parents in their evaluations of the "boys' toys" and "girls' toys" in the study. It was predicted that psychologically androgenous parents would not feel as compelled to provide sex

Table 12. Number of "Boys' Toys," Girls' Toys," and "Neutral Toys" Owned by Boys and Girls, by Purchaser

		Toy Gender			
Purchaser*	Child Gender	"Boys' Toys"	"Neutral Toys"	"Girls' Toys"	Total
Parent	Boy	7	9	5	21
	Girl	4	10	8	22
	Total	11	19	13	43
Other	Boy	6	7	0	13
	Girl	1	12	4	17
	Total	7	19	4	30

*Based on mothers' recollection.

appropriate toys for their children and thus would rate "boy's toys" and "girl's toys" as equally desirable for their children, regardless of the child's biological sex.

As Table 13 shows, the predicted tendency of psychologically androgynous parents to show the least difference in their evaluations of sex-appropriate and sex-inappropriate toys did not emerge. These findings were consistent whether the child was a girl or a boy. While psychologically androgynous fathers did not significantly differ in their evaluations of the two sets of toys, the small number of such fathers reduced the opportunity to find the difference obtained to be statistically significant. For the females, the psychologically androgynous mother showed the *most* difference in evaluation of sex-appropriate and sex-inappropriate toys for her preschool child. What emerges from the findings in Table 13, instead of a lack of sex bias in the toy selections of psychologically androgynous parents is a tendancy for *all* parents, regardless of sex-role preferences, to favor sex-appropriate toys for their children. For both mothers and fathers, the least difference between ratings of sex-appropriate and sex-inappropriate toys is found among the more masculine individuals in terms of the Bem scale. In retrospect, this may be partly due to the characteristics of a nonmasculine individual on the scale. In terms of the 60 adjectives of the Bem scale, this person is more likely than a masculine person to be "yielding," "gullible," and "soft-spoken." A masculine person, on the other hand, is one whose self-description is characterized as "assertive," "forceful," and "individualistic." Thus it may paradoxically be the masculine individual who is most likely to break convention and present "boys' toys" to a daughter and "girls' toys" to a son.

3. *Children's Sex-Role Preferences Related to Toy Ownership and Parental Sex-Role Preferences.* With the recognition again that gifts of toys are not the sole means of sex-role socialization, it is useful to examine the sex-role preference of children owning different proportions of "boys' toys" and of children

Table 13. Mean Ratings of Toys by Parents' Sex-Role Preference

Mean Rating* of Toys for Which:	Mother			Father		
	Masculine	Psychologically Androgynous	Feminine	Masculine	Psychologically Androgynous	Feminir
Toy Gender = Child Gender	2.70	3.65	2.95	3.00	3.15	3.80
Toy Gender ≠ Child Gender	2.30	2.45	2.05	2.10	2.15	2.30
Difference	.40	1.20**	.90**	.90**	1.00	1.50**
n	6	8	8	14	4	4

*5-point scale; higher scores = more desirable.
**Difference significant by correlated means t-test at 2-tailed p ≤ .05.

whose parents may be classified as masculine, feminine or psychologically androgynous. These comparisons are presented in Tables 14 and 15, using both the paper and pencil measure of sex role (the modified Brown It Scale) and the behavioral measure of sex role (toy choice). As Table 14 indicates, ownership of "boys' toys" is related to the child's sex role preference. The Brown It Scale scores show that girls with fewer of the "boys' toys" relative to "girls' toys" had a stronger feminine sex-role preference. Using the behavioral measure, boys owning relatively more of the "boys' toys" were also found to be more likely to choose the "male" prize toy. This evidence is not as strong as it might be, but it does suggest that toy ownership plays a part in the development of sex-role preference.

In Table 15 the same dependent measures are contrasted for children whose parents have different sex-role preferences. The only feminine It Scale scores for boys occur for those with psychologically androgynous fathers. But when boys' mothers are psychologically androgynous, It Scale scores instead appear to be more masculine for the sons. For girls, the only masculine It Scale scores occur for those with psychologically androgynous fathers and for those with masculine mothers. These findings generally parallel those involving the toy choices which are shown in the lower half of the table. These results may suggest that parents of the same sex as the child may cause their sex-role preference to be reflected in the child by acting as a same-sex model. The effect of psychological androgyny, however, appears opposite for mothers and fathers. Psychologically androgynous fathers tend to have more feminine boys and more masculine daughters. Psychologically androgynous mothers instead tend to have more masculine sons and more feminine daughters. This same pattern was observed in the parental toy evaluations in Table 13. The explanation again appears to be that it is the masculine mothers who are most individualistic (a "masculine" trait) in encouraging nontraditional sex roles.

While these results are based on a limited sample and may only be taken as tentative, it is apparent that parental sex preferences are related to children's sex-role preferences. Given this finding, together with the findings that a) parental sex-role preferences are related to parental toy preferences, and that b) children's toy ownership is related to children's sex-role preferences, it seems rea-

Table 14. Sex Role Preferences of Children Owning Different Proportions of Male Toys from Test Set

		Proportion of Test Toys Owned Which Are "Boys' Toys"	
Dependent Measure	Child's Sex	<50%	>50%
Mean Brown It Scale	Boy	6.25 (n=4)	6.29 (n=7)
Score (of 8; >4 = male)	Girl	3.33 (n=9)	4.50 (n=2)
Proportion choosing	Boy	.25 (n=4)	.86 (n=7)
"male" prize toy	Girl	.67 (n=9)	.50 (n=2)

Table 15. Sex Role Preferences of Children by Parental Sex Role Preferences

		Mother's Sex-Role Preference			Father's Sex-Role Preference		
Dependent Measure	Child's Sex	Masculine	Psychologically Androgynous	Feminine	Masculine	Psychologically Androgynous	Feminine
Mean Brown It Scale Score (of 8; >4 = male)	Boy	6.5 (n=4)	7.3 (n=3)	6.3 (n=4)	6.9 (n=6)	3.0 (n=1)	5.5 (n=4)
	Girl	4.5 (n=2)	2.6 (n=5)	2.3 (n=4)	2.6 (n=8)	5.0 (n=3)	(none)
Proportion choosing a "male" prize toy	Boy	.75 (n=4)	.33 (n=3)	.75 (n=4)	.67 (n=6)	0.0 (n=1)	1.0 (n=4)
	Girl	.50 (n=2)	.20 (n=5)	.25 (n=4)	.38 (n=8)	0.0 (n=3)	(none)

sonable to conclude that parental selections of toys as gifts to children play a direct and effective role in communicating parental expectations for their children's sex-role preferences. A causal role for toy gifts in this process cannot of course be established with the present data.

III. ISSUES FOR GIFT-GIVING RESEARCH

The two studies presented have explored the communication and socialization functions of gift-giving more thoroughly than the other functions noted. This research suggests that gift selections depend upon the giver's ideal self-concept, the nature of the occasion, and the giver's relationship to the recipient. The inclusion of considerations of occasion and relationship characteristics makes gift selection a more complex choice act than the selection of comparable products for personal consumption. It is also clear, however, that there are a number of relevant theoretical perspectives which may be applied to understanding gift-giving behavior. Viewing gift-giving as a means of interpersonal communication suggests the application of theories of social judgment, ingratiation, balance, self-concept, and power. In focusing on the communication involved in gifts to children, theories of socialization as well as general theories of learning also become relevant. While the theoretical perspectives just noted focus on the symbolic functions of gift-giving, the process of gift exchange may also be considered using the less symbolic theories of reciprocity and distributive justice in a gift-giving context. Based on both the inherent interest of the subject area and the availability of relevant theoretical perspectives, gift-giving appears to be an area of consumer behavior which is ripe for research.

In researching consumer gift-giving behavior some of the more interesting questions which we might hope to answer outside of the theoretical framework just noted include these:

1. Are giver perceptions of recipient needs and tastes accurate (veridical perceptions)?
2. Under what situational conditions, and for what types of givers, recipients, and giver-recipient relationships are these perceptions most accurate?
3. Is gift-giving autonomy among children related to feelings of self-worth?
4. Are differences in risk reducing strategies apparent between one-sided and mutual gift exchange occasions?
5. Does more giver satisfaction occur when the giver selects a gift without the aid of hints or suggestions?
6. Are children who receive more gifts than others learning to be more generous or less so?
7. Do givers with more positive self-concepts tend to be more generous givers?
8. If gift-giving is generally pleasurable, is gift-receiving necessarily unpleasurable, as reciprocity theory would imply?

9. Does expending more effort on gift selection or creation necessarily lead to greater giver satisfaction, or does this merely heighten the effect of recipient feedback about the gift?

10. Is the selection of gifts which require recipient commitment through wearing or displaying the gift related to the giver's desire to change the recipient?

While these are only a few examples of the issues of interest in consumer gift-giving behavior, they are indicative of the scope of the relevant considerations and the importance of gift-giving behavior in many facets of communication, social exchange, economic exchange, and socialization. Furthermore, these issues are specific to the subset of gift-giving to which this report has restricted itself. By also considering gifts to and from organizations, medical donations, and gifts not directly conveyed to the recipient, the scope of gift-giving research issues is multiplied. Obviously, therefore, the opportunities for gift-giving research are abundant.

FOOTNOTES

[1]The author wishes to thank the staff, parents, and children of the Institute for Child Development Preschool at the University of Illinois for their cooperation in "study two" reported in this paper. The preschool is supported by a training grant in child psychology, Public Health Service Grant No. HD0244, from the National Institutes of Child Health and Human Development. The author also wishes to thank Steven M. Warshaw, who aided in carrying out this project.

2. As Howard and Sheth (1969) point out, verbal communication is itself "symbolic" and subject to multiple interpretations. However, compared to gift-giving, verbal messages are much more overt in having communication as their primary rationale and their content and structure also benefit from the consensus of accepted usage which allows dictionaries and language manuals. While selected stereotypical gifts may sometimes acquire such formalized meanings (see Hitchings, 1976), most potential gifts suffer substantial communicational ambiguity.

3. Since religion may affect gift-giving occasions, it is useful to note that approximately 15 percent of the sample claimed Judaism as their primary religious belief and between 6 and 7 percent claimed to be agnostic or atheistic. Based on previous studies in the communities involved, both figures seem to be reasonable approximations of the population.

4. For expositions of three-mode factor analysis, see Tucker (1964) and Vavra (1972).

REFERENCES

Adams, J. S. (1963), "Toward an Understanding of Inequity," *Journal of Abnormal and Social Psychology* 67: 422–436.

Alpert, M. I., and Peterson, R. A. (1972), "On the Interpretation of Canonical Analysis," *Journal of Marketing Research* 9: 187–92 (May).

Andrews, F. E. (1953), *Attitudes Toward Giving,* New York: Russell Sage Foundation.

Belk, R. W. (1976), "It's the Thought that Counts: A Signed Digraph Analysis of Gift-Giving," *Journal of Consumer Research* 3: 155–62.

Belshaw, C. S. (1965), *Traditional Exchange in Modern Markets,* Englewood Cliffs, N.J.: Prentice-Hall.

Bem, S. L. (1974), "The Measurement of Psychological Androgyny," *Journal of Consulting and Clinical Psychology* 42: 155–62 (April).

Benedict, R. (1960), *Patterns of Culture,* New York: Mentor Books.

Bills, R. E., Vance, E. L., and McLean, O. S. (1951), "An Index of Adjustment and Values," *Journal of Consulting Psychology* 15: 257–261.

Brown, D. G. (1956), "Sex-Role Preference in Young Children," *Psychological Monographs* 70.

Bussey, J. et al. (1967), "Patterns of Gift Giving," London: Bradford University Press.

Caron, A. and Ward, S. (1975), "Gift Decisions by Kids and Parents," *Journal of Advertising Research* 15: 15–20.

Cherry, C. (1961), *On Human Communication,* New York: Science Editions, Inc.

DeFleur, M. L. (1970), *Theories of Mass Communication,* 2nd ed., New York: David McKay.

DeLucia, L. A. (1963), "The Toy Preference Test: A Measure of Sex-Role Identification," *Child Development* 34: 107–117.

Dillon, W. (1968), *Gifts and Nations: The Obligation to Give, Receive, and Repay,* The Hague: Mouten.

Fagot, B. I., and Patterson, G. R. (1969), "An In Vivo Analysis of Reinforcing Contingencies for Sex-Role Behaviors in the Preschool Child," *Child Development* 1: 563–58.

Fein, G., Johnson, D., Kosson, N., Stork, L., and Wasserman, L. (1975), "Sex Stereotypes and Preferences in the Toy Choices of 20-month Old Boys and Girls," *Developmental Psychology* 11: 527–528.

Fling, S., and Manosevitz, M. (1972), "Sex Typing in Nursery School Children's Play Interests," *Developmental Psychology* 7: 146–152.

Green, R., Fuller, M., Rutley, B. R., and Hendler, J. (1972), "Playroom Toy Preferences of Fifteen Masculine and Fifteen Feminine Boys," *Behavior Therapy* 3: 425–429.

Goffman, E. (1961), "Fun in Games," in *Encounters,* New York and Indianapolis: Bobbs-Merrill.

Grubb, E. L., and Grathwol, H. L. (1967), "Consumer Self-Concept, Symbolism, and Market Behavior: A Theoretical Approach," *Journal of Marketing* 31: 22–27 (October).

Hitching, S. B. (1976), "Beware When Bearing Gifts in Foreign Lands," *Business Week*: 91–92 (December 6).

Homans, G. C. (1961), *Social Behavior: Its Elementary Forms,* New York: Harcourt, Brace and World.

Howard, J. A., and Sheth, J. N. (1969), *The Theory of Buyer Behavior,* New York: John Wiley.

Jones, E. E. (1964), *Ingratiation,* New York: Appleton-Century-Crofts.

Kerton, R. K. (1971), "An Economic Analysis of the Extended Family in the West Indies," *Journal of Developmental Studies* 9: 423–434 (July).

Laswell, H. (1948), "The Structure and Function of Communication in Society," in Lyman Bryson (ed.) *The Communication of Ideas,* New York: Harper.

Lambert, L. V., and Durand, R. M. (1975), "Some Precautions in Using Canonical Analysis," *Journal of Marketing Research* 12: 468–475 (November).

Levi-Strauss, C. (1969), *The Elementary Structures of Kinship,* revised ed. translated by James Harle Bell, John Richard von Sturmer, and Rodney Needham (eds.), Boston: Beacon Press.

———— "The Principle of Reciprocity," in L. A. Coser and B. Rosenberg (eds.), *Sociological Theory,* New York: MacMillan (1965).

Lowes, B., Turner, J., and Wills, G. (1971), "Patterns of Gift-Giving," in G. Wills (ed.), *Explorations in Marketing Thought,* London: Bradford University Press, pp. 82–102.

Malinowski, B. (1932), *The Sexual Life of Savages in North-Western Melanesia,* London: Routledge.

Mauss, M. (1954), *The Gift,* London: Cohen and West.

Rabban, M. (1950), "Sex-Role Identification in Young Children in Two Diverse Social Groups," *Genetic Psychology Monographs* 42: 81–158.

Rheingold, H. L., and Cook, K. V. (1975), "The Contents of Boys and Girls Rooms as an Index of Parents' Behavior," *Child Development* 46: 459–463.

Ross, D. M., and Ross, S. A. (1972), "Resistance by Preschool Boys to Sex-Inappropriate Behavior," *Journal of Educational Psychology* 63: 342–346.

Ryans, A. (1977), "Consumer Gift Buying Behavior: An Exploratory Analysis," in D. Bellinger and
    B. Greenberg (eds.), *Contemporary Marketing Thought,* Chicago: American Marketing Associ-
    ation, Series No. 44, 99–104.
Schwartz, B. (1967), "The Social Psychology of the Gift," *American Journal of Sociology* 73:
    1–11.
Seipel, C-M. (1971), "Premiums—Forgotten by Theory," *Journal of Marketing* 35: 26–34.
Sherif, M., and Sherif, C. W. (1963), "Varieties of Social Stimulus Situations," in S. B. Sells (ed.),
    Stimulus Determinants of Behavior, New York: Ronald Press, pp. 82–106.
Stewart, D., and Love, W. (1968), "A General Canonical Correlation Index," *Psychological
    Bulletin* 70: 160–63 (September).
Tesser, A., Gatewood, R., and Driver, M. (1968), "Some Determinants of Gratitude," *Journal of
    Personality and Social Psychology* 9: 233–236.
Tucker, L. R. (1964), "The Extension of Factor Analysis to Three-Dimensional Matrices," in
    Norman Fredericksen and Harold Gulliksen (eds.), *Contributions to Mathematical Psychology,*
    New York: Holt, Rinehart and Winston, pp. 110–127.
Vavra, T. G. (1972), "An Application of Three-Mode Factor Analysis to Product Perception," in
    Fred C. Allvine (ed.), *Marketing in Motion/Relevance in Marketing,* Chicago: American Mar-
    keting Association, Series No. 33, pp. 578–583.
Veblen, T. (1934), *The Theory of the Leisure Class,* New York: Modern Library.
Ward, S., and Wackman, D. (1972), "Children's Purchase Influence Attempts and Parental Yield-
    ing," *Journal of Marketing Research* 9: 316–319 (August).

A PROCESS MODEL OF INTERORGANIZATIONAL RELATIONS IN MARKETING CHANNELS

Ernest R. Cadotte, UNIVERSITY OF TENNESSEE

Louis W. Stern, NORTHWESTERN UNIVERSITY

I. INTRODUCTION

While a number of empirical studies have focused on the existence, usage, and consequences of power and conflict in distribution channels [see, for example, El-Ansary and Stern (1972), Etgar (1976a; 1976b; 1977), Hunt and Nevin (1974), Lusch (1976a, 1976b), Rosenberg and Stern (1971), Shuptrine and Foster (1976), Stern, Sternthal, and Craig (1973)], none has fully treated these social phenomena comprehensively in concert. In order to do so demands the formulation of a process model in which the dynamic interactions of power and conflict are depicted.

Research in Marketing—Volume 2, 1979, pages 127–158.

The objective of this paper is to present such a model. In brief, a process model of dyadic channel, socio-political relations should take into account Pondy's (1967) and Walton's (1969) observation that conflict in a dyadic relationship tends to occur in cycles—that each conflict episode (see Thomas, 1976) is particularly shaped by the results of the previous episode and in turn lays the groundwork for subsequent episodes. Therefore, in the dynamic model described below, five critical elements have been interrelated: *conflict potential, dependence* (and its obverse *power*), *conflict perception, resultant force,* and *conflict aftermath* (see Figure 1).

The process elaborated upon in this paper begins with the *potential* for conflict between two channel members who occupy positions on different levels of distribution (e.g., a manufacturer and a wholesaler). The level of potential conflict is determined by the degree of goal, domain, and perceptual incompatibility existing between the channel members as well as the extent of their interdependence. For the sake of exposition only, if one assumes that one channel member is the focal organization and the other its target, then it is possible to assert that the level of the focal organization's *dependence* on the target organization, and hence the latter's *power* over the former, is determined by the benefits received from, and the costs incurred in behalf of, the target organization as well as the viability of the focal organization's alternatives to its exchange relationship with the target organization.

The rate at which the various areas of potential conflict become *perceived* or recognized by the focal organization depends upon the level of benefits received relative to costs incurred via its dependency relationship with the target organization. As a result of the perception of conflict, the focal organization will initiate efforts to influence the target organization's goals, domain conceptions, and perceptions.

The degree to which the target organization will experience effective pressure

Figure 1.   The Process Model of Dyadic Interorganizational Relations.

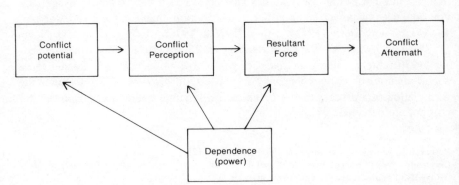

Figure 2. The Dynamic Process of a Conflict Episode in Dyadic Interorganizational Relations.

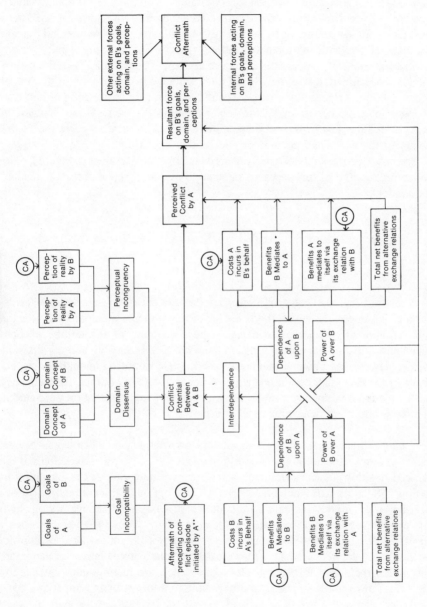

*The conflict episode portrayed here is taken from organization A's perspective.

**The variables which change during the aftermath stage of the conflict process are designated by "CA".

to shift its position on these dimensions depends upon the level of *power* of the focal organization relative to the power of the target organization and the rigidity of the latter's goals, domain conceptions, and perceptions. Its ultimate stance relative to these dimensions will also be affected by its own internal processes as well as by forces stemming from other dyadic relations both within and outside the channel of which the focal and target organizations are only a part.

The *aftermath* of a successful influence attempt ("power play") on the part of the focal organization will include not only a change in one or more of the target organization's critical dimensions (goals, domain, or perceptions) but also changes in costs, benefits, and the power relationship itself. These changes, in turn, affect the level of conflict potential, perceived conflict, and the future ability of the organizations to alter one another's positions.

The entire process model briefly described above is displayed in Figure 2. The following sections of this paper are devoted to discussing each of the elements of the model.

II. ELEMENTS OF THE MODEL

A. Conflict Potential

Assuming that the potential exists for the attainment of satisfactory performance, the degree to which the behavior of one channel member frustrates the goal attainment of another is likely to be a function of the degree of *goal incompatibility, domain dissensus, perceptual incongruency,* and *interdependence* between the channel members. While there is not an unqualified acceptance of the necessary conditions which precede a state of conflict, the frequency with which these dimensions appear in the literature suggests that they are among the more important determinants of conflict.[1]

1. Goals. Each channel member has its own goals and objectives. A goal refers to a future position an organization *wishes* to occupy and exists only if the desired position "differs from the actual or expected state at the inception of action" (Schmidt and Kochan, 1972). The concept of goal incompatibility does not, however, merely indicate a situation where goals are different among channel members but rather indicates a situation where there exist simultaneously unattainable goals. Thus, incompatible goals are a potential cause of conflict because they are generally the criteria by which alternative courses of action are evaluated; they tend to promote decisions which are incongruent and thereby conflict. For example, manufacturers wishing to improve their competitive positions are often stymied by a lack of growth motivation on the part of small distributors who have little interest in opening more territories, soliciting new accounts, or developing new product lines (Webster, 1976). The potential for conflict in such situations due to the obvious incompatibility of goals is high.

The level of goal incompatibility between two channel members depends not only on the degree to which specific goals are incompatible but also on the relative value of these goals to the organizations (Thomas, 1976, p. 917). Clearly, in the above example, market share is likely to be a goal of high value to growth oriented manufacturers while the desire for a "quiet life" may be heavily weighted by certain distributors. Thus, the potential for conflict in such a circumstance is even higher.

Taking channel member A's perspective, goal incompatibility can be stated formally in proposition form as follows:

Proposition 1: *The level of goal incompatibility between channel members A and B can be expressed in terms of the degree to which specific goals are incompatible weighted by the relative value of these goals to A and summed over the set of goals held by A.*

Notationally:

$$G_{Iab} = \sum_{i \epsilon G_a} g_{iab} \cdot \theta_{ia} \tag{1}$$

where: G_{Iab} = the degree to which channel member A's goals are incompatible with channel member B's goals $(0 \leq G_{Iab} \leq 1)$,

g_{iab} = the level of incompatibility between channel members A and B on the ith goal $(0 \leq g_{iab} \leq 1)$,

θ_{ia} = the relative value of the ith goal to A $(0 \leq \theta_{ia} \leq 1$ and $\sum_{i \epsilon G_a} \theta_{ia} = 1)$, and

G_a = the set of goals held by A.

The degree of goal incompatibility between channel members A and B is described in Eq. (1) as the product of the level of incompatibility between the two organizations on each goal held by A weighted by the importance of each goal to A, summed over all A's goals. Assuming the level of incompatibility on a specific goal can be defined on a scale from zero to one and that the total weights of all the goals held by A sum to one, then the degree to which channel member A's goals are incompatible with B's goals will vary over the interval from zero to one, where zero indicates complete goal compatibility or a lack of incompatibility and one indicates complete goal incompatibility.

2. Domain. The concept of domain, according to Thompson (1967), refers to the claims an organization stakes out for itself in terms of (1) range of products, (2) population served, and (3) services and/or functions performed. The applicability of the concept, or of closely related concepts, to distribution channels has been shown in a number of studies (Assael, 1968; Burley, 1975; Carlson and Kusoffsky, 1966; Dutton and Walton, 1966; Hunt and Nevin, 1975; Kriesberg, 1955; Levine and White, 1972; Lusch, 1976a; Palamountain, 1955; Stern et al., 1976; Thomas et al., 1972; Thompson, 1967). Domain consensus is important among channel members because, as Thompson (1967, p. 29) has observed, a domain "defines a set of expectations for members of an organization and for others with whom they interact, about what the organization will or will not do. It provides, although imperfectly, an image of the organization's role in a larger system, which, in turn, serves as a guide for the ordering of action in certain directions and not in others." The greater the dissensus over which products, populations, and functions are prescribed for interdependent organizations, the greater will be the opportunity for conflict to exist between the organizations. In other words, the greater the domain dissensus, the greater will be the potential for B's performance to be inconsistent with A's expectations and hence increase the likelihood that A's goal attainment would be impaired.

Domain dissensus can be expressed in proposition form in a manner similar to that used for goal incompatibility.

Proposition 2: *The level of domain dissensus between channel members A and B can be expressed as the product of the degree to which dissent exists over the proper assignment of products, populations, and functions weighted by the relative value of these elements to channel member A and summed over A's domain set.*

Notationally:

$$R_{Dab} = \sum_{i \in R_a} r_{iab} \cdot \beta_{ia} \qquad (2)$$

where: R_{Dab} = the degree to which dissent exists between A and B over the proper prescription of products, populations and functions ($0 \leq R_{Dab} \leq 1$),

r_{iab} = the level of dissent between A and B on the ith element in A's conception of its and B's domains ($0 \leq r_{iab} \leq 1$),

β_{ia} = the relative value of the ith element in A's conception of its and B's domains ($0 \leq \beta_{ia} \leq 1$ and $\sum_{i \in R_a} \beta_{ia} = 1$), and

R_a = the set of products, populations and functions which A perceives as prescribed for either itself or B.

3. *Perceptions.* Incongruent perceptions of the environment are important sources of conflict because they indicate that there will be differing bases of action in response to the same situation. As a result, behaviors stemming from these perceptions are likely to frustrate and produce conflict. Differences in

perceptions of reality have been attributed to technical problems of communication, such as number and types of information sources, information dispersion mechanisms, information accuracy, semantics, etc. (e.g., Carlson and Kusoffsky, 1966; March, 1966; Smith, 1966; Thomas et al., 1972) and/or to differences in goals and orientations such as different predispositions, values, and attitudes (Assael, 1968; Dutton and Walton, 1966; McCammon and Little, 1965; Palamountain, 1955; Smith, 1966; Stern and Gorman, 1969; Wittreich, 1962).

Like goal incompatibility and domain dissensus, perceptual incongruence can be stated in proposition form:

Proposition 3: *The level of perceptual incongruence between channel members A and B can be expressed in terms of the degree to which specific perceptions are incongruent weighted by the relative value of these perceptions to A and summed over the set of perceptions held by A.*

Notationally:

$$V_{Nab} = \sum_{i \in V_a} v_{iab} \cdot \pi_{ia} \qquad (3)$$

where: V_{Nab} = the degree to which A's perceptions of the environment are incongruent with B's perceptions $(0 \leq V_{Nab} \leq 1)$,

v_{iab} = the level of incongruence on the ith perception of the environment as formulated by A $(0 \leq v_{iab} \leq 1)$,

π_{ia} = the relative value of the ith perception to A $(0 \leq \pi_{ia} \leq 1$ and $\sum_{i \in V_a} \pi_{ia} = 1)$, and

V_a = the set of perceptions of the environment held by A.

4. Interdependence. In a very general sense "interdependence" means "that two or more organizations must take each other into account if they are to accomplish their goals" (Litwak and Hylton, 1962).[2] In general, the greater the level of interdependence, the greater will be the opportunity for interference of goal attainment (Schmidt and Kochan, 1972), and hence the greater the potential for conflict between channel members (Assael, 1968; Dutton and Walton, 1966; March and Simon, 1958; Schmidt and Kochan, 1972; Robicheaux and El-Ansary, 1976–1977). This generalization is particularly important in understanding the rupture of a number of joint ventures involving distribution both in the United States (Skaggs-Albertson, 1977) and abroad (Thorp, 1977).

In order to obtain a mathematical equivalent of interdependence, it is useful to draw upon Emerson's concept of "cohesion," which he defines as the average of A's dependence on B plus B's dependence on A (Emerson, 1972, p. 34). Used in this sense, cohesion indicates the potential for mutual interference of goal attainment between A and B. If we assume cohesion to be equivalent to interdependence, then the level of interdependence between A and B can be defined in proposition form.

Proposition 4: *The level of interdependence between channel members A and B is equivalent to the average of A's dependence on B plus B's dependence on A.*

Notationally:

$$I = \frac{D_{ab} + D_{ba}}{2} \tag{4}$$

where: I = the degree of interdependence between A and B $(0 \leq I \leq 1)$,
    D_{ab} = the level of dependence of A on B $(o \leq D_{ab} \leq 1)$, and
    D_{ba} = the level of dependence of B on A $(0 \leq D_{ba} \leq 1)$.

If D_{ij} is defined over the interval 0 to 1, where 0 is equivalent to complete independence and 1 is equivalent to complete dependence, then I will also be defined over the interval 0 to 1.

5. Conflict Potential Defined.   Based on the reasoning above, it is hypothesized here that the level of potential conflict between two channel members is determined by their degree of goal incompatibility, domain dissensus, perceptual incongruency, and interdependence.[3] Because the social science literature has treated the first three conditions as separate and distinct causes of conflict, it suggests that their relationship to conflict is additive. That is, conflict potential could exist if any one of these three conditions were present and would increase proportionately with the addition of either one or both of the remaining conditions.

Interdependence, on the other hand, has been pervasively recognized as a necessary precondition for conflict under all circumstances. That is, if two organizations are not interdependent, then there is no opportunity for interference of goal attainment and hence no potential for conflict.[4] This conclusion suggests that the relationship between interdependence and the other three determinants of conflict is multiplicative. In other words, if interdependence is zero, the potential for conflict is zero. If any one of the other three sources of conflict is zero, then the potential for conflict is reduced proportionately, no matter what the level of interdependence between the organizations.

Following the above reasoning, the authors can now offer a formal definition of potential conflict:

Proposition 5: *The level of conflict potential is defined as the degree to which the behavior of one channel number could potentially destroy, thwart, or hinder the goal attainment of another. Conflict potential increases additively with increasing levels of goal incompatibility, domain dissensus, and perceptual incongruency but only in proportion to the level of interdependence between the two channel units.*

Notationally, Proposition 5 can be stated as follows:

$$C_{Pab} = \frac{(G_{Iab} + R_{Dab} + V_{Nab})}{3} \cdot I \tag{5}$$

C_{Pab} = the level of conflict potential between A and B taken from A's perspective $(0 \leq C_{Pab} \leq 1)$.[5]

B. Dependence

Extending Emerson's (1972, p. 32) concept of dependence into a channel setting,[6] the dependence of channel member A upon channel member B (D_{ab}) "is (1) directly proportional to A's motivational investment in goals mediated by B, and (2) inversely proportional to the availability of those goals to A outside the A-B relation." In equation form, Emerson's definition of dependence would read:

$$D_{ab} = \frac{\text{A's motivational investment in goals mediated by B}}{\text{The availability of A's goals outside the A–B relation}} \tag{6}$$

While Eq. (6) is a conceptually satisfying definition of dependence, it lacks the explicitness needed for a mathematical model of interorganizational relations in marketing. In this section, a more rigorous definition of this concept is developed by critically examining first the numerator and then the denominator in Eq. (6).

1. A's Motivational Investment in Goals Mediated by B.   Goals were defined earlier to be future positions a channel member wishes to occupy. Parsons (1966) points out that in practically all cases "goals admit of degrees of attainment" rather than being all or nothing instances. It would seem, therefore, that A's motivational investment in goals mediated by B would vary directly with B's contribution to A's goal attainment and inversely with A's current level of goal attainment. In equation form:

$$\begin{array}{c} \text{A's motivational investment} \\ \text{in goals mediated by B} \end{array} = \frac{\text{B's contribution to A's goal attainment}}{\text{The current level of A's goal attainment}} \tag{7}$$

a. *B's Contribution to A's Goal Attainment*—In order to define mathematically the phrase "B's contribution to A's goal attainment," it is necessary to understand why two or more organizations engage in exchange relations in the first place. On this point Levine and White (1972) concluded from their study of health agencies that few, if any, organizations have access to all the resources required to enable an organization to attain its objectives. Therefore, an organization will select, on the basis of expediency or efficiency, a limited set of functions to perform and rely on outside organizations for the remaining resources it needs to achieve its objectives. As long as the benefits the organization receives from these relationships remain greater than those it could achieve by working independently, it will maintain the exchange relationship (p. 343; see also Alderson, 1969).

Transferring this finding to a channel context, it is possible to argue that the benefits which one channel member receives from another form the basis of the second's contribution to the first's goal attainment. That is, the more A's resource requirements are met by B, the greater B's contribution to A's goal attainment. For example, Table 1 lists the types of services frequently made available to franchisees by franchisors when a franchise is initially established

Table 1.   Initial Services and Continuing Services to
Franchisees, as Reported by Franchisors.

Type of Service Provided	Franchisors Reporting (n=182)
Initial Services	
Operating manuals	100.0%
Management training	100.0
Franchisee employee training	88.3
Market surveys and site selection	84.4
Facility design and layout	80.6
Lease negotiation	62.7
Franchisee fee financing	37.7
All other services	21.1
Continuing Services	
Field supervision	96.1%
Merchandising and promotion materials	94.5
Franchisee employee retraining	85.1
Quality inspections	79.6
Advertising	66.4
Centralized purchasing	65.3
Market data and guidance	62.6
Auditing and record keeping	51.0
Group insurance plans	48.9
All other continuing services	13.1

Source: National Industrial Conference Board, Franchised Distribution (New York: National Industrial Board, 1971), pp. 23–24.

and those which are extended over the life of the franchise relationship. Each of these services is a benefit which the franchisee receives from the franchisor. In addition to the franchised product and/or system, each service contributes to the franchisee's ability to attain its goals. Similarly, the franchisee may contribute a building, fixtures, inventory, warehousing space, local promotion, retail personnel, management abilities, etc., all of which contribute to the franchisor's ability to attain its goals.

To measure goal contribution, it is not sufficient, however, to restrict the analysis to the benefits which one channel member mediates to another. In order to determine B's contributions to A's goal attainment, one must also consider the costs A incurs in B's behalf. While it is generally recognized that in a reciprocal exchange relation[7] both A and B receive benefits from each other, these benefits also involve costs on the part of the mediator. B's contribution to A's goal attainment would be equal to the difference between these benefits and costs. In the franchise example, the franchisor's contribution to the franchisee's goal attainment would be equal to the sum of the total benefits mediated by the franchisor less the sum of the total costs the franchisee incurs in the franchisor's behalf.

The above consideration suggests a corollary to the previously stated necessary condition for an exchange relationship: As long as the benefits mediated by channel member B for A's goal attainment are greater than the costs A incurs in B's behalf, A will maintain the exchange relation with B (Corollary 1). Assuming that Corollary 1 is true, it is possible to state the following proposition:

Proposition 6: *In an exchange relationship between channel members A and B, B's contribution to A's goal attainment is equal to the difference between the benefits mediated by B to A and the costs incurred by A in B's behalf.*

Notationally:

$$\text{B's contribution to A's goal attainment} = B_{ba} - C_{ab} \qquad (8)$$

where: B_{ba} = the benefits mediated by B to A,
C_{ab} = the costs incurred by A in B's behalf, and

$$B_{ba} - C_{ab} > 0 \text{ by Corollary 1.} \qquad (9)$$

The benefits[8] channel member A receives from B are broadly defined to include utilitarian (e.g., research funds, sales volume and margins, promotional allowances, technical and administrative assistance, and manpower), coercive (e.g., withdrawing rewards, blacklisting, initiating antitrust actions, and doing physical harm to another organization's assets or personnel), and normative resources (e.g., the allocation of symbols of esteem, prestige, and acceptance). The costs channel member B incurs in A's behalf include B's actual expenditure of its utilitarian, coercive, and normative resources.

The costs B incurs will generally be less than the benefits A actually receives from B. That is,

$$B_{ba} - C_{ba} > 0. \tag{10}$$

The difference between B_{ba} and C_{ba} is due to A's perception of these benefits. For example, the scarcity of raw materials and sub-assemblies which occurred in late 1973 and early 1974 caused the value of these items to be substantially magnified among prospective users, especially where these products represented a vital link in a production or distribution process ["Politics of Scarcity" (*Wall Street Journal*, 1973); "Price Gouging" (*Wall Street Journal*, 1973)].

A is also likely to perceive extra benefits in its relationship with B because of task specialization on B's part (Mallen, 1973). In other words, to the extent that economies of scale are possible in the tasks B performs and A cannot possibly achieve these economies acting on its own, then A is likely to perceive, as extra benefits of the A-B relation, the savings it enjoys by farming out these tasks to B. For example, many of the services listed in Table 1 would probably be prohibitively expensive for an individual franchisee to purchase in the open market. The franchisor, on the other hand, can spread the high absolute costs of these services over many franchisees so that the cost of providing them to any individual franchisee is relatively small. Consequently, the value of the services to the franchisee may be considerably more than their relative cost to the franchisor.

In addition, A may attribute "objective" resources to B which B does not possess simply because B's claims to these resources seem credible to A, or because A believes B possesses these resources (Lehman, 1969, p. 344). Thus, the difference between the "sent" benefits and the "received" benefits is equivalent to the "psychic" or "symbolic" benefits A perceives in the A-B relation.[9]

The relationship between the costs incurred for another channel member and the benefits received as a result of that expenditure can be stated in proposition form as follows:

Proposition 7: *The level of the benefits B mediates to A varies with the costs B incurs in A's behalf. The degree to which the benefits received exceed the "objective" resources expended will depend upon A's perception of these benefits.*

Notationally:

$$B_{ba} = C_{ba}^{\Gamma} \tag{11}$$

where: Γ = the symbolic elasticity of expenditures ($\Gamma > 1$).

   b. *The Current Level of A's Goal Attainment*—If B's contribution to A's goal attainment is defined to be equal to ($B_{ba} - C_{ab}$), then it seems reasonable to sum the net contributions of all the organizations in A's task environment to obtain A's current level of goal attainment. This conclusion unfortunately assumes that A is a passive actor in the determination of its benefits. While A is ultimately dependent upon its task environment for all its resources, it is also capable of managing this dependence in order to enlarge the benefits it receives. On this point, Thompson (1967) observes that, under norms of rationality, a focal organization will attempt to increase its power relative to members of its task environment in order to reduce the contingencies and constraints imposed by the task environment. A reduction in contingencies and constraints will simultaneously reduce the uncertainties of the task environment and thereby enable the focal organization to achieve higher levels of goal attainment.[10] While these additional benefits pass through the other organizations, they are mediated only by the focal organization.

For example, the services provided by franchisors in Table 1 tend to reduce the uncertainties which stem from dealing with independent franchisees. The reduction in uncertainty (risk) in turn increases the potential profitability of the entire franchise system to the franchisor. Similarly, Webster has observed in industrial distribution:

> Most manufacturers have developed a variety of training programs and supporting services to make the distributor as effective as possible, thus strengthening the distributor and the commitment to him. There is also greater emphasis on the distributors market development and account solicitation functions. Thus, it appears that the trend will sustain itself for some years to come, producing larger, more effective, better managed industrial distributors, who will perform a broader variety of functions for their suppliers... A final word of caution is in order. Even though the industrial distributor is becoming stronger and more effective, he still depends heavily on the manufacturer for his strength and effectiveness (Webster, 1976, p. 15).

Based upon the above-observations, the following proposition is stated:

Proposition 8: *The current level of A's goal attainment is equal to the sum of the net contributions it receives from each member of its task environment plus the benefits it mediates for itself in the management of its relationship with these members.*

Notationally:

$$\text{The current level of A's goal attainment} = \sum_{i \in T} [(B_{ia} - C_{ai}) + B_{aai}] \qquad (12)$$

where: B_{ia} = the benefits mediated by i to A,
    C_{ai} = the costs incurred by A in i's behalf,
    B_{aai} = the benefits mediated by A to A via the A-i relationship, and
    T = the set of organizations in A's task environment.

Thompson's discussion of managing dependence suggests that the benefits a focal organization mediates for itself are directly related to the power of the focal organization relative to the power of target organizations (Thompson, 1967). However, Ridgeway (1957) has observed that automobile manufacturers prefer autonomously owned dealerships (where the power ratio is lower relative to company-owned outlets) because the dealerships: 1) provide the company with a local image, 2) generate higher sales volumes, 3) create fewer management problems, and 4) are more desirable under federal and state legislation. Similarly, Bucklin (1973) and El-Ansary and Robicheaux (1974) suggest that, at some point, a channel member's tolerance for further interference in its activities by a second channel member decreases with the second's increasing control over the first. These observations lead to the conclusion that self-mediated benefits increase as the relative power of the focal organization increases but at a decreasing rate. Furthermore, the observations of several students of channel relations (Bucklin, 1973; El-Ansary and Robicheaux, 1974; Mallen, 1963; Ridgeway, 1957; Webster, 1976; Weiss, 1958) imply that the focal organization's ability to mediate its own benefits increases directly with the costs it incurs in behalf of target organizations (which are benefits from the target organizations' perspective). Based upon these observations, the following proposition is stated:

Proposition 9: *The benefits channel member A mediates in its own behalf via the A-B relationship increase directly with the increasing costs it incurs in B's behalf. The rate at which these costs are translated into benefits for A is determined by the A-B power ratio and increases as A's power increases relative to B's but at a decreasing rate.*

Notationally:

$$B_{aab} = \left(\frac{P_{ab}}{P_{ba}} \right)^{\lambda} \cdot C_{ab} \tag{13}$$

where: P_{ab} = the power of A over B,
       P_{ba} = the power of B over A, and
       λ = the elasticity of power
       $(0 < \lambda < 1)$.

2. The Availability of A's Goals Outside the A-B Relation. The availability of A's goals outside the A-B relation refers, according to Emerson, "to alternative avenues of goal-achievement, most notably other social relations" (Emerson, 1972, p. 32). In support of this conclusion, Litwak and Hylton (1962, p. 401) observed that the more alternatives a fund-raising agency had for sources of funds, the less its dependence on other agencies in the community. In a channel of distribution context, Webster observed:

> The presence of second lines is especially annoying to those firms that make major investments in their distributors, as with training programs, market development expenses, and the like. Such commitments are made in an attempt to become the distributor's single most important and profitable line; second lines frustrate the achievement of those objectives (Webster, 1976, pp. 15-16).

Emerson also argues, however, that the number of alternatives an organization has is not sufficient to properly assess dependency. He states that the cost associated with each alternative must likewise be included (Emerson, 1972,

p. 32). On this same point, Thibaut and Kelley (1959) state that an entity's willingness to sever a relationship (an indicator of dependency) is determined by the value of the current relationship relative to the value of its available alternatives. With these observations in mind, the following proposition can be stated:

Proposition 10: *The availability of A's goals outside the A-B relation varies directly with the number and viability of alternatives available to A. The viability of an alternative is determined by the ratio of the total net benefits obtainable via an alternative relationship to the total net benefits of the current relation.*

Notationally:

$$\text{The availability of A's goals} \atop \text{outside the A–B relation} = \sum_{k \in S} \frac{(B_{ka} - C_{ak}) + B_{aak}}{(B_{ba} - C_{ab}) + B_{aab}} \qquad (14)$$

where: S = the set of alternatives available to A.

Assuming that channel member A will maintain its exchange relation with B if, and only if, the total net benefits it receives from B are greater than the total net benefits it could receive from its alternatives (Corollary 2), then the right-hand side of Eq. (14) will always yield a fraction less than or equal to one for each alternative. Summed across all alternatives, including B, Eq. (14) will always equal a value greater than or equal to one. Thus, the smaller the opportunity cost of switching to one or more alternatives, the greater will be the value of Eq. (14), and hence the smaller A's dependence upon B as measured in A's motivational investment in goals mediated by B.

3. Dependence Defined.   Via Propositions 6–10, it is now possible to define dependence in more rigorous terms:

Proposition 11: *The dependence of channel member A upon channel member B is 1) directly proportional to B's net contribution to A's current level of goal attainment and 2) inversely proportional to the number and viability of A's alternatives for goal attainment.*

Notationally[11]:

$$D_{ab} = \frac{\dfrac{\text{B's net contribution to A's goal attainment}}{\text{A's current level of goal attainment}}}{\displaystyle\sum_{k \in S} \dfrac{\text{The total goal contribution of a}}{\text{relation with alternative } k} \Big/ \dfrac{\text{The total goal contribution of a}}{\text{relation with B}}} \qquad (15)$$

$$D_{ab} = \frac{\dfrac{B_{ba} - C_{ab}}{\displaystyle\sum_{i \in T} [(B_{ia} - C_{ai}) + B_{aai}]}}{\displaystyle\sum_{k \in S} \left[\dfrac{(B_{ka} - C_{ak}) + B_{aak}}{(B_{ba} - C_{ab}) + B_{aab}} \right]}$$

$$\qquad (16a)$$
$$\qquad (16b)$$
$$\qquad (16c)$$
$$\qquad (16d)$$

where: D_{ab} = the level of dependence of A on B ($0 \leqslant D_{ab} \leqslant 1$).

4. *Power and Dependence.* Thompson (1967) has applied Emerson's (1972) conceptualization of the power-dependence relation to interorganizational relations by stating that organization B has power relative to A to the extent that B has the capacity to satisfy the needs of A and to the extent that B monopolizes that capacity. B's capacity is determined by the resources it possesses or is attributed to possess which A perceives as being necessary for its goal attainment. Therefore, the sources of A's dependence on B are simultaneously the sources of B's power over A. If one accepts Emerson's premise that the power of B over A is equal to, and based upon, the dependence of A upon B ($P_{ba} = D_{ab}$), then Eq. (16) also defines P_{ba}. Such a definition is in line with Lehman's analysis of power potential, because the benefits B mediates in A's behalf have already been defined in terms of the symbolic and objective power sources identified by Lehman (1969). If these benefits increase, then B's relative contribution to A's goal attainment increases, the attractiveness of A's alternatives declines, and therefore B's power over A increases. It is now possible to define B's power over A more precisely:

Proposition 12: *The power potential of B over A is equal to and based upon the dependence of A upon B.*

Notationally[12]:

$$P_{ba} = D_{ab} \tag{17}$$

$$P_{ba} = \dfrac{\dfrac{B_{ba} - C_{ab}}{\displaystyle\sum_{i \in T} [(B_{ia} - C_{ai}) + B_{aai}]}}{\displaystyle\sum_{k \in S} \left[\dfrac{(B_{ka} - C_{ak}) + B_{aak}}{(B_{ba} - C_{ab}) + B_{aab}} \right]} \tag{18}$$

where: P_{ba} = the level of potential power of B over A ($0 \leqslant P_{ba} \leqslant 1$).
Eq. (18) provides a more inclusive definition of potential power than was afforded by Lehman (1969). Whereas Lehman only considers the sources of B's power, Eq. (18) also considers A's cost of the relationship, B's share of A's goal attainment, and the viability of A's alternatives.

C. Perceived Conflict

The rate at which one member of a channel perceives[13] the behavior of another to be interfering with its goal attainment is determined by the level of costs it incurs in behalf of the other channel member relative to the total benefits it receives in its relationship with it. To illustrate, after analyzing the distribution systems of the automotive, drug, food, and liquor industries, Assael (1968) concluded that "A declining economic position of any segment of the channel will further stimulate conflict. . . . A retailer may regard a manufacturer's policy as coercive in a period of decline, yet the identical policy may be dismissed as a minor irritant during prosperity." Similar situations have been observed in the toy industry (Carberry, 1963). Finally, studies of various franchising relationships suggest that a franchisee's satisfaction with a franchise relationship increases with increasing benefits from the franchisor (the quality of the franchisor's assistance) and decreases with the franchisor's increasing ability to withdraw or with the actual withdrawal of benefits[14] (Hunt and Nevin, 1974, p. 172; Lusch, 1976a, p. 387; Lusch, 1976b, p. 10).[15]

The important point is that because goals speak primarily of degrees of attainment (Parsons, 1966), organizations experience varying degrees of dissatisfaction with regard to relationships with their task environment. The greater the costs a channel member incurs in behalf of another channel member compared with the total benefits received from the relation, the less the latter's contribution toward the former's goal attainment and, therefore, the greater the former's dissatisfaction with the relationship. This perceived dissatisfaction, in turn, encourages the former channel member to look outside its organizational boundaries and determine how other members of the channel are impeding its goal attainment (Assael, 1969). In the final analysis, the likelihood that a channel member will be able to identify behavior conflicting with its goal attainment will depend upon the degree to which other channel members are interdependent with it, and the extent to which they disagree on goals, domains, and perceptions.

The above point can be stated more formally as follows:

Proposition 13: *The level of conflict A perceives in the A-B relation varies directly with the level of potential conflict that exists from A's perspective. The rate at which the potential conflict becomes perceived is determined by the ratio of the costs A incurs in B's behalf relative to the total benefits A receives in the A-B relation.*

Notationally:

$$\hat{C}_{Pab} = \frac{C_{ab}}{B_{ba} + B_{aab}} \cdot C_{Pab} \qquad (19)$$

Substituting Eq. (5) into Eq. (19) yields:

$$\hat{C}_{Pab} = \frac{C_{ab}}{B_{ba} + B_{aab}} \cdot (G_{Iab} + R_{Dab} + V_{Nab}) \cdot I \qquad (20)$$

where: $\hat{C}_{Pab}$ = the level of conflict A perceives in its relation with B.
$(0 \le \hat{C}_{Pab} \le 1)$

As a note of explanation, the term

$$\frac{C_{ab}}{B_{ba} + B_{aab}} \qquad (21)$$

will vary from 0 to 1 inclusive. When the ratio approaches 1, this means the degree of A's dissatisfaction with the A-B relation will be high and practically all of the potential areas of conflict between A and B will be perceived. When the ratio approaches 0, this means the degree of dissatisfaction will be low, and A will perceive very little conflict between the two.

D. Resultant Force

A channel member which desires to reduce the uncertainty within its task environment will do so by pressuring other channel members to change their goals, domain conceptions, and perceptions of reality to be more in line with its own. The nature of the pressure applied may be in the form of either a coercive or a noncoercive act. Recent studies conclude that coercive pressure may be more disruptive to channel relations than noncoercive acts (Hunt and Nevin, 1974; Lusch, 1976b) but that coercion may be more effective in obtaining compliance (at least in the short run). This finding is supported in research conducted in other contexts (see Raven and Kruglonski, 1970).

The degree to which a channel member is successful in eliciting the desired change will determine the extent to which it is able to increase its power relative to other organizations and thus to achieve higher levels of goal attainment. In other words, the desire to reduce uncertainty within the task environment and thereby increase the current level of goal attainment is the *motivating force* behind the exercise of power. The *focus* of its application is the target organization's goals, domain, and perceptions. The *intent* of the focal organization (hereafter called power initiator) is to overcome *resistance* on the part of the target organization (hereafter called power resistor) and elicit a readjustment in the latter's goals, domain, and perceptions in a direction favorable to the power initiator.

French and Raven (1960) define the resultant force of an intentional and impositional act to be the change an entity feels pressured to make in its current state as a result of the power initiator's intervention into its life space. Whether or not the state of the system will, in fact, change will depend upon the *resultant forces* the entity experiences from other sources. French and Raven also maintain that the resultant force of the power initiator's intervention consists of two components: a force to change the system in the direction induced by the initiator and an opposing resistance set up by the same act. In this regard, Thomas explicitly recognizes that in a conflict episode any action taken to resolve the perceived conflict will result in reactive behavior by the party affected. Moreover, the initial reaction to the conceptualization of conflict may initiate a prolonged interaction between the two parties where "each party's behavior serves as stimulus for the other's response" (Thomas, 1976, p. 895).

Marketing scholars have also recognized the need to consider both the notion of power intervention and that of an opposing resistance when evaluating channel influence attempts or "power plays" (Etgar, 1976b, p. 254; Stern et al., 1973–1974). The resistance of a channel member may be caused by several factors, including a concern for the uncertainty of the outcome of the proposed change, a desire for pattern maintenance (Parsons, 1966) within the channel, a belief that at some point increased control by a second channel member will result in reduced payoffs to the resistor (Bucklin, 1973; El-Ansary and Robicheaux, 1974), or a concern for establishing a precedence with the initiator which would increase the initiator's propensity to apply pressure again in the future (Stern et al., 1973–1974, p. 405).

French and Raven (1960) define the resultant force to be the difference between the two forces which implies that every time the resistor is more forceful than the initiator, the resistor will move in a direction opposite to that intended by the initiator.[16] Under these conditions, the initiator could never have a positive influence. It is preferable, therefore, to use the quotient of the force of the resistor because doing so assumes that an initiator, no matter how great or small its power, will always exert a positive pressure on the state of the resistor. It does not imply anything about the extent to which this influence will be exhibited in a system change. The ultimate change will be dependent upon the direction and magnitude of all other forces acting simultaneously.

In the conflict process being modeled here, the organization is taken to be the entity under study. The state of the organization is determined by the position of its goals, domain conceptions, and perceptions of the environment. These elements, rather than an organization's behavior, have been selected to measure state changes because behavior in a dyadic relation is largely determined by an organization's goals, domain conceptions, and perceptions.

Along with power, a second factor which determines the magnitude of the resultant force is the distance the target channel member would have to move with respect to its goals, domain conceptions, and perceptions of reality in order to eliminate the uncertainty the focal organization experiences via its exchange relation with the target channel member. In order to reduce uncertainty, one would expect the initiator to pressure the resistor to shift its positions with respect to its goals, domain conceptions, and perceptions by the magnitude of the incompatibility the initiator perceives in these dimensions. The greater the perceived incompatibility of the two channel members' positions, the greater the change the resistor will feel pressured to make in its positions. Conversely, the smaller the distance, that is, the more compatible their positions, the smaller the change an intervening act will elicit from the resistor, even under the same or similar power structures. The importance of the distance between the initial positions of the initiator and the resistor in a power play has been widely recognized in experimental studies of power (March, 1966).

A third factor which determines the resultant force of an intervening act is the rigidity of specific goals, domains, and perceptions. This rigidity would appear to be a function of the differential inertness of the three dimensions, the nature of specific conflict issues, and the nature of the original intervening act. The notion of the differential inertness recognizes that each of the dimensions are not likely to be equally responsive to pressure. The work of Wittreich (1962), Ridgeway (1957), and Mallen (1963) on interorganizational relations in channels of distribution suggests that it is easier to change an organization's activities than to change its goals. In addition, it is probably easier to change an organization's perceptions of reality than to change its domain, although there is no available evidence to support this contention. In general, we would expect to find that the time and effort needed to change a channel member's goals would be greater than the time and effort needed to change its domain, which would, in turn, be greater than the time and effort needed to change its perceptions of reality, regardless of the power structure or the incompatibility in the dimensions.

The rigidity of the dimensions would also appear to be a function of the specific nature of the conflict issue. Drawing from the literatures of labor negotiations and international politics, Thomas points out that depending upon a party's conceptualization of the concern, alternative courses of action, and possible outcomes associated with a specific issue, the issue may be perceived as having an "either-or," "zero-sum," "indeterminant," or an "unresolvable" outcome. Moreover, depending upon party's attitude towards assertiveness and cooperativeness, he may assume an orientation which is either competitive (domination), avoidant (neglect), accommodative (appeasement), sharing (compromise) or collaborative (integration) (Thomas, 1976, pp. 895–901).

Finally, the rigidity of a conflict issue appears to be a function of the nature of the original intervening act to change a channel member's goals, domain conceptions, or perceptions. Stern and Gorman argue that "when one party establishes the use of coercion, the other is likely to respond in kind, intensifying conflict rather than resolving" (1969, p. 161). Likewise, Lusch's (1976b) review of the use of coercive and noncoercive sources of power in the conflict process suggests that the use of coercive sources of power tends to intensify and increase conflict whereas the noncoercive sources tend to have the opposite effect. Thomas et al. (1972, p. 905) has concluded that the behavior elicited from another is to some extent a response to one's own behavior. In other words, cooperative behavior tends to elicit cooperative behavior and hostile behavior tends to elicit hostile behavior. In light of these observations, it would appear that the use of coercive power would tend to solidify or increase the rigidity of a channel member's position regarding a conflict issue, while the use of noncoercive sources would tend to lessen or reduce the rigidity of the channel member's position.

In summary, the magnitude of the resultant force experienced by a power resistor will vary inversely with the rigidity of the conflict issues. That is, as the rigidity of a conflict issue increases, the actual force being applied to the resistor's position will decline, and the time and effort required to cause a change in position will increase.

In light of the above discussion, it is now possible to define formally the resultant force the resisting channel member will experience on its goals, domain conceptions, and perceptions of reality:

Proposition 14: *The resultant force of an intentional and impositional act initiated by channel member A is defined to be the amount of pressure B experiences on its goals, domain conceptions and perceptions of reality as a result of an intervening act. The magnitude of the resultant force is 1) directly proportional to the power of the initiator, A, relative to the power of the resistor, B; 2) directly proportional to the perceived distance over which B would have to shift its goals, domain conceptions, and perceptions in order to be compatible with A's concept of these elements; and 3) inversely proportional to the rigidity of goals, domain conceptions, and perceptions. The resultant force B experiences is always in the direction of the initiator A.*

Notationally:

$$F_{bae} = \frac{P_{ab}}{P_{ba}} \cdot \frac{\hat{C}_{Pabe}}{T_e} \tag{22}$$

where: F_{bae} = the resultant force B experiences on e as a result of A's intervening act,

 e = the element upon which B is experiencing pressure for change; G for goals, R for domain, V for perceptions,

 P_{ab} = the power of the initiator A over the resistor B,

 P_{ba} = the power of the resistor B over the initiator A,

 $\hat{C}_{Pabe}$ = the level of conflict or incompatibility in e perceived by A in the A-B relation,[17] and

 T_e = the time required to elicit a complete shift in an organization's position with regards to e (rigidity) under equivalent power levels (i.e., $P_{ab} = P_{ba}$).

In order to illustrate how Eq. (22) operates, we define the "adjustment time" (T'_e) to be the time required under varying power ratios for the initiator to cause the resistor to shift completely its position in the initiator's direction on a given element. In symbols:

$$T'_e = \frac{P_{ba}}{P_{ab}} \cdot T_e \tag{23}$$

Substituting Eq. (23) into Eq. (22) yields

$$F_{bae} = \frac{\hat{C}_{Pabe}}{T'_e} \tag{24}$$

For example, if T_e were equal to 100 time units, the power of the initiator were equal to .6 and the power of the resistor were equal to .3, then T'_e would be equal to 50 time units. Under these conditions, the power resistor would experience pressure to move 1/50th of the perceived distance between its and initiator's position on element e during a conflict episode. On the other hand, if the power relation were reversed, then T'_e would be equal to 200 time units, and the power resistor would experience pressure to move 1/200th of the perceived distance. In other words, as the power of the initiator declines, the time and effort required for the resistor to adjust completely to the initiator's demands increases and consequently the amount of force the resistor experiences on its goals, domain conceptions, and perceptions during any conflict episode decreases.

E. Conflict Aftermath

The final event in the process model of conflict is the outcome of the conflict episode. In a channel of distribution context, the aftermath of a conflict episode may include termination of the channel relationship (in extreme circumstances), change in the target channel member's goals, domain conceptions and perceptions, or simply a perceived need to change accompanied by a recognition by the target of its inability to accommodate the pressure due to other forces acting upon it. Because the channel relationship is terminated in the first case thereby allowing no further opportunity for exchange, only the latter two cases will be considered in detail below.

At the outset, it should be recognized that while a change in the target channel member's goals, domain conceptions, and perceptions is the most direct result of a conflict episode, it is by far not the only change. The aftermath of a conflict episode in dyadic channel relations is so extensive that none of the initial conflict conditions is left unaltered. Unfortunately, there is little theoretical discussion or empirical research to suggest the impact of a conflict episode beyond the initial change in goals, domain conceptions, and perceptions. However, by merely indicating some of the likely occurrences in the aftermath stage of this process model, the authors hope to provide a feeling for the scope and usefulness of the model in determining outcomes. As constituted, therefore, this final section serves as a brief indication of the model's potential.

1. The Change in Goals, Domain Conceptions, and Perceptions.   French and Raven (1960) have argued that the ultimate change an entity will undergo as a result of an intentional effort to influence its state will depend upon the magnitude and direction of all forces acting upon the entity at that point in time. In the present context, the ultimate magnitude and direction of force the target channel member will experience on its goals, domain conceptions, and perceptions will be determined by the sum of all forces acting upon these dimensions at the time of the conflict episode. These forces include not only those initiated by the focal channel member, but also forces stemming from other dyadic relations, the extra-channel environment, and the internal processes of the target channel member itself.

To illustrate the above point, consider the hypothetical case where a large discount retailer begins to pressure a manufacturer to offer it price breaks above and beyond those available to small independent retailers. The manufacturer may feel compelled to lower its prices to the discounter but is restrained from doing so due to the simultaneous pressures from independent retailers to maintain the current price relationship. Moreover, pressures from the Federal Trade Commission in the form of possible antitrust investigations may further inhibit the manufacturer's willingness to accommodate the discounter. Finally, while the sales department may attempt to react favorably to the discounter's pressure, the finance and accounting departments may apply counterpressure to resist the change out of their concern for the firm's profitability and their accountability.

The importance of the channel environment in determining the aftermath of a conflict episode and, more importantly, its effect on the fundamental nature of the channel relations has only recently been touched upon in the channel literature. At the very least, government policy, regulation, and enforcement will tend to circumscribe the range of acceptable intervening acts and responses (Stern and El-Ansary, 1977). Etgar takes the importance of the environment in determining channel relations an additional step. He hypothesizes that the power-generating resources of a channel member may in part reflect the particular characteristics of the environmental forces impinging upon his channel (demand, technology, competition, legal constraints, etc.) and its ability to capitalize upon these forces and to mitigate their effects upon other channel members (Etgar, 1977, p. 70). The results of his study of the environmental and control structure conditions of several distributive channels led him to conclude "that channel leaders tend to emerge in distributive channels when those channels face threatening environments" (ibid., p. 75).

The important point to recognize from the above discussion is that resultant forces which prompt changes in a channel member's position may be mitigated by other forces within the channel, the firm, and the environment. Moreover, forces from the environment may by themselves cause a shift in goals, domain conceptions, and perceptions within the channel which, in turn, may affect future power and conflict relations.

Proposition 15 restates the relationship between the ultimate change in goals, domain conceptions, and perceptions and the pressures brought to bear upon them:

Proposition 15: *The ultimate magnitude and direction of force (a vector) the target channel member will experience on its goals, domain conceptions, and perceptions will be determined by the sum of all forces acting upon these elements at the close of the conflict episode.*

Notationally:

$$F_{be} = \sum_{i \epsilon T} F_{bie} \qquad\qquad (25)$$

where: F_{be} = the composite force B experiences on element e at the close of the
     conflict episode,

   F_{bie} = the resultant force B experiences on e from the ith organization in
     B's task environment, and

    T = the set of organizations comprising B's task environment.

2. *The Change in Benefits and Costs.*   The degree to which the goals, domain conceptions, and perceptions of the target channel member change in the direction intended by the focal channel member will determine the extent to which the benefits, costs, and power of each organization will change. Illustrative of the direction of these changes, Assael (1969) observed that, in the automobile industry, "the conflict period of the mid-1950s resulted in a reallocation of responsibility. General Motors refined dealer responsibilities by allocating to the dealer marketing functions it had previously performed: administration of local advertising was left entirely to the dealers; service and warranty policies were liberalized to provide dealers with greater independence in allowances and administration of claims; dealers were given greater latitude in ordering new cars, parts, and accessories and in determining additional investment; and they were allotted greater sales responsibilities to enhance profit potentials" (Assael, 1969, p. 579). Thus, as a result of the conflict process, the benefits which the dealers mediated to General Motors increased as did the costs the dealers incurred in behalf of General Motors as they took on additional responsibilities. Also, the dealers were able to reduce the contingencies and constraints of their task environment by gaining some control over their relation with General Motors. They would therefore be expected to increase the benefits they mediate for themselves. And, finally, the power of General Motors relative to its dealers declined. Thus, GM's ability to mediate benefits in its own behalf would also be expected to decline.

Although not as explicit, similar observations could also be drawn from several other sources which have described interorganizational relations in distribution (Mallen, 1963; Weiss, 1958). If it is possible to generalize from these examples to other channel situations, then, assuming a successful power play by the power initiator A, the following changes would be expected in the A-B relation:

 1) $+\Delta\ B_{ab}$

 2) $+\Delta\ C_{ab}$

 3) $+\Delta\ B_{aab}$

 4) $-\Delta\ B_{bba}$

It is worthwhile to note that by assuming a successful power play by A will result in an increase in the benefits it will mediate to B, one could predict, using the model developed in this paper, the latter three changes.[18]

3. The Change in Power (Dependence). Equations (26) and (27) are provided to illustrate how the changes in costs and benefits will ultimately affect the power of the focal and target channel members. Taking Eq. (26) first, it can be demonstrated that B's motivational investment in goals mediated by A will always increase (26-A) as a result of the changes in benefits it receives from and through A. Consequently, the power of A over B will tend to increase. The increase in P_{ab} will, however, be tempered or enhanced depending upon whether or not the additional benefits B receives from A outweigh the decline in benefits it experiences due to the unfavorable change in the power ratio in Eq. (13). The net change in B_{ab} and B_{bba} will determine the viability of B's alternatives (26-B) and therefore the ultimate level of A's power over B.

In Eq. (27), it can also be demonstrated that A's motivational investment in goals mediated by B will decline (27-A) as a result of the changes in costs it incurs for B and the benefits it receives through B. However, by Eq. (13), the total benefits it receives in its relation with B will increase and consequently the viability of its alternatives will decline (27-B). Therefore, it is difficult to predict *a priori* exactly how P_{ba} will change.

$$P_{ab} = D_{ba} = \cfrac{\cfrac{B_{ab} - C_{ba} \qquad\qquad\qquad + \Delta B_{ab}}{\sum_{i \in T}[(B_{ib} - C_{bi}) + B_{bbi}] + \Delta B_{ab} - \Delta B_{bba}}}{\sum_{k \in S}\left[\cfrac{(B_{ka} - C_{bk}) + B_{bbk}}{(B_{ab} - C_{ba}) + B_{bba} + \Delta B_{ab} - \Delta B_{bba}}\right]}$$

$$\text{(26a)}$$
$$\text{(26b)}$$

$$P_{ba} = D_{ab} = \cfrac{\cfrac{B_{ba} - C_{ab} \qquad\qquad\qquad - (+\Delta C_{ab})}{\sum_{i \in T}[(B_{ia} - C_{ai}) + B_{aai}] - (+\Delta C_{ab}) + \Delta B_{aab}}}{\sum_{k \in S}\left[\cfrac{(B_{ka} - C_{ak}) + B_{aak}}{(B_{ba} - C_{ab}) + B_{aab} - (+\Delta C_{ab}) + \Delta B_{aab}}\right].}$$

$$\text{(27a)}$$
$$\text{(27b)}$$

4. The Changes in Conflict Potential, Perceived Conflict, and the Resultant Force. It was observed above that a successful power play will result in the closing of the distance between channel members A and B with regards to their goals, domain conceptions, and perceptions. As a result, the level of conflict attributable to these sources will decline. It was also observed that the changes in the goals, domain conceptions, and perceptions of channel member B will simultaneously change the costs, benefits, and consequently the power relationships of both organizations. To the extent that the power of A and possibly B increases, so will their obverse dependencies. Therefore, the level of interdependence could increase, and simultaneously increase the potential for one channel member to interfere with goal attainment of another. The ultimate change in conflict potential between two channel members is difficult to predict without the benefit of simulation. Where it should decline because goals, domain conceptions, and perceptions of the channel members are more compatible, it may, in fact, increase because there is more opportunity for interference.

The change in the conflict perceived by each channel member will vary directly with the change in the conflict potential between the organizations. In addition, because the benefits A receives through B will increase faster than the costs it incurs in B's behalf, the level of conflict A perceives may decline. B, on the other hand, may experience an increase in the level of conflict it perceives, if the additional benefits it receives from A do not offset the decline in benefits it mediates for itself.

The magnitude of force which future intervening acts may generate in subsequent conflict episodes is difficult to predict due to the complexity of the conflict model. Where the resultant force originating with A would tend to increase because A's power relative to B has increased, it may in fact decline because the level of conflict A perceives in the A-B relation has declined. The converse would be true for resultant forces originating with B.

III. SUMMARY

The objective of this paper has been to develop a dynamic, mathematical model of conflict and power in dyadic interorganizational relations. The model has been formulated in terms of a conflict episode which is comprised of a chain of events beginning with conflict potential, passing through perceived conflict and resultant forces, and ending in conflict aftermath. The intensity of each stage is a function of the level of dependence (power) between channel members or their cost-benefit components.

Conflict potential has been defined in terms of goal, domain, and perceptual incompatibility and the interdependence which exists between two organizations. Dependence and its obverse power have been formulated in the model in terms of the costs and benefits a channel member incurs and receives from and through another channel member operating on a different level in the distribution chain. The level of conflict perceived in an exchange relationship was found to be a function of the conflict which potentially exists between two channel members and the extent to which the benefits of the relationship exceed its costs.

It was also argued that a channel member will attempt to cause another channel member to change its goals, domain conceptions, and perceptions to be in line with its own conception of these elements in order to reduce the contingencies and constraints within its environment, and thereby increase the level of its goal attainment. The level of force which a channel member can generate by intentionally intervening in the life space of the second channel member was defined in terms of the relative power of the two organizations, the perceived incompatibility of their goals, domain conceptions, and perceptions, and the rigidity of these elements.

Finally, the aftermath of an intentional and intervening act was postulated to be determined by not only the resultant force of the act, but also by all forces impinging on the target channel member at that point in time. However, the complexity of the conflict process portrayed by the model prevented the prediction of the direction and magnitude of the changes which would occur during the aftermath stage of the conflict episode. A tentative analysis of the model did reveal that the aftermath would be so extensive that none of the initial conflict conditions would be unaltered.

In a sense, the model proposed here has been a synthesis and an integration via mathematical notation of much of the literature on conflict and power as it pertains to interorganizational relations in marketing. It is necessarily tentative because of the relative dearth of empirical findings on interorganizational conflict and power generally. It is clear that a next step in the development of the model would be to put it to an empirical test. At the very least, the multiplicative components of the model should be compared to the additive models recently employed in the literature in terms of their relative ability to explain variation in channel relations. In addition, new, and perhaps innovative, research efforts should be undertaken to attempt to measure, first, the variables defined here and, second, the relationships between these variables. Finally, the model should be translated into a Forrester-type simulation (Forrester, 1961, 1968, 1969) in order to allow the logic of the model to be carefully evaluated, as well as make possible the complete description of a conflict aftermath.

FOOTNOTES

1. The relevant literature in this case includes theoretical and empirical studies which have focused on interorganizational and intergroup conflict and power relations. Ideally only the literature on interorganizational behavior should be cited in the development of this model. Unfortunately, this literature is so sparse that it is necessary to consult the work done on intergroup behavior. In support of this decision, March and Simon (1958) and Thomas et al. (1972) point out that the conditions affecting intergroup conflict also appear to be factors influencing interorganizational conflict. On the other hand, both Sherif (1958) and Evan (1966) have argued that intraorganization theory cannot be applied to interorganizational situations.

Finally, and with reluctance, it will occasionally be necessary to draw upon studies of interpersonal conflict and power relations. While this practice is limited only to the borrowing of certain concepts to add clarity to the discussion, the authors recognize that the generalizing of interpersonal theory to interorganizational theory is questionable and is therefore a limitation of the model to be presented.

2. In a footnote, Litwak and Hylton (1962) point out that in the definition of interdependence used here "the phrase 'take into account' is meant in a very immediate sense for in a broad sense all organizations must take each other into account." Similar definitions of interdependence can also be found in Emerson (1972) and Walton and McKersie (1965).

3. While these variables are not the only determinants of conflict, the authors consider them to be among the most important. For a more extensive listing of the causes of conflict, see Fink (1968).

4. This notion has been adapted by the authors from Schmidt and Kochan's (1972) discussion of the relationship between interdependence and goal incompatibility as necessary preconditions for conflict.

5. The definition of conflict potential offered here implicitly assumes that goal incompatibility, domain dissensus and perceptual incongruence are all equally important as indicated by their equal one-third weighting. It may be more realistic to assign unequal weights to the three elements. Unfortunately, there is insufficient evidence in the literature to suggest the relative importance of each element.

In terms of a further refinement of Eq. (5), it should be noted that the effect of the weighting scheme is to reduce the scale of the importance dimension of each source of conflict to 1/3 (e.g., $0 \leq \theta'_{ia}, \beta'_{ia}, \pi'_{ia} \leq .333$). Consequently, the sum of the relative importance of all potential incompatibilities across the three sources of conflict is one. That is,

$$\sum_{i \in G_a} \theta'_{ia} + \sum_{i \in R_a} \beta'_{ia} + \sum_{i \in V_a} \pi'_{ia} = 1$$

6. Thompson (1967) also found Emerson's concept of dependence to be useful in analyzing interorganizational relations (see Chapter IV, especially pp. 29–32).

7. Unlike Levine and White (1972), the authors would argue that all exchange relations are reciprocal. The authors consider the intangible benefits which an organization receives via an exchange relation to be as important as the tangible benefits in terms of contribution to goal satisfaction. Levine and White, however, do not treat intangible benefits in their analysis.

8. The following categorization of benefits is taken from Lehman's (1969) expansion of Etzioni's (1961) typology of power sources. Other typologies include French and Raven (1960) and Katz and Kahn (1972).

9. In an analogous situation on the interpersonal level, Kahn et al. (1964) speak of an objective environment and a psychological environment. The objective environment consists of "real" objects and events, verifiable outside a person's conscious experience. The psychological environment consists of conscious and unconscious representations of the objective environment.

10. Katz and Kahn (1972) have also observed that "In adapting to their environment, systems will attempt to cope with external forces by ingesting them or acquiring control over them."

11. As the total goal contribution of the A-B relation increases due to increases in B_{aab}, so will the dependence of A on B, even if B's net contribution to A's goal attainment is relatively low and/or stable. The reason A's dependence increases is that the total goal contribution of the A-B relation [Eq. (16-d)] is used to divide into the total goal contribution of each alternative [Eq. (16-c)]. The greater Eq. (16-d), the less the value or viability of the alternatives and hence the greater the dependence. Equation (16-a) measures only those contributions B mediates and is only one determinant of A's dependence.

12. Observe that the power of B over A (P_{ba}) is defined in terms of the benefits A mediates to itself via its relationship with B (B_{aab}) and vice versa. Therefore, it is necessary to solve Eqs. (13) and (18) simultaneously in order to arrive at values for B_{aab} and P_{ba}.

13. The use of the concept "perceived conflict" is slightly different from that used by Pondy. According to Pondy (1967), perceived conflict refers to both the perception of conflict where no latent conflict exists, as well as the lack of perception of the latent conflict conditions (p. 301). The first element of this definition is contained in the authors' conceptualization of perceptual incongruence. The second forms the basis of the interpretation adopted in this paper. The authors prefer to define perceived conflict as the acknowledgment or cognition of conflictual behavior which stems from goal incompatibility, domain dissensus, and perceptual incongruency.

14. The reader is cautioned to recognize that the authors cited here employed an additive model and not a multiplicative model as proposed here.

15. For other case examples relative to this relationship, see Kahn et al. (1964); Katz and Kahn (1972).

16. Our definition of resultant force is an adaptation of Lewin's definition of power. See Lewin (1951).

17. Recall that conflict potential is additive in terms of goal incompatibility, domain dissensus, and perceptual incongruency. Consequently, the level of conflict A perceives in its relation with B ($\hat{C}_{Pab}$) can be broken down into its component sources of conflict. For example, by isolating the goal element of conflict in Eq. (20), it is possible to define the level of conflict perceived by A due to goal incompatibility ($\hat{C}_{Pabg}$) to be as follows:

$$\hat{C}_{Pabg} = \frac{C_{ab}}{B_{ba} + B_{aab}} \cdot I \cdot G_{Iab}$$

Similar definitions can be obtained for the level of conflict perceived by A due to domain dissensus ($\hat{C}_{Pabr}$) and perceptual incongruency ($\hat{C}_{Pabv}$).

18. To illustrate the above observation, ΔC_{ab} can be predicted from ΔB_{ab} with the help of Prop. 7. The inclusion of ΔB_{ab} and ΔC_{ab} into the definitions of power (Prop. 12) for A and B, respectively, indicates that the power of A will tend to increase and the power of B decrease. Consequently, B_{aab} will tend to increase (it will also increase because C_{ab} has increased) and B_{bba} will tend to decline (Prop. 9). However, in order to determine exactly what the P_{ab}, P_{ba}, B_{aab}, and B_{bba} will be after a successful power play, it would be necessary to solve four equations in the form of Eqs. (18) and (13) simultaneously.

REFERENCES

Alderson, Wroe (1969), "Cooperation and Conflict in Marketing Channels," reprinted in Louis W. Stern (ed.), *Distribution Channels: Behavioral Dimensions,* Boston: Houghton Mifflin, p. 204.

Assael, Henry (1969), "Constructive Role of Interorganizational Conflict," *Administrative Science Quarterly* 13: 216 (December).

———— (1968), "The Political Role of Trade Associations in Distributive Conflict Resolution," *Journal of Marketing* 32: 573–582 (April).

Bucklin, Louis P. (1973), "A Theory of Channel Control," *Journal of Marketing* 37: 42 (January).

Burley, James R. (1975), "Territorial Restriction in Distribution Systems: Current Legal Developments," *Journal of Marketing* 39: 52–56 (October).

Carberry, James F. (1973), "Valley of the Dolls," *Wall Street Journal,* pp. 1 and 16 (June 20).

Carlson, Bjorn, and Kusoffsky, Bertil (1966), *Distributor Brands Versus Producer Brands,* English translation, Stockholm, Sweden: The Economic Research Institute at the Stockholm School of Economics, pp. 114–120.

Dutton, John M., and Walton, Richard E. (1966), "Interdepartmental Conflict and Cooperation: Two Contrasting Studies," *Human Organization* 25: 207–220.

El-Ansary, Adel J., and Robicheaux, Robert A. (1974), "A Theory of Channel Control: Revisited," *Journal of Marketing* 38: 2–7 (January).

El-Ansary, Adel J., and Stern, Louis W. (1972), "Power Measurement in the Distribution Channel," *Journal of Marketing Research* 9: 47–52 (February).

Emerson, R. M. (1972), "Power-Dependence Relations," *American Sociological Review* 27: 32 (February).

Etgar, Michael (1976b), "Channel Domination and Countervailing Power in Distributive Channels," *Journal of Marketing Research* 13: 254–262 (August).

———— (1977), "Channel Environment and Channel Leadership," *Journal of Marketing Research* 14: 69–76 (February).

_____ (1976a), "Effects of Administrative Control on Efficiency of Vertical Marketing Systems,"
Journal of Marketing Research 13: 12–24 (February).

Etzioni, Amitai (1961), "A Comparative Analysis of Complex Organizations," *A Sociological Reader on Complex Organizations,* 2nd edition, New York: Holt, Rinehart and Winston, pp. 59–76.

Evan, William M. (1966), "The Organization Set: Toward a Theory of Interorganizational Relations," reprinted in Merlin B. Brinkerhoff and Phillip R. Kunz, *Complex Organizations and Their Environments,* Dubuque, Iowa: Wm. C. Brown Publishers, pp. 326–340.

Fink, Clinton F. (1968), "Some Conceptual Difficulties in the Theory of Social Conflict," *Journal of Conflict Resolution* 12: 414–466 (December).

Forrester, Jay W. (1961), *Industrial Dynamics,* Cambridge, Mass.: M.I.T. Press.

_____ (1968), *Principles of Systems,* 2nd preliminary edition, Cambridge, Mass.: Wright-Allen Press, Inc.

_____ (1969), *Urban Dynamics,* Cambridge, Mass.: M.I.T. Press.

French, J. R. P., and Raven, B. (1960), "The Bases of Social Power," in Darwin Cartwright and Alvin Zander (eds.), *Group Dynamics: Research and Theory,* New York. Harper and Row, pp. 607–623.

Hunt, Shelby D., and Nevin, John R. (1974), "Power in a Channel of Distribution: Sources and Consequences," *Journal of Marketing Research* 9: 186–193 (May).

_____, and _____ (1975), "Tying Agreements in Franchising." *Journal of Marketing* 39: 20–26 (July).

Kahn, R. L., et al. (1964), *Organizational Stress: Studies in Role Conflict and Ambiguity,* New York: John Wiley and Sons, p. 12.

Katz, Daniel, and Kahn, Robert L. (1972), "Organizations and the System Concept," reprinted in Merlin B. Brinkerhoff and Phillip R. Kunz, *Complex Organizations and Their Environments,* Dubuque, Iowa: Wm. C. Brown Publishers, p. 42.

_____ and _____ (1966), *Social Psychology of Organization,* New York: John Wiley and Sons.

Kriesberg, Louis (1955), "Occupational Controls Among Steel Distributors," *American Journal of Sociology* 61: 203–212 (March).

Lehman, Edward W. (1969), "Toward a Macrosociology of Power," *American Sociological Review* 34: 453–464 (August).

Levine, Sol, and White, Paul E. (1972), "Exchange as a Conceptual Framework for the Study of Interorganizational Relations," reprinted in Merlin B. Brinkerhoff and Phillip R. Kunz, *Complex Organizations and Their Environments,* Dubuque, Iowa: Wm. C. Brown Publishers, pp. 341–355.

Lewin, Kurt (1951), *Field Theory in Social Sciences,* New York: Harper and Row, p. 336.

Litwak, Eugene, and Hylton, L. F. (1962), "Interorganizational Analysis: A Hypothesis on Coordinating Agencies," *Administrative Science Quarterly* 6: 395–426 (March).

Lusch, Robert F. (1976a), "Channel Conflict: Its Impact on Retailer Operator Performance," *Journal of Retailing* 52: 3–12 (Summer).

_____ (1976b), "Sources of Power: Their Impact on Intrachannel Conflict," *Journal of Marketing Research* 13: 382–390 (November).

Mallen, Bruce (1973), "Functional Spin-Off: A Key to Anticipating Change in Distribution Structure," *Journal of Marketing* 37: 18–25 (July).

_____ (1963), "A Theory of Retailer-Supplier Conflict, Control and Cooperation," *Journal of Retailing* 39: 24–32 (Summer).

March, James G. (1966), "The Power of Power," in David Easton (ed.), *Varieties of Political Theory,* Englewood Cliffs, N.J.: Prentice-Hall, pp. 39–70.

_____, and Simon, Herbert A. (1958), *Organizations,* New York: John Wiley and Sons, p. 131.

McCammon, Bert C., and Little, Robert W. (1965), "Marketing Channels: Analytical Systems and

Approaches," in George Schwartz (ed.), *Science in Marketing,* New York: John Wiley and Sons, p. 322.

Palamountain, Joseph C. (1955), *The Politics of Distribution,* Cambridge, Mass.: Harvard University Press.

Parsons, Talcott (1966), "The Political Aspect of Social Structure and Process," in David Easton (ed.), *Varieties of Political Theory,* Englewood Cliffs, N.J.: Prentice-Hall, p. 72.

"The Politics of Scarcity" (1973), *Wall Street Journal,* p. 4 (December 31).

Pondy, Louis R. (1967), "Organizational Conflict: Concepts and Models," *Administrative Science Quarterly* 12: 296–320 (September).

"Price Gouging Spreads as Suppliers Seek Ways to Profit on Shortages" (1973), *Wall Street Journal,* pp. 1 and 14 (November 2).

Raven, Bertram H., and Kruglonski, Arie W. (1970), "Conflict and Power," in Paul Swingle (ed.), *The Structure of Conflict,* New York: Academic Press.

Ridgeway, Valentine F. (1957), "Administration of Manufacturer-Dealer Systems," *Administrative Science Quarterly* 7: 464–483 (March).

Robicheaux, Robert A., and El-Ansary, Adel (1976–1977), "A General Model for Understanding Channel Member Behavior," *Journal of Retailing* 52: 13–30, 93–94 (Winter).

Rosenberg, Larry J., and Stern, Louis W. (1971), "Conflict Measurement in the Distribution Channel," *Journal of Marketing Research* 8: 437–442 (November).

Schmidt, Stuart M., and Kochan, Thomas A. (1972), "Conflict: Toward Conceptual Clarity," *Administrative Science Quarterly* 17: 359–370 (September).

Sherif, M. (1958), "Superordinate Goals in the Reduction of Intergroup Conflict," *American Journal of Sociology* 63: 349–356 (January).

Shuptrine, Kelly F., and Foster, Robert J. (1976), "Monitoring Channel Conflict with Evaluations from the Retail Level," *Journal of Retailing* 52: 55–74 (Spring).

"Skaggs-Albertson's 'Amicable Separation' " (1977), *Business Week,* pp. 32–33 (February 7).

Smith, Clagett G. (1966), "A Comparative Analysis of Some Conditions and Consequences of Intraorganizational Conflict," *Administrative Science Quarterly* 11: 504–529.

Stern, Louis W., Agodo, Oriye, and Firat, Fuat A. (1976), "Territorial Restrictions in Distribution: A Case Analysis," *Journal of Marketing* 40: 69–75 (April).

————, and El-Ansary, Adel (1977), *Marketing Channels,* Englewood Cliffs, N.J.: Prentice-Hall.

————, and Gorman, Ronald H. (1969), "Conflict in Distribution Channels: An Exploration," in Louis W. Stern (ed.), *Distribution Channels: Behavioral Dimensions,* Boston: Houghton Mifflin, pp. 288–305.

————, Schultz, Robert A., and Grabner, John R. (1973–1974), "The Power Base-Conflict Relationship: Preliminary Findings," *Social Science Quarterly* 54:412–419.

————, Sternthal, Brian, and Craig, Samuel C. (1973), "Managing Conflict in Distribution Channels: A Laboratory Study," *Journal of Marketing Research* 10: 169–179 (May).

Thibaut, J. W., and Kelley, H. H. (1959), *The Social Psychology of Groups,* New York: John Wiley and Sons.

Thomas, Kenneth W. (1976), "Conflict and Conflict Management," in Marvin D. Dunnette (ed.), *Handbook of Industrial and Organizational Psychology,* Chicago: Rand McNally, pp. 889–935.

Thomas, Kenneth W., Walton, Richard E., and Dutton, John M. (1972), "Determinants of Interdepartmental Conflict," in M. Tuite, R. Chisholm and M. Radnor (eds.), *Interorganizational Decision-Making.* Chicago: Aldine, p. 69.

Thompson, James D. (1967), *Organizations in Action,* New York: McGraw-Hill, p. 26.

Thorp, Might (1977), "Marketing in Japan Takes Twenty Turns Foreign Firms Find," *Wall Street Journal,* pp. 1 and 19 (March 7).

Walton, R. E. (1969), *Interpersonal Peacemaking: Confrontations and Third Party Consultation,* Reading, Mass.: Addison-Wesley.

Walton, Richard E., and McKersie, Robert B. (1965), *A Behavioral Theory of Labor Negotiations,* New York: McGraw-Hill, p. 362.

Webster, Frederick E., Jr. (1976), "The Role of the Industrial Distributor in Marketing Strategy," *Journal of Marketing* 40: 10–16 (July).

Weiss, Edward B. (1958), "How Much of a Retailer Is the Manufacturer," *Advertising Age* 29: 68.

Wittreich, Warren J. (1962), "Misunderstanding the Retailer," *Harvard Business Review* 40: 147–159 (May–June).

THE PRODUCT AUDIT SYSTEM AS A TOOL OF MARKETING PLANNING

C. Merle Crawford, UNIVERSITY OF MICHIGAN

Product managers, marketing managers, and general managers are increasingly using revolutionary versions of what were once called "product comparisons" or "competitive evaluations." These new versions, essentially systems of analyses, are still rather confidential and still in their early developmental stage. But we now know enough about them to prepare this research report, designed to show what these Product Audit Systems tend to consist of, how companies are organizing to manage them, and how they are operating them to maximize input to decision making.

A Product Audit System is an arrangement of resources and activities designed to elicit carefully measured comparisons of a firm's products (or product line) with those of its competitors. Simplistic audits have been around as long as we have had marketing, but today's audits are:

1. More comprehensive, as regards the assortment of dimensions compared.
2. More thorough and systematic, keyed essentially to the many superior sources of data today.

Research in Marketing—Volume 2, 1979, pages 159–189.
Copyright © 1979 by JAI Press Inc.
All rights of reproduction in any form reserved.
ISBN 0-89232-059-1

3. More critical, in that marketing planning can now utilize product comparisons in more creative ways.
4. More likely to involve organizational levels and units far beyond marketing. In fact, the new pressures from nonmarketing departments of business firms may have been the major reason for the sharp improvement in most audits.

Unfortunately, product audit systems are also still evolving, and evidence indicates this evolutionary progress will continue. We cannot know where they will ultimately settle down, but we do have a fairly good picture of where the technology stands today. No study has as yet attempted to quantify practices in this area, but enough reports have come out for a good qualitative understanding.

Throughout this paper, we will call on these reports of company practice. However, the reader should be advised that these practices have rarely been systematically evaluated by their company users. Some efforts have aborted, some are serving political rather than decision-making purposes, and none have been consolidated at the total-organization level, to my knowledge. They are experimental and developmental or just tiny fragments of what could be. A great deal of research needs to be done, and even now it appears few firms are aware of what other firms are doing along these lines. Dominguez (1) gives as good a status report as we now have, though he relies principally on life cycle measurements.

Because of the general trend today to blur functional lines in corporate organization, this report of product audit systems is not clearly a "marketing" account. Corporations are more than ever interested in performance and cost-effectiveness—they care not at all whether marketing functions are independent from production or finance. Safety, service, information systems, and consumer affairs are examples of other operations that have been de-functionalized.

Thus we will see in this report that the marketing department often provides the key impetus for a product audit system, it is perhaps the major user of the system output, and its special needs are a powerful determinant of operations methodology. But the fact remains that the auditing operation is increasingly responsible to other corporate officers and increasingly serves a wide range of nonmarketing needs.

I. REASONS FOR GROWTH IN AUDITING SYSTEMS

The reasons for such widespread interest in product audit systems are probably many. We can isolate several as the key ones, however, the first four being those which have produced increased *demand* for the systems outputs—social pressures, growth of the marketing concept, increased use of strategic planning, and inflation. Another four changes have occurred to help *permit* the development of the appropriate technologies—attitude measurement methodologies, the computer, organizational concepts and testing services. Each will be described in turn.

A. Social Pressures

The consumerism movement has brought pressure for information on product performance, safety, cost-effectiveness, etc. Unit pricing, product life, warranty coverage, ingredient listings, and comparative characteristics are just a few of the specific areas where product managers, advertising managers, public relations directors, quality control departments and many more have been forced to develop and publish more data about products.

Additionally, ecological and environmental pressures have caused product interests. Biodegradability, harmfulness of smoke residues, atmosphere damage, and visual pollution are examples. Increasingly companies will have to measure product impact on publics other than consumers. The Federal government announced in 1973 a special program to develop specifications for products such as air conditioners, which specification would then be used to force industry compliance (2).

Although these two, consumerism and ecology, comprise most of the social pressure on products, there are others. Finance personnel must frequently report sales, cost, and profit data by product lines. The personnel department is interested in how various products or product lines utilize various types of employees. Plant managers are increasingly concerned about the safety of various ingredients or processes or by-products. Multinational managers review product extension opportunities in entirely new ways today.

B. Marketing Concept and the Product Manager

After going through a lengthy period of experimentation, the marketing concept and its mechanism of execution, the product manager, have finally come into their own. Virtually every company of commercial significance has accepted the idea that profit maximization comes from dedicating the firm's total resources to customer satisfaction. This approach forces attention onto products as the key mechanism for the resource/customer interface. It has also brought about a surge of interest in product line extensions, market segmentation and product positioning. All require thorough study of product attributes and customer attitudes toward those attributes. Hanan (3), especially, demonstrates the relevance of attributes to market segmentation.

C. Strategic Planning

Concomitant with the intensified interest in products by the marketing division has been a new interest by top management. Just as marketing planning has become more sophisticated, so has total corporate planning—it is rare to find a corporation of any significance today without an annual planning process.

This planning almost inevitably involves an analysis of opportunities and resources—what strengths and weaknesses must the planning process recognize.

Since a firm's product line is often one of its key resources, or at least it *may* be, that product line requires the same intensive study as does any other important asset. Optimizing the exploitation of the product resource requires that it be thoroughly understood—measured and evaluated. Thus top managements have been throwing a new spotlight onto products, and the spotlight is intended to disclose attributes on a far broader scope than historically provided by the marketing department.

D. Inflation

Apparently most of the world's economies are in a permanent state of inflation. If so, the recent spate of "Operations Economy" or "Cut Cost" or "Do It Cheaper" programs will continue and become more demanding. In the process, corporate managements are calling on a technique long established in the engineering department, called Value Analysis. But instead of several engineers challenging every single cost on a product to prove itself or be eliminated, management offers a similar challenge to every dimension of the entire business. This includes products, of course, but now the focus is on much more than the physical aspects that are of engineering concern. And persons from several divisions of the business are participating.

These four forces of social pressure, the marketing concept, strategic planning and inflation have produced an entirely new interest in products, especially as regards their characteristics, or attributes. But the interests are now so diverse that they frequently conflict—for instance cost vs. safety vs. advertisability.

Such a range of critical concerns has forced today's product appraisers to seek techniques for making far more systematic and thorough product audits than in the past. Fortunately, and perhaps not just coincidentally, several developments of a permissive nature have been occurring simultaneously.

E. Attitude Measurement

As stated above, a product's attributes hold different interests to different persons. Moreover, any given attribute may be subject to different measurements, and even a single measurement may receive conflicting interpretations. The problem is, partly, a matter of attitudes, and a key attitude input on a product audit is that of a product purchaser or a product user.

Without accurate assessments of attitudes toward various product attributes, a product audit degenerates into a shouting match. So it is fortunate that for perhaps the past fifteen years marketing research theoreticians have put more energy into attitude measurement than any other facet of their craft. We now have a very sophisticated set of devices for uncovering and recording user attitudes toward various product attributes. We also have a still-developing set of analytical mechanisms for evaluating those attitudes, based partly on new scaling techniques to provide the data and partly on mathematical methodologies to manipulate the data. It now appears that we have most of what we need to provide the user data portion to an overall product evaluation system. See Wilkie and Pessemier (4) and Kinnear and Taylor (5) as examples.

F. Computer

As in so many other fields, the computer brings to product audits the capacity for dealing with diverse inputs, large numbers of complex relationships, and multiple and changing outputs. Most firms have too many products for anything less than computer processing, and most products now have a set of attribute dimensions that requires complex data-handling mechanisms. Lastly, the sheer diversity of the product evaluation situation argues for an on-line, up-to-date capability which three-ring binders or 5×8 cards could never yield.

G. Organization

Simultaneous with the development of data and the computer, we have seen a fortitudinous growth in organizational capability for performing the new task. First of all, there has been a rapid development of what is generally called corporate staff. Legal departments, planning groups, specialists in public relations, safety controllers, legislative experts, etc., are growing in number and importance coincident with the divisionalized form of general organization. Such staffs provide resources, interest, and a ''home'' for whatever firm-wide product audit system may develop.

A second organizational change key to this situation is the growth of the product manager concept. Although posing many problems and coming in a full range of responsibilities, the product manager is the marketing job of the moment. The position represents the largest single interest in product auditing and can either provide locus for the activity or else be the major impetus to get it located somewhere else. Virtually no organization can say it has no convenient place to locate a product audit system.

H. Testing Services

Primarily as a direct result of the many outside pressures discussed earlier, we have seen a burst of activity by product-testing organizations. The National Bureau of Standards, Consumers Union, the U.S. Testing Service, Underwriters' Laboratories, and literally thousands of state, county, city, semiprivate and private testing organizations now exist. Many more are needed and will be forthcoming. We may even see one that business generally feels is not needed—a Federal version of the Consumers Union. Regardless, a vast array of services now exists to assist business in the measurements they increasingly need. See ''Testing'' (6) as an example of one and see *Business Week* (7) for a recent summary of the situation.

The natural consequence of these two sets of trends, increasing demands for product measurements and increasing capabilities for such measurements is pressure for company-wide, centralized systems of product assessment and evaluation.

Until recently, most actions have been fragmented, and primarily in reaction to specific needs. Most departments collect product data, and most store it, but most publish only parts of it, and most see it as a vested interest resource. The R & D group studies products to be sure they meet governmental safety standards or industry standards, for example; manufacturing gathers data on quality as against R & D specifications; marketing has customer preference data; finance has costs.

Much duplication exists, some data are even destroyed or purposefully hidden, some analyses are distorted, and all are fragmented and incomplete. Different definitions are used for similar attributes, different standards are used to measure product performance, and the entire function is seen as a cost imposed by outside pressures unjustifiably. One large electrical apparatus firm found that its technical departments were systematically collecting and analyzing comparative product information on scores of products, yet its marketing people were not compiling even the most simplistic comparative profiles. Unfortunately, its major—and much more successful—competitor was using a highly integrated and imaginative system of product comparisons in its marketing departments.

What we have then, is a rather typical multi-disciplinary or cross functional opportunity being forged out of a series of originally unrelated but not highly convergent trends. Although no one term for this activity has become accepted, the single most frequently used is Product Audit System, and this name is used here.

II. PRODUCT AUDIT SYSTEM: ESSENTIAL ELEMENTS

Most product audit systems which have been described consist of three parts. The first part is Inputs—the products, persons and other things which constitute the system's resources. The second part is the set of operational relationships between the various inputs. Third is the output or results that are produced by the operations.

These three elements are common to systems generally, but are unique in each application. We will now look at the specific character they have in product audit systems, and will then contrast product audit systems with several other business systems before going into a detailed description of how corporations are actually using them.

A. System Inputs

Company practices have varied greatly in detail, but almost all of them have made use of the following inputs:

1. *Auditors*. People or devices which are trained to measure product attributes.
2. *Products*. The obvious part, but still somewhat complex. Practices vary as to whether to include all items in a line or only the volume leaders, whether to include some or all of the packaging and cartoning, and whether to include presale or postsale service as part of the product. There are several other such variations.
3. *Funds*. Product auditing can be very thorough or very slapdash. Apparently managements have found widely diverging values from product audits because they have varied greatly in their expenditures.
4. *Computer facilities* and other data storage capability.

B. Operations

The actual practices involved here will be described in detail later—they consist essentially of deciding what attributes will be audited, selecting the measuring units, making the measurements, and then analyzing the data. However, certain principles seem to be at work here, as different companies have established their policies.

The first one is a strong desire for *impartiality*—that is, the system must be free from the distorting influence of any one vested interest. Even the product manager, most popular locus for product audit, is not above bias, which has created argument for putting the system at corporate staff or some other position outside of marketing.

Two, audits benefit from a *long-time-frame commitment*. Key values come from data comparisons over multiple periods, and start-up costs are high.

Three, managements are demanding, and fully expect, the utmost *integrity* from the system—accuracy, reliability, honesty.

Four, special efforts are frequently taken to keep the audit system *efficient*—to reduce the tendency toward bureaucracy. The system needs independence of data, but as a service system it needs to remain especially responsive to changes in output demands.

C. System Outputs (Results)

The output of a product audit system consists of data—descriptions, comparisons, trends, whatever, but data. Persons served by the systems use the data to make judgments, change operations, undertake special studies, etc. The output of the product audit system thus constitutes the input to scores of other systems around the firm.

For example, a product system may call for an annual usage test of a line of products compared with competition. If the products are tennis rackets, all of a year's models may be tested to determine durability, power, resistance to weather, etc. The resulting report goes to manufacturing, quality control, R&D,

the internal industry standards committee, marketing, and perhaps others—each uses the data differently.

The data themselves are stored in the system and become a resource or an input for the next analysis on tennis rackets. The system thus is a provider of data, in virtually unlimited variety thanks to the growing supply of original data and data-handling equipment, but it leaves to the various functional areas the judgments and the decisions following from use of the data.

Naturally, when the auditing is done by the marketing group it is but a part of the marketing planning process—one cannot delineate the audit system from the higher-order planning system.

But some firms see value in having the auditing process be independent from data usage, so they see system output as data. A product manager/auditor sees output as plans, or at least strategy recommendations.

However stipulated, outputs are highly situational. Most are scheduled, periodic, and routine, though of course there will be many special ones, a good example of which was General Electric's request of its product audit system to review the energy utilization characteristics of a major portion of its product line at the time of the energy crunch (8).

III. HOW THE PRODUCT AUDIT SYSTEM DIFFERS FROM OTHER BUSINESS SYSTEMS

Several other business practices utilize the term audit, or audit system. Obviously there is no confusion between the operations being described here and the accountant's "audits." But there will be some confusion with two other concepts of audit, especially in marketing.

First, the product audit is not a marketing audit. The latter is far more comprehensive, tends to serve the needs of top marketing or corporate management only, may be performed only when required by a special situation, and is really an analytical task, not a data-handling task.

A thorough marketing audit, such as the one Shrello Associates report (9) explained in a very usable fashion, calls for a special output from the Product Audit System as one of the key inputs to the marketing audit. Thus the two audits have a powerful relationship in that a meaningful marketing audit must have valid product data, else there is no base for conclusions on quality of past marketing effort, competitive strength, etc. Yet many marketing audits are based on cursory and incomplete, if not actually incorrect, product data. Some of the most glaring examples have come from marketing audits conducted as parts of acquisition analyses. Many "acquirers" are surprised to find the low quality of products that looked good during the negotiations.

A second possible confusion comes from firms where the term "product audit" has actually meant only a look at each product's profit or each product's income statement (10), (11), (12). This is actually a very limited concept of product audit and an unfortunate use of the term, since profit and costs are but a small portion of the output of a fully effective product audit system.

The now classical market-share/market-growth matrix developed by the Boston Consulting Group makes clear the limitation of a profit-only product line audit. See (13) and *Business Week* (14). In their consulting work the BCG found that current profitability was a poor predictor of future profitability, and in seeking better predictors they fell upon the idea of adding two more product attributes to the measuring system—the current share of market held by each product and the growth rate of each market.

This was a very productive step, but it also demonstrates the value of going

Figure 1. A sorting of products by comparison of audited values with market performance.

Overall Product Audit Score

as Percent of Market Leader's Score

	Under 70%	Over 70%
Below Average Share-of-Market	A. Justifiable Loser: Revise product or forget it.	C. Potential Gainer: Why isn't it higher in sales? Poor strategy?
Above Average Share-of-Market	D. Risky Winner: It shouldn't be doing this well-- why is it?	B. Justifiable Winner

beyond the very simplistic descriptions of a product's situation. If a firm uses a full product audit system rather than one of these limited analyses, it arrives at an *overall* evaluation of product—a weighted total score on the product. Westinghouse, for example, uses a system whereby each major product line is evaluated on a series of factors from product features all the way through to distributor support. So is each competitor's line. The weighted total for each Westinghouse line is percented to the market "score" leader—not sales leader. The Westinghouse product may be 100 percent if it is the best, or it may be only 20 percent if the line is very weak.

Plotting these scores against market share, as shown in Figure 1, demonstrates how the total product audit being described in this writing differs from the limited, financial type of analysis frequently called a product line audit. If *all* characteristics of a product are audited, the resulting analyses lead more directly to actions than do the partial audits.

IV. THE PRODUCT AUDIT SYSTEM: OPERATING POLICIES AND PRACTICES

Having seen 1) the forces tending to produce product audits, 2) the essential elements of such systems, and 3) the contrasts between the analysis being described here and other analyses sometimes called audits, we can now examine in detail the range of operating policies and practices currently being used to produce the audit outputs. We will first look at the various organizational options that exist, then the operations actually carried on, and then the range of system outputs seen so far. The analysis will conclude with an examination of several special facilitating policies frequently found useful and a call for further research on the general subject of product audit systems.

A. Organizational Options

Figure 2 shows a skeleton organization of the typical divisionalized company. Indicated on the chart by numbers are the following options for locating the product audit function.

1. Centralized Corporate Staff. This option is always the most attractive to system designers because it clearly delineates responsibilities, frees the operation of conflicts with other tasks, tends to assure top management attention and support, and in general gives it the optimum status so important to a new function. These are real advantages but corporate staffs can also become isolated and even terribly bureaucratic. They are also expensive if they just duplicate much of the effort at division levels. Finally, they may become myopic and forget their role.

In general a good product audit system can be defined on the corporate staff

Figure 2. Various possible organizational locations for the product audit function.

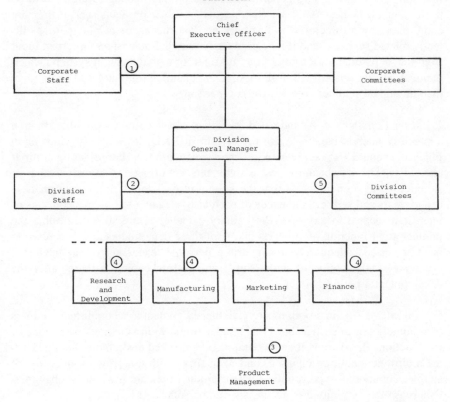

level if the firm's policy is to keep divisions lean, and if various other functions are so centralized. Division thinking is kept close to corporate thinking by a full flow of vertical communication. But if the divisions are essentially operating companies with only fiscal ties to corporate, the product audit system is delegated too.

2. Division General Staff. The second of three successful options is to put the system under the direct control of the division general manager—separate from the other functions. This position lets it be responsive to all needs, yet keeps it from coming under the influence of any one function.

3. Product Management Department. A third viable option is to assign the function to the one other group with a general management focus—the product management department. This assumes the function really does have such a focus—that it is not simply a group of product specialists, a product service function, or an advertising department. If the product managers are held to be profit centers, if they really are "presidents" of their products, and if they are coordinated by a director who has only product management plus perhaps directly related services, and if new product activity has at least an important input from that department, then conditions are right for a product audit system located there. If not, the system will lose its strategic planning role, and will be no more than an annual product competitive comparison.

4. Other Functions.   As indicated in Figure 2, it is certainly possible, though apparently inadvisable, to locate the system in R&D, in Manufacturing, or in Finance. It could also be given to a corporate new products coordinating group if one exists. The drawback to these assignments, set off against the advantages of simplicity and economics, is that the system utilizes inputs from each of these departments and services the needs of each also—leading to obvious conflicts of interest if located in any one. Preliminary evidence seems to indicate that the product audit function often starts in one of these departments and *can* serve to meet the needs adequately under strong personal leadership of an interested executive. Only "pride of authorship" argues for keeping it there, after the developmental period is over.

5. Committee   A final option is to give the assignment to a committee, and it is occasionally felt to be feasible 1) in smaller firms, 2) in situations where one of the functional heads runs it and a committee is deemed desirable to help guarantee multifunctional participation, and 3) in firms with a narrow product line of simple, commodity-type products where product data are few and unchanging. Otherwise the committee is needlessly cumbersome.

6. Internal Structure.   Within the unit assigned the task of a continuous product audit, there are still more organizational options—practice becomes highly situational. Generally speaking, the function is kept lean, utilizing the personnel and resources of other units. Thus, for instance, the product audit system pulls inputs from marketing research, from R&D, from manufacturing, etc. For this function one needs data format stipulation and computer interface management. But, if the system managers assume responsibility for actually making the measurements, a good analog organizational format is that of Consumers Union, particularly now that they are increasing their use of consumers for inputs.

It should be apparent therefore that the internal structure is a function of 1) the technical nature of the product evaluations to be made, for example toys vs. pharmaceuticals, 2) the strengths of the supporting staffs around the firm, 3) the sophistication of the system, for example the complexity of outputs, and 4) the organizational unit assigned the overall task, for example committee vs. a corporate staff position. Much experimentation is going on, and more innovation is sure to result.

B. Operations

The actual operating of a product audit system, regardless of where it is organizationally located, has several definite facets, each of which will be taken up in turn: 1) Selecting the products to be audited; 2) Selecting the attributes to be measured; 3) Defining the attributes; 4) Compiling the information; 5) Determining the organizational involvement; 6) Setting the timing and sequence of output; and 7) Determining the methodology of data collection.

1. Selecting the Products to Be Audited. The essence of the product audit system as industry is currently trending is that *all* product informational needs are integrated into one product audit—one source to provide the service more effectively and more professionally than having it scattered throughout the firm. Marketing, for example, is principally interested in those products with large volumes and large budgets. Manufacturing is especially interested in those with unique or difficult raw materials, parts or processing characteristics. The Environmental Affairs Officer, however, must be alert for real or perceived problems on any product, whether it sells well or not. A simple, minor product whose key ingredient comes from Rhodesia would concern Purchasing.

So it is reasonable to expect that every product a firm sells will warrant attention for one reason or another and will be a candidate for inclusion. Of course, if some products actually have no important attributes, if a firm decides to centralize less than 100 percent of the product auditing, or if the start-up period is to be gradual or trial run, then less than total product coverage is perfectly acceptable. Cost/benefit analyses have also restricted audit lists. Some firms have audited only *groups* of products for now, hoping to get into greater detail later.

2. Selecting the Attributes to Be Measured. Seemingly a simple task but actually one that is quite complex is the listing of specific attributes to be audited for each product or product line. It is terribly inefficient to include all attributes, and poor marketing management to accidently exclude any significant ones. Therefore some heuristic is needed, and a common one is the trichotomy of *Feature, Performance, and Effect. Feature* is descriptive of what is—the physical or psychological facts about a product at rest. Color, size, shape are examples, and almost every product yields quite a list easily. Getting the *complete* list is another matter, however, because attribute listing is actually a creative task. Features are often reflective of one's professional interest in a product. An engineer, a child safety expert, an agency artist, a botanist, and a marketing planner will cite different features of a packaged tea rose, for example.

Putting a product into action yields its *performance* attributes. How does it function, operate, perform? Every item does something and those somethings can be audited. A mixer mixes, a car runs, a flag flutters, a pencil writes. Each performance can be analyzed in detail, using motion study methodology, to register those attributes to add to the list. Again we are dealing with a creative task, apparently, because attribute lists differ widely.

Third, the "use" of any product creates *effects*—good and bad, sought and unwelcome, expected and unexpected. The rose, just mentioned, yields beauty, adds decoration, emits aroma or allergic reaction, occupies space, etc. A bicycle yields distance coverage, better health, sore feet, happiness, pride, fear. . . . Again, just listing the effects of a product is a creative task, and a list changes almost continuously, as producers of Freon-based spray products noticed a couple of years ago. Selecting the effects to actually audit is a key management decision, because no system could audit everything, but the selection should be made from a complete list.

Table I shows feature, performance and effect attributes for a very simple product, facial tissues, and even a cursory look at the list will disclose many omitted attributes. Such a list for a tractor will run perhaps a hundred pages.

Furthermore, the attribute selection decision must also deal with the problem of *reality vs. perception of reality*. In general there is no reality short of that perceived to exist, so most attribute audits add measurements of perceptions to those of absolutes, and thus will vary from audience to audience. On some dimensions, of course, government scientists or Consumers Union testers may think perceptions irrelevant, so the issue may become complicated.

But the basic idea of a Product Audit System is to maximize the *usefulness* of output, and for this, marketing decision-makers need perceived attribute data; this fact contributes heavily to the organizational problem discussed earlier, because manufacturing people, for example, tend to be more interested in physical reality than in consumers' misconceptions of reality [see Twedt (15)].

The difficulty of dealing with perceptions introduces the problem of *measurability* and the issue of whether the system should include attributes which are not

Table 1.   Attribute List for Facial Tissues

Features	Performance	Effect
Softness	Scratchiness	Abrasion
Aroma	Absorbency	Allergic reaction
Purity	Tear strength	Completeness
Tear direction	Ease of crushing	of absorbency
Number of plies	Size-coverage	Disposability
Number of folds	Popability	Biodegradability
Location of folds	Attractiveness	
Size sq. inches	Taste	
Color	Filtering capability	
Shape		
Thickness		
Flavor		
Chemical content		
Transparency		
Compressibility		

measurable, or should it confine itself to the so-called tangible factors? Consumers Union eschews the unmeasurable, implying that the status of a brand name, the beauty of a car's lines, or the confidence one might place in a Bayer's Aspirin are factors irrelevant to the decision process and should be ignored (16).

A marketer feels differently, and very much wants the system to output measurements on all attributes that customers actually consider. Getting agreement on how these intangibles will be scored is difficult, and the techniques used lead to controversy, but bringing such differences to the surface is one of the key values of a Product Audit System.

As a final question on attribute inclusiveness, it is worth noting that putting an attribute into the system does not predetermine any costs or outputs. Other inputs are necessary to determine what information is actually collected on each attribute, since listing an attribute doesn't necessarily disclose its measurement. For example, if a bicycle is to be measured on a simple attribute like speed, is this under test conditions or out on the roads? Which roads? What weather conditions? Which riders? How long sustained? Obviously, listing the attribute won't determine its costs until its unit of measurement is stipulated.

Moreover, having an attribute in the system and defining its unit of measurement still is not enough. How often will the data be collected? And for which output uses will the attributes be included? If the governmental affairs office wants a "safety" score on each of the firm's bicycles, the speed attribute would presumably be factored in somehow, but a report scoring products on "in-store promotability" or on "scarce resource utilization" would probably factor speed at zero and thus exclude it—the difficulties of measuring speed would be no problem.

The essence is, if an attribute is conceivably of use to any user of the audit system then it is listed and its measurement data collected and stored. A company has to make trade-off decisions here—one with thousands of products and hundreds of attributes for each has to become selective, but they apparently feel it is better to cut down willfully and knowingly than to put some arbitrary ceiling on attribute numbers. Besides, large firms with many products spend huge sums on product information—centralizing the function may reveal the costs without increasing them.

To decide that full attribute lists are desirable as a starting point raises the question of how they are obtained. A common starting point is a review of all product data reports and records used in the firm. Lengthy lists result from this effort alone, because, to the surprise of most auditors, companies compile product information in many places.

Surveys also help. Kiser, Rao, and Rao (17) demonstrated this approach in another setting when they first reviewed the literature, and then conducted in-depth interviews with purchasing agents, and then ran a mail survey of several hundred purchasing departments, all in an effort to get attributes of vendors. Surveys of customers work equally well on products.

Other outside sources are:

- Suppliers—who frequently can help because of their own audit systems on parts, packaging, raw materials, etc.
- governments—if they do any product testing
- testing organizations—private companies, National Bureau of Standards, etc.
- trade associations—some of whom may also do the auditing, e.g., on service
- consumers' groups—who sometimes provide new insight on how product attributes can be listed.

But most product attributes come from product auditors who simply study products directly, observe them, run experiments on them, and even use some of the more common idea-generating techniques. For instance, brainstorming yields new insights on almost any situation if used properly. These in-house methods include all concerned points of view, from R&D to Customer Service, Quality Control to Public Relations, Advertising to Shipping. Various nonproduct attribute listing and evaluating situations exist and can offer analogous help in conceptualizing the situation here—e.g. vendor evaluation and judging of all types (18), (19), (20).

3. *Defining the Attributes.*   Once the attributes are listed, the next step is to define them—as a basis for the measurement to follow. This step is often quite complex. Consumers Union recently decided to study reel-to-reel and cassette recording tapes, and their report in the October 1976 issue of *Consumer Reports* (21) represents a near ultimate in careful and thorough attribute definition on a really simple and unsophisticated consumer item. They measured maximum output level, weighted tape noise, relative bias, record sensitivity, print-through, asperity modulation noise, harmonic distortion, output uniformity, and freedom from dropouts. It took only two pages to record the results, but four pages of extra-fine print just to define the listed attributes. Every issue of *Consumer Reports* demonstrates the problem of definition.

The important point is that more time is probably spent defining attributes in terms of their measurement than in actually making the measurements. Although there is a temptation to start with available data and then work back to attribute definitions, this is felt to be a mistake. It is also a mistake to use a quantitative measurement as an attribute definition in preference to a scaled qualitative one just on the basis that it is more tangible.

As an example of the general problem of attribute definition, contemplate the attribute of softness in a towel. An engineer's definition would focus on the towel's surface, perhaps; a dermatologist might measure by skin depression or abrasion; and an advertising agency might prefer an arbitrary scale of consumer impressions. Each could well be a good measurement of softness until softness is carefully and thoroughly defined. Then only one will work. Wallace and Sherret (22) demonstrated the problem, and a solution, with great clarity when they audited Modes of Travel. Murphy and Enis (23) demonstrated the public or macro point of view on attribute definition, quite different from the usual firm view.

Fortunately, although the problem is real, operating economics tends to simplify it. Even though the towel auditor above might want softness defined three ways, and measured accordingly, he will probably have to settle for the one definition most closely related to system outputs and uses. Auditors produce to serve their markets, and usually operate under tight cost constraints.

4. Compiling the Information. Once the operational demand—attribute list and measurement—has been stipulated, we go to the actual compilation of the data. This phase is somewhat mechanical, and certainly is highly situational. The system used by Eli Lilly to cover hundreds of pharmaceutical products will obviously differ from that used by the Hertz Company. But there are some principles involved, particularly regarding the Who, When, and How, and these will be discussed here. Many reference sources have dealt with this question, also, since the new auditing systems utilize information handling technologies that are widely available. Day (24), for example, recently published an excellent general discussion of attribute measurement, especially on the competitive comparison aspects.

5. Determining the Organizational Involvements. Although the overall system responsibility may be clear, arriving at the actual data compilation point raises new organizational questions. The task must be fragmented—sometimes into scores of pieces, and out of complexity comes a search for simple decisions. Experience seems to show that at least one of them must be resisted—that is, assigning data collection to the person or department most intimately involved with the attributes being measured. Cost and time argue for it, but objectivity argues against it. Thus, for example, quality control has traditionally been free of responsibility to the manufacturing unit it assesses, since objectivity is critical, yet manufacturing may report its own labor hour data. Likewise, an audit system would want physical product data to come from some unit outside manufacturing. An advertising agency might be asked to provide a regular flow of data on consumers' physical attribute awareness, but not used for scoring perceived positionings.

The matrix in Figure 3 shows a decision rule that has been used. One dimension is "importance of the attribute" and the other is "likelihood of bias in measurement." Cell A attributes can be measured by anyone—the lowest cost rules. Cell B also is no problem because measurement offers no fear of distortion. Cell C is a problem only in that the sytem should be alert for changes in attribute importance—minor bias may become ruinous if the attribute suddenly is perceived as critical by someone using system output.

Cell D attribute measurement is the problem, of course, and such instances are

Figure 3.   Measurement assignment matrix.

Importance of Attribute

	Low	High
Low	Category A: ● No danger-- ● Assign to lowest cost unit.	Category B: ● Attribute important but no bias concern. ● Assign to lowest cost unit.
High	Category C: ● Attribute not important, so bias is no threat. ● Assign to lowest cost unit.	Category D: ● The critical cell ● Measurement must be assigned to group with no vested interest.

Liklihood of Bias

the reason for the matrix. Every measurement here must be made carefully, so carefully in fact that governmental regulators often decree attribute measurement technology or actually do the measuring—e.g., fresh meat quality ratings. Other times, law has made provision for protected persons within the firm—pollution, safety, etc.—so they can report objectively, without fear of internal pressure to alter their data. And even if not required by law, most product audit systems designers see the need for Cell D measurements as being well met by outside firms or specially insulated internal departments. In some cases, trade associations have pooled resources to set up independent test centers. In others, private testing companies have come into being to meet the need.

What results, then, is a systems organizational blend—a flow of assessments from many different sources within the firm and without. Since many of these will be somewhat emotional and rarely completely free of self-interest, special skill is needed to bring them to constructive compilation and resolution. Chambers, Mullick, and Goodman (25) once described a technique they developed at

Corning Glass Works for handling this type of problem, and they claimed it was working well.

6. Setting the Timing and Sequence of Output. Given the inflow of required data on various product attributes, and moving past the routine questions of information storage, we can next look at the matters of timing and sequence of output reports from the system. The basic principle lying behind the theory of sophisticated systems is "on-line" access—reports whenever needed, and this is a good statement of goal for product audit systems—ultimately. When new, however, they usually operate in response to the needs of only one functional group. If that group is marketing planning, and it usually is, the output is geared to an annual schedule. Data are collected, processed, and published according to the dates in the firm's annual planning manual.

However, this beginning simplicity ultimately yields to a three-way classification of outputs.

Frequent-periodic—where the nature of the variable is critical—e.g., safety— and subject to unexpected change. An obvious example is quality control data, but so would be a taste of margarine or level of service by a major appliance dealer. Infrequent or erratic testing of such attributes makes for unpleasant surprises.

A 1975 review by *Business Week* (26) of competitive espionage techniques— the legal ones—pointed out that IBM and Texas Instruments were among companies which designated special departments to maintain an up-to-the-minute knowledge of competitive products, feature by feature. In these high technology areas the information compilation and release has to be continuous.

Infrequent-periodic—based on cycles of need by users of the system. The period may be annual, as for marketing planning; or quarterly, as for plan reviews and revisions; or monthly, as for federal reporting purposes. Sometimes the period is determined at the point of supply, as when an outside organization makes an annual compilation on a group of products.

On demand—the theoretical goal category mentioned earlier. This level of system service is actually of two subtypes. First is the case where the data are critical and the system must maintain an absolutely up-to-the-minute state of knowledge. Some products are so potentially dangerous, e.g., parenteral solutions, that 100 percent quality control sampling is required. But these are quite rare, and the more common type of on-demand reporting is where system users cannot predict their information needs and thus cannot ask for periodic reporting. The data they get is "what is available"—not necessarily current, but rather whatever has been reported into the system.

7. Determining the Methodology of Data Collection. The techniques used for the various individual attribute assessments are, of course, highly situational, and most are well established by traditional practice in the various industries. This is especially true for physical measurements of entirely tangible attributes, and most firms have been measuring certain aspects of their products since their first day of production.

But two aspects have caused problems; the first one concerns the measurement of perception, especially when the factor being perceived is not directly quantifiable, and the second concerns the matter of cost/benefit analysis. Perceptions are personal. There is no "correct" score on the beauty of a refrigerator, yet refrigerator manufacturers must include esthetic factors in their audit system. Fortunately, some of the most meaningful advances in marketing research over the past fifteen years have come in attitude measurement and particularly in use of scaling techniques. There is no reason to exclude a factor from the system just because it is difficult to measure. Swan and Combs (16), for example, recently published an excellent review of this problem; they discuss methods for handling reality vs. perceptions especially well. This is not to say that research skills have overcome the problem, however. In fact, they probably never will because of the emotionalism within a firm on the issue of attribute quality. It remains a fact in most audit systems, apparently, that the methodology of attribute measurement is the single greatest controversy still surrounding the product auditing idea.

To the extent that accurate and acceptable measurements are a function of the dollars expended, we come to the second of the two major measurement questions—cost/benefit appraisals. Since the measurement costs, the problem lies with the benefit factor. To help evaluate the costs of various measurement methodologies, the following typology of output accuracies has evolved.

• *Mandatory accurate.* Those few assessments—e.g., radiation from microwave ovens or TVs which have legal bases, major damage potential, fraud potential, or governmental reporting requirements. They are to be accurate regardless of the cost.

• *Decision-desirable accurate.* Those attributes which play a key role in strategic decisions—e.g., positioning—and thus which everyone wants to be accurate but which at some point will become too expensive for precise measurement. To contrast with the previous category, a pharmaceutical company *must* know the incidence of severe medical reaction to a new chemical entity, but it only badly wants to know whether consumers feel the new product works more quickly than a leading competitive product.

• *Reasonably accurate.* Those where tactical decisions rest on the accuracy of the data, but where the firm's experience with the products gives it a basis for detecting any major errors by the auditing system. The figures are important but the probability of undetected error is low, so measurements can be less thorough. By exception, of course, any attribute in this third category can suddenly move up to "category two" importance.

• *Estimates sufficient.* Those attributes which complete a picture, which are occasionally helpful on certain rather routine decisions, or which satisfy some personal whim. Experienced audit personnel can make judgments on these attributes—and they do—as the counterpart of marketing research's "quick and dirty" studies.

Because of the influences introduced by these two methodological decision problems, actual company practice varies greatly, firm to firm. They collect, compile, and publish in an endless array of systems. The following two examples display some of this heterogeneity.

William E. Finney, then president of Oxford Laboratories, credited its continuing Product Audit with a major role in its success (27). In fact, the auditing, a part of an overall planning and review program, helped increase the firm's profits to the point where G. D. Searle moved to acquire Oxford. In addition to a Product Planning Committee which evaluated new product ideas and a Scheduling Committee which kept tabs on product projects as they came along, Finney had a Product Audit Committee that was charged with looking at current products and deciding whether to keep, change, or kill them. Every product got a review at least once a year.

The Product Audit Committee, like the other two committees, consisted of members of top management, and was chaired by the then general manager of Oxford's international division. Some time in advance of the monthly meeting the chairman announced which products would be reviewed at that meeting, and various units produced appropriate data. Cost accounting, quality control, complaint files, and the sales department were among the key groups involved. Some of the data were perpetually maintained, but most of the review was on situational factors. In fact, a special situation, such as an increase in complaints, may have put the product up for review, although a review would have been held on an annual schedule if no special need arose.

At the meeting, the products were attacked and defended in a free-working style. No significant attribute was spared, as Oxford management sought to find ways to enhance the product's usefulness or reduce its costs. The overall immediate purpose of each review was to arrive at action conclusions calling for product modifications, price changes, further research, actual abandonment, etc.

Finney recognized the informality and flexibility of his system, but he also noted the key features of scheduled periodicity, comprehensiveness, and total functional involvement.

A contrasting example is offered by a large corporation which manufactured heavy earth-moving and construction equipment. Every three years its president called a world-wide product conference. Some twenty-five top executives were involved in this meeting, the purpose of which was to review all products in the line and all products under development. Reports were prepared and presented covering such dimensions as quality, performance, design, and price. Every product was continued, modified, or scheduled for discontinuance.

In between the three-year conferences, a special committee consisting of the Assistant to the President, two Executive Vice Presidents, the Vice Presidents of

Marketing and Engineering and Research, and the Director of Economics met on an unscheduled basis for interim reviews on various products.

This firm, too, demonstrates the wide range of options. It, too, demonstrates, however, that managements tend to think in terms of *periodic* reviews rather than *continuous* reviews. Both of these organizations might benefit from—and both may today be using—a system which has tabbed particular attributes of particular products for continuous review.

C. System Outputs

The composite of outputs produced by a Product Audit System can best be explained by looking at three dimensions—the frequency or timing schedule, the specific content of reports on individual products, and special output considerations on product lines or subsets of products.

1. Schedule of Reports.   Product auditors occasionally cite an analogy between products and human bodies. If one thinks of the body as one's "product line" we can quickly see a rationale for a system of product assessments around a time frame. First of all, for a normal, healthy patient, a physician will probably order a periodic examination, the length of the period being primarily a function of the likelihood of trouble developing.

The purpose of this examination is also analogous to products—the physician is scanning the horizon. He is not looking for specific troubles—just any trouble. Furthermore, he is trying to *predict* them, not find them. He wants the periodicity of his measurements to be self-predicting, letting him tell the patient that he is heading for certain difficulties, and that action needs to be taken to avoid them.

The product auditor tries to do exactly the same thing, and he selects his time periods accordingly. Just as the pediatrician wants to see a newborn after thirty days, a product auditor schedules more frequent reviews for new products than for those in more mature phases of the life cycle.

The medical analogy also yields the second timing category of outputs, stemming from situations where the physician has discovered a possible problem and wants a more frequent scan on that particular attribute—X-rays, blood tests, EKGs, etc. These are still diagnostic, but of a situational periodicity.

A third category of report frequencies traces to results of the special scans—a truly acute problem calling for an intensive study of the product situation and leading to short-term action for resolving it.

These three types of reporting frequencies can be called *Routine Periodic, Special Periodic,* and *Special Investigative.* The Routine Periodic studies are most common, and are exemplified by the two company examples in the previous section. Special Periodic studies are typical of only the more sophisticated systems except for those particular functions of a business which regularly face this type situation—e.g., quality control. Special Investigative reports are rare today, only because few product audit systems are geared up to produce them quickly and economically. The need is frequent, but the auditor typically must start from scratch in gathering and updating the relevant data.

2. Content of Reports. The content of any output is quite obviously geared to the perceived needs—what people are going to do with the data, what decisions are pending, etc. The opening parts of this writing noted the many pressures and changes tending to focus attention on product auditing, each of which calls for certain outputs from the system. Thus, purely as examples, the environmental affairs director may call for emissions data, the product manager wants attribute superiorities, the strategic planner looks for growth situations, and the controller looks at costs.

The life cycle of product audit systems is still developing, so output practice has not stabilized. However there are several different types of outputs that various companies have disclosed.

The first is the most obvious—a straight summary of factual descriptive information about one product. It is represented by Column 2 of Table 2. More helpful analytically, however, is a Competitive Comparison report represented by Columns 3 through 5 of Table 2. And, since decision-makers are rarely content with data only in a descriptive framework, and only on factually assessable attributes, reports also cover judgmentally assessed attributes, e.g., esthetics of comfort—the assessments representing the customers' value judgments, not just technical fact.

For clarification, a bicycle might be recorded factually and technically as:

Gears: 10-speed
Wheels: 26 inches'
Weight   4 pounds

Relatively:

Gears: Same as competitive touring bikes
Wheels: Same as competitive touring bikes
Weight: One-third pound lighter than all brands except Acme
         Two pounds heavier than Acme

Judgmentally or evaluatively:

Gears: Customers see no difference, except that our type is seen as more durable than the Apex-Circle-Acme type
Wheels: Possibly because of more squared frames, our models are seen as lower than most
Weight: Customers see no difference, and claim that all of the six leading brands weigh the same.

Actually, outputs are usually mixtures of these. Some absolutes are more meaningful than relatives, e.g., product contamination. Some relatives are more important than facts, e.g., perceived beauty. Sometimes firms keep all three

Table 2.   Summary of Attribute Ratings

Product: Peps Childrens' Vitamin Tablets

Product Line(s): 1st order: Children's Vitamins
                 2nd order: Vitamins

Date: June, 19xx

Attribute	Our Product	Relative to Competition			Comments
		Zeds	Vitans	Chews	
Features					
1. Shape	Beveled rectangle	=	=	=	Shapes differ but doubtful that consumers perceive any meaningful difference.
2. Size	4 mm × 8 mm	=	=	=	All are probably small enough to satisfy consumer.
3. Color	Pink	+	+	=	Our pink is much preferred over the two green ones.
4. Vitamin level	Exactly meets minimum daily requirements	=	=	=	All do.
Performance					
1. Taste	Scores 90% acceptable in monadics	+	+	++	We're better, but all score high on monadics.
2. Mouth feel	Smooth—no grit	+	+	+	A big advantage over the gritty competitors.

data, but since product managers have stimulated most of the product audits to date, the published data are usually in relative form, and are usually evaluative, particularly in any case where perceptions differ from reality.

Rarely are the basic periodic reports that list attributes sufficient, since firms want overall summary or composite scores on the products; thus, weighting columns are added. Each attribute is given a weight and each brand is then scored, attribute by attribute. Multiplying and adding yields a composite number for each brand, very similar incidently to the numerical checklist system often used to evaluate new product ideas.

Table 3 shows this weighting process. Sometimes firms have used different sets of weights to get different composite scores—e.g., the attribute weights to determine short-term competitiveness may be different from those for long-term assessments. But weighting becomes very controversial. Morris and Bronson (28) report an experience of Consumers Union on electric frying pans where they surveyed consumers to get the weights and allocated 100 points to the various attributes. Twenty-five of the 100 points went to "legibility of the thermometer," an allocation sharply criticized by the authors.

Beyond weightings there are other variables in output content. Swan (29) published an analysis in 1974 which demonstrated how product performance ratings can be compared with prices to yield insight on customers' use of price-quality association, or to indicate high-risk overpricing situations, or to reveal opportunities for price increases. Martilla and James (30) updated this by comparing attribute performance scores with consumers' ratings of attribute importance, in a matrix-style diagram.

Another variation stems from this type of matrix because the question of product support is raised whenever one evaluates a product's attributes against

Table 3. Weighted Composite Scores
(Simplified for Demonstration Purposes)

Products

Attribute	Weight	Ours Rating	Score	A Rating	Score	B Rating	Score
Speed	6	6	36	10	60	10	60
Durability	8	9	72	4	32	6	48
Service required	8	5	40	8	64	9	72
Adaptability	3	9	27	4	12	2	6
Energy efficiency	2	8	16	2	4	3	6
Size	3	6	18	6	18	8	24
Movability	1	9	9	4	4	2	2
Noise	4	4	16	5	20	10	40
			234		214		258
Percent of Top Value			91%		83%		100%

price or preference. So some audit systems have added a factor called *Support* to the file—dollars spent, improvements made, distribution achieved, relative price, etc. All marketing factors other than product can be added—a *relative* basis is used, because competitive conclusions are sought.

This compiling of Product Attributes and Support leads directly then to still another data set frequently included—*Results*. Sales, margins, profit, shares of market, conquests, etc., are all seen from time to time. And again, matrices sometimes show dramatic opportunities or dangers, as for example when market shares are contrasted with return on investment. Many people are convinced that the best route to profits is via market share, and a share/profit matrix sheds light on this controversy within the setting of a particular product line.

Finally, there is the question of source, or authority for audit data. One position says, compile the best data you can and go with it—work to improve it as often as possible, but accept it as accurate in the meantime. The other position says that the outputs are only as good as the inputs and thus the "quality" of the data put out from the system should always be on display—either by citing the exact source, or simply identifying weak or questionable data with an asterisk. Table 4, Source Listing, shows a report of the source-citing type, but a data user has to know each source's reliability quite well to use this type of listing. The asterisk approach gives the audit system manager the responsibility of determining reliability and thus makes the reader's task easier. But the responsibility is a heavy one, with political overtones, particularly at those times when internal data must be classified as weak or unreliable.

3. Product Line or Subsets Output. To this point we have discussed the data provided for individual products. But various sets of products also have attributes—attributes of the set, or line, not just attributes of the individual items in the set. For example, in 1977 Ford's two luxury cars, the Continental and the Continental Mark IV, were individually well regarded. But Ford's *line* of luxury

Table 4.   Source Listing
(For Attribute Ratings in Table 2)

Shape ------------------	Product Manager appraisal, April 1977
Size----------------------	Product team assessment, including Medical, May 1977
Color--------------------	General study of children's color preferences, National Color Institute, May 1975
Vitamin level ----------	Control Lab. Report 6390-C, January 1977 Confirmed label claims
Taste --------------------	User monadic test, Kansas City and Charlotte, June 1976
Mouth feel -------------	Employee test panel, January 1976, plus some personal experience with several children of employees.

cars had a major weakness in that it lacked a counterpart of Cadillac's highly successful Seville. So, Ford added the Versaille, just as the producer of a single camera might add a new viewing mechanism to match a competitor's addition.

One product line attribute which has received a great deal of attention is age, or maturity, and various techniques have been used to disclose and display the age of a product line. Figure 4 shows one such effort, a plotting of every product in each of three product lines, giving its age in an absolute, factual, profile-

Figure 4. Partial output from audit system for three product lines—analysis of line maturity.

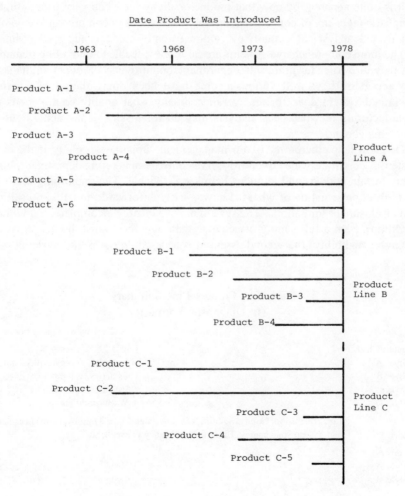

format, character. Even casual observation shows that Product Line A has a much greater potential maturity problem than do lines B and C. A similar listing showing dates of last significant improvement could be equally revealing.

But maturity is only one attribute of a product line. Some others are completeness, cost, effectiveness, availability, improvability, promotability, and attractiveness to the trade.

Table 5 Product Line Summary, shows a simplified adaptation of a report used by one product auditor to draw attention to lines as a whole.

D. Special Facilitating Policies

It is quite apparent by now that product audit systems can vary from a highly simplistic reporting of competitive product evaluations to comprehensive compilations and analyses of virtually every dimension of products and product lines.

The more comprehensive systems are far more valuable to marketing planners, but they also offer far more intradepartmental controversy. Product audits actually report on how well various people have been doing their jobs—a fully integrated system does for an overall company what quality control does for manufacturing or what sales analysis may do for a sales department. Political problems abound.

Of great help, therefore, is top management support, especially if the audit system is corporate-wide. Even if it serves only the marketing department, however, certain policies and attitudes help keep it viable. The main thing seems to be faithful presentation of what is known—straightforward, no frills, no selling, full disclosure of limitations. The system may be terribly incomplete, but without credibility even a full supply of accurate data will accomplish little.

Given credibility, the second essential is accessibility. On-line retrieval is an

Table 5.   Product Line Summary
(In Diagnostic Format)

Product	Deficits on Rating Forms
Vacuum Cleaners	
Style A	Esthetics, serviceability, storage
Style B	Esthetics, weight
Style C	Esthetics, serviceability
Style D	We have no entry

Line conclusion: Good possibilities for line extension and improvements in esthetics and exterior mechanics. Basic unit efficiency is excellent.

Scrubbers	
Style A	None
Style B	Weight

Line conclusion: No major gaps or general deficiencies.

ideal, and some data in every system warrant such costs, but most access is not on-line. Strong guidance is needed to keep usage easy, quick, and operationally efficient, not bureaucratic.

Third, only reasonably secure and competent managements can maintain the necessary blend of totally accurate data, reasonably accurate data, sound estimates, and rough estimates. The product audit system doesn't call for massive new data collecting—rather, it collects, compiles, arranges, and publishes data generally available in such a way that usage is optimized. If rough estimates are adequate, then rough estimates should suffice; there is always the temptation to increase data quality—to increase system integrity—even when not needed.

Finally, the management of the system is itself a growing specialty, and deserving of special training and special techniques. For example, one firm found it valuable to evaluate their attribute evaluation (25). Statistical analyses were made of individuals' attribute scorings, partly to learn which persons were closer to overall scores and partly to get an indication of variation within each scorer's set. Such internal quality improvement efforts are especially useful in these early days of product audit systems.

V. CURRENT RESEARCH NEEDS

As of now, a number of rather major questions about product audit systems have surfaced. Each of them deserves some comment.

First, we need to know in greater detail exactly what different firms are doing today in the area of product auditing. Essentially, the first order of business is a *Census* of product auditing practice. Such a census would show variations by industry, by size, and by sophistication in planning generally. The information gathered should cover all facets of the operation—organization, purpose, and techniques.

Second, and simultaneously with the census, we need to know what managements feel about the *economic success* of these activities. What have they cost? What benefits have they produced? How measured? Furthermore, how successful do they look to the outsider? Is there a macro position different from that of management's?

Third, what do the managers of these systems feel are their *future needs?* Where are they now failing to meet reasonable goals set for them? What can be done to make their operations more effective or more efficient?

Fourth, we need to know a great deal more about *several specific areas* of product auditing practice. Specifically which organizational arrangements are best? Can the function remain under marketing control, or do the potential users and political problems mandate a nonfunctional location in general management?

Other specific areas are many, but we should cite 1) attribute definition, 2) attribute measurement, 3) attribute weighting, to produce more useful overall product scores, and 4) data handling and processing. Right now product data are too often gathered at many locations in a firm, and take whatever form best suits the needs of persons at those locations. The data must be standardized if they are to be optimally processed, stored, and retrieved, but this would require that attribute definitions be developed to meet these diverse needs. It would appear that we do not currently know how to do this.

Fifth, better data handling will also require a more thorough *integration* of the product audit system with the many other information systems in a firm. How should the audit relate to the annual planning schedule? With reporting to governmental units? With the accounting system? With the quality assurance system? With R&D's planning system?

Sixth, some work will have to focus on the role and methodologies of outside testing organizations. If we look at all of the various federal, state, and local governmental units which currently assess products in one way or another, that group alone gives great cause for concern. Not that the politics of that situation are necessarily good or bad, but rather that the goals of such auditing units are substantially different from those of the business firms involved. Furthermore, there is too little control exercised over those units, conceptually and methodologically.

Likewise, and in some ways more critically, product auditors must also deal with *non*government, outside auditing firms such as Consumers Union (31). Their role needs to be appraised, their success measured, and their future more clearly outlined. Given reliable, objective outside testing, product auditing systems can become more efficient solely via the economics such outside pooling of testing permits. But as of right now, few outside firms have achieved such a status, and these are typically profit-making enterprises not committed to lowest cost, pooled auditing. In this connection, the possible role of trade associations needs to be studied.

Seventh, given progress in structure, role, and methodology, we should then be able to make some good *forecasts* of what product auditing systems will ultimately become. It seems inconceivable, given the causal forces listed at the start of this report, that such systems can ever be less complex, less critical, or less active than they are now. The forecast would be for pronounced future growth, though a great deal more information is needed to be precise in those forecasts.

REFERENCES

1. Dominguez, G. S. (1971), *Product Management*, The American Management Association, especially Chapter 7, "Monitoring and Controlling the Product," New York.
2. "A Federal Spur to Product Development" (1973), *Business Week* pp. 68 ff. (August 25).
3. Hanan, M. (1968), *Market Segmentation*, American Management Association, New York.
4. Wilkie, W. L., and Pessemier, E. A. (1973), "Issues in Marketing's Use of Multi-Attribute Attitude Models," *Journal of Marketing Research* X: 428–441 (November).

5. Kinnear, T. C., and Taylor, J. R. (1971), "Multivariate Methods in Marketing Research: A Fuller Attempt at Clarification," *Journal of Marketing* 35: 56–59 (October).
6. *Testing For Public Safety* (1965), Underwriters Laboratories Inc., Chicago.
7. "A Surge of Business for Independent Labs" (1977), *Business Week:* 116–123 (April 11).
8. "Marketing Newsletter" (1974), *Sales Management Magazine:* 17 (March 4).
9. *Improving Your Competitive Position* (1974), Schrello Associates, Long Beach, Calif.
10. Stiritz, P. (1976), "Monitoring Product Line Performance," speech delivered to 1976 Annual Marketing Conference, The Conference Board, New York City (October).
11. Tibbetts, H. M. (1976), "Profit Oriented Marketing and the Profit Line Audit," speech delivered to the 1976 Annual Marketing Conference, The Conference Board, New York City (October).
12. Wind, Y., and Claycamp, H. J. (1976), "Planning Product Line Strategy," *Journal of Marketing* 40: 2–9 (January).
13. Day, G. S. (1977), "Diagnosing the Product Portfolio," *Journal of Marketing* 41:29–38 (April).
14. "Mead's Technique to Sort Out the Winners," *Business Week*: 124–129 (March 11).
15. Twedt, D. W. "How to Plan New Products, Improve Old Ones, and Create Better Advertising," (1969), *Journal of Marketing* 38: 53–57 (January).
16. Swan, J. E., and Combs, L. J. (1976), "Product Performance and Consumer Satisfaction: A New Concept," *Journal of Marketing* 40: 25–33 (April).
17. Kiser, G. E., Rao, C. P., and Rao, S. R. G. (1974), "Perceptual Differences and Similarities of Vendor Attributes Between Purchasing and Non-Purchasing Executives," *Journal of Purchasing*: 16–29 (August).
18. Dickson, G. W. (1966), "An Analysis of Vendor Selection Systems and Decisions," *Journal of Purchasing*: 5–17 (February).
19. Hinkle, C. L., Robinson, P. J., and Green, P. E. (1969), "Vendor Evaluation Using Cluster Analysis," *Journal of Purchasing*: 49–58 (August).
20. *The Training of Judges For Girls' Gymnastics,* (1971), American Association for Health, Physical Education and Recreation, Washington, D.C.
21. "Recording Tape: Reels and Cassettes" (1976), *Consumer Reports:* 594–599 (October).
22. Wallace, J. P., and Sherret, A. (1973), "Estimation of Product Attributes and Their Importances," *Lecture Notes in Economics and Mathematical Systems,* M. Beckman and H. P. Kunzi, (eds.), Berlin: Springer-Verlag.
23. Murphy, P., and Enis, B. M. (1974/1975), "Let's Hear the Case Against Brand X," *Business and Society Review*: 82–89 (Winter).
24. Day, R. L. (1968), "Preference Tests and the Management of Product Features," *Journal of Marketing* 32: 24–29 (July).
25. Chambers, J. C., Mullick, K., and Goodman, D. A. (1971), "Catalytic Agent for Effective Planning," *Harvard Business Review* 49: 110–119 (January–February).
26. "Business Sharpens Its Spying Techniques" (1975), *Business Week*: 60–63 (August 4).
27. "Putting Products Through An Audit Wringer" (1974), *Business Week*: 60–61 (February 2).
28. Morris, T. R., and Brownson, C. S. (1969), "The Chaos of Competition Indicated by Consumer Reports," *Journal of Marketing* 33: 26–27 (July).
29. Swan, J. E. (1974), "Price-Product Performance Comparisons Between Retailer and Manufacturer Brands," *Journal of Marketing* 38: 59–69 (July).
30. Martilla, J. A., and James, J. C. (1977), "Importance-Performance Analysis," *Journal of Marketing* 41: 77–79, (January).
31. Strickling, H. L. (1965), *Implications of the Existence of Consumers Union For Marketing of Major Appliances and Related Durables,* Ph.D. dissertation, New York University, published by Consumers Union of U.S. Inc.

RUDIMENTS OF NUMERACY*

A.S.C. Ehrenberg, LONDON BUSINESS SCHOOL

INTRODUCTION

People who say they are not numerate usually do not mean that they cannot do arithmetic. Nor should they mean that they cannot do mathematics. Instead, they are really saying that they cannot cope with numerical data—tables, graphs, percentages, and so on. But such data are often badly presented—requiring much effort even for sophisticated users to understand—and the fault is that of the *producers* of the data. It is as if they either did not know what their data were saying or were not letting on. That is the starting point of this paper.

Numeracy has two facets—reading and writing, or *extracting* numerical information and *presenting* it. The skills of data presentation may at first seem ad hoc and judgmental, a matter of style rather than of technology. But certain aspects can be formalized into explicit rules, the equivalent of elementary syntax. Such precepts have largely been ignored in statistical practice and teaching.

In this paper I therefore put up for discussion some rules or guidelines for

*Read to the Royal Statistical Society in London on March 2, 1977 (*J. Royal Statist. Soc. A*, 140, 277–297).

Research in Marketing—Volume 2, 1979, pages 191–216.
ISBN 0-89232-059-1

improved data presentation. In doing so, my immediate concern is not with the general public but with supposedly numerate people like ourselves—producers and more or less regular users of numerical information. I stress that I am not so agitated about the less numerate fringe (e.g., backward school-children or apocryphal company chairmen); they also need help but will not do much with numerical information however well it is presented.

The paper is in five sections. Section 1 gives two examples of how the presentation of data can be improved. Specific rules for doing so are then set out in Section 2, followed by a brief assessment of the relevant literature in Section 3. Possible objections and problems of implementing the rules are discussed in Sections 4 and 5.

I. SEEING THE DATA

The criterion for a good table is that the patterns and exceptions should be obvious at a glance, at least once one knows what they are. But most tables do not meet that standard.

To illustrate, Table 1 reproduces a small table of data on UK merchant vessels from *Facts in Focus* (1), table 63, a typical "official" publication of statistical information for general use. The table may at first appear reasonably well laid out. But in forming this view one's attention probably has centered not on the numbers but on the items, such as Passenger vessels, Dry cargo, Gross and Deadweight tonnages, the types of vessels, and so on.

The numbers themselves are not as easy to take in. What are their main

Table 1. United Kingdom Merchant Vessels in Service (500 Gross Tons and Over)

	1962	1967	1973
Number			
All vessels	2,689	2,181	1,776
Passenger*	242	173	122
Dry cargo	1,847	1,527	1,165
Tankers	600	481	489
Thousand gross tons			
All vessels	20,554	20,375	29,105
Passenger*	2,504	1,709	920
Dry cargo	10,562	10,757	13,520
Tankers	7,488	7,908	14,665
Thousand deadweight tons			
All vessels	26,577	27,448	46,763
Passenger*	1,467	919	349
Dry cargo	13,990	14,362	20,115
Tankers	11,120	12,167	26,299

*All vessels with passenger certificates.
Source: Facts in Focus (1).

features? How can they be summarized? How can one tell someone over the phone? What is one likely to absorb or remember? Looked at with these questions in mind, the table now appears like a fairly undigested jumble of numbers. But it need not have been like that.

Table 2 gives an improved presentation of the same data. It is easier to see major patterns and exceptions:

— The *numbers* of vessels declined over the years by 30 to 50 percent, but less for tankers.

— The *tonnages* jumped dramatically by up to 100 percent during 1967–1973, except for passenger vessels.

— Dry cargo vessels accounted for the largest numbers of vessels and also the biggest tonnages, with tanker tonnages overtaking the dry cargo ones in 1973. Passenger vessels differed from the others in having larger gross than deadweight tonnages.

Few of these patterns seem as clear in Table 1, even now that one knows what to look for. The original table therefore fails both the strong and the weak versions of the criterion for a good table, whereas Table 2 certainly passes the weak version if not entirely the strong one:

The Strong Criterion for a Good Table: The patterns and exceptions should be obvious at a glance.

The Weak Criterion: The patterns and exceptions in a table should be obvious at a glance once one has been told what they are.

The weak criterion is much the more important one. It applies automatically to all situations which are repetitive, i.e., ones where the probable pattern of the

Table 2. An "Improved" Version of Table 1

Vessels of 500 Gross Tons and Over	1962	'67	'73
Number			
Dry Cargo	1,800	1,500	1,200
Tankers	600	480	490
Passenger*	240	170	120
ALL VESSELS	2,700	2,200	1,800
Gross Tons ('000)			
Dry Cargo	11,000	11,000	14,000
Tankers	7,500	7,900	15,000
Passenger*	2,500	1,700	900
ALL VESSELS	21,000	20,000	29,000
Deadweight Tons ('000)			
Dry Cargo	14,000	14,000	20,000
Tankers	11,000	12,000	26,000
Passenger*	1,500	900	300
ALL VESSELS	27,000	27,000	47,000

*All vessels with passenger certificates.

new data is known beforehand. It can therefore cover more complex tables and apply to the experienced user.

The strong criterion sounds fine. But it says nothing more than that the naive newcomer should gain instant insight, unaided. This will seldom work. With data that are altogether new, or at least new to the expected reader, the producer of the table can not merely announce that "the results are shown in the table" and expect every reader to work out the story line himself. Instead, he should guide the reader by a brief verbal commentary and tell him what he knows.

This process represents the *weak* criterion in operation again. It is illustrated by Paul Samuelson's *Economics* (2) where every table and graph is accompanied by a short paragraph commenting on what it says, as exemplified in Table 3. While Samuelson's format need not be copied slavishly (usually one would simply comment in the main text) and some of his tables are none too good, his care to communicate is no doubt correlated with the book's phenomenal success over the years.

A common doubt about trying to improve the layout of a table is whether the presentation should not depend on the particular use to be made of the data. But an "improved" version like Table 2 is easier for virtually *any* purpose than is the original Table 1. The data could perhaps be displayed in a way even more suited to some specific purpose, but that would merely mean taking the procedures of this paper yet further.

The main steps in going from Table 1 to Table 2 (such as rounding and reordering the rows, and possible objections to them) will be discussed in the later sections. At this stage I only want to illustrate how some marked improvements in data presentation are possible even with a small and fairly simple table:

Table 3.   A Table with Commentary
[Table 2.5 from Samuelson's *Economics* (2)]

U.S. and Soviet populations gain relative to rest of Europe:

	ANNUAL GROWTH	1964	1975	1980
United States	1.6%	192	229	247
United Kingdom	0.7%	54	57.5	59.2
France	1.3%	48	56	60
Soviet Union	1.6%	228	269	290
Sweden	0.6%	7.7	8.2	8.4
Italy	0.7%	51	54	56
Japan	1.0%	97	107	112

Estimated Future Population of Different Countries in 1980 (in millions). Note the different rates of growth (1958–1964 average) in the first column, showing the U.S. and the Soviet growing fastest and Sweden and Italy slowest.
Source: United Nations *Statistical Year Book.*

Table 4.   Adults Who "Really Like to Watch": Correlations to 4 Decimal Places
(Programs Ordered Alphabetically Within Channel)

		PrB	ThW	Tod	WoS	GrS	LnU	MoD	Pan	RgS	24H
ITV	PrB	1.0000	0.1064	0.0653	0.5054	0.4741	0.0915	0.4732	0.1681	0.3091	0.1242
"	ThW	0.1064	1.0000	0.2701	0.1424	0.1321	0.1885	0.0815	0.3520	0.0637	0.3946
"	Tod	0.0653	0.2701	1.0000	0.0926	0.0704	0.1546	0.0392	0.2004	0.0512	0.2437
"	WoS	0.5054	0.1474	0.0926	1.0000	0.6217	0.0785	0.5806	0.1867	0.2963	0.1403
BBC	GrS	0.4741	0.1321	0.0704	0.6217	1.0000	0.0849	0.5932	0.1813	0.3412	0.1420
"	LnU	0.0915	0.1885	0.1546	0.0785	0.0849	1.0000	0.0487	0.1973	0.0969	0.2661
"	MoD	0.4732	0.0815	0.0392	0.5806	0.5932	0.0487	1.0000	0.1314	0.3267	0.1221
"	Pan	0.1681	0.3520	0.2004	0.1867	0.1813	0.1973	0.1314	1.0000	0.1469	0.5237
"	RgS	0.3091	0.0637	0.0512	0.2963	0.3412	0.0969	0.3261	0.1469	1.0000	0.1212
"	24H	0.1242	0.3946	0.2432	0.1403	0.1420	0.2661	0.1211	0.5237	0.1212	1.0000

The golden rule is that the next step or two in looking at the figures in a table must be visually easy.

The 10 × 10 correlation matrix in Table 4 is another small but more analytical table. The variables here are whether people in a sample of 7,000 UK adults said they "really liked to watch" a range of ten TV programs like World of Sport (WoS), Match of the Day (MoD), Panorama (Pan), and so on [from data in Goodhardt et al. (3), Chapter 9].

Again the patterns and exceptions are not clear. But appropriate reordering of the variables, rounding, better labeling and better spacing lead to a marked improvement, as shown in Table 5. Now we can see that there is a cluster for the five Sports programs, another cluster for the five Current Affairs programs, and three locally high correlations of .2 between Panorama and the Sports programs.

I am not concerned in this paper with how the appropriate ordering of the variables was initially discovered (although this can be greatly helped by good data presentation). What concerns me here is our ability to see, understand, and

Table 5.   The Correlations for the 10 TV Programs Rounded and Reordered

Programs		WoS	MoD	GrS	PrB	RgS	24H	Pan	ThW	Tod	LnU
World of Sport	ITV		.6	.6	.5	.3	.1	.2	.1	.1	.1
Match of the Day	BBC	.6		.6	.5	.3	.1	.1	.1	0	0
Grandstand	BBC	.6	.6		.5	.3	.1	.2	.1	.1	.1
Prof. Boxing	ITV	.5	.5	.5		.3	.1	.2	.1	.1	.1
Rugby Special	BBC	.3	.3	.3	.3		.1	.1	.1	.1	.1
24 Hours	BBC	.1	.1	.1	.1	.1		.5	.4	.2	.2
Panorama	BBC	.2	.1	.2	.2	.1	.5		.4	.2	.2
This Week	ITV	.1	.1	.1	.1	.1	.4	.4		.3	.2
Today	ITV	.1	0	.1	.1	.1	.2	.2	.3		.2
Line-Up	BBC	.1	0	.1	.1	.1	.2	.2	.2	.2	

communicate such a pattern once it has been established. Even now that we know the pattern, it is still not apparent in Table 4. In contrast, anyone can see it in Table 5 (especially anyone already familiar with the notion of a correlation matrix). In fact, Table 5 is largely redundant, as with all tables which satisfy the *strong* criterion of a good table. Its main pattern could be described in words alone, as consisting of two clusters: correlations of .3 to .6 between the five Sports programs and of .2 to .5 between the five Current Affairs, with correlations of .1 or so between these two clusters. Yet some deliberate redundancy in communication usually helps.

Experience indicates that most people would agree that the improved tables illustrated here are somehow better than the original versions. But more formal assessment of this also seems desirable—not merely to "prove" the difference, but to see in what *ways* the improvements work, for what kinds of people, and under what circumstances. Some exploratory studies in this direction are summarized elsewhere (Chakrapani and Ehrenberg, 4).

II. SIX BASIC RULES

The table improvements illustrated so far involved a combination of factors (subsumed by the golden rule that the *next* steps in looking at a table should be visually easy). These factors can be considered separately, and in this section I outline six specific rules or guidelines which deal in turn with drastic rounding, marginal averages, choosing between rows and columns in a table, ordering the rows or columns, the use of space, and the differing roles of graphs and tables.

These rules will be illustrated with another example from *Facts in Focus* (1), Table 97, concerning the level of unemployment in Great Britain over four selected years, as reproduced in Table 6.
Although this is again a small and simple table (chosen for conciseness of exposition here), the numerical details are once more not obvious at a glance. Suppose we now look away from this table. What do we remember having seen, *without looking back?* What can we say about the numbers of unemployed?

Rule 1: Rounding to Two Effective Digits

Understanding any set of numbers involves relating the different numbers to each other. But in Table 6 this is not easy. For example, mentally subtracting the

Table 6.   Unemployment in Great Britain—Original Version

	1966	1968	1970	1973
Total unemployed (thousands)	330.9	549.4	582.2	597.9
Males	259.6	460.7	495.3	499.4
Females	71.3	88.8	86.9	98.5

Source: Facts in Focus (1)

1966 total from the 1973 total and remembering the answer is relatively difficult (330.9 from 597.9 = 267.0). Taking ratios mentally (330.9 *into* 597.9) is virtually impossible. Most of us can do such mental arithmetic only by first rounding the figures to one or two digits in our heads.

In Table 7 this rounding has been done for the reader. The general rule is to round to two effective digits, where "effective" here means digits which vary in that kind of data. (Final 0's do not matter, as the eye can readily filter them out.)

Now we can see that the difference between 330 and 600 for total unemployed is 270, and that 330 *into* 600 is almost 2, i.e., an increase of almost 100 percent. We can also see that the increase for males from 260 to 500 is again nearly 100 percent and that the corresponding increase for females is about 40 percent, from 71 to 99. Total unemployed up by almost 100 percent, males up by almost 100 percent and females up by less than 50 percent: that is something one *can* remember. It is also easier to recall that the range for total unemployed is from about 330 to 600 than that it is from 330.9 to 597.9.

Returning to Table 6, we see how any comparable assessment of the figures would necessarily involve mental rounding. Pocket calculators are not the answer, since knowing that 597.9/330.9 = 1.8069 does not greatly help us to see and absorb the patterns in the table. For better or for worse, drastic rounding is necessary if we are to see and internalize the data. Whether rounding to two effective digits is "going too far" is a possible objection considered in Section 4.

A lesser problem is that the male and the female numbers are shown to the nearest ten thousand and the nearest thousand, respectively, by being rounded to two effective digits *in their own context*. This avoids overrounding when different groups of figures vary greatly in size (as also occurred in Table 2). The consequence is that the figures do not add up exactly. This is an undoubted nuisance, but a lesser one than the perceptual difficulties of the unrounded data in Table 6—anyone who cannot learn to cope with rounding errors will probably not get much out of such statistical data anyway.

Rule 2: Row and Column Averages

The next rule concerns the use of row or column averages to provide a visual focus and a possible summary of the data. Table 8 illustrates this by giving the row averages across the four years. (The column totals in this table serve almost the same purpose as column averages.)

Even with a small table such averages prove useful. Noting that the average

Table 7. Unemployed in GB—Rounded

000's	1966	'68	'70	'73
Total unemployed	330	550	580	600
Male	260	460	500	500
Females	71	89	87	99

Table 8.   With Averages

000's	1966	'68	'70	'73	Ave.
Total unemployed	330	550	580	600	520
Male	260	460	500	500	430
Female	71	89	87	99	86

Male/Female ratio is 5 to 1 (i.e., 430/86), we can see more readily how this ratio varies over the years, from less than 4 to 1 in 1966 to just over 5 to 1 in the three succeeding years. Put in statistical jargon, by making the "main effects" explicit (here the row averages and column totals) we can see more easily any "interactions" between rows and columns (here sex by the years). The general rule is to work out row and column averages before scrutinizing the detailed figures.

Rule 3: Figures Are Easier to Compare in Columns

Figures are easier to follow reading down a column than across a row, especially for a large number of items. Even for our small example here, Table 9 makes it easier to see that each category of unemployed was substantially lower in 1966 than in the three later years.

We also notice minor variations and subpatterns more, for example that contrary to the total trend, the female figures leveled off only for 1968 and 1970 (in fact dropping slightly in the latter year), and that the 1973 figure of 99 is markedly high. Compared with Table 8, more of the data become visible to us.

The improvement is a perceptual one. To see in Table 8 that the main variation for total unemployed is from roughly 300 to 600, the eye first had to take in and then partly ignore the symbols and gaps in the sequence

330   550   580   600

and it had to travel relatively far to do so. But in Table 9 the hundreds are close together. The eye can run down the first digit in each column and totally ignore the rest, i.e.,

Table 9.   Rows and Columns Interchanged

GB	Unemployed (000's)		
	Total	Male	Female
1966	330	260	71
'68	550	460	89
'70	580	500	87
'73	600	500	99
Average	520	430	86

3..
5..
5..
6..

It could also marginally take in the second digits while still concentrating on the first

33.
55.
58.
60.

This we tend to do anyway when we read long strings of longer numbers, whether across the page

330.9   549.4   582.2   601.9   261.3   734.6   790.2

or, preferably, *downward*

330.9
549.4
582.2
601.9
261.3
734.6
790.2

where the blip (a copying or typing error?) typically stands out more clearly.

Rule 4: Ordering Rows and Columns by Size

Ordering the rows and/or columns of a table by some measure of the size of the figures (e.g., their averages) often helps to bring order out of chaos. It means using the dimensions of the table to enable us to see the structure of the *data* rather than merely reflecting the structure of the row or column labels (which is usually already well known). The tables in Section 1 gave striking examples.

The present unemployment data already have the rows and columns in an effective order of size because the trends happen to coincide with the order of the years. But to illustrate the rule further, Table 10 gives the data with the rows in another order, A to D. Even with such a small table it is less easy to see that the Row C (or 1966) figures are generally the smallest. Interactions are even harder to spot, e.g., that the male figures in Rows B and D are identical at 500 while the female ones differ markedly at 87 and 99.

Table 10.   Rows in Some Other Order

Unemployed (000's)

GB	Total	Male	Female
A	550	460	89
B	580	500	87
C	330	260	71
D	600	500	99
Average	520	430	86

When ordering rows or columns by size, a subsidiary question is in which *direction* the figures ought to be ordered. People differ in their predilections here. Some like to have figures running from large on the left (as in Table 9), or from large at the top, whereas others prefer the opposite. With time series, some like to have time progress from the left or the top of the tabulations, whereas others prefer to have the latest figures there. But these views are usually not held very strongly, nor do they appear to have any marked perceptual consequences when ordering *columns*. But for the *rows* of a table, showing the larger numbers above the smaller numbers (as in Table 11) helps because we are used to doing mental subtraction that way.

The combinations of consecutive numbers in Table 11 happen to be simple and hence fairly easy to subtract either way round. But in other cases the effect is more marked. If the first two numbers had been 640 and 580 instead of 600 and 580, the arrangement would matter more:

$$\begin{matrix} 580 \\ 640 \end{matrix} \text{ compared to } \begin{matrix} 640 \\ 580 \end{matrix}$$

With less rounded numbers the effect is even stronger. For example, subtracting 583 from 637 is easier in the form

$$\begin{matrix} 637 \\ 583 \end{matrix} \text{ than } \begin{matrix} 583 \\ 637 \end{matrix}$$

Facilitating such mental arithmetic is important when one is scanning large sets of data.

Rule 5: Spacing and Layout

Table 12 illustrates a form of table layout widely used in typed reports and prestigious printed documents. The rows are given in double or triple spacing and the columns are spread right across the page.

Table 11. Rows in Decreasing Order of Totals

Unemployed (000's)

GB	Total	Male	Female
1973 (D)	600	500	99
'70 (B)	580	500	87
'68 (A)	550	460	89
'66 (C)	330	260	71
Average	520	430	86

Such tables look nice but are counterproductive. The data are not easy to read because the eye has to travel too far. The rule is that figures which are meant to be compared should be placed close together. Single spacing is particularly effective in making the eye read down columns. But there also need to be deliberate gaps to guide the eye *across* the table (e.g., between groups of five or so rows) as was illustrated in Tables 2 and 5.

Rule 6: Graphs vs. Tables

Graphs are widely thought to be easier on the reader than tables of numbers, but this is only partly true. Graphs are of little use in communicating the *quantitative* aspects of the data, but they can highlight *qualitative* results (such as that something has gone up, is a curve rather than a straight line, or is small rather than large). For example, the bar graph of the unemployment data in Figure 1 shows dramatically that

(i) Unemployment increased most from 1966 to 1968;

(ii) Female unemployed were much fewer than male.

But these are *qualitative* features of the data which can also be conveyed quite well verbally, as in (i) and (ii). But a graph can make the points more "graphic," and hence graphs can be very useful at the beginning or end of an analysis.

However, graphs are of little if any use for quantitative detail. In Figure 1 the size of the increase from 1966 to 1968 is not obvious at a glance (one has to

Table 12. Widely Spaced Figures

Unemployed

	Total	Male	Female
1973	600	500	99
'70	580	500	87
'68	550	460	89
'66	330	260	71

Figure 1.   A Bar Chart of the Unemployment Data.

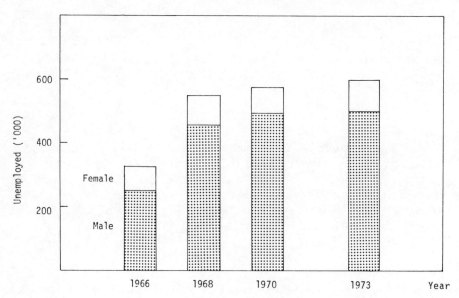

project the blocks onto the vertical scale and interpolate). Nor is it clear just how small a proportion the female unemployed were, nor whether this proportion went up or down over the years, let alone by how much. This quantitative failure of graphs has led to some of the numbers often being shown as well, as illustrated in Figure 2 [though this is not done in *Facts in Focus* (i), say].

One then mostly looks at the numbers (e.g., to see that the proportion of female unemployed actually went *down*) rather than at the graph, so that graphs with numbers inserted are often little more than badly laid-out tables. Arithmetical manipulation of the readings is made difficult rather than easy (e.g., taking averages, differences, ratios, or deviations from an average or a trend-line). Hence well-designed or "graphic" tables are better than graphs for any detailed numerical analysis, especially with extensive ranges of data.

III. THE LITERATURE

The literature relating to the successful presentation of statistical data seems to be sparse. The possible sources are psychological, typographical and statistical.

A good deal of work on information processing has been reported in psychology [e.g., Shroeder et al. (5), Lindsay and Norman (6)]. But little of it seems directly relevant to our narrow area of highly structured numerical tables and graphs—not even most of the work on pattern recognition and attention span.

Figure 2.   With Numbers Added.

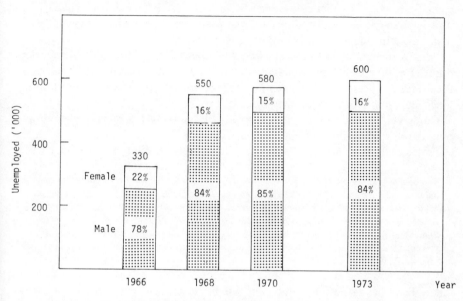

However, in writing about formal mathematical rather than *empirical* tables, Wright (7) has noted that it is helpful to space related columns of figures closer than unrelated ones, and to arrange items so they can be scanned vertically rather than horizontally.

More fundamentally, Herbert Simon (8), in discussing short-term memory, noted not only that we can generally recall numbers of up to seven or even ten digits correctly if we are not interrupted in any way (i.e., not even by our own thoughts), but that there is also now experimental evidence that if we *are* interrupted by any task (however simple) the number of digits we retain in our short-term memory generally drops to *two*.

This would explain our need in Rule 1 to round figures to two significant (or variable) digits if we are to be able to perform mental arithmetic with them, i.e., to keep the figures accessible for immediate recall while being "interrupted" through having to relate one figure to another. (More than two significant digits being retained across an interruption can usually be explained parsimoniously either by our having recoded the information into two larger "chunks," or by having taken enough time—about five seconds per chunk—to fixate the information in our *long-term* memory.)

The study of *typography*, Spencer (9), has centered on the legibility of type faces and sizes, on page design and problems of reduction and degradation, rather than the interrelation of different aspects of a numerical table. Yet some precepts apply, like the well-established typographical rule such as that strings of capitals are relatively difficult to read (BEING ALL OF THE SAME HEIGHT). This is often ignored for headings and captions in statistical tables, especially by many manufacturers of peripheral computer equipment.

Some statistical writers have stressed the importance of limiting the number of digits. But they almost invariably continued to use unnecessarily large numbers themselves. Giffen (10), for example, greatly stressed rounding but used up to nine digits himself—"to the nearest acre."

Golde (11) referred to a loss in accuracy of "only 3.41 percent" when dropping the third digit in a certain number.

Professor Ray Bauer (12) has a splendid diatribe on digits in his Chapter 5:

> The data should not pretend to be more than they are. One of the most misleading practices indulged in by pretentious researchers is to present complex tables with the percentages carried out to the third, or even fourth, significant figures. Sometimes this is done because a researcher is lazy and he does not want to round out the figures which come out of the computer. Sometimes he is afraid to round his percentages because they won't add to precisely 100 percent. Other times he actually believes that the third figure is important: this is virtually never true.

Yet nobody has taken much notice of this because Bauer has still only stressed the pointlessness and lack of precision of the later digits, rather than the *positive* advantages of eliminating them—that we can see, manipulate, and communicate two-digit numbers much better.

Graphics are currently attracting a good deal of attention [see Beniger and Robyn (13) for a bibliography], but there seems to be nothing new to help in communicating quantitative information effectively. The *Council for Social Graphics* in Washington, D.C. has recently been assessing people's "graphicacy" (how well one can read graphs), but their target audiences are mainly the innumerate or inexperienced (e.g., school children) rather than professional or regular users of numerical information.

On the whole, the presentation of numerical data to facilitate its use has been a relatively neglected area. Perhaps people have not realized how unnecessarily incomprehensible their supposedly competent tables usually are.

IV. SPECIFIC OBJECTIONS

A number of objections and problems have been raised while using and teaching the present approach to data presentation during the last few years [e.g., Ehrenberg (14), Part I]. I now discuss these, taking the six rules in turn.

Rounding (Rule 1)

Rounding is the rule which tends to raise the most (or the most heated) objections. It is the only rule wherein information is actually discarded and many people seem to feel that observed data should be treated as sacrosanct, e.g., that if some clerk or computer happens to have recorded the data to five digits, then that is how the data should always remain.

Yet rounding is readily accepted in graphical presentations and also in fitting mathematical models to the data. Nor would most people object to reducing statistical data to *three or four* effective digits. But they often feel that rounding to only two effective digits is overdoing it. Unfortunately, such rounding is necessary to facilitate mental arithmetic. For example, few of us can divide 17.9 percent into 35.2 percent in our heads (most percentages are reported as "per mille" rather than as "per centum"). Of several thousand people asked to do this over the years only two U.S. mathematicians at Purdue have claimed success. But they got different answers, so at least one of them was wrong. In contrast, dividing 18 percent into 35 percent is obviously about 2. Thus two digits are better.

The finding noted earlier that our short-term, quick-access memory is limited to manipulating two-digit numbers applies even to a simple arithmetical task like scanning a column of more or less equal figures against their average, and even when all the figures remain in front of us as in the following examples:

549.2	550	549
582.2	580	582
601.9	600	602
621.3	620	621
734.6	730	735
617.9	620	618

With *four* digits in the first column we can hardly recall the average of 617.9 as we run down the column from one entry to the next (unless we go in for mental rounding). With *two* significant digits there is no problem—we can check the trend while readily holding the average of 620 in our head. With *three* digits there is still quite a problem of recalling the average as we go down the column, although we can cope better by transforming the 618 into two "chunks" like 6 18 (six eighteen) or into a "singsong" *six*-one-eight. (With three digits we could also take the time to transfer the average of 618 to our longer-term memory, but this would hardly work when scanning a table with many such columns.)

Instead of asking for any particular data, "Can we possibly round them to two digits?" we need to check only whether there is some specific reason why we should *not* do so. One can think of exceptional situations, e.g., where large multipliers might be involved, where rounding errors can build up as in compound interest calculations, or where we are analyzing deviations from a model. One would then often keep a third digit for working purposes in calculating averages, slope coefficients or other parameters to avoid minor problems with rounding errors, but round again when actually reporting the results. Again, one can round the sequence 186, 97, 93 to 190, 97, 93 without effective loss, but with our decimal system one might not round 106, 97, 93 to 110, 97, 93 because the error of rounding the 106 is large compared with the range of 13. But such cases are exceptions.

One safeguard is that no information need be *completely* lost by rounding. The two-digit rule is a guideline for statistical working tables and the final presentation of results, not necessarily for basic data records. One can put the more precise data in an appendix or, better still, in a filing cabinet or other data bank just in case somebody should want it sometime.

The more precise data are, however, unlikely ever to be used. When would the earlier unemployment figures really be needed to the nearest 100 persons as in Table 13, rather than rounded to the nearest 1,000 or 10,000? The degree of precision that might be required can be judged against the range of the observed variation that has to be explained, the size of the residuals in any formal model-building, and the likely requirements of any deeper analysis (not to mention the inherent inaccuracy of the data).

For example, in Table 13 the average error in rounding the female unemployed to two digits would be 300. This is trivial when assessed against the overall increase of almost 30,000 in the female figures from 1966 to 1973, and the contrary drop of about 2,000 from 1968 to 1970. The rounding errors are also trivial when compared with the residuals from a mathematical model like F = 0.1M + 43. This represents the relationship between Female and Male unemployed quite well, the correlation being .85. But the residuals average at 3,000.

Finally, the rounding errors are trivial in the context of any fuller analysis of unemployment. This would never mean digging deeper into the eight selected readings in Table 13. Instead, it would necessitate taking account of vastly *more* data: for other years, different regions of the country, different industries, different age groups (treating school dropouts and students separately), plus figures for employment, reported vacancies, inflation, investment, stock-piling, dumping, Gross National Product, the money supply, birth rates, immigration, mechanization, business cycles, world trade, unemployment in other countries, and so on, as well as intensive comparisons of figures based on different definitions and measuring procedures (i.e., the whole question of the "quality" of the data).

Each monthly issue of the *Department of Employment Gazette* in the UK gives about 8,000 two-to-four digit numbers on unemployment, and *Employment and*

Table 13.   Unemployment in Great Britain
(Table 5 Repeated)

	1966	1968	1970	1972
Total unemployed (thousands)	330.9	549.4	582.2	597.9
Males	259.6	460.7	495.3	499.4
Females	71.3	88.8	86.9	98.5

Earnings gives several thousand more. They may be mostly the same as in the previous month, but the need to see the wood for the trees becomes even more urgent than with the eight figures in Table 13. Hoping to explain variation to the third digit (less than 1 percent) becomes even more absurd. People who object to rounding to two significant digits because they feel that "there may be something there" can have had no experience of *successfully* analyzing and understanding extensive empirical data.

Averages (Rule 2)

Averages are not always directly descriptive or "typical" of the readings in question. Including such averages in a table is often criticized as useless or even misleading. But they can still provide a visual focus for inspecting the data, and also useful parameters when comparing different distributions of the same type.

To illustrate, I use the slightly more complex example shown in Table 14 (a re-presentation of the earlier TV data in Table 5). It says how many adults who "really liked to watch" one TV program also really liked to watch another. Thus 39 percent of adults really liked to watch World of Sport (WoS), and of these, 73 percent really liked to watch Match of the Day, 72 percent Grandstand, and so on. (The earlier correlations of Table 5 can be calculated from the data in Table 14; the new table involves no change in empirical content but only in language or model.) Writing in the row and column averages by hand, as one would do with

Table 14. Duplication Analysis: Percentage of Adults Who Like One TV Program Who Also Like Another

% of Adults Who Really Like to Watch

	Wrld of Sprt 39	Mtch of the Day 38	Grnd stnd 35	Prof Box ing 32	Rgby Spec ial 16	24 Hrs 31	Pan- or- ama 31	Ths Wk 27	To- day 24	Line- up 9	Av. 28
% who also really like to watch	%	%	%	%	%	%	%	%	%	%	%
World of Sport	(100)	75	80	75	74	49	52	51	47	50	61
Match of the Day	73	(100)	77	72	75	47	48	45	41	46	58
Grandstand	72	71	(100)	68	75	47	48	45	41	47	57
Prof. Boxing	61	60	62	(100)	65	41	49	40	38	44	51
Rugby Special	28	30	32	31	(100)	21	23	19	18	25	25
24 Hours	39	38	40	39	44	(100)	68	61	50	66	49
Panorama	41	38	42	42	42	67	(100)	58	47	59	48
This Week	34	31	34	34	33	53	50	(100)	48	53	41
Today	29	26	28	28	29	39	37	43	(100)	44	34
Line-up	12	11	12	13	16	20	18	19	17	(100)	15
Average (excl. 100's)	43	42	45	45	50	42	44	42	39	48	44

computer output or other working tables, we quickly see that none of the averages represent the data at all well. They are not typical or modal of the individual figures in the corresponding row or column.

Nonetheless, the averages provide a useful focus. By fixing first on the average for each row and ignoring the 100s in the diagonal, we see four above-average figures followed by five below-average figures in each of the first five rows, and the opposite pattern in the last five rows (five *below*-average figures followed by four *above*-average ones). Blocking out the row averages on the right by hand dramatizes their effectiveness in providing this visual focus.

Correspondingly, the column averages help us to see that there is no such simple pattern in the columns. But we also note that these column averages are all virtually equal. Focusing first on the overall average of 44 helps to see this.

This suggests checking whether the figures in each column follow the same form of distribution (having the same means). Starting with the overall average of 44 and the column of row averages on the right, we see a "High-Low-About average-Low" pattern. Inspecting the individual columns in the body of the table against their averages (with the 100s in parentheses so that the eye can ignore them more easily) shows the same pattern in the first five columns, but a somewhat different pattern for the last five: "About average-Low-High-Low." We now see that the virtual equality of the column averages across all ten columns was a coincidence.

Thus used critically as a working tool, averages are of value in getting to know the data even when they do not summarize the data as simple "typical" figures. Calculating marginal averages for a table generally remains a helpful first step to see which way the data go. But they need not always be retained in the final presentation.

Using Columns for Figures to Be Compared (Rule 3)

An objection often raised about interchanging rows and columns is the difficulty of fitting long row-captions into column headings. This can usually be done by abbreviation, by spreading the headings over two or three lines (as in Table 14), and by relegating detail to footnotes. (Some people are said to object to having to look at the footnotes to a table, but they are probably not the sort of people who would get much out of a complex-looking table anyway.)

It is important to get one's priorities right. The design of a table must be determined by the data that are being displayed, not by the logic of the row and column labels. Yet tables often are designed without taking any account of the data. For example, some recent proposals by the *Business Statistics Office* (15) for interchanging rows and columns in its regular *Business Monitor* series were judged unconvincing, but the dummy tables that were prepared contained no numbers. In practice, if a table layout is designed without reference to the data, that is what the final table will probably look like.

To illustrate, Table 15 clarifies the patterns in Table 14 by interchanging the rows and columns, omitting the 100s, and inserting appropriate averages (in this table *row* averages do not seem to help). We now see that the figures in each column tend to be similar within each of the two program categories, and hence close to the averages shown at the bottom of each block. For example, World of Sport (WoS) in the first column is liked by about 76 percent of those who liked one of the other Sports programs (the individual figures varying between 74 and 80 percent), and by about 50 percent of those who liked one of the Current Affairs programs.

Since World of Sport (WoS) is liked by about 39 percent of *all* adults (as shown in the last row of the table), we can see now that it was about twice as popular among those who liked another Sports program, and about 1.3 times as popular among those who liked a Current Affairs program, than among the population as a whole (76/39 and 50/39).

The same pattern holds for the other Sports programs shown in the next four columns (MoD to RgS). From the averages we estimate "duplication ratios" of $63/32 = 2.0$ within the Sports cluster and $41/32 = 1.3$ between the Sports and Current Affairs programs. The pattern also applies to the Current Affairs programs in the last five columns of the table. The duplication ratios here are again 1.3 for Current Affairs versus Sports and 1.9 within the Current Affairs cluster itself.

Table 15 may appear more complex than the earlier correlation matrix in Table

Table 15. Duplication Analysis: Rows and Columns Interchanged and Subgroup Averages

Percent Who Also Really Like to Watch

Adults Who Really Like to Watch		WoS	MoD	GrS	PrB	RgS	AV.	24H	Pan	ThW	Tod	LnU	AV.
World of Sport	%		73	72	61	28		39	41	34	29	12	
Match of the Day	%	75		71	60	30		38	38	31	26	11	
Grandstand	%	80	77		62	32		40	42	34	28	12	
Prof. Boxing	%	75	72	68		31		39	42	34	28	13	
Rugby Special	%	74	75	75	65			44	42	33	29	16	
AVERAGE		76	74	71	62	30	63	40	42	33	28	13	31
24 Hours	%	49	47	47	41	21			67	53	39	20	
Panorama	%	52	48	48	49	23		68		50	37	18	
This Week	%	51	45	45	40	19		61	58		43	19	
Today	%	47	41	41	38	18		50	47	48		17	
Line-Up	%	50	46	47	44	25		66	59	53	44		
AVERAGE		50	45	46	42	21	41	61	58	51	41	18	46
ALL ADULTS	%	39	38	35	32	16	32	31	31	27	24	9	24

$$(63/32 = 2.0) \qquad (31/24 = 1.3)$$
$$(41/32 = 1.3) \qquad (46/24 = 1.9)$$

14 but it provides much more insight into the data. It is an instance of the so-called "duplication law," which says here that the percentage of people who like program P among those who like program Q is directly proportional to the percentage of the whole population who like program P, the proportionality factor or "duplication ratio" being a constant for a particular grouping of programs. This form of relationship has already been found to occur in a wide range of choice situations [e.g., Goodhardt (3), Ehrenberg (16)], and also has strong theoretical backing (Goodhardt, 17 and 18).

Table 15 may not seem obvious at a glance if one is seeing it for the first time. But it brings out the duplication pattern clearly enough for anyone already knowledgeable in the area, and in particular for anyone involved in using the model in question. This typically involves examining and communicating literally hundreds of thousands of such figures over the years. A form of layout meeting the weak criterion for a good table which allows one to scan and grasp extensive data then becomes essential.

A common query about changing rows into columns is whether all users of the table will want to compare the figures in the columns rather than those in the rows. In practice they must always do *both*. But the main pattern in the data should be looked at first and hence in columns because that is easier. Then, having seen the main pattern, one can look at the rows and at any row-and-column interactions. Again, with a table of time series one usually looks first at each series on its own (which is easier in columns) and only then correlates the different series.

Ordering by Size (Rule 4)

Ordering the rows or columns of a table by some measure of size raises two problems. One is that different measures of size can be used, resulting in different possible orders. The criticism is that readers (especially *other* readers) might be misled by the particular order chosen.

For example, in Table 2 ordering the rows of the shipping data by the numbers of vessels led to the sequence Cargo/Tanker/Passenger. Ordering by the *1973 tonnages* would have led to the sequence Tanker/Cargo/Passenger. But users of a table do not have to accept the chosen ordering as sacrosanct. One order will show up the conflict with another, and *some* visible ordering is always better than none (as in the original Table 1). In Table 2 anyone can see that the 1973 tonnages *were* out of step. (Were you, the reader, in any way misled, or would you only be worrying about the possible effect on *others?*)

The second problem arises when there are many different tables with the same basic format. Straight application of the rule would lead to different orders for different tables. In such cases the same order should be used in every table.

A good example occurs with tables giving various social and economic statistics for different countries, or for different regions or towns within the same country. A useful common order for all such tables might be population size. This provides an instant visual rank correlation between the absolute and per capita rates for each variable.

Such an ordering is often criticized as departing from the alphabetical listing of the countries, making it difficult to look up the result for a particular country. But a statistical table is not a telephone directory. To use an isolated figure one must understand the context of the surrounding ones and see the general pattern of the data. If there are many such tables and they are large, an alphabetical key will be worth giving. In any case it is probably easier to find an isolated name in a nonalphabetical listing than to interpret an isolated number from an unstructured table.

Spacing and Layout (Rule 5)

The basic guidelines for table layout may seem simple: single-spacing and occasional deliberate gaps to guide the eye; columns spaced evenly and close together; and occasional horizontal and vertical rules to mark major divisions. But many typists, printers, and computers are programed differently. Double-spacing in tables is common, as are columns spaced unevenly according to the width of the headings, and occasional irregular gaps between single-spaced rows because some row captions ran to two lines. One needs not only good typists or printers, but also thoughtful *control* of these facilities.

The traditional printer's embargo on vertical rules is widely accepted (as illustrated by the tables in this paper) but can be sidestepped increasingly through modern offset and duplicating methods. However, ruling off every column routinely, as in Table 1 is counterproductive. In contrast, a few well-chosen rules can have a startling effect, as the reader may see by drawing a vertical and a horizontal rule by hand to separate the two sets of five programs in Table 15.

The niceties of good spacing and layout are many and complex. Some specific ones are illustrated by Table 15. A good general example (not illustrated here) occurs with tables where the data come in pairs of related figures, e.g., "observed" and "theoretical" values, or "last year" and "this year": The use of closely spaced *pairs* of columns is then very effective. More work is needed to make the possible variety of such procedures more explicit.

Graphs vs. Tables (Rule 6)

A claim often made in supposed contradiction to Rule 6 is that people (especially "other people") find graphs easier to look at than tables, e.g., Figure 1 rather than Table 13. They probably do, but this is misleading because it does not reflect that people usually extract and retain little information from a graph.

It's no use merely saying, "Here are some complex data—let's put them on a graph.'' What does one learn even from simple graphs (like Figures 1 or 2)? They are supposed to be easy, but suppose one looks away, what does one remember? Some shapes or qualitative features perhaps, but seldom any quantities. Success in graphics seems to be judged in producer rather than consumer terms: by how much information one can get on to a graph (or how easily), rather than by how much any reader can get off again (or how easily).

V. SOME PROBLEMS OF IMPLEMENTATION

Perhaps the most frequent comment on the rules of data presentation discussed here is that they are ''mere common sense,'' with the insidious implication that real statisticians do not have to bother with them. But at this stage the rules reflect neither common knowledge nor common practice. In that sense they are decidedly uncommon.

The rules seem obvious only once they have been stated. No particular skills or knowledge are then required to assess them—only one's common senses, i.e., whether they feel, look, and sound right. The procedures therefore lack the technical mystique of a Durbin-Watson test or non-Euclidian space that tends to guarantee a certain instant popularity.

Implementation of such presentation rules is often thought to depend on two factors: (1) the data, (b) one's purpose. But in this final section I show that the rules generally transcend these factors.

The Nature of the Data

The data to be presented can be classified along several dimensions, namely whether they are:
— Simple or complex
— New or repetitive
— Reliable or uncertain
— To tell a particular story, or presented only ''for the record.''
I now consider these four aspects.

Complexity. The tables illustrated in this paper have been mainly small and simple, for reasons of space. Nonetheless, Table 1 was in effect a *three-way* table, and the Table 2 version made it much easier to correlate the three different variables (i.e., the numbers of vessels and the two types of tonnages). Table 15 was another fairly complex example. More generally, my experience is that the six rules also apply to still more complex or extensive data, where they are in fact needed even more. Some examples have been considered elsewhere (e.g., Ehrenberg, 14, 19, 20, 21).

New or Old? The analytic situations discussed in the statistical literature mostly follow the ''exploratory'' approach, where a new data set is to be analyzed as if that kind of data were being looked at for the first time ever. Good data presentation then takes a fair amount of work, since one seldom gets a new table completely right the first time round. But the real problem with new data is not that of presenting it well, but of having first to understand it. Luckily this is (or should be) relatively rare. Most situations faced by professional or frequent users of data are *repetitive,* in that they have already seen a good deal of similar data before and therefore know the probable structure (Ehrenberg, 22).

To take Table 15 as an example, one's usual task is not to discover the basic duplication pattern for the first time [that can strictly happen at most once, and did so about ten years ago in this instance—Goodhardt, 15; Ehrenberg and Twyman, 23].

Instead, one needs to assess these particular data against one's prior knowledge of the duplication law, to establish and understand any apparent anomalies, to communicate the results to others, and to *use* the results (e.g., for theoretical model-building, practical decision-making, prediction or control). In such well-understood repetitive situations the rules of data presentation can be applied routinely. Their use becomes highly efficient.

The Quality of the Data. It is often said that the "quality" of the data should affect how they are presented. This presumably refers to outliers, sampling errors and basic measurement problems. But given that certain numbers are to be reported at all, it is better to present them clearly rather than obscurely, so the rules still apply. Good data presentation makes outliers and misprints stand out: Twyman's Law—that any reading which looks interesting or different is probably wrong—can only be applied if we first see that a reading *is* out of step.

Sampling errors occur if sample sizes are small. Most modern statisticians are of course highly trained to deal with this (if with nothing else) and such issues can, I hope, largely be taken as read. I only add that some analysts' habit of attaching a standard error to every reading in the body of a table is both visually obnoxious and statistically naive. If standard errors or other devices of statistical inference need to be explicitly quoted, this should be done either in a separate display, or in footnotes, or in the text.

The basic problem with data is what the variables in question actually measure. In our unemployment example the figures are for registered unemployed (with a good deal of small print in the definitions), and do not properly represent "unemployment," whatever that may be. Female unemployed tend for example to be markedly underrepresented, especially at times of high general unemployment. Learning to understand what one's variables mean usually depends on comparing different *types* of measurement (e.g., the official figures of registered unemployed with sample survey data of supposedly "actual" unemployed). This is usually a complex task and the need for effective data presentation remains. Even if our measurements are known to be biased, that is no reason for leaving the numerical results obscure.

For the Record or . . . ? Three main types of empirically based data tables can be distinguished:

— working tables, for the use of the analyst and his immediate colleagues, with no wider communication in mind;
— the final presentation to a more or less specific audience, to support or illustrate some specific conclusion or findings;
— tables set out "for the record" (as in official statistics) in case someone wants to use the data.

In the first two cases the structure of the data needs to be apparent both to the analyst himself and to others. Hence the rules of this paper apply. With data presented "for the record," however, it is sometimes argued that the data will contain so many different stories, for different kinds of uses and users, that its presentation must vary accordingly. But few real instances have been quoted and this conclusion seems to be the exception rather than the rule. In any case, it does not follow that the data must be presented to tell *no* story, as is so often the case.

One frequently cited illustration of the use of such data is the politician who wants to quote a single number in some speech (e.g., the number of doctors in his home town) and who appears profoundly uninterested in general patterns and laws, e.g., of the incidence of doctors in different towns and places. But this is wrong. No meaningful use can be made of an isolated number. What good is it knowing that there are 57 doctors in the town without some idea of whether this 57 is high, low or normal—as *many* as 57, or *only* 57, or what? Without aiming to turn politicians or other users of the odd statistic into full-fledged statisticians, we need not pander to the mindless misuse of statistical data. In any case, most occasional users would be happy to see, or be told, that 57 *is* high (or low) on a per capita basis and after allowing for the local age distribution, or whatever. Bringing out general patterns in official statistics can do little harm, and may do much good.

Applying the present rules to official statistics will take time and effort, but this will be more than balanced by savings in paper and printing costs, not to mention the fuller and better use that will be made of the data. Yet the practical problems of implementing these rules of data presentation must not be underestimated. There can be very substantial setup and upset costs in changing from traditional practices. The methodology is still underdeveloped. People are not only unfamiliar with the techniques, but also with the fundamental notion that most tables can be improved to communicate better.

The Purpose of the Analysis

It is commonly suggested that one should formulate one's purpose explicitly before tackling the analysis or presentation of some data. Sir Maurice Kendall (24), for example, has said that if he had some data and wanted in some sense to describe their structure, he would do nothing except store the original observations until someone could specify the object of the exercise. This reads like a denial of the purpose of ordinary science, i.e., to understand a system, and to do so before attempting to make practical applications.

In a recent review in this journal Pridmore (25) extended this view to the novice, complaining that apparently he had not been told to ask himself such questions as "What am I going to do with the results? Why am I doing this? Why are the data wanted?" before starting his analysis. But I doubt if a novice could answer these questions, or should be expected to do so. More generally, I feel that the emphasis on establishing a purpose prior to first studying one's data is unrealistic.

I am not saying that one should not have a purpose, but only that one cannot formulate a realistic purpose if one knows nothing yet about one's data (i.e., no prior knowledge and also no peeking). But as mentioned earlier, most analyses are of a repetitive kind, so that one usually has prior experience of other, similar data to influence how one approaches the new data.

Formulating a purpose without knowledge of the data would in any case mean that the analyst's uninformed perception of his purpose would determine how he analyses and presents his data. This would be very subjective. The contrary view, which I support, is that the detailed analysis and presentation of the data should be dominated by the facts. One's personal objectives or purpose should mainly determine how one then *uses* the results.

The kind of presentation rules discussed in this paper are themselves often regarded as subjective because the presentation is to be deliberately influenced by one's knowledge of the data. This is an anathema to some statisticians, due to a misunderstanding of certain technical problems in statistical inference for small samples. But if the presentation rules are made explicit, any reasonably experienced person can follow them and obtain more or less the same results, which is the touchstone for achieving objectivity.

The presentation of data of course involves judgment. But that is true of any form of analysis (e.g., in choosing one's variables, measurement techniques, conditions of observation, sample sizes, cleaning-up procedures, analytic techniques and models, significance levels, etc.). Judgment is largely what distinguishes a good analyst from a lesser one. But this judgment must have knowledge, experience and techniques to bite on, and subsequently be replicable by others. The main aim in this paper has been to discuss rules or guidelines for data presentation which can be applied more or less routinely, with judgment.

REFERENCES

1. Central Statistical Office (1974), *Facts in Focus,* 2nd edition, Baltimore: Penguin Books.
2. Samuelson, P. (1976), *Economics,* 10th edition, New York: McGraw-Hill.
3. Goodhardt, G. J., Ehrenberg, A. S. C., and Collins, M. A. (1975), *The Television Audience: Patterns of Viewing,* Lexington, Mass.: D. C. Heath.

4. Chakrapani, T. K., and Ehrenberg, A.S.C. (1976), "Numerical Information Processing," (working paper).
5. Shroeder, H. M., Driver, M. J., and Streufort, S. (1967), *Human Information Processing,* New York: Holt, Rinehart & Winston.
6. Lindsay, P. H., and Norman, D. A. (1972), *Human Information Processing,* New York: Academic Press.
7. Wright, P. (1973), "Understanding Tabular Displays," *Visible Language 7:* 351.
8. Simon, H. A. (1969), *The Sciences of the Artificial,* Cambridge, Mass.: M.I.T. Press.
9. Spencer, H. (1969), *The Visible Word,* London: Lund Humphries.
10. Giffen, Sir Robert (1913), *Statistics,* Henry Higgs and George Udny Yule, eds., London: Macmillan.
11. Golde, R. A. (1966), *Thinking with Figures in Business,* Reading, Mass.: Addison-Wesley.
12. Buzzell, R. D., Cox, D. F., and Brown, R. V. (1969), *Marketing Research and Information Systems: Text and Cases,* New York: McGraw-Hill.
13. Beniger, J. R., and Robyn, D. L. (1976), "The History and Future of Graphics in Statistics," in *Social Statistics Proceedings,* Washington, D.C.: The American Statistical Association.
14. Ehrenberg, A. S. C. (1975), *Data Reduction,* London and New York: John Wiley.
15. Fessey, M. C. (1976), private communication.
16. Ehrenberg, A. S. C. (1972), *Repeat-Buying: Theory and Applications,* New York: Elsevier.
17. Goodhardt, G. J. (1966), "The Constant in Duplicated Television Viewing," *Nature* 212: 1616.
18. Goodhardt, G. J., Chatfield, C., and Ehrenberg, A. S. C. (1977), "The Dirichlet Choice Model" (in preparation).
19. Ehrenberg, A. S. C. (1976), "Communicating Market Data," *J. of Adv. Research* 16: 27.
20. Ehrenberg, A. S. C. (1976), "Annual Reports Don't Have to Be Obscure," *J. of Accountancy* 88 (August).
21. Ehrenberg, A. S. C., and Goodhardt, G. J. (1977), "Developing and Using a Model," *Proceedings of the 20th Annual Conference of the Market Research Society.* London: The Market Research Society.
22. Ehrenberg, A. S. C. (1976), "We Must Preach What Is Practised," *The Statistician* 25: 195.
23. Ehrenberg, A. S. C., and Twyman, W. A. (1967), "On Measuring Television Audiences," *J. Roy. Statist. Soc. A.* 130: 1.
24. Kendall, Sir Maurice (1969), private communication.
25. Pridmore, W. A. (1976), "Review of Data Reduction," *J. Royal Statist. Soc. A,* 139: 268.

EVALUATING THE COMPETITIVE ENVIRONMENT IN RETAILING USING MULTIPLICATIVE COMPETITIVE INTERACTIVE MODEL

Arun K. Jain, STATE UNIVERSITY OF NEW YORK AT

BUFFALO

Vijay Mahajan, OHIO STATE UNIVERSITY

I. INTRODUCTION

Marketing planning by a firm starts with the development of a well-defined set of corporate objectives and their pursuit by a sound competitive strategy. The formulation of a competitive strategy depends upon an understanding of the nature of the competition, the competitors and their strategies in the marketplace.

Research in Marketing—Volume 2, 1979, pages 217–235.
Copyright © 1979 by JAI Press Inc.
ISBN 0-89232-059-1

217

This is necessitated by the fact that the market response is a function of the efforts of the competitors and those of an individual firm.

Each firm occupies a position in the market that is unique in some respects. Its location, the product it sells, its operating methods, or customers it serves tend to distinguish it to some extent from all others in the market. The firm competes in the market by making the most of its individuality and its unique character. It is continuously attempting to establish some competitive superiority to secure a strong relative position in the market. A firm that has been excelled by its competitors on some dimension(s) of the value to the customers always has the possibility of reversing the trend by developing something new on other dimensions. However, this requires that the firm develops an understanding of the dynamics of the market. For example, it would need a decision model to evaluate the impact of its alternative marketing mix strategies on its relative position in the market. Furthermore, such a model would assist the firm in simulating the impact of competitors' anticipated marketing strategies on its relative position.

Models of competition have been developed in economics literature. In a purely competitive market, a firm has no problem of marketing strategy, only a problem of best production level. Marketing mix variables, such as advertising, do no good since consumers buy strictly according to price. The development of marketing strategies becomes extremely important in an oligopolistic industry. Such a condition calls for explicit consideration of competitive behavior in the development of marketing strategy since one firm's marketing action can adversely affect the performance of another firm. However, in real markets a firm may also enjoy some elements of monopolistic competition even when few competitors exist in the marketplace. Because of its unique offerings in quality, reliability, and service, a firm may have some competitive independence which may enable it to increase its sales with an increase in its marketing efforts without provoking competitive retaliation. Therefore, to achieve a competitive position in the market, it is necessary for a firm to develop a decision model that would help to identify and evaluate alternative marketing mix, contributing to competitive independence and competitive retaliation (Kotler, 1, 2).

Understanding of the dynamics of competition is particularly important in retailing since the securing of a competitive advantage over a retail rival is often an ephemeral matter, and the development of an effective marketing strategy is essential in order to permit retention of small advantages for a longer period. The absence of such understanding, especially for small retail stores, has contributed to high bankruptcy rates and amount of ownership turnover (Duncan, 3). The various marketing mix variables which retailers tend to use for differentiating themselves generally include a) price, b) the services offered to consumers (e.g., credit facility, shopping atmosphere, parking space, etc.), c) the product assortment made available (breadth, depth, quality, etc.), and location (Stern and El-Ansary, 4). Among these elements of competitive strategy, the site selection decision is extremely difficult and a critical factor in influencing customer patronage and, hence, the market position. Once the site for the store has been selected, the management can no longer amend their decision without undesirable financial consequences. Furthermore, through a strategic location, a firm achieves advantages which are unique to the firm. In the development of competitive strategy prices could be met, services could be extended and improved, merchandise may be duplicated, and promotion can be imitated; but a retailer's locational advantages are difficult to assail or neutralize. In a way, the site of the store offers a firm monopolistic advantage over others maintaining an oligopolistic competition in terms of the other marketing mix variables. This forces the competitors to evaluate the impact of such a decision on their relative position in the market given certain anticipated strategies of competitors.

The objective of this paper is to model the competitive environment in retailing. More specifically, this paper models the competition in food retailing. The model is next applied to simulate and evaluate the impact of 18 alternative strategies of a new store entry on the existing competition and market-share shifts. The data for the study were obtained in a large northeastern metropolitan area where a new store entering the market was supposed to generate market-share shifts.

II. THE MODEL

Several models have been proposed in the marketing literature to examine site selection in retailing. Examples of such models include Checklist methods, Analog methods, Multiplicative Competitive Interactive (MCI) models, Environmental models, Additive models, Sectogram techniques, and Microanalytic models (Stern and El-Ansary, 4; Openshaw, 5). Attempts have also been made to combine the various approaches (Openshaw, 5; Nakanishi, 6). Of the various approaches proposed, Analog and MCI models seem to be the most popular. A review of the application of the Analog models can be found in the works of Applebaum et al. (7) and Green and Applebaum (8). Briefly, this approach involves (a) identification of the trading area for the proposed site using customer spotting techniques, (b) selection of "analogs" among the existing stores, i.e., those stores which best match the description of the proposed store in terms of store types, site/area characteristics, and competitive situation, (c) estimation of per capita sales volume for the proposed store from the sales volume figures for the "analogs," and (d) forecasting the sales of the new store from its projected trading area and estimated per capita sales volume. This approach does not directly deal with the competitive influences in the evaluation of a site. The accuracy of the results depends upon the selection of the analogs and analyst's own judgments.

Alternatively, the MCI model explicitly incorporates the competitive environment in the evaluation of the store sites. The applications of MCI model, which is an extension of the Gravitational market-share model of the consumer spatial behavior originally suggested by Huff (9), and Huff and Batsell (10), has been limited because of the difficulty in the estimation of its parameters (Haines et al., 11; Hlavak et al., 12; Lalond, 13; Mahajan et al., 14; Stanley and Sewall, 15). However, it has recently been demonstrated by Teekens (16) and Nakanishi and Cooper (17) that the MCI model can be calibrated using the least squares procedures. In the modeling of consumer choices, the superiority of the MCI model over Additive model has also been demonstrated in a nonmarketing application of predicting outcome of election results (Nakanishi et al., 23; Mahajan et al., 18; Muller, 19). In the coming years we would expect a much wider use of the model due to the ease of estimation and sophistication of the model. Furthermore, since the MCI model as compared to other models systematically handles competitive influences, it offers a great potential for examining the impact of competitive strategies. This paper uses the MCI model to describe the competition and examine the market-share shifts.

The MCI model has been developed from an analog with Newton's Law of Gravitation. This law states that the gravitation force, F_{ij}, between two masses, M_i and M_j, separated by distance, D_{ij}, is

$$F_{ij} = c[M_i (M_j/D_{ij}^2)] \tag{1}$$

where c is a constant.

If the mass M_i is being attracted by m number of masses, the relative force by which M_i will be attracted to M_j is

$$p_{ij} = F_{ij}/ \sum_{j=1}^{m} F_{ij} \tag{2}$$

$$= (M_j/D_{ij}^2)/ \sum_{j=1}^{m} (M_j/D_{ij}^2).$$

In general, the gravitational-type models may take the following form:

$$F_{ij} = c \ M_i \ M_j^{\beta_1} \ D_{ij}^{\beta_2} \tag{3}$$

where, β_1 and β_2 are the sensitivity parameters. For example, in Eq. (1) β_1 is equal to 1 and β_2 is equal to -2. Similarly, the general form of Eq. (2) is:

$$p_{ij} = (M_j^{\beta_1} \ D_{ij}^{\beta_2})/ \sum_{j=1}^{m} (M_j^{\beta_1} \ D_{ij}^{\beta_2})) \tag{4}$$

The sensitivity parameters in Eq. (4) in different applications of the model can be estimated by the ordinary least squares methods on the log-transformed-centered form of Eq. (4) as suggested by Nakanishi and Cooper (17), i.e.,

$$\ln p_{ij} = \beta_1 \ln M_j + \beta_2 \ln D_{ij} - \ln \left(\sum_{j=1}^{m} (M_j^{\beta_1} D_{ij}^{\beta_2}) \right) \tag{5a}$$

or

$$1/m \sum_{j=1}^{m} \ln p_{ij} = \beta_1/m \sum_{j=1}^{m} \ln M_j + \beta_2/m \sum_{j=1}^{m} \ln D_{ij}$$

or

$$- 1/m \sum_{j=1}^{m} \ln \left(\sum_{j=1}^{m} (M_j^{\beta_1} D_{ij}^{\beta_2}) \right)$$

or

$$\ln \left(\overline{\prod_{j=1}^{m}} p_{ij} \right)^{1/m} = \beta_1 \ln \left(\overline{\prod_{j=1}^{m}} M_j \right)^{1/m} + \beta_2 \ln \left(\overline{\prod_{j=1}^{m}} D_{ij} \right)^{1/m}$$

$$- m/m \ln \left(\sum_{j=1}^{m} (M_j^{\beta_1} D_{ij}^{\beta_2}) \right)$$

or

$$\ln \hat{p}_i = \beta_1 \ln \hat{M} + \beta_2 \ln \hat{D}_i - \ln \left(\sum_{j=1}^{m} (M_j^{\beta_1} D_{ij}^{\beta_2}) \right) \tag{5b}$$

Subtracting (5b) from (5a) yields:

$$\ln (p_{ij}/\hat{p}_i) = \beta_1 \ln (M_j/\hat{M}) + \beta_2 \ln (D_{ij}/\hat{D}_i) \tag{5}$$

where:

$$\hat{p}_i = \left(\overline{\prod_{j=1}^{m}} p_{ij} \right)^{1/m}$$

$$\hat{M} = (\prod_{j=1}^{m} M_j)^{1/m}$$

$$\hat{D}_i = (\prod_{j=1}^{m} D_{ij})^{1/m}.$$

Huff (9) first proposed the use of Eq. (2) to model the consumer choice behavior in the selection of stores. His model suggests that the probability (p_{ij}) of consumers in region i (i, $i = 1, 2, \ldots, n$) choosing a particular retail facility j (j, $j = 1, 2, \ldots, m$) is in proportion to the ratio of their utility to disutility derived from the facility. More formally, the model states:

$$p_{ij} = (\text{Utility})(\text{Disutility})^{-1} \tag{6}$$

The utility and disutility of retail facilities emanate from two sets of characteristics:

1. The characteristics which are independent of the consumer's point of origin such as sales area in the store, quality of product and service, in-store convenience level, etc.
2. The characteristics which are dependent on the consumer's point of origin such as the distance (or travel time) involved in getting from a consumer's travel base i to a given retail facility j.

The relevant characteristics may include categorical—presence or absence of certain characteristics (e.g., location in a shopping plaza, type of the store—independent or chain store) and inverval scaled information (e.g., number of aisles in the store, size of the parking lot). Extending Eq. (4), the consumer's choice from among m alternative stores may be described as follows:

$$p_{ij} = (\prod_{k=1}^{q} A_{kj}^{\beta_k}) \cdot (\prod_{e=1}^{r} B_{eij}^{\beta_e}) / \prod_{j=1}^{m} [(\prod_{k=1}^{q} A_{kj}^{\beta_k}) \cdot (\prod_{e=1}^{r} B_{eij}^{\beta_e})] \tag{7}$$

where,

$i = 1, 2, \ldots, n$ and $j = 1, 2, \ldots, m$

p_{ij} = The probability that a customer at location i will shop at retail facility j

A_{kj} = The k-th attribute of the retail facility j which is *independent* of the consumer's point of origin; $k = 1, \ldots, q$

B_{eij} = The e-th attribute of the retail facility j which is *dependent* on the consumer's point of origin i, $e = 1, 2, \ldots, r$

β_k, β_e = Empirically determined parameters which reflect the sensitivity of the retail outlet characteristics on the probability to shop at a particular store.

The MCI model, Eq. (7), can be calibrated by least squares methods using the following log-transformed-centered form of Eq. (7):

$$\ln (p_{ij}/\hat{p}_i) = \sum_{k=1}^{q} \beta_k \ln (A_{kj}/\hat{A}_k) + \sum_{e=1}^{r} \beta_e \ln (B_{eij}/\hat{B}_{ei})$$

$$= \sum_{k=1}^{q} \beta_k Z_{kj} + \sum_{e=1}^{r} \beta_e Z_{eij}$$

(8)

where,

$\hat{p}_i = (\prod_{j=1}^{m} p_{ij})^{1/m}$ = Geometric mean of the probabilities of consumer in point of origin i shopping at m retail facilities

$\hat{A}_k = (\prod_{j=1}^{m} A_{kj})^{1/m}$ = Geometric mean of k-th attribute of m retail facilities which is independent of the consumer's point of origin

$\hat{B}_{ei} = (\prod_{j=1}^{m} B_{eij})^{1/m}$ = Geometric mean of e-th attribute of m retail facilities which is dependent on the consumer's point of origin

Z_{kj} $= \ln (A_{kj}/\hat{A}_k)$

Z_{eij} $= \ln (B_{eij}/\hat{B}_{ei})$.

As discussed by Mahajan and Jain (20), the calibration of Eq. (7) by means of Eq. (8) although intuitively appealing and operationally simple, may pose two serious computational problems for the analyst. First, if consumers from any region i ($i = 1, 2, \ldots , n$) do not shop at a retail facility j ($j = 1, 2, \ldots , m$) the resulting p_{ij} and the geometric mean, $\hat{p}_i$, for the region will be equal to zero. In such an event, the transformation of the ratio $p_{ij}/\hat{p}_i$ will not be possible for parameter estimation. The popular approach of discarding the corresponding observations may result in reduction of the total number of observations which may effect the magnitude and sign of the estimated parameters (Johnson, 21; Young and Young, 22). This warrants extreme care in sample selection and study design to ensure that the data closely approximates the market conditions. The reduction in the degrees of freedom caused by discarding of observations may be compensated by increasing the number of origins (n) in the study. Second, the multiplicative character of the model requires that all the explanatory variables be coded as interval or ratio-scaled. This excludes the use of variables in the model which can only be assigned values of zero or one to reflect their absence or presence in the environment being analyzed. The use of such variables in the model will make their geometric mean, $\hat{A}_k$ or $\hat{B}_{ei}$, zero and log transformation of their ratio, $A_{kj}/\hat{A}_k$ or $B_{eij}/\hat{B}_{ei}$, undefined and parameter estimation impossible.

Nakanishi, Cooper and Kassarjian (23) have proposed the following transformation to handle the binary variables in the model Eq. (8):

A. $B_{eij} = m/C_{ei}$ if the retail facility j patronized by consumers at region i possess the characteristic e

$= (1 - C_{ei}/m)$, otherwise

Where, C_{ei} is the number of retail facilities among the m facilities patronized by consumers at region i which possess the characteristic e.

B. $A_{kj} = m/C_k$ if the retail facility j possesses the characteristic k

$= (1 - C_k/m)$, otherwise

Where, C_k is the total number of retail facilities among the m facilities which possess the characteristic k.

Mahajan and Jain (20) have evaluated exponential transformation, likert scale and the above transformation by Nakanishi, et al., and demonstrated that all three will yield the same values of the standardized beta coefficients in Eq. (8) for a data structure. This paper will use exponential transformation to convert binary variables, i.e.,

$$x_{kj} = \exp(A_{kj})$$

or

$x_{kj} = \exp(1) = e$, if facility j possesses attribute k $(A_{kj} = 1)$
$= 1$, otherwise

Furthermore, as derived in Mahajan and Jain (20) the log transformed-centered term in Eq. (8) of such a binary variable is

$Z_{kj} = (1 - C_k/m)$, if facility j possesses attribute k
$= - (C_k/m)$, otherwise

Where, C_k is the number of facilities that possesses attribute k.

III. MARKET SHARE MODEL FOR FOOD RETAILING

Data for this study was generated from the suburb of a large northeastern metropolitan area. According to the recent census reports, the region has 14,671 households with an average 3.45 members per household. The region is predominantly white and the approximate annual median family income in the region is $11,000. Five supermarket chains operate 18 stores in the region.

In order to determine the household market-share distribution across these stores and obtain store image information, the area was divided into 23 subblocks according to the traffic patterns. Using a Haines directory, which lists telephone numbers by street address, a random sample of 300 households was drawn. Trained interviewers conducted telephone interviews with the selected population. During the course of the interview, the respondents were asked to provide, among other information, the name of the store they go to for most of their grocery shopping. Next, information about characteristics of the stores patronized by the sample was obtained through a survey. The particular characteristics considered in the survey included the dimensions of store image, layout, appearance, accessibility, service, and employee composition. A brief discussion of these follows:

A. *Store Image*. Store image is the "personality" a store represents to the public—a complex of meanings and relationships serving to characterize the store for people. It summarizes the information that consumers have about the store and its characteristics, their feelings toward it, and of any other impressions of the store which they have formed over time as shoppers. The image that a store projects has considerable impact on the shopping decisions of the consumers, the more favorable the store image the more likely are the consumers to shop and buy in a particular store (Doyle and Fenwick, 24).

B. *Layout*. The layout of a store refers to the number and placement of display tables and counters, location of various types of merchandise in the outlet, and allocation of space to selling and nonselling area. It affects customer patronage by making the store an attractive, inviting, and convenient place to shop. The studies by Super Market Institute and retail trade journals (Kotler, 2; *Progressive Grocer,* 25, 26) indicate that layout of supermarkets has great influence on their sales and profit performance.

C. *Appearance*. The appearance of a store often sells it. It suggests what a customer might expect from the store. It typifies the spirit of the organization, nature of the activity, and stability and performance of the organization. An attractive front and exterior creates confidence and goodwill among customers (Duncan, 3). An attractive interior serves as an invitation to customers to explore the facilities inside the store, search for new and different items and spend longer time within the store.

D. *Accessibility*. An important feature of any location is the volume, nature and flow of traffic past the site. The greater the number of passers-by the better, since a convenient location ordinarily is very important to consumers. Sites which are highly visible and convenient to turn into enhance the prospects of customer patronage.

E. *Service*. Services are nonprice devices used to help the retailer differentiate his offerings in order to achieve higher sales and thereby maintain a certain segment of the market. Customer services are an important part of retailing because they can so powerfully affect customer patronage. Indeed, when the products and prices among retailers are not strongly differentiated,

competition among retailers is quickly reduced to which of them can offer
the service mix that is most appropriate for a particular market segment.

F. *Employee Composition*. Employees of a store are the first point of contact
between the store and its customers. Shoppers tend to form impressions
about the store on the basis of their assessment of the employees. A
favorable impression of the employees by customers would increase the
prospect of continued patronage of the store.

Table 1 lists the particular variables used to measure the various dimensions of
store characteristics. The distance from the center of each block to the various
stores using city-block metric provided the average distance traveled by a household to the patronized store.

The survey revealed that one particular chain dominates in the region and
holds 54 percent of the household market through seven independent locations.
Two of the supermarket chains hold household share of 20 percent each through a
total of ten independent locations. The balance of the household market is
equally divided between two chains. On the average, the stores in the region have
a sales area of 20,612 square feet, approximately eleven aisles and eight checkout counters. Table 2 gives the coefficient of variation (standard deviation ÷
mean) for the store characteristics across the eighteen stores. A high value of
coefficient of variation indicates greater differences across the store on the given

Table 1. Characteristics of Stores

Dimension	Variable
I Store Image	1. Consumers' perception of product freshness, variety and quality**
	2. Consumers' perception of product prices**
	3. Consumers' perception of store service levels (e.g., friendliness of the personnel, store cleanliness, ease of checking out, etc.)**
II Layout	4. Sales area (square feet)
	5. Number of aisles
	6. Number of checkout counters
III Appearance	7. Inside appearance**
	8. Outside appearance**
IV Accessibility	9. Location at an intersection*
V Service	10. Credit card service*
	11. Personal check cashing service*
	12. Maintains a deli counter*
	13. Maintains a meat counter*
VI Employee Composition	14. Predominantly white employees*
	15. Predominantly black employees*

*Ceded as 1 or 0 to indicate the presence or absence of the attribute.
**Evaluated on a five-point scale with a value of 1 indicating high evaluation and the value 5
indicating low evaluation.

characteristics. Values in the table indicate that the eighteen stores in the region
tend to predominantly differ in terms of:

   i. location at an intersection,
  ii. sales area,
 iii. credit card service,
 iv. number of checker counters, and
  v. number of aisles.

The table indicates that appearance and image differences across the stores are
not very predominant. Furthermore, all the stores provide personal check-
cashing service, maintain a deli and meat counter and have predominantly white
employees.

In order to model the competitive environment in the region and explain the
variation in the market-share distribution across the stores, the MCI model, Eq.
(8), was calibrated using the characteristics which differentiated the stores most
as given above along with the distances from blocks to the stores. The explicit
assumption here is that since MCI is a consumer choice model, the differences in
the market shares across the stores are attributable to the characteristics on which
stores differ. This assumption does not imply that other characteristics are not
important. All that is being suggested is that among all the characteristics,
irrespective of their importance to consumers, only the characteristics on which
stores differ should be relevant in the selection of a store by a consumer, affecting the market share distribution at the aggregate level. This approach is similar
to the approach suggested by Zeleny (27) in the development of Attribute-
Dynamic Attitude Model (Mahajan and Jain et al., 28).

The Ordinary Least Squares results for Eq. (8) are:

$$\ln\left(\frac{p_{ij}}{\hat{p}_i}\right) = \beta_0 + \beta_1 \ln\left(\frac{S_{ij}}{\hat{S}_i}\right) + \beta_2 \ln\left(\frac{D_{ij}}{\hat{D}_i}\right)$$

$$+ \beta_3 \ln\left(\frac{H_{ij}}{\hat{H}_i}\right) + \beta_4 Z_{i1j} + \beta_5 Z_{i2j}$$

(9)

where,

   p_{ij} = Market share of the j-th store in block i
   S_{ij} = Sales area (in square feet) of the j-th store patronized by the
            residents in block i
   D_{ij} = Distance of the j-th store from i-th block
   H_{ij} = Number of the checkout counters in the j-th store patronized by
            the residents in block i
   Z_{i1j} = $(1 - C_{il}/m_i)$, if the j-th store patronized by the residents of
            block i offers credit card services
           = $-(C_{il}/m_i)$, otherwise.
            Here m_i is total number of stores patronized by the residents of

the i-th block and

Cil is the number of stores that offer credit-card services.

Z_{i2j} $= (1 - C_{i2}/m_i)$, if the j-th store patronized by the residents in block i is located at an intersection

$= - (C_{i2}/m_i)$, otherwise.

C_{i2} is the number of stores that are located at an intersection among the m_i stores patronized by the residents of the i-th block

$\hat{P}_i, \hat{S}_i,$
$\hat{D}_i, \hat{H}_i$ = Geometric means as defined earlier in Eq. (8)

β_0 = 0.554
β_1 = 0.021
β_2 = −0.298
β_3 = 0.086
β_4 = 0.557
β_5 = 0.256

From Eq (9), predicted market share is given by:

$$p_{ij} = \frac{\exp\left[\begin{array}{c} \beta_0 + \beta_1 \ln\left(\frac{S_{ij}}{\hat{S}_i}\right) + \beta_2 \ln\left(\frac{D_{ij}}{\hat{D}_i}\right) \\ + \beta_3 \ln\left(\frac{H_{ij}}{\hat{H}_i}\right) + \beta_4 Z_{i1j} + \beta_5 Z_{i2j} \end{array}\right]}{\sum_{j=1}^{m} \exp\left[\begin{array}{c} \beta_0 + \beta_1 \ln\left(\frac{S_{ij}}{\hat{S}_i}\right) + \beta_2 \ln\left(\frac{D_{ij}}{\hat{D}_i}\right) \\ + \beta_3 \ln\left(\frac{H_{ij}}{\hat{H}_i}\right) + \beta_4 Z_{i1j} + \beta_5 Z_{i2j} \end{array}\right]} \quad (10)$$

The correlation coefficient between the market share predicted by Eq. (10) and the observed is 0.70 (significant at $\alpha = 0.01$ level). The Eq. (10) models the competitive environment. This model may be used now to simulate the effect of competitive marketing strategies on the market share shifts.

IV. MARKET SHARE SHIFTS UNDER COMPETITORS STRATEGY

The market share model, Eq. (10), provides a vehicle to examine the effects of alternative strategies, in terms of the explanatory variables used in the model, of different competitors. Particularly, this model can assist a new entering firm in the market in selecting a marketing strategy for maximizing penetration in the trading area. Not only can the firm obtain information about the market share it can capture from different blocks, the firm can also forecast the market share of its competitors as well as the sources of its gain in the market under the existing and anticipated competition. We will now illustrate the application of the model, Eq. (10), and its usefulness in developing a competitive strategy for a specific case.

In the region studied in this report, a new supermarket chain is planning to open a store at a preselected location at an intersection. It is anticipated that the new supermarket would present a direct competition to the largest existing supermarket chain in the region. Furthermore, it is anticipated that to be competitive, the new store will have to adopt the strategy of the existing stores in terms of employee composition, convenience and personal check-cashing service (see Tables 1 and 2). Since all the supermarkets in the region are very competitive and image conscious (as shown by the low values of the coefficient of variation of image variables in Table 2), the new store plans to develop a competitive image and thereby position itself near all other stores.

In order to determine an optimal competitive strategy in terms of the variables that differentiate the existing supermarkets and to forecast the market share shifts, 18 different marketing strategies for the new store were developed and their effects simulated using the model, Eq. (10). These eighteen strategies are given in Table 3 and the respective forecast market-share shifts are presented in Tables 4, 5, and 6.

The three values for the sales area and checkout counters selected for simulating competitive strategies represent the average values for all supermarkets in the region (20612/8), the value for the largest competitor in the region (22586/11), and average values for the stores of the new chain in the region they are coming from (32000/15).

Table 2.   Characteristic Variation Across Stores

Variable*	Coefficient of Variation
Location at an intersection	0.73
Sales area	0.59
Credit-card service	0.36
Number of checkout counters	0.34
Number of aisles	0.32
Outside appearance	0.23
Inside appearance	0.18
Consumers' perception of product prices	0.16
Consumers' perception of store service levels	0.13
Consumers' perception of product freshness, variety and quality	0.11
Personal check-cashing service	0.00
Maintains a deli counter	0.00
Maintains a meat counter	0.00
Predominantly black employees	0.00
Predominantly white employees	0.00

*Variables are listed in the decreasing magnitude of the coefficient of variation.

Table 3. Alternative Simulated Strategies

Strategy	Sales Area (sq. ft.)	Number of Checkout Counters	Credit-Card Service	Location at an Intersection
I	32,000	15	Yes	Yes
II	32,000	15	No	Yes
III	32,000	8	Yes	Yes
IV	32,000	8	No	Yes
V	32,000	11	Yes	Yes
VI	32,000	11	No	Yes
VII	20,612	15	Yes	Yes
VIII	20,612	15	No	Yes
IX	20,612	8	Yes	Yes
X	20,612	8	No	Yes
XI	20,612	11	Yes	Yes
XII	20,612	11	No	Yes
XIII	22,586	15	Yes	Yes
XIV	22,586	15	No	Yes
XV	22,586	8	Yes	Yes
XVI	22,586	8	No	Yes
XVII	22,586	11	Yes	Yes
XVIII	22,586	11	No	Yes

The simulated market share for the new store under the eighteen strategies for the 23 blocks in the region are presented in Table 4. The following evaluative remarks about the strategies can be made:

A. The store is expected to capture the within block highest market share from the block in which the location is planned, i.e., block 10. Furthermore, the distance effect is also reflected in other neighborly blocks, viz., 8, 9, and 11. The within block market share for the furthest block, i.e., block 17, is negligible.

B. The effect of credit-card service is very consistent across all the blocks. The strategies with no credit-card service consistently yield lower within block market share when the values of other variables are held constant. This is evident from a comparison of projected market shares between strategies I and II, III and IV, and so on across the 23 blocks. This suggests that the new store, to be competitive, should offer this service.

C. A comparison among strategies I, III and V; strategies II, IV, and VI; strategies VII, IX and XI; strategies VII, X, and XII; strategies XIII, XV and bxvii; and strategies XIV, XVI, and XVIII indicates that in general higher number of checkout counters contribute to higher within block market shares. Strategies with the highest number of checkout counters yield the largest within block market share.

D. In terms of the sales area the results in Table 4 suggest that higher sales area in general do not necessarily yield significantly larger within block

Table 4. Simulated Market Share for the New Store

Strategy												Blocks											
	1	2	3	4	5	6	7	8	9	10	11	12	13	14	15	16	17	18	19	20	21	22	23
I	.12	.06	.10	.10	.24	.15	.09	.38	.42	.63	.44	.13	.09	.11	.02	.08	.01	.1	.11	.08	.08	.04	.08
II	.11	.04	.05	.09	.20	.15	.09	.36	.37	.59	.41	.12	.08	.08	.00	.06	.00	.05	.09	.08	.02	.01	.05
III	.11	.05	.08	.09	.22	.14	.08	.35	.40	.60	.42	.11	.08	.09	.00	.07	.00	.08	.10	.07	.06	.03	.07
IV	.10	.02	.03	.08	.17	.13	.08	.34	.34	.57	.40	.10	.07	.07	.00	.04	.00	.02	.07	.06	.00	.00	.03
V	.12	.05	.09	.09	.23	.14	.08	.36	.41	.62	.43	.12	.08	.10	.01	.08	.00	.09	.10	.08	.07	.04	.07
VI	.11	.03	.04	.07	.18	.14	.08	.35	.35	.58	.40	.11	.08	.08	.00	.05	.00	.04	.08	.07	.01	.00	.04
VII	.13	.07	.11	.10	.25	.15	.09	.38	.43	.63	.45	.13	.09	.11	.02	.09	.02	.11	.12	.09	.05	.09	.12
VIII	.12	.05	.07	.10	.21	.15	.09	.37	.39	.51	.42	.12	.09	.09	.01	.07	.00	.06	.10	.08	.03	.02	.06
IX	.12	.05	.09	.09	.23	.14	.08	.36	.41	.61	.43	.12	.09	.10	.01	.08	.00	.09	.10	.08	.07	.04	.07
X	.10	.03	.04	.09	.19	.14	.08	.35	.35	.58	.40	.11	.08	.07	.00	.05	.00	.04	.08	.07	.01	.00	.04
XI	.12	.06	.10	.10	.24	.15	.09	.38	.42	.62	.44	.12	.09	.11	.02	.09	.01	.10	.11	.08	.08	.04	.08
XII	.11	.04	.05	.09	.20	.14	.08	.36	.37	.58	.41	.12	.08	.08	.00	.06	.00	.05	.09	.08	.02	.01	.05
XIII	.12	.05	.09	.09	.23	.14	.08	.36	.41	.62	.43	.12	.08	.10	.01	.08	.01	.09	.10	.08	.07	.04	.07
XIV	.11	.03	.04	.08	.19	.14	.08	.35	.35	.58	.41	.11	.08	.08	.00	.05	.03	.04	.08	.07	.01	.00	.04
XV	.10	.04	.08	.08	.21	.13	.08	.34	.39	.60	.41	.11	.07	.08	.00	.06	.00	.07	.09	.07	.05	.02	.06
XVI	.09	.01	.02	.07	.16	.12	.07	.33	.32	.56	.39	.09	.07	.06	.00	.03	.00	.01	.06	.06	.00	.00	.02
XVII	.11	.05	.08	.09	.22	.14	.09	.35	.40	.61	.42	.11	.08	.09	.01	.07	.00	.08	.10	.07	.06	.03	.07
XVIII	.10	.02	.03	.08	.17	.13	.08	.35	.33	.57	.40	.10	.07	.07	.00	.04	.00	.02	.07	.06	.00	.00	.03

Table 5. Market Share Aggregate in the Trading Area

Strategy	Store 1	2	4	6	9	50	51	12	16	18	21	22	23	52	53	29	30	36	New Store
I	.0429	.0115	.0303	.0499	.0104	.2157	.1604	.0151	.0509	.0938	.0132	.0148	.0025	.0994	.0152	.0000	.0299	.0219	.1225
II	.0454	.0095	.0311	.0533	.0105	.2286	.1668	.0144	.0500	.0936	.0124	.0140	.0020	.1003	.0162	.0000	.0252	.0221	.1048
III	.0435	.0119	.0307	.0503	.0106	.2189	.1624	.0153	.0517	.0952	.0135	.0150	.0026	.1010	.0155	.0001	.0307	.0222	.1088
IV	.0460	.0100	.0313	.0539	.0105	.2327	.1695	.0147	.0510	.0952	.0127	.0142	.0021	.1024	.0163	.0000	.026	.0224	.0892
V	.0432	.0117	.0305	.0501	.0105	.2173	.1512	.0152	.0513	.0945	.0133	.0149	.0025	.1002	.0153	.0001	.0303	.0221	.1157
VI	.0457	.0098	.0312	.0536	.0105	.2307	.1682	.0145	.0505	.0944	.0125	.0141	.0020	.1013	.0163	.0000	.0256	.0222	.0969
VII	.0426	.0115	.0302	.0495	.0104	.2140	.1590	.0150	.0506	.0932	.0131	.0147	.0025	.0987	.0151	.0000	.0298	.0218	.1282
VIII	.0450	.0095	.0309	.0529	.0104	.2261	.1654	.0143	.0496	.0930	.0123	.0139	.0020	.0994	.0160	.0000	.0251	.0220	.1122
IX	.0432	.0118	.0305	.0500	.0105	.2172	.1612	.0153	.0514	.0947	.0134	.0150	.0026	.1004	.0153	.0002	.0307	.0221	.1147
X	.0456	.0100	.0312	.0535	.0105	.2303	.1681	.0146	.0507	.0946	.0126	.0142	.0021	.1015	.0163	.0000	.0260	.0223	.0960
XI	.0429	.0117	.0303	.0498	.0105	.2156	.1601	.0151	.0510	.0939	.0133	.0148	.0025	.0995	.0152	.0001	.0302	.0220	.1216
XII	.0454	.0097	.0311	.0532	.0105	.2282	.1667	.0145	.0501	.0938	.0124	.0141	.0020	.1004	.0162	.0000	.0256	.0221	.1039
XIII	.0432	.0116	.0305	.0502	.0105	.2175	.1613	.0152	.0512	.0944	.0133	.0149	.0025	.1001	.0154	.0000	.0302	.0221	.1160
XIV	.0458	.0097	.0312	.0537	.0105	.2310	.1683	.0145	.0504	.0943	.0125	.0140	.0020	.1012	.0163	.0000	.0254	.0222	.0970
XV	.0438	.0120	.0308	.0506	.0106	.2207	.1635	.0154	.0520	.0958	.0136	.0151	.0026	.1018	.0156	.0002	.0310	.0224	.1028
XVI	.0463	.0101	.0314	.0543	.0105	.2351	.1709	.0148	.0514	.0958	.0128	.0143	.0021	.1033	.0163	.0000	.0263	.0225	.0818
XVII	.0435	.0118	.0307	.0504	.0106	.2191	.1624	.0153	.0516	.0951	.0134	.0150	.0025	.1010	.0155	.0001	.0306	.0222	.1892
XVIII	.0460	.0099	.0313	.0540	.0105	.2330	.1696	.0147	.0509	.0950	.0126	.0142	.0020	.1023	.0163	.0000	.0259	.0223	.0894
Present Share	.0400	.0100	.0100	.0600	.0100	.2400	.1900	.0100	.0500	.1100	.0100	.0400	.0100	.1100	.0100	.0300	.0500	.0300	

Table 6. Market Share Shifts Within Block Number 8

Strategy	Store 8	Store 16	New Store
Prior	0.80	0.20	0.0
I	.41	0.21	0.38
II	.39	0.25	0.36
III	0.42	0.23	0.35
IV	0.40	.26	0.34
V	0.42	0.22	0.36
VI	0.40	0.25	0.35
VII	0.41	0.21	0.38
VIII	0.39	0.24	0.37
IX	0.42	0.22	0.36
X	0.40	0.25	0.35
XI	0.40	.22	.38
XII	0.40	0.24	.36
XIII	.42	.22	.36
XIV	0.40	.25	.35
XV	.43	.23	.34
XVI	.41	.26	.33
XVII	.43	.22	.35
XVIII	.40	.25	.35

market share. In fact, if the new store decides to keep the sales area at the average value of the existing stores, i.e., 20,612 squre feet, it can do as good if not better if it builds a store with the sales area of 32,000 square feet. (The average value of the sales area of the new chain in the region in which it is currently operating.)

To summarize, the simulated within block market shares for the new store in Table 4 suggests that the competitive strategy for the new store should consist of a sales area of 20,612 square feet, fifteen checkout counters and credit-card services. This further suggests that, in this particular region, the convenience offered at the stores in terms of services contribute more to the market share than the size of the store.

Table 5 gives the aggregate market shares of the existing 18 stores and the new store under the eighteen different marketing strategies. Again a comparison of the strategies indicates that the optimal strategy for the new store is strategy VII which consists of a sales area of 20,612 square feet, fifteen checkout counters, and credit-card services. The stores least affected by the strategies of the new store are the ones located farther away from it. The stores located within the blocks neighboring the site of the new store are most affected as reflected in the market share shifts in Table 5.

With the help of the model, Eq. (10), it is also possible to simulate the market-share shifts across the stores within a block. For example, Table 6 gives the market share shifts within block 8 across the eighteen marketing strategies.

The results indicate that the new store is capturing most of its market share from store 8. In fact, store 8 loses almost 50 percent of its within block market share to the new store. The store 16, by and large, maintains its market share with a slight gain under the strategies in which the new store does not offer credit-card services.

V. CONCLUSIONS

Competition in the market is an important facet of retailing. It is a real problem that retailers must face and accept as part of their operation. The firm which shows a lack of understanding and assessment of its competitive environment usually finds itself struggling for existence. It is not sufficient for a firm to collect information about its competitors and the environment. It has to continuously evaluate the information and develop competitive strategies. Development of competitive strategies is particularly important in site selection since such decisions are long term decisions and any errors made may result in undesirable consequences.

This paper has proposed the utilization of MCI model to model competition in food retailing. A systematic method of selecting variables to be included in the model was proposed and a simulation approach was used for selecting an optimal strategy. The proposed procedure would enable the management in examining the market-share shifts under varying market strategies. Although the example discussed in the paper was for a new entering firm, its application for the existing firms to evaluate the impact of their own strategies and the anticipated strategies of their competitors are obvious.

REFERENCES

1. Kotler, Philip, (1971), *Marketing Decision Making: A Model Building Approach,* New York: Holt, Rinehart and Winston.
2. _____ (1965), "Competitive Strategies for New Product Marketing Over the Life Cycle," *Management Science*: 104–119 (December).
3. Duncan, D. J., and Hollander, S. C. (1977), *Modern Retailing Management: Basic Concepts and Practices,* Homewood, Ill.: Richard D. Irwin.
4. Stern, Louis W., and El-Ansary Adel I. (1977), *Marketing Channels,* Englewood Cliffs, N.J.: Prentice-Hall.
5. Openshaw, S. (1975), *Some Theoretical and Applied Aspects of Spatial Interaction Shopping Models,* London: The Institute of British Geographers.
6. Nakanishi, M. (1976), "A New Technique for Forecasting New Store Sales," *Proceedings,* Fall Conference, American Marketing Association, pp. 224–229.
7. Applebaum, William, (1968), *Guide to Store Location Research with Emphasis on Supermarkets,* Reading, Mass.: Addison-Wesley.
8. Green, Howard L., and Applebaum, William (1976), "The Status of Computer Applications to Store Location Research," *AIDC Journal* 11: 33–52 (April).
9. Huff, David L. (1963), "A Probabilistic Analysis of Consumer Spatial Behavior," in William S. Decker, ed., *Emerging Concepts in Marketing,* Chicago: American Marketing Association, pp. 443–461.

10. _____, and Batsell, Richard L. (1976), "Conceptual Operational Problems with Market Share Models of Consumer Spatial Behavior," in Mary J. Schlinger, ed., *Advances in Consumer Research,* Vol. 2, Chicago: Association for Consumer Research, pp. 165–172.
11. Haines, George H., Simon, Leonard S., and Alexis, Marcus A. (1972), "Maximum Likelihood Estimation of Central City Food Trading Areas," *Journal of Marketing Research* 9: 154–159 (May).
12. Hlavac, T. E., Jr., and Little, J. D. C. (1966). "A Geographic Model of an Automobile Market," Working Paper 180–66, Cambridge: Alfred P. Sloan School of Management, Massachusetts Institute of Technology.
13. Lalond, Bernard J. (1962), "Differentials in Supermarket Drawing Power," Marketing and Transportation Paper 11, East Lansing, Mich.: Bureau of Business and Economic Research, Michigan State University.
14. Mahajan, Vijay, Jain, Arun K., and Bergier, Michel (1977), "Parameter Estimation in Marketing Models in the Presence of Multicollinearity: An Application of Ridge Regression," *Journal of Marketing Research* 14: 586–591 (November).
15. Stanley, Thomas J., and Sewall, Murphy A. (1976). "Image Inputs to Probabilistic Model: Predicting Retail Potential," *Journal of Marketing* 40: 48–53 (July).
16. Teekens, R. (1972), *Prediction Methods in Multiplicative Models.* The Netherlands: Rotterdam University Press.
17. Nakanishi, M., and Cooper, L. G. (1974), "Parameter Estimate for Multiplicative Competitive Interactive Model—Least Squares Approach," *Journal of Marketing Research* 11: 303–311 (August).
18. Mahajan, Vijay, Jain, Arun K., and Ratchford, Brian T. (1978), "Use of Binary Attributes in the Multiplicative Competitive Interactive Choice Model," *Journal of Consumer Research* 5: 210–215 (December).
19. Muller, John E. (1970), "Choosing Among 133 Candidates," *Public Opinion Quarterly* 34: 395–402 (Fall).
20. Mahajan, Vijay, and Jain, Arun K. (1977), "An Examination of Operational Problems with Multiplicative Competitive Interactive Model," in Barnett A. Greenberg and Danny N. Bellenger, eds., *Contemporary Marketing Thought,* Chicago: American Marketing Association, pp. 319–323.
21. Johnston, J. (1963), *Econometric Methods,* New York: McGraw-Hill.
22. Young, Han H., and Young, Lin Y. (1975), "Estimation of Regressions Involving Logarithmic Transformation of Zero Values in the Dependent Variables," *The American Statistician* 29: 118–120 (August).
23. Nakanishi, M., Cooper, L. G., and Kassarjian, H. H. (1974), "Voting for a Political Candidate under Conditions of Minimal Information," *Journal of Consumer Research* 1: 36–43 (September).
24. Doyle, P., and Fenwick, I. (1974), "How Store Image Affects Shopping Habits in Grocery Chains," *Journal of Retailing* 50: 39–52 (Winter).
25. "Super Markets of the 70's" (1969), *Progressive Grocer*: 58 (July).
26. "How Customers Shop the Super Market" (1960), *Progressive Grocer*: 50 (August).
27. Zeleny, M. (1976), "The Attribute-Dynamic Attitude Model (ADAM)," *Management Science* 23: 12–26 (September).
28. Mahajan, Vijay, Jain, Arun K., Thangaraj, A., Ravichandran, B., and Acito, F. (1977), "An Experiment with the Attribute-Dynamic Attitude Model (ADAM)," *Proceedings,* The Fourth International Research Seminar, Sennaque Abbey, Gordes, France (May).

THE PARAMETRIC MARGINAL DESIRABILITY MODEL*

John F. McElwee, Jr., UNIVERSITY OF LAVERNE

Leonard J. Parsons, GEORGIA INSTITUTE OF

TECHNOLOGY

INTRODUCTION

The Parametric Marginal Desirability Model is a member of the family of adequacy-importance, compositional, multi-attribute models of brand preference. Specifically, the PMD Model employs a dual ideal point concept on the belief continuum of each brand's attribute belief measurements. The most unique feature of the PMD Model is the use of a function of the purchase importance of the product to parametrically modify the model specification as applied to different products.

Research in Marketing—Volume 2, 1979, pages 237–257.
Copyright © 1979 by JAI Press Inc.
All rights of reproduction in any form reserved.

Since the PMD Model is part of the adequacy-importance family, the basic model is of the class

$$A_{jk} = \frac{1}{n} \sum_{i=1}^{n} I_{ij} B_{ijk} \qquad (1)$$

where

A_{jk} = attitude of consumer j toward brand k,

I_{ij} = importance weight given to attribute i by consumer j,

B_{ijk} = belief by consumer j as to the extent to which attribute i is offered by brand k, and

n = number of salient attributes.

This formulation assumes that judgements are averaged (Troutman and Shanteau, 1976). To describe the specific PMD Model requires some quantitative definition of the belief scale with its two critical points and the manner in which the purchase importance is to be included.

TWO IDEAL POINTS

Belief Scale

Traditional adequacy-importance models can be described as having linear belief and importance scales. Even more basic is the use of measures of belief and importance that are non-negative. This means the higher the perceived amount of an attribute in a brand, the higher the attitude score. The fact that more of an attribute is not always more desirable has led some researchers to discard the monotonic belief scale in favor of a scale containing a global maximum or a point on the scale giving maximum satisfaction. The Parametric Marginal Desirability Model pursues the foregoing issue to its logical conclusion by including two ideal points on the belief scale to establish the presence of both the "most ideal" value and the "least ideal" value of each attribute.

The two ideal point belief continuum is constructed on the idea that a prospective buyer bases his evaluation on both attraction of a desired level of the attribute and repulsion of another undesirable level he knows the product can contain. His belief perception of a brand then becomes a function of how much of a desirable amount of the attribute he believes he will receive and how much of the undesirable level he thinks he will avoid. The attribute's contribution to the desirability of a brand can thus be made positive, zero, or negative depending upon its positioning on the belief scale. (This is one difference between the PMD Model and any model incorporating the Minkowski r metric.) There is no restriction that ideal points be at the extremes of the belief scale.

In order to avoid bias in the belief measurement, it has been found that the importance measurement should be made after a commitment is made to the belief. Wilkie and McCann (1972) proved experimentally that measuring brands within attributes was a more consistent procedure than measuring attributes within brands. In addition, they found that a pre-belief measurement statement warning respondents that their brand could not possibly be best in all attributes served to significantly reduce halo effect surrounding the measurement.

Nonlinear Coding

Elaborating on the concept of two critical belief points, the Parametric Marginal Desirabiliy Model recognizes the possibility that coding between the critical points may not be linear. Microeconomic utility theory criticizes the concept of ever increasing utility gained from increasing possession of a good. Practically, a point of saturation can be reached beyond which either no additional utility will be achieved or possibly even decreased utility will accrue. Therefore, included in the PMD Model is the recognition of changing marginal utility as a critical point on the belief continuum is approached. It is anticipated that the fashion in which the ideal points are approached on the belief continuum of each attribute will be dependent upon the particular product class being modeled.

Figure 1 shows a belief continuum where the two critical points are approached with *diminishing* marginal belief. It is hypothesized that the belief scale used by a given consumer will resemble this type of nonlinear scale for an unimportant purchase closer than it will resemble a linear scale. This response is meant to be in concert with the idea of consumer insensitivity to changes in attribute values near the ideal points for a purchase that does not really concern him. In this study, a sinusoidal function will be employed to simulate the diminishing marginal belief scale shown in Figure 1 because of its convenient mathematical form. If the belief scale is coded linearly in the variable θ measured in radians with $\theta = \pi/2$ at the ideal point and $\theta = -\pi/2$ at the least ideal point, then the scale coding will be shown. To simulate diminishing marginal belief, the belief scores are then interpreted as the sine of the value of θ given each bin on the belief scale. This process results in the belief scores shown in Figure 1. For example, a consumer showing a perceived brand belief of "6," his ideal point, would be given a belief score of 1. If his perception of the amount of attribute contained in the brand changed to "5," his brand score would change to 0.707 instead of 0.500 as in the linear case. A further change to "4" would then change his belief score to zero as in the case of a linear scale. The sine function thus simulates the concept of diminishing marginal belief for an unimportant purchase.

One maintained hypothesis in the Parametric Marginal Desirabiliy Model is that the zero point on the belief scale corresponds to the true point of indif-

Figure 1.   Belief Scale and Resultant Coding for the PMD Model with Two
Critical Points and Nonlinear Coding.

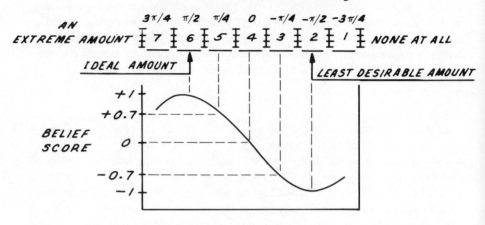

ference. Schmidt and Wilson (1975) provide a reminder that the use of a multiplicative composition rule requires existence of a rational zero point on both measures entering into the product.

Approximate Belief Scale

Henry (1975) and Henry and Zahn (1975) have commented on the difficulties of measuring the ideal point. An *approximation* of the PMD belief scale may be obtained by using a belief scale which is somewhat easier for the consumer to handle. In addition, any given transformation will yield the same values for all consumers.

However, the approximation does have important limitations. The key difference between the original model and its approximation is that the approximation implicitly weights each attribute by the reciprocal of the distance between the most ideal point and least ideal point for that attribute. Moreover, critical diagnostic information is lost. No longer is the consumer's perception of the ideal amount of an attribute or of the least ideal amount of an attribute known. The consumers' perceptions about a brand are not ambiguous. For those brands not containing an ideal amount of an attribute, it is not known whether they contain too much or too little of an attribute. Nonetheless, the approximation does allow an initial test of the PMD Model to be made.

The approximate belief scale resembles that used by Bass and Talarzyk (1971). They measure belief as Tab's caloric content is (VERY SATISFACTORY: 1 2 3 4 5 6 : VERY UNSATISFACTORY). Bass and Talarzyk assume that any belief value for an attribute will add to the aggregated attitude about that brand. Thus, there is no consideration that a particular belief value may be very undesirable to the consumer and may actually reduce the desirability of the brand to him. The PMD Model through the coding scheme discussed previously approaches the problem of attribute undesirability by a concept of belief evaluation which provides for a subtraction from overall brand desirability.

ATTRIBUTE IMPORTANCE

Measurement

Attribute importance can be measured by using the use/motive context and associated ideal attribute level approach advocated by Pessimier and Wilkie (1974). In this method, the respondent is asked to allocate among a comprehensive list of use/motive contexts the percentage of usage to which he would apply the product if he were to acquire it. Then, having allocated his use/motive contexts, he is asked to indicate the amount of each attribute he would desire in the product for each of his identified use/motive contexts. The importance score for each attribute is obtained by:

$$I_{ij} = \sum_{u=1}^{U} M_{uj} C_{iuj} \qquad (2)$$

where

I_{ij} = importance of attribute i to consumer j,
M_{uj} = percentage of time to which consumer j would apply the product to use u,
U = number of use/motive contexts identified by consumer j,
C_{iuj} = the amount of attribute i that consumer j would wish in in the product if he were to apply it to use/motive context u.

(Comparison of the use/motive context method with a simple ranking of the importance of the attributes demonstrated a high rank correlation in our study.)

The significance of the inclusion of the importance component to form an importance-belief product for each attribute as opposed to employing belief scores only is ambiguous. Some studies (Beckwith and Lehmann, 1973; Sheth and Talarzyk, 1972) have found that the inclusion of importance actually reduces the predictive ability of the model while others (Hansen, 1969; Hughes and Guerrero, 1971; Lehmann, 1971; Wilkie and Weinrich, 1973) have found the inclusion of importance to have either no effect or to actually improve the model. Therefore, the necessity for the entrance of the importance component into the model is also considered during PMD Model testing.

Number of Attributes

Empirical evidence is mixed on how many salient attributes to include; Wilkie and Weinrich (1973) found that including all salient attributes in multi-attribute models does not necessarily produce the best predictions. Nakanishi and Bettman (1974) entered the attributes into a model in the order of their importance scores and found that the inclusion of more than the first attribute did not increase the predictive ability of the model. Since the only product they examined was of the frequently purchased, low-cost variety, their conclusion was not necessarily inductive to all product classes. The PMD Model hypothesizes the inclusion of all salient attributes.

THE PURCHASE IMPORTANCE PARAMETER

The PMD Model posits that brand desirability or preference is a *function* of the sum of the importance and belief products of the attributes. The means by which the individual attribute products are combined is hypothesized as a function of the importance of a purchase in that product class to the individual consumer. Specifically, it is hypothesized that a less important purchase will result in comparatively less sensitivity to brand differences near the ideal brand. A parameter is incorporated into the PMD Model to capture the impact of differences in purchase importance across product classes.

Functional Form

The simplest functional form which possesses the properties posited by the PMD Model is a power function. Consequently, the PMD Model is specified as

$$d_{jk} = (-1)^\delta \, (|A_{jk}|)^p \qquad (3)$$

where

d_{jk} = the desirability of brand k to consumer j, $-1 \leq d_{jk} \leq 1$

A_{jk} = the total contribution by the n salient attributes to consumer j's attitude about brand k.

p = purchase importance parameter, $p \geq 0$.

δ = 1 for $A_{jk} < 0$, 0 for $A_{jk} \geq 0$.

The value A_{jk}, and consequently d_{jk}, is required to lie in the unit circle. This is guaranteed by the appropriate coding of the importance and belief scales ($0 \leq I_{ij} \leq 1$ and $-1 \leq B_{ijk} \leq 1$). The PMD Model assumes that positive and negative attitudes having the same magnitude will have equal effects except for sign. Thus the presence of the absolute value of attitude and the delta constant. The global measure of brand preference, d_{jk}, used as the criterion variable, should be interval scaled. This is achieved by employing the compared judgment or "dollar metric" method (Pessemier and Wilkie, 1974).

Figure 2 shows the effect on the brand desirability versus attitude sum as the purchase importance parameter is varied. Parameter values less than 1 decrease marginal desirability as the ideal brand desirability is approached. This characteristic is hypothesized to be typical of a less important purchase. Parameter values of 1 and greater are conversely hypothesized to be a typical of a very important purchase.

Related Theories

A behavioral basis for the Parametric Marginal Desirability Model might be sought in the approach-avoidance gradient theory of conflict put forth by Miller (1971), which itself evolved out of earlier work by Lewin and by Hull. Miller's theoretical analysis was based upon four assumptions:
   a) The tendency to approach a goal is stronger the closer an individual is to it.
   b) The tendency to go away from an object avoided is stronger the closer the object is to it.

Figure 2.   Effect of the Purchase Importance Parameter on Brand Desirability.

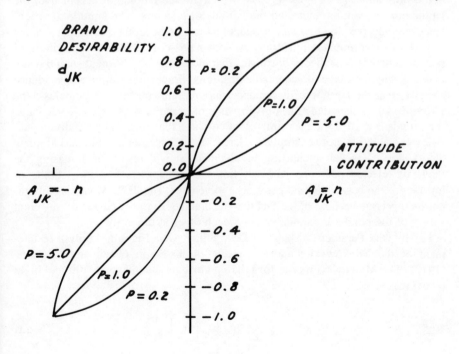

    c) The strength of avoidances increases more quickly with closeness than does that of approach.

    d) The strength of the tendencies to approach or avoid varies with the strength of the drive upon which they are based.

Miller verified these assumptions by a series of animal experiments. However, he found that the greater strength of the avoidance gradient postulated in assumption (c) was situation specific and depended upon the relative strengths of the underlying drives. The PMD Model will be consistent with this theory only for values of the purchase importance parameter greater than one. Even then, the current version of the PMD Model assumes that the basic avoidance and attraction strengths are equal. However, the PMD could be extended to relax this assumption.

The purchase importance parameter is related to the individual's involvement with the attitude object, that is, the product. Involvement describes the general level of interest in the product class. For a given product, the degree of involvement will vary among consumers. Nonetheless, the discrimination among products on the basis of the mean level of involvement with the products should be possible.

Involvement is a key concept in the social judgment theory of Sherif, Sherif, and Nebergall (1965). According to this theory the consumer's attitude toward a brand falls into one of three regions, which are the latitude of acceptance, the latitude of noncommitment, and the latitude of rejection. The latitude of acceptance contains position toward a product that is most acceptable toward a product and all other acceptance positions. All other positions fall into the latitude of noncommitment. The theory postulates that increasing involvement should result in decreasing the range of acceptable positions. Fragmentary empirical evidence suggests that the latitude of acceptance may remain constant. Nonetheless, the PMD Model implies that, for a given value of brand desirability, a lower value for attitude is needed for a less important purchase than for a more important one. A lower value for attitude implies a larger acceptance region. Social judgment theory postulates that increasing involvement should result in increasing the range of rejected positions. Indeed, this theory suggests that the latitude of rejection is the best single indicator of involvement. The PMD Model is ambiguous on this issue because of the fact that the brand desirability curves for different values of the purchase parameter cross each other at the origin.

Finally, the Parametric Marginal Desirability Model is *not* simply a restatement of the Minkowski r-metric concept discussed in Green and Carmone (1970). The Minkowski metric for relating attribute judgments to attitude might be expressed as

$$A_{jk} = \left[\sum_{i=1}^{n} |I_{ij} B_{ijk}|^{r} \right]^{1/r} \tag{4}$$

where r = Minkowski metric. Pessemier and Wilkie (1974) note that variations in r change model predictions; that is, value of r less than one give lower ratings proportionally greater weight while values of r greater than one give higher ratings proportionally greater weight in the summated index. In contrast, the PMD's purchase importance parameter p acts only on the summated index and not on individual product terms. The relative weights of the ratings remain constant regardless of the value of p.

DATA

Preliminary surveys were used for the selection of product classes, for the ascertainment of brand familiarity, and for the determination of salient attributes. The product class study revealed that U.S. compact automobiles and cola drinks were quite different in terms of purchase importance. Consequently, these two product classes were chosen for analysis. The repertory grid technique (Kelley, 1955; Frost and Braine, 1967) was used to determine salient attributes for each product class.

The main mail questionnaire was sent to 450 employees of a large private industrial organization. In this organization of 4,000 employees, approximately 3,000 were listed in the company telephone directory. The questionnaire was sent through the company's internal mail system to approximately 100 employees not listed. The 350 selected from the directory were randomly selected by the use of a table of random numbers. The 100 other employees were selected at random in a similar manner from lists of hourly employees. Of the 450 questionnaires sent out, 298 were returned, but 21 of these were either incomplete or partly incomplete and of no use to the study. Because of the large number of computations involved and in order to have a validation sample, a subset of 131 questionnaires were randomly selected for complete analysis from among the 277 usable questionnaires.

The cola drink product class was found to have four salient attributes. These attributes were sweetness, carbonation, cola flavoring, and calorie content. Six brands were selected for analysis. They were Coca Cola, RC Cola, Diet Rite, Tab, Pepsi-Cola, and Diet Pepsi. The repertory grid identified eight salient attributes for domestic compact automobiles. They were economy of operation, handling ease of traffic, styling and design, reliability, roominess, power and pickup, safety, and accessories. As in the case of the cola drink products, six brands were arbitrarily chosen for study. These brands were AMC Hornet, Dodge Dart, Ford Maverick, Chevrolet Nova, Pontiac Ventura, and Plymouth Valiant.

ANALYSIS

The analysis was conducted on the level of the individual. The global measures of brand preference given by each subject were correlated with his attitude scores toward each brand. Six brands were analyzed for each of the two chosen product classes. As a result of having only six brands for each individual to evaluate, insufficient data points were available for the correlation coefficients to be significant or reliable in most cases. However, the distribution of the correlation coefficients can be considered as an estimate of the distribution of the correlation coefficients of the population. The distribution of r's is likely to be positively skewed. Such a distribution can be transformed into an approximately normal, mound-shaped distribution of z's by use of the Fisher r to z transformation (Fisher, 1954).

The number of different specifications of the PMD Model examined was equal to the product of the number of salient attributes times the number of values of the exponent of importance times the number of codings of the belief scale times the number of values of the purchase parameter. The number of salient attributes was n, which varied across product classes. There were two values of the exponent of importance, zero or one, corresponding to the exclusion or inclusion of importance in the model. The number of codings of the belief scale was three. A cosine coding was included as well as the sine and linear codings. The purchase importance parameter was varied systematically over a wide range of values. Nine values of the parameter were picked so that the logarithm of the values would be symmetrically arrayed about zero. The specific values of the purchase importance parameter selected were 0.2, 0.4, 0.6, 0.8, 1.0, 1.25, 1.67, 2.50, and 5.00. For each product, a total of $n \times 2 \times 3 \times 9 = 54n$ correlations were calculated for each respondent.

Identification of the order in which to enter attributes was necessary. In the case of the "importance-belief" models, the attributes were entered in the order of decreasing score. In the case of the "beliefs-only" models, the belief values were entered in the order of decreasing corresponding importance. It was sometimes necessary to decide about the entering order of the attributes when equal importance scores were encountered. In those cases it was decided that ties would be broken based on the variance of the belief scores applicable to the tied attributes. The criterion of selecting tied attributes in order of decreasing belief score variance was based on the intuitive logic that a consumer would be more brand discriminating for attributes more important to him.

The analysis of these individual correlations involved three steps. For each combination of belief scale type and purchase importance value, the significance of the inclusion of increasing numbers of attributes and the significance of the inclusion of the attribute importance component was determined using two-way factorial analysis of variance with repeated measures. The repeated measures ANOVA design is described in Winer (1971). The next step was to determine if any of the nine models created by the different purchase importance parameter values were significantly better than the others. To test this significance a single-factor (parameter value) experiment having repeated measures was employed. Finally, separate analyses of variance were conducted to determine the candidate model for each belief scale specification. In order to select from the three models, a one factor (belief scale), repeated measures analysis of variance was employed. Whenever the analysis variance results indicated a significant difference on a factor containing more than two levels, each pair of levels was tested for a difference in the means. The Newman-Keuls procedure (Winer, 1971) was employed because of sample dependence.

The results of these various analyses for cola drinks were that the best PMD Model was one which included all attributes, included importance, used a sine belief scale, and had a purchase importance parameter value of 0.2. (ANOVA tables for these and other analyses reported here are available from the authors.) The mean correlation coefficient squared for this version of the PMD Model was 0.727. The null hypothesis of an importance-belief model could not be rejected in favor of a beliefs-only model. In practice, since all attributes are included, the principle of parsimony would suggest that there is no gain in collecting importance-component information.

For U.S. compact automobiles, the best PMD Model was an all-attributes, beliefs-only model with a linear belief scale and a purchase importance parameter of 0.8. The value of the mean correlation coefficient squared for this version was 0.659. The Newman-Keuls procedure revealed that the linear and sine belief scales were not significantly different from each other. A Wilcoxon matched pair signed rank test established that the linear and sine belief scales were not significantly different from each other. A Wilcoxon matched pair signed rank test established that the linear belief scale was superior. The sine scale still might be preferred since it would apply to less important purchases as well.

In determining if any of the nine models created by the different purchase importance parameter values were significantly better than the others, a single factor (parameter value) experiment having repeated measures was employed. The resultant F test statistic was 24.73 for cola drinks and 9.15 for U.S. compact cars. The Geisser and Greenhouse (1958) conservative critical F value at the 0.05 level of significance with 1 and 130 degrees of freedom is 3.91. Therefore, a significant difference in the effect of parameter values was demonstrated for both products.

PURCHASE IMPORTANCE

The PMD Model has been defined to include a parameter p which was referred to throughout the ensuing discussions as the "purchase importance parameter." Our analysis has shown that the parameter did have an effect on the model's performance and that the optimal value of the parameter varied for different product classes. The final step is to test the hypothesis that the p parameter is a function of the purchase importance of a given product class to a consumer.

A "dollar metric" approach was used to obtain a ratio-scaled global purchase importance value. As would be expected, the mean purchase importance value across the 131 subjects was greater for compact U.S. autos than for cola drinks, i.e., 17.1 for autos and -34.2 for cola drinks on a scale anchored at $+95$ and -95. The standard deviations for these two sample populations were 22.2 and 30.2, respectively.

The information available about each individual consisted essentially of two data points in p-b space, where b is the symbol for purchase importance value. Since only two data points were available, individual correlations across products were not conducted. Since the PMD Model analysis indicated that the estimate of the population p value for compact U.S. autos was greater than that for cola drinks and since the mean value of b was greater for compact U.S. autos than for cola drinks, the expected slope of a line connecting the two data points was positive. Therefore, the approach used for analysis was to calculate slopes between the two p-b data points for each individual and to form a distribution of these slopes. The analysis was then completed with a test of whether the mean of the slope distribution was significantly greater than zero.

The effect of the purchase importance parameter on the shape of the brand preference curve suggested that the relationship between p and purchase importance could be a logarithmic one instead of a linear one. The hypothesis test resulted in the rejection of the null hypothesis with .01 significance. In other words, the mean of the individual ln p vs b slopes did differ significantly from zero in a positive direction.

As a result of the analysis of this section, the parameter p, which has been previously demonstrated to have a significant effect on the performance of the PMD Model and to vary with product application, has been shown to be a function of the measure of individual purchase importance. Although p has been determined to be a significant exponential function of the purchase importance, this relationship is not necessarily the optimum one. The addition of product classes would be highly instrumental in determining the relationship between p and b.

A COMPARISON WITH OTHER MULTI-ATTRIBUTE MODELS

The performance of the Parametric Marginal Desirability Model is compared to three leading compositional, multi-attribute models of attitude structure. These models are an expectancy-value model, an adequacy-importance model with monotonic belief scales, and an adequacy-importance model employing an ideal point on the belief scale. The comparison is made on the level of the individual using correlation analysis.

The Expectancy-Value Model

The expectancy-value theory has many variations, but they are all based upon an individual's expectancy that an act will be followed by a consequence and on the value of that consequence to the individual. The expectancy component is the likelihood that an act will be followed by good or bad outcomes. The value component is a measure of how good or bad those outcomes are conceived to be by the individual.

A commonly employed example of an expectancy-value model is the "Fishbein" model which, when used as a determinant of brand preference, is interpreted (Cohen et al., 1972) as:

$$A_{jk} = \frac{1}{n} \sum_{i=1}^{n} E_{ijk} V_{ij} \qquad (5)$$

where

A_{jk} = attitude of consumer j about the act of purchasing brand k

E_{ijk} = expectancy, the belief by consumer j of the likelihood that brand k contains attribute i

V_{ij} = value, the goodness or badness of attribute i to consumer j in this product

n = number of attributes salient to consumer j in this product line.

This model has usually been recognized as the expectancy-value model of brand preference.

The expectancy-value model is made operational in the following manner. The strength of belief E_{ijk} about a cola drink might be measured as:

That Tab has calories is (HIGHLY PROBABLE: 7 6 5 4 3 2 1: HIGHLY PROBABLE).

This scale would be recoded from +1 (very likely to possess) to −1 (very unlikely to possess). The evaluative aspect V_{ij} might be measured as:

It is (DESIRABLE: 7 6 5 4 3 2 1: UNDESIRABLE) for a cola drink to contain calories.

This scale would be recoded from +1 (very good attribute) to −1 (very bad attribute).

A brand felt very likely (positive E_{ijk}) to possess a very undesirable attribute (negative V_{ij}) would receive a negative contribution toward the attitude of consumer j about the act of purchasing the brand. Conversely, a brand felt very unlikely (negative E_{ijk}) to possess a very desirable attribute (positive V_{ij}) would also receive a negative contribution toward the attitude. By similar consideration of all possible products of values and beliefs, a structure evolves which defines the bipolar multiplying concept. The employment of the expectancy-value model as operationalized by Fishbein in equation (5) has been limited in marketing studies due to the semantics of the model definition as pointed out by Ahtola

(1975). The belief statements which were defined by Fishbein to describe only the direction of belief have been consistently confused to mean the degree of perceived possession of a given attribute. In other words, when a respondent is asked to determine his strength of belief about the likelihood that a given brand contains an attribute, he doesn't know whether he should state probability of any amount of the attribute or whether he should evaluate the amount of the attribute contained.

Analysis of alternative specifications of the expectancy-value model for cola drinks yielded a best model which included the expectancy component, but which included only the three most important attributes instead of all four salient attributes. For U.S. compact cars, the best candidate model was determined to be expectancy-only with all eight attributes included.

Regular Adequacy-Importance Model

Adequacy-importance models equate attitude about a brand to the sum of a number of multiplicative terms, one for each attribute determined to be salient to the product line. This relationship has already been expressed algebraically in equation (1). The belief scales are cognitive (how many calories?) rather than evaluative (how desirable are calories?). The belief measurement could be carried out on a seven point scale:

Tab has (VERY MANY CALORIES: 7 6 5 4 3 2 1: NO CALORIES AT ALL).

This scale would be recorded from $+1$ (maximum amount of attribute present) to $+1/7$ (minimum amount of attribute present). The regular adequacy-importance model employed the importance measurements used by the PMD Model.

One way in which the adequacy-importance models differ from the expectancy-value models lies in the interpretation of how the component attribute effects combine. Bass and Talarzyk (1971) contend that any attribute, no matter how unimportant, will add something to the overall value accruing to the attitudinal object. Therefore, in operationalizing this model, the importance term I_{ij} is coded over a range of positive value, say $+1$ for "very important" and $+1/7$ for "unimportant." At the same time, the belief component B_{ijk} is also coded over a range of positive values which may be framed by $+1$ for highly perceived attribute content and $+1/7$ for the opposite. As a result, any salient attribute adds to the additudinal score regardless of its desirability.

The regular adequacy-importance model for cola drinks included all the attributes since the value of mean correlation coefficient squared increased with the number of attributes included. At the same time, the model was a beliefs-only model since the response to that model was superior to that of the importance-belief model. This same model, beliefs-only and all eight attributes included, was the best specification for U.S. compact cars.

Ideal Point Adequacy-Importance Model

More of an attribute is not always more desirable to consumers. Consequently, the monotonic belief scales might be discarded in favor of a scale containing a global maximum. An adequacy important model employing an ideal point on the belief scale could be written as

$$A_{jk} = \frac{1}{n} \sum_{i=1}^{n} I_{ij} (|B_{ijk} - P_{ij}|)^{\phi} \tag{6}$$

where P_{ij} = perception by consumer j of the ideal amount of attitude i, and
ϕ = 1 for city block distance, 2 for Euclidean distance.
This model has been studied by Lehmann (1971) and Bass, Pessemier, and Lehmann (1972). They coded the belief scale from high (1) to low (6) and importance from very important (1) to very unimportant (6). Under this coding lower values of attitude index correspond to greater brand desirability. This coding means that a value of the parameter ϕ equal to one implies constant marginal utility for the attributes while a value of two implies diminishing marginal utility. Lehmann found that the city block measure fit data on television show preference best. A result that was also found by Bass, Pessemier, and Lehmann.

For the ideal point model, the importance values used in the PMD Model evaluation were combined with belief measurements obtained by a scale calibrated around the stated ideal point. The ideal point was coded as +1 while the other scale positions were coded linearly under the assumption that the first scale positions beyond those positions measured were always zero.

The analysis for cola drinks revealed that the number of attributes entering the model was not significant, the adequacy-importance model with one ideal point on the belief scale was found to be an "importance-belief" mode with only the most important attribute entered. However, for U.S. compact automobiles, the inclusion of more than one attribute was significant. For this product class, the model selected was an importance-belief one with all eight attributes included.

Comparison of Selected Models

The characteristics of the candidate PMD Model and the selected forms of the three alternative models are summarized in Table 1 for both products. To assess the difference among these candidates a single factor (model), repeated measures analysis of variance was performed. The F ratio obtained indicated a significant difference among the mean correlation coefficient squared of the four models. There was no adjustment in degrees of freedom for the fact that the PMD involved one parameter while the other models contained no parameters. This is potentially a serious problem. However, the issue will be shown in the next

Table 1.   Comparison of Selected Candidate Models for Cola Drinks
(Compact Cars)

Model	Number of Attributes	Belief or Expectancy-Only?	Importance Parameter	Belief Scale	Mean r^2
PMD	4 (8)	No (yes)	0.2 (8)	Sine (Linear)	.727 (.659)
Regular Adequacy-Importance	4 (8)	Yes (Yes)	—	Linear (Linear)	.495 (.606)
Ideal Point Adequacy-Importance	1 (8)	No (No)	—	Linear (Linear)[a]	.093 (.308)
Expectancy-Value	3 (8)	No (Yes)	—	Linear (Linear)	.507 (.577)

[a] Discontinuity at the ideal point.

section to be immaterial to the conclusions reached in our analysis. The Newman-Keuls method was used to study the differences in individual pairs of mean correlation coefficients squared.

The results of the comparison among models for cola drinks are given in Table 2. The PMD Model produced a significantly larger mean correlation coefficient squared than did any of the other models at the .05 level. The expectancy-value and regular adequacy-importance models produced results that were not significantly different from each other. However, the performance of both models was superior to the ideal point adequacy-importance model.

For U.S. compact cars, the Newman-Keuls test of the difference of the means indicated that the mean correlation coefficient squared of the PMD Model was significantly larger than that of either the expectancy-value model or the adequacy-importance model with ideal point at the .05 level. However, the test statistic for the difference between the mean correlation coefficient squared of the PMD Model and the adequacy-importance model with linear belief was not quite significant at the .05 level. However, significance did exist at the 0.10 level. The adequacy-importance model with linear belief was not significantly better than the expectancy-value model. Both models, however, were significantly better than the adequacy-importance model with ideal point belief scale. The results of the model comparison are shown in Table 2.

The comparison of the candidate versions of the PMD Model for the two products against the candidate forms of three alternate models resulted in a clear demonstration of the superiority of the PMD Model within the bounds of this research. The optimum PMD Model was overwhelmingly better than the alternatives when explaining brand preference of cola drinks. Although not as strongly, the PMD Model was also shown to be better than the alternatives in predicting brand preference of U.S. compact automobiles. When the characteristics of the

Table 2. Significance of the Difference in Mean Correlation Coefficients
Squared of Models for Cola Drinks
(Compact Cars)

Model Superiority	Mean r^2	PMD Model	Expectancy- Value Model	Regular Adequacy- Importance Model	Ideal Point Adequacy- Importance Model
PMD Model	.727 (.659)	—	*(*)	*(**)	*(*)
Expectancy- Value Model	.507 (.577)		—	n.s. (n.s.)	*(*)
Regular Adequacy- Importance Model	.495 (.606)			—	*(*)
Ideal Point Adequacy- Importance Model	.093 (.308)				—

*Significant at the .05 level.
**Significant at the .10 level.
[n.s.] Not significant.

"best" PMD Model are considered for each of the two products, the compact auto product was optimum with a linear belief scale and parameter value of 0.8 compared to a sine belief scale and a parameter value of 0.2 for the less important cola product. Since a parameter value of 1.0 converts the PMD Model into a linear compensatory model similar to the regular adequacy-importance and the expectancy-value models and since both the latter models employ linear belief scales, a great deal of similarity is seen to exist between the structure of the four models in the case of the U.S. compact car product. From this point of view the superiority of the PMD Model for the important product is impressive.

It may also be noticed that the performance of the regular adequacy-importance model and the expectancy-value models are somewhat similar for both products. If the work of Bettman, Capon, and Lutz (1976) is considered, then this phenomenon is understandable. These authors found that about 45 percent of consumers employ cognitive algebra either the same or very similar to that of the adequacy-importance model algebra when faced with an importance-belief task. On the other hand, they found that about 60 percent of consumers employ cognitive algebra either the same as or similar to that of the expectancy-value model algebra when faced with an expectancy-value task. When one meaning of the expectancy-value attribute components (Ahtola, 1975), it is not difficult to comprehend the similarity of the performance of these two models in the PMD Model comparison.

The comparative inability of the ideal point adequacy-importance model to explain brand preference is obvious for both products studied. Since the same belief scale and importance measurements were employed for both this model and the regular adequacy-importance model, the most likely cause of the poor performance of the ideal point model is in the measurement and treatment of the ideal point itself. Several articles (Henry, 1975; Henry and Zahn, 1975) have pointed out the difficulty in obtaining consistent and correct identification of ideal point location on the belief scale. Perhaps using the techniques of Srinivasan and Shocker (1973) for deducing the location of an ideal point would have yielded better results. In any event, the PMD Model approximation eliminates this possible source of difficulty by anchoring the belief scale at the two critical points regardless of their location thus eliminating the need for absolute critical point location. Another difficulty in treating the ideal point belief scale measurement, even if the ideal level itself is correctly identified, lies in the scale coding. The scale between "none of the attribute" and the ideal point can be scaled linearly to be in consonance with the coding of the regular adequacy-importance model, but how to code the section of the scale on the other side of the ideal point is a difficult decision, because how much less than ideal is an "extreme amount of the attribute"?

ADDITIONAL ANALYSIS

One of the hypotheses underlying the theory of the PMD Model is that each consumer possesses two critical points on his belief continuum for each salient attribute, one for each of his most liked and most disliked levels of that attribute. Since the PMD Model was optimum when the summation of attribute components was modified by parameter values of 0.2 and 0.8 for cola drinks and U.S. compact cars, respectively, it was not possible to separate the effects of the dual ideal point hypothesis from the second involving the effects of purchase importance. By setting the value of p equal to 1.0, the model attains the form of the regular adequacy-importance model and differs only in the way the belief scores are obtained. Therefore, in order to assess the dual ideal point hypothesis, the PMD Model with parameter set equal to 1.0 was compared to the three alternative models for each of the products.

With $p = 1.0$ the mean correlation coefficient squared of the PMD Model when applied to cola drinks was 0.631, a value revealed by the Newman-Keuls method to be still significantly greater than that obtained with any of the alternate models at the $\alpha = 0.05$ level. When the parameter was set equal to 1.0 and the U.S. compact car data was applied, the mean correlation coefficient squared obtained with the PMD Model was .664. Since this value was slightly greater than the mean $r^2 = .659$ obtained with $p = 0.8$, the PMD Model in this case remained superior at the $\alpha = 0.10$ level.

The results of removing the purchase importance factor from the PMD Model did not change its superiority over the alternate models, thus substantiating the hypothesis concerning the two ideal points. The hypothesis concerning the effect of the purchase importance parameter had previously been supported by findings showing a significant difference among the mean correlation coefficients squared obtained from the nine different parameter values tested.

DISCUSSION

One of the basic hypotheses underlying the creation of the Parametric Marginal Desirability Model was that the consumer's determination of brand preference within a given product class is influenced by his perceived purchase importance of that product. In order that this hypothesis be implemented, a parameter representing a function of purchase importance was introduced into the model in such a fashion as to adapt model performance to coincide with the postulated effect of purchase importance processing system. Specifically, the parameter p was introduced in such a manner as to create increasingly diminishing marginal desirability near the ideally desirable and undesirable preference levels of the product as purchase importance decreases. Values of p equal to 1 reduce the model to a linear adequacy-importance relationship where the attitudinal effect is the sum of the contributions of the salient attributes. On the other hand, $0 < p < 1$ provides the effect of decreasing marginal desirability previously described. Conversely, p values greater than 1 were employed to test the possibility that some products may be so important as to create large marginal desirability near the ideal and least ideal levels.

From the behavioral aspect, the PMD Model employs the concept that the consumer employs two critical reference points to determine his belief component to the importance-belief product. These two critical points are located at the points on his belief scale for each attribute which give him his most ideal and least ideal amount of that attribute, respectively, for the product under consideration. His belief measurement is a function of the difference in the influences of these two critical levels as the point on the belief scale where he perceives the brand in question to be located. A basic assumption throughout this research was that the resultant influence of the two critical levels as a point midway between them was zero, thus obviating the contribution of that particular attribute to attitudinal affect. Moving the perceived location of the brand to a point on the belief scale closer to the ideal point results in an influence from that point exceeding that from the more distant least ideal point and provide a positive contribution to attitudinal affect. A similar positioning of the brand closer to the least ideal point conversely provides a negative belief score and a negative contribution to attitudinal affect as a consequence.

The initial belief scale coding was such that belief scores were obtained from a linear relationship, i.e., belief score is obtained from a linear function with 0 in the middle of the range. However, if one were to consider the previous discussion regarding the p parameter and attempt to apply it to the case of only one attribute, it is apparent that the linear belief scale would be inappropriate for products of low purchase importance and corresponding values of p much less than 1. In order to test this point, the belief scale was coded in such a manner as to provide diminishing marginal belief near the critical points, a similar concept to that of diminishing marginal desirability for total attitudinal affect. The coding employed to achieve this effect was obtained by scaling the belief scale between the critical points linearly in radians and performing a sine transformation on the resultant scores. It was found on the less important purchase that the low population p value of 0.2 provided a model that was improved by use of the sine coded belief scale which was in concert with the idea behind the transcendental coding. However, the more important produce with a p value of 0.8 performed somewhat better using a linear belief scale than when the sine transformation was employed.

Our initial examination of the Parametric Marginal Desirability Model has indicated its feasibility. However, additional investigation is necessary. For instance, we treated the purchase importance parameter for a product as being homogeneous for all consumers. We need to assess the costs and benefits of allowing this parameter to be heterogeneous among consumers. Perhaps individual parameters would provide a useful basis for segmentation or other marketing policies. A comparison should be made with the exponential discrepancy model of Einhorn and Gonedes (1971). Most importantly, we need to examine a wide range of products and to determine the functional relationship between purchase importance (and other product related variables) and the purchase importance parameter.

FOOTNOTE

*John F. McElwee, Jr. is an Engineering Specialist at the Pomona Division of General Dynamics. He is also a Lecturer in Business and Economics at University of LaVerne. Leonard J. Parsons is Professor of Industrial Management at Georgia Institute of Technology.

REFERENCES

Ahtola, Olli T. (1975), "The Vector Model of Preferences: An Alternative to the Fishbein Model," *Journal of Marketing Research* 12: 52–59 (February).
Bass, Frank M. (1972), "An Attitude Model for the Study of Brand Preference," *Journal of Marketing Research* 9: 92–96 (February).
_____. (1972), "Fishbein and Brand Preference: A Reply," *Journal of Marketing Research* 9: 461 (November).
_____, Pessemier, Edgar A., and Lehmann, Donald R. (1972), "An Experimental Study of Relationships Between Attitudes, Brand Preference, and Choice," *Behavioral Science* 17: 532–541 (November).
_____ and Talarzyk, W. Wayne (1971), "Using Attitude to Predict Individual Brand Preference," *Occasional Papers in Advertising* 4: 63–72 (May).
Beckwith, Neil E., and Lehmann, Donald R. (1973), "The Importance of Differential Weights in

Multiple Attribute Models of Consumer Attitude,'' *Journal of Marketing Research* 10: 141-145 (May).

Bettman, James R., Capon, Noel, and Lutz, Richard (1976), "Cognitive Algebra in Multi-Attribute Models," *Journal of Marketing Research* 12: 151-165 (May).

Cohen, Joel B., Fishbein, Martin, and Ahtola, Olli T. (1972), "The Nature and Uses of Expectancy-Value Models in Consumer Attitude Research," *Journal of Marketing Research* 9: 456-460 (November).

Einhorn, Hillel J., and Gonedes, Nicholas J. (1971), "An Exponential Discrepancy Model for Attitude Evaluation," *Behavioral Science* 16: 152-157 (March).

Fisher, Sir Ronald A. (1954), *Statistical Methods for Research Workers,* New York: Hafner.

Frost, W. A. K., and Braine, R. L. (1967), "Application of the Repertory Grid Technique to Problems in Market Research," *Commentary* 9: 161-175 (July).

Geisser, S., and Greenhouse, W. G. (1958), "An Extension of Box's Results on the Use of the F Distribution in Multivariate Analysis," *Annals of Mathematical Statistics* 29: 885-891.

Green, Paul E., and Carmone, Frank J. (1970), *Multidimensional Scaling and Related Techniques in Marketing Analysis,* Boston: Allyn and Bacon.

Hansen, Flemming (1969), "Consumer Choice Behavior: An Experimental Approach," *Journal of Marketing Research* 6: 436-443 (November).

Henry, Walter A. (1975), "Utility Theory: A Fundamental Frame of Reference for Attitude Structure Models," unpublished paper, University of California, Riverside.

_____ and Zahn, G. Lawrence (1975), "A Cautionary Note on Measure Validation of Direct Measures of Ideal Points," unpublished paper, University of California, Riverside.

Hughes, G. David, and Guerrero, J. L. (1971), "Testing Cognitive Models Through Computer Controlled Experiments," *Journal of Marketing Research* 8: 232-244 (August).

Kelley, G. A. (1955), *Psychology of Personal Constructs,* New York: Norton.

Lehmann, Donald R. (1971), "Television Show Preference: Application of Choice Model," *Journal of Marketing Research* 8: 47-55 (February).

Miller, Neal E. (1971), *Neal E. Miller: Selected Papers,* Chicago: Aldine.

Nakanishi, Masao, and Bettman, James R. (1974), "Attitude Models Revisited: An Individual Level Analysis," *Journal of Consumer Research* 1: 16-21 (December).

Pessemier, Edgar A., and Wilkie, William L. (1974), "Multi-Attribute Choice Theory—A Review and Analysis," in G. David Hughes and Michael L. Ray, eds., *Buyer/Consumer Information Processing,* Chapel Hill: University of North Carolina Press, pp. 288-330.

Schmidt, Frank L., and Wilson, Terry C. (1975), "Expectancy Value Models of Attitude Measurement: A Measurement Problem," *Journal of Marketing Research* 12: 366-368 (August).

Sherif, Carolyn W., Sherif, Muzafer, and Nebergall, Roger E. (1965), *Attitude and Attitude Change,* Philadelphia: W. B. Saunders.

Sheth, Jagdish N., and Talarzyk, W. Wayne (1972), "Perceived Instrumentality and Value Importance as Determinants of Attitudes," *Journal of Marketing Research* 9: 6-9 (February).

Srinivasan, V., and Shocker, Allan D. (1973), "Linear Programming Techniques for Multidimensional Analysis of Preferences," *Psychometrika* 38: 337-369 (September).

Troutman, C. Michael, and Shanteau, James (1976), "Do Consumers Evaluate Products by Adding or Averaging Attribute Information?," *Journal of Consumer Research* 3: 101-106 (June).

Wilkie, William L., and McCann, John M. (1972), "The Halo Effect and Related Issues in Multi-Attribute Models—An Experiment," Institute Paper No. 377, Institute for the Behavioral, Economic and Management Sciences, Krannert Graduate School of Industrial Administration, Purdue University.

_____, and Weinrich, R. P. (1973), "Effects of the Number and Type of Attributes Included in an Attitude Model: More is Not Better," Institute Paper No. 385, Krannert Graduate School of Industrial Administration, Purdue University.

Winer, B. J. (1971), *Statistical Principles in Experimental Design.* New York: McGraw-Hill.

CARRY-OVER EFFECTS IN ADVERTISING COMMUNICATION*

Alan Sawyer, OHIO STATE UNIVERSITY

Scott Ward, HARVARD UNIVERSITY

MARKETING SCIENCE INSTITUTE

INTRODUCTION

This paper examines the question of how long effects of advertising last. This topic is obviously of importance to marketing managers, who must make advertising budget decisions—e.g., how much to spend, what media schedule to use, or when to change campaigns—that depend in part on the carry-over effects of previous advertising. The nature and extent of carry-over effects is also crucial to current policy issues, such as the regulation of television advertising.

To date, most studies on this question have consisted of econometric analyses

Research in Marketing—Volume 2, 1979, pages 259–314.
ISBN 0-89232-059-1

of aggregate data (Clarke, 1975) or have been limited to particular stimuli or conditions of exposure, the sampling characteristics of which are unknown (Zielske, 1959). In the more general behavioral science literature—particularly in social psychology and communication research—studies are often limited in scope and are carried out with nonadvertising stimuli under conditions that cannot be simply generalized to the question of the duration of mass media advertising. Virtually absent are longitudinal studies focusing on advertising effects, similar to the econometric studies reviewed by Clarke.

Despite these shortcomings, behavioral science research is useful in providing information on what processes underlie carry-over effects—especially within individuals—and what circumstances make duration of advertising effect longer or shorter, i.e., the mediating and contingent conditions that may influence the duration of advertising effects. A major goal of this paper is to set forth micro-theoretical notions (Ray, 1969b) from the behavioral science literature that can be used to formulate propositions or hypotheses to be tested in advertising contexts.

Defining Carry-Over Effects

Conceptually, the question of how long advertising lasts seems to imply more specific questions of what particular aspects or effects of advertising may last in an individual's cognitive structure for varying lengths of time. Important issues are: (1) What *portion* of communication effects remains after exposure, i.e., is there less than 100 percent decay of effects? (2) What *kind* of effect is carried over or left in an individual's cognitive structure following exposure? (3) How easy is it to re-evoke a particular communication effect? (4) What is the incremental value of previous communication effects in terms of the ability to create other effects in subsequent communications?, and (5) How long do each of these conditions last?

In the advertising context, the presence of subsequent communications is implied. Therefore, theories of the residual effects of communication must consider the interaction of a particular communication with subsequent communications.

Estimates of advertising carry-over vary, and the processes by which carry-over occurs are controversial and not well understood. Krugman (1975) describes the controversy well, in contrasting two views of human attention, perception, and retention of communication effects. Some evidence suggests what he calls a "hard in/easy out" model, which says that attention requires effort, perception mediates selection for short-term or long-term memory, and rapid forgetting means advertisers must spend relatively more money to "get into perceptions or to get back in." This model is the prevalent one in advertising circles, but Krugman suggests that evidence exists for some opposing hypotheses (an "easy in/hard out" model). In the latter case, there is selective perception and much input to, and easy retrieval from, memory; later associated stimuli can trigger stimuli stored much earlier, which would mean that advertisers can spend fewer dollars to "get into" (memory) or "remind."

Research Approaches

This paper consists of two sections. The first focuses on the *processes* by which some communications have more persistent effects than others, and draws heavily on studies of attitude changes. The second section examines research on *factors affecting the processes,* e.g., marketing and advertising characteristics, such as message appeals, media scheduling, and consumer segment differences.

Our conceptual approach for organizing the research and theory bearing on the question of carry-over effects draws heavily on information-processing notions. That is, we are interested in understanding the interaction of personal factors (e.g., intelligence, prior knowledge level) and cognitive responses as they occur in response to a communication. The particular kinds of cognitive responses go beyond recall, comprehension or attitude effects specified in most hierarchy of effects models of communication processes. We expect cognitive responses such as counterarguing, curiosity and "connections" to occur also, and relate to varying persistence effects.

For example, individuals may differentially recall message content and may differentially counterargue against message claims. Such cognitive responses may in turn be influenced by the content and structure of memory related to the message. Finally, personal factors, such as intelligence and predispositions, may influence what messages and/or aspects of messages are attended to, and the kinds of effects which occur.

The factors affecting information-processing of advertising communication, which in turn relate to varying persistence effects, include advertising messages factors (e.g., nature of appeals, amount of information, etc.) and situational factors (e.g., brand reputation, message timing and repetition). For example, fear appeals may evoke effects that are not particularly strong initially but that are relatively persistent. Situational factors, such as familiarity with past advertising for a brand, or message repetition, may also influence carry-over effects.

Finally, the responses of interest are the learning, attitude and behavior effects resulting from communication exposure.

PROCESSES AFFECTING PERSISTENCE OF COMMUNICATION EFFECTS

Persistence of Learning

A logical first question to ask is, What do we know about the retention of learned information? Much has been written on this question (e.g., Barnard, 1975; Hunter, 1964; Norman, 1969; Wood, 1961), so only a brief review is offered here. One of the first researchers to delve deeply into learning and memory was Ebbinghaus (1885), who used lists of nonsense syllables as test stimuli and himself as sole subject. His findings included the: *negatively accelerated forgetting curve, serial position learning and forgetting effects and overlearning.*

Ebbinghaus's memory results have been replicated many times since. Researchers have also added to his findings. For example, the estimated absolute level of retention has been found to depend upon the particular measure of learning. Generally, estimates of retention are lowest if measured by unaided recall, intermediate if by the amount of time taken in relearning, and highest if by recognition (Luh, 1922; Postman and Rau, 1957; Greenberg and Garfinkle, 1962). The general negatively accelerated shape of the forgetting curve has been confirmed for many types of stimuli, including both consumer (Simmons, 1965) and industrial advertisements (McGraw-Hill, 1964).

What processes have been postulated to account for the decay of learned information? The most prevalent explanation is the *interference theory* of forgetting, which postulates that the learning of a stimulus is interfered with by items preceding (proactive inhibition) or following (retroactive inhibition) that stimulus. Stimuli at the beginning or end of a series suffer from only one inhibition, retroactive or proactive, respectively, whereas items in the middle encounter both types of interference. Most contemporary learning researchers believe that interference is the only mechanism underlying memory loss. Other researchers subscribe to a *decay or disuse theory* which hypothesizes that time alone, not intervening events, accounts for retention losses.

One other theoretical aspect of retention involves a distinction between short-term and long-term memory. *Short-term memory* (STM) concerns periods between input and retention measurement of about one minute or less, whereas *long-term memory* (LTM) involves longer time periods. Some researchers (e.g., Hebb, 1949) ascribe to a two-factor theory of memory, with decay accounting for STM and interference determining LTM. Others (e.g., Melton, 1963) believe that interference is the only operation in both memory stores.

Waugh and Norman (1965) offer a different view of memory that may be relevant to our concern with the persistence of communication effects. They distinguish between primary memory (PM) and secondary memory (SM). Items still in consciousness represent PM, whereas events that can be recalled but are not conscious at the time of the recall test constitute SM. All events must pass through PM, but since PM has a limited capacity, old items may be displaced when new items are presented. Older items may be forgotten permanently or, if rehearsed, they can hold on to their positions in PM and also become more permanent by moving into SM. The likelihood that an item is in PM depends on retroactive inhibition, whereas SM is influenced by factors that influence rehearsal, such as the number of exposures.[1]

In addition to the research on processes underlying differences in individuals' learning retention, much research has examined various factors that affect the rate of learning and retention. Many important variables have been isolated, including meaningfulness of the stimuli (Underwood and Schultz, 1967), similarity of items (Underwood and Ekstrand, 1967), past subjects' experimental experiences (Underwood, 1957), time devoted to viewing the stimuli, and spatial size of the advertising message (Strong, 1914). However, variables that have powerful effects on initial learning or acquisition do not appear to produce differences in retention when the degree of original learning is equated. When certain variables appear to affect retention, it is usually because the degree of original learning is unequal, thus creating the retention differences. Therefore, by far the most important variable in the persistence of learning is the level of original learning itself (Underwood, 1964).

In summary, two findings are particularly pertinent to the present study. The above observation regarding the prime importance of original learning for retention decay rates suggests that, if original learning is controlled for, differential retention results as a function of the time of measurement are likely to be very rare. Second, research on the underlying memory processes hints that processes occurring right at and immediately following the time of exposure and attention to a communication are likely to be extremely important in determining any persistence of learning effects.

Persistence of Attitude Change and Behavior

In the last few decades, social psychologists and communication researchers have focused considerable attention on attitude change phenomena. In this section, we review and assess studies which have examined the duration of attitude change effects.

In an extensive literature review, McGuire (1968c) found studies in which induced opinion change persists for up to ten months, while other studies show very little persistence. McGuire concluded that a very rough estimate of the average half-life of initial attitude change was about six months, but cited little evidence to support his estimate. A major problem is a lack of studies that examine persistence effects for longer than a few weeks. Such estimates are probably premature and perhaps misleading. Unlike learning, there are no "typical" retention curves of yielding or attitude change.

One of the complexities involved in determining changes in attitude yielding over time is the not uncommon phenomenon of actual temporal *increases* in attitude change. See Figures 1a, b and c. For example, Peterson and Thurstone (1933) found effects varying from rapid decay to actual increases in attitude change among school children over time periods as long as two or eight months. Other studies have reported *absolute* increases in attitudes in certain conditions (e.g., Hovland and Weiss, 1951; Holt and Watts, 1973; Insko, Arkoff, and Insko, 1965). Also, there appear to be many variables that lead to *relative* persistence of attitude effects, such that attitude effects in one message condition decay less rapidly than in another situation. For example, Weiss (1953) measured attitude change among individuals who were exposed to an antismoking communication that was followed by a message that discounted its truthfulness. Decay in attitude change over six weeks was less for this group than for a comparable group which did not receive the discounting message. Other studies that have reported relative differences in persistence of attitude change include Kelman and Hovland (1953), Whittaker and Meade (1968), Schulman and Worrell (1970), and Johnson and Watkins (1971).

What are the processes and situations that retard decay of attitudes and attitude change? Seven hypotheses have been advanced to account for either absolute increases in attitude levels or relative persistence of attitude change:

1. the discounting cue hypothesis;
2. the general conclusions only hypothesis;
3. the "Bartlett" effects hypothesis;
4. the delayed filtering of complex implications hypothesis;
5. the intervening activities hypothesis;
6. the uninvolved learning hypothesis; and
7. the "boomerang" hypothesis.

Discounting cue hypothesis. The most popular explanations of increased attitude change over time involve some version of the discounting cue hypothesis. The essential notion is that if there is some aspect of a message that causes the message to be initially discounted or resisted, the passage of time may lead either to forgetting of the inhibiting cue or to dissociation of it from the original communication so that the impact of the persuasive content may gradually take effect. For example, Hovland, Lumsdaine, and Sheffield (1949) reported an experiment in which soldiers were shown "The Battle of Britain," a World War II propaganda film; their opinion change was measured either five days or nine weeks afterwards. For a subset of eight opinion items, the difference between the experimental group and a control group who did not see the film was larger after nine weeks than after five days. The authors coined the since heavily used term "sleeper effect" to describe this delayed buildup of the film's impact (see Figure 1a).

The discounting cue hypothesis might assert the following explanation of the sleeper effect: The Army, which sponsored the film, was viewed as a discredited or biased source of war-relevant information. This discredited source led to an initial discounting of the filmed message and a reduction of the initial persuasive impact. As time passed, the change-inhibiting discredited source was either forgotten or dissociated from the message. Where memory of the initial persuasive content had not totally dissipated nine weeks later, the full attitudinal impact—then uninhibited by the discounting cue—asserted itself, thus producing the observed sleeper effects. Subsequent research by Kelman and Hovland (1953) lent support to the explanation that the discounted source was not forgot-

Figure 1a. Absolute Increase of Advertising Effects (Sleeper Effect).

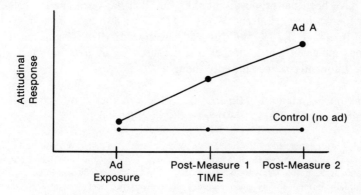

Figure 1b. Total Persistence of Advertising Effects.

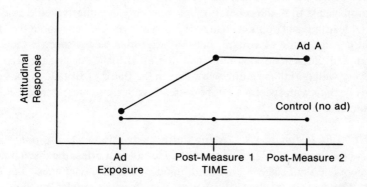

Figure 1c. Relative Persistence of Ad A over Ad B; Partial Persistence of both Ad A and Ad B.

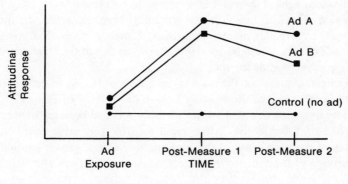

Adapted from Cook and Flay (1975)

ten but rather was dissociated from the message itself. Although negative source effects have been the prime discounting cue that has been studied, other cues such as forewarning (Holt and Watts, 1974) have also been examined. Recent research (Cook et al., 1974; Gillig and Greenwald, 1974; Capon and Hulbert, 1973) has indicated that a sleeper effect caused by discounting cues may not occur so frequently as was initially thought.

General Conclusions Only Hypothesis.   One hypothesis, offered by Hovland, Lumsdaine, and Sheffield (1949), p. 198) speculates that:

> forgetting is accompanied by loss of specificity of content—the details drop out and only the "general idea" or "substance" of the material remains. This "general idea" that is retained is of a more generalizable form, so that the individual has a greater tendency to go beyond the facts initially learned. In this sense, attitudes are to a certain extent 'general ideas' that lack specificity and generalize more broadly than is justified by the evidence.

Instead of a "sleeper effect" mechanism to explain delayed reactions to the Army propaganda film, the general conclusions only hypothesis would assert that the initial learning and opinion change focused on specific facts about the British RAF during the Battle of Britain, but that after nine weeks specific facts were forgotten and the general idea remained that all British, not just the RAF, had fought very well during the entire war, not just the Battle of Britain. Although the opinions dealing with specifics might decrease with time, more general attitudes might increase over time.

"Bartlett" Effect Hypothesis.   Many current advertisements use qualified arguments (see Preston, 1977). For example, Geritol first offers the disclaimer that "most people do not suffer from 'tired blood' " and then continues "but if *you* do ..." The success of this appeal may stem from unequal forgetting of the qualification and the main argument.

Bartlett (1952) predicted a delayed-action effect for persuasive communications that argue for one side of an issue but that also present some qualifications and reservations against the main arguments. It was predicted that the qualifying details would, in effect, inhibit initial attitude change. However, the qualifying details would be forgotten more quickly than the main conclusion. Consequently, more attitude change would be observed after a passage of time than immediately following presentation of the message.

For example, assume that the main argument about British soldiers performing at least their full share of the fighting load in the "Battle of Britain" had been qualified by the admission that a few cowardly acts had been reported and some fighting had been ineffective. More rapid forgetting of these qualifying statements than of the main point of the film might lead to a greater attitude change after a passage of time than immediately when the qualifiers were still remembered. Papageorgis (1963) tested the "Bartlett" effects hypothesis on qualified and unqualified messages, measuring effects immediately after exposure and 2 days, 14 days, and 41 days after exposure. Significant delayed effects on recall and opinion change were found for up to 14 days. As predicted, losses in recall were significantly greater for the qualified arguments than for the unqualified message. Although the delayed attitude change was greater, as predicted, for the qualified message than for the unqualified one, this effect was statistically significant for only one of the two issues used in the study.

Delayed Filtering of Complex Implications Hypothesis. Another hypothesis originally set forth by the Hovland group was that complex implications of initially learned content may not be perceived by the audience at the outset but may become more apparent later on when the learned material becomes relevant in some new context. Direct conclusions of a message would decay with forgetting. However, time may allow more remote, subtle, perhaps even unmentioned ramifications of the message to filter through from the direct conclusions of the message. The delayed impact on the indirect issues would lead to a delayed decay relative to that of the direct impact.

For example, the "Battle of Britain" film showed directly how the outnumbered British defeated the German Luftwaffe. However, there were no direct assertions that the Germans were militarily weak or that the war would subsequently end soon, and no immediate effects on this opinion item were found. However, it might later have occurred to viewers that the Germans' inability to defeat the British implied that they certainly could not defeat the entire Allied Force and that the war would soon end—a delayed opinion effect that was found in the study.

Other evidence supporting this hypothesis was reported by McGuire (1960a, 1960c), who found that, compared to the opinion change on explicitly mentioned target issues, there was an increase over a one-week period on opinions regarding unmentioned, indirect conclusions. Delayed attitude effects, which also support the "filter" hypothesis, were reported by Cohen (1957) for confusingly ordered messages (information before need arousal) and by Stotland, Katz, and Patchen (1959) for complex antiprejudice messages which contained subtle, self-insightful appeals. However, not all studies have found that indirect conclusions persist longer than direct ones. Null findings were reported by McGuire (1960b) and Dillehay, Insko, and Smith (1966).

Intervening Activities Hypothesis. The previous hypothesis predicts that some delayed attitude effects may occur because of conscious or subconscious internal processing of retained information. Other, more active, intervening activities could also account for differences in persistence of attitudinal effects. Two such activities are discussion and new-information seeking. For example, if viewers discussed the propaganda film after its showing, both the repetition of the previously perceived arguments and the opportunity to discover forgotten as well as new facts and ideas could account for a delayed effect on attitude. Similarly, the film might have spurred some of the audience to find out new information from other information sources.

There is much research support for this hypothesis. For example, Watts (1967) compared the effects of inducing subjects to write out a point of view versus simple exposure to written arguments for the same point of view. Immediate comparisons revealed no differences between the two experimental conditions. However, after six weeks, there was significantly greater persistence of attitude change for subjects who wrote arguments than for those who simply read them—the former group showed a slight nonsignificant increase in attitude change, whereas about half of the initial change had dissipated in the latter group. Watts decided that at least part of this difference was due to the fact that 63 percent of the subjects in the first group reported discussing the key issue in the six-week period whereas only 38 percent of the other group reported doing so.

Janis and Hoffman (1971) manipulated whether the two subjects were asked to telephone each other daily after five weekly antismoking information sessions or to contact each other only at the weekly sessions. The results showed no significant differences in the immediate attitude and behavior changes but significantly greater attitude and behavior change (fewer cigarettes smoked per day) for subjects in the frequent contact condition.

Other studies relevant to the intervening activities hypothesis include Mitnick and McGinnies's study (1958) of racial attitudes, and Lewin's (1958) classic study of group support for opinion change regarding food preferences. In the former study, complete persistence of attitudes for one month was found when subjects viewed an antiprejudice film, followed by interpersonal discussion. However, subjects in the film-only group showed complete loss of opinion change over the same time period. Lewin's study found group discussions about adopting new foods were more effective than lectures after delays of one, two and four weeks.

Maccoby et al. (1961) examined the effects of intervening social support on persistence of attitude change induced in young mothers who read a booklet advocating late toilet-training schedule. When the women's opinions and discussions were monitored over a six-month period, much evidence of selective exposure (or retention) was found. The young mothers tended to have discussions with people who expressed agreement with their own current toilet-training opinions. The major effect of these conversations was to prevent attitude decay. People who did not engage in discussions supporting the new attitudes tended to revert to their initial positions. Likewise, Newcomb (1963) concluded that a type of selective process accounted for the fact that Bennington students who were more liberal in college than their background might indicate tended to marry more liberal people and remain more liberal when compared to liberal colleagues who married conservatives.

Although selective exposure may not be a common phenomenon (Freedman and Sears, 1965; Sears, 1968), heightened awareness and retention of any available social support factors may aid longer persistence. Cook and Wadsworth (1972) found some support for this mechanism in an experiment where some subjects were exposed seven times (overlearning) and some subjects were exposed only once to the conclusion of a message. Four days later, subjects learned that either 90, 50, or 10 percent of their peers thought the earlier message was convincing. Only the overlearned group was affected by the "peer support."

Mere exposure to the original post-measurements may be sufficient to maintain learned behavior. This was impressively demonstrated in an experiment by Evans et al. (1965) in which improved toothbrushing behavior was measured at one, two, five, and ten weeks following either exposure to a persuasive message or the feedback of results at time of measurement, or neither. No treatment group exhibited better toothbrushing behavior than control subjects who received no message and whose performance was measured but not fed back to them. However, all groups, including the control, showed improved behavior which persisted after ten weeks. The authors concluded that merely the repeated measures themselves may have been sufficient to maintain the desired behavior—a fact that may pose methodological problems for repeated measures designs.

Uninvolved Learning Hypothesis. Certainly a most important intervening activity affecting attitude persistence would be consistent behavior such as a purchase. Krugman (1965) has offered an important explanation of the advertising process for situations in which delayed attitude effects are quite probable. Comparing the learning curves of television advertising for many low-priced packaged goods to that of nonsense syllables (e.g., Krugman, 1962; Ray, 1969a), Krugman asserts that the main parallel between the two types of typically often repeated stimuli is a lack of viewer involvement. In such uninvolving situations as exposure to a persuasive television commercial for, say, chewing gum, advertising researchers may overestimate the degree of conscious, active perceptual defense.

> Instead, as trivia are repeatedly learned and repeatedly forgotten and then repeatedly learned a little more, it is probable that two things will happen: (1) more simply, that so-called "over-learning" will move some information out of short-term and into long-term memory systems, and (2) more complexly, that we will permit significant alterations in the *structure* of our perception of a brand or product, but in ways which may fall short of persuasion or of attitude change. One way we may do this is by shifting the relative salience of attributes suggested to us by advertising as we organize our perception of brands and products (Krugman, 1965).

Krugman continues his thesis to suggest that, due to the uninvolved nature of the response to the commercial, most or all of the measurable perceptual and attitudinal effects are very likely to be delayed.

> Sociologists have met "sleeper effects" before, and some psychologists have long asserted that the effects of "latent" learning are only or most noticeable at the point of reward [e.g.,

Hovland (1951)]. In this case, it would be at the behavioral level involved in product purchases rather than at some intervening point along the way. That is, the purchase situation is the catalyst that reassembles or brings out all the potentials for shifts in salience that have accumulated up to that point. The product or package is then suddenly seen in a new "somehow different" light although nothing verbalizable may have changed *up to that point*. What we ordinarily call "change of attitude" may then occur after some real interval, however minute. Such change of attitude after product purchase is *not,* as has sometimes been said, in "rationalization" of the purchase but is an emergent response aspect of the previously changed perception. We would perhaps see it more often if products always lived up to expectations and did not sometimes create negative interference with the emerging response (Krugman, 1965).

As a measure of involvement, Krugman offers measures of cognitive responses he calls "personal connections" or the number of conscious bridges or personal references a viewer expresses between his own life and the advertisement (see Krugman, 1966–1967).

The significance of conditions of low or high involvement is not that one is better than the other, but that the processes of communication impact are different. That is, there is a difference in the change processes that are at work. Thus, with low involvement one might look for gradual shifts in perceptual structure, aided by repetition, activated by behavioral-choice situations, and *followed* at some time by attitude change. With high involvement one would look for the classic, more dramatic and more familiar conflict of ideas at the level of conscious opinion and attitude that precedes changes in overt behavior (Krugman, 1965).

Empirical results reflecting on Krugman's fascinating conjecture are quite scant. However, Ray and his colleagues (Ray et al., 1973) have consistently found from laboratory studies that the uninvolved learning hierarchy is common in advertising-repetition response curves. Ray and Sawyer (1971) found a learning-purchase-intention-brand-evaluation sequence of change for less involving convenience goods products, while a classic learning-attitude-purchase-intention change order was found for more involving shopping goods. Rothschild and Ray (1973) found similar orders in, respectively, a less involving local political campaign and a more involving national presidential election campaign. More research in this area is needed.

"Boomerang" Effect Hypothesis. A tentative hypothesis regarding the persistence of recall and attitude change has emerged from a recent study in marketing communication. Ray, Sawyer, and Strong (1971) found a "boomerang" effect in which biweekly exposures for the same direct-mail print advertisement produced negative effects, perhaps due to irritation caused by repeated exposures. Although increases in brand preference during exposure weeks and decreases during nonexposure weeks were found for three of the first four exposures, an opposite effect was found for exposures five, six, and seven.

An extensive advertising persistence study by Marder Associates (1968) also found a boomerang effect on attitude. Twelve test ads were inserted in an issue of *Life*. Four days after arrival of the test issue, recall and attitude were measured for different sets of test and control groups every day for eleven days. Generally, attitude increased and then decayed. However, one particular ad for Sprite exhibited a highly significant initial *decrease* in attitude change (in comparison to the no-exposure control sample). This initial decrease slowly "decayed" up to the point where the attitude of the test group was equal to that of the control after eleven days.

This phenomenon deserves further study, both to assess its reliability, and to identify the mechanism and conditions by which it occurs. The potential significance of such a boomerang effect is that, without a control group, a researcher might mistakenly conclude that there is a type of "sleeper effect" in operation when, in fact, the delayed increase is merely a recovery from the initial *negative* effects of the advertising.

The Relationship Between Persistence of Learning and Persistence of Attitude Change

To this point, we have examined separately the evidence regarding persistence of learning of the content of communications and the evidence regarding persistence of attitude changes induced by communication. It is commonly assumed in communication research and advertising effects models that the two phenomena are related: acquiring and retaining some information (learning) from a message is thought to be a necessary condition for intitial and persisting attitude change. In this section, we review evidence regarding how the persistences of these two cognitive phenomena are related.

Understanding the relationship between persistence of learning and persistence of attitude change is important for practical reasons. For example, one reason marketers repeat advertising is to increase learning, which is assumed to be related to increasing and maintaining attitude change. Learning measures, such as copy point recall, are frequently taken as criteria for the effectiveness of advertising campaigns. But the key marketing issue is whether retention, or learning, is related to consumer attitudes and, ultimately, to sales. It could be, for example, that learning decays quickly but that positive attitudes persist. On the other hand, learning may persist, but consumer attitudes and behavior may not. In either case, learning would be a poor predictor of campaign effectiveness, unless learning is related directly to sales, and not to attitudes.

Four views of the relationship between persistence of learning and persistence of attitude change are found in the literature. These are:
1. They are directly and exactly related;
2. They are indirectly related;
3. The relationship depends on subsets of messages; and
4. The relationship depends on the receiver's cognitive responses during communication.[2]

Direct, Isomorphic Relationship. The first view is that both the learning and attitude decay curves follow Ebbinghaus's negatively accelerating decay curve, i.e., that decay of learning and of attitude change is isomorphic. Empirical evidence for this point of view is scant.

Miller and Campbell (1959) examined the relationship in a different way. They exposed subjects to competing persuasive messages at different points in time, and measured the effects of the messages on attitudes either immediately after exposure, one week, or two weeks later. This procedure yielded four conditions:

Condition 1: Second message given immediately after the first; immediate measurement.

Condition 2: Second message given immediately after the first; measurement made one week later.

Condition 3: Second message given one week after the first; followed immediately by measurement.

Condition 4: Second message given one week after first; delayed measurement.

Based on the assumed negatively accelerated learning decay curves and a direct attitude-learning relationship, the greatest advantage of the second message over the first was predicted for Condition 3, the least advantage for Condition 2, and an intermediate advantage for Conditions 1 and 4. These predictions were confimed in separate tests of both learning of message content and attitude change.

However, although the correlations between content recall and immediate attitude change (Condition 1) were quite positive (r = .38), the correlations of delayed content recall and delayed attitude change were negative (r = −.45). Similar results were obtained by Insko (1964) with a different type of recall measure. Wilson and Miller (1968) also found decreased recency with delayed measurement but did not find an increase in recency with an increased interval between messages.

The previously mentioned Marder Associates (1968) advertising persistence study offered some indirect evidence for a direct recall-attitude relationship. A top-of-mind awareness measure taken every day for eleven days (expressed as change from no-exposure control groups) showed a pattern of no change for the first three days, an increase which peaked at five days, and then rapid decline to zero remaining effect by days ten and eleven. Marder hypothesized that the delayed increases in awareness were due to delays in actual ad exposure (*Life* is not read cover-to-cover as soon as it arrives). For the only three ads which exhibited any significant attitude change, the pattern of delayed increase, peaking (at seven days), and rapid decline to zero after eleven days closely resembled that of the awareness data. Unfortunately, all the data presented were in aggregate form; no awareness-attitude correlations across individuals were reported.

Indirect Relationship. A second view holds that learning accounts for some of the variance in persistence of attitude change, but not for all, or even most of it, as the first view would have. That is, the decay curves for the two phenomena need not be isomorphic.

One of the more extensive investigations of the relationships of learning and attitude change over time was conducted by Watts and McGuire (1964). They proposed two alternative hypotheses: the "functional dependence" view and the "functional autonomy" view. The former hypothesis views recall and attitude as analogous to a "doorbell" model, where as soon as pressure is removed from the bell (forgetting), the noise (attitude) also stops. In contrast, the functional autonomy hypothesis views recall and attitude as acting like a "light-switch" model. Initial learning of the inducing content is necessary for producing the opinion change. But once the change is made, it is as if a switch were thrown and the new opinion persists—regardless of the retention of the content—unless subsequently some countercontent is received, thus throwing the opinion "switch" back again.

The results of measuring opinion change and various aspects of recall of messages exposed immediately, one week, two weeks, or six weeks before measurement are shown in Figure 2. It can be seen that all of the recall curves show the expected negatively accelerated decay predicted by past learning research. Induced opinion change also decreases with time; however, the fact that the shape of the opinion decay curve is much more linear suggests a less than perfect learning-attitude relationship over time. Further analysis revealed that persistence of opinion change was functionally autonomous of recall of the message topic and recall of which side was advocated, whereas enduring attitude change was functionally dependent upon recall of the three specific arguments in the message. It should be noted that these results directly conflict with the "general conclusions only" hypothesis, which would predict a functionally dependent relationship of persisting attitude with recall of the conclusions and a functionally autonomous relationship with recall of the specific arguments.

Watts and McGuire (1964) speculate that a discounting cues type of sleeper effect might explain the results. People who immediately forgot even the topic of the message were likely to have incorrectly perceived the message in the first place and, hence, were unaffected. As time passed, people who did not recall the topic were more likely to be people who actually forgot the initially properly received content. A sleeper effect might be likely to occur for these actual "topic forgetters" who would initially discount the specific arguments since they heard them in a persuasion session. With time, however, dissipation of the discounting cue (recall of exposure to a persuasive message on a given topic) would enable a fuller persuasive impact of the still retained message content. Recall of the positive source (source was experimentally manipulated as either positive or negative) was positively related to attitude, but no effects of recall of the negative source were found. No evidence of a source-as-a-discounting-cue hypothesis was

Figure 2.   Percentage of Induced Opinion Change Retained and Percentage of
Subjects Recalling Specific Aspects of the Communication.

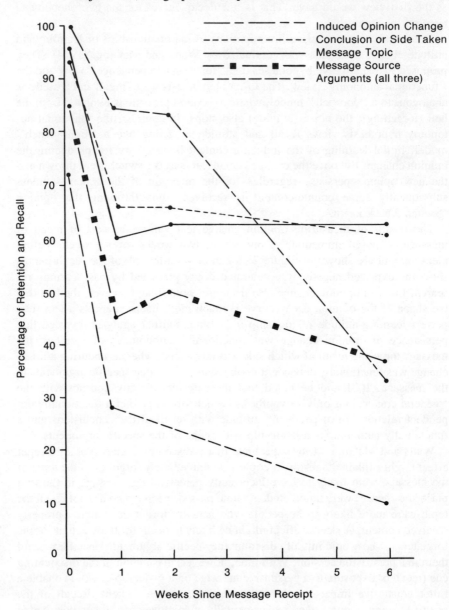

Source: Watts and McGuire (1964)

found since this relationship of source recall and attitude change did not differ over time.

Other research supporting this hypothesis of an indirect learning-attitude relationship includes Miller and Campbell's (1959) above-cited correlational findings of a positive relationship between attitude and recall when measures were taken immediately after exposure, and negative relationships when measures were taken after a week. Levanthal and Niles (1964) found behavioral intentions regarding automobile driving to be positively related to the number of minutes spent viewing films. When measures were taken later, they found that the higher the opportunity for learning (measured by number of minutes viewing films), the more prolonged was attitude over time.

As Kapferer (1976) notes, manipulations of exposure probably do increase retention of the message, but it cannot be assumed that the amount of information retained necessarily mediates attitudinal persistence. In fact, longitudinal analyses of panel data (e.g., Aaker and Day, 1971) have found weak support for the advertising-learning-brand-attitude relationship.

Effects of Message Subsets.   A third view of the relationship between learning persistence and attitude persistence, consistent with the Watts and McGuire (1964) research, holds that only some parts of messages are relevant to persuasion. The persistence of learning and attitude change may depend upon the persistence of learning and yielding cues in messages; these cues form a link in the broader persuasion process (cf. McGuire's theory discussed earlier). Investigators have focused on learning of *arguments* and learning of message *conclusions,* as message elements which may mediate the learning-attitude relationship.

Message *arguments* may contain yielding cues and, consequently, may be related to persistence. Calder et al. (1974) found in a jury simulation study that, with more learning, initial attitude change was greater; furthermore, the absolute level of change persisted for two weeks. Watts and McGuire (1964) examined opinion change among subjects who were ex post facto divided into two groups depending on the number of arguments recalled. Those in the high-recall group showed more change than the low-recall group one week after exposure and six weeks later. Other research has shown that repetition has an impact, partly because it contributes to less rapid decay of message arguments, not only because repeated arguments have a higher initial impact (Wilson and Miller, 1968).

Other investigators have examined message *conclusions* as mediators of attitudinal persistence. As mentioned earlier, Cook and Wadsworth (1972) found that repetition of a conclusion was sufficient for attitude persistence—but only when linked by subjects to social support, i.e., the perception that many others had evaluated the message as conclusive.

The focus on message elements may hold some promise for better understanding of the relationship between learning and attitude persistence. As Kapferer observes, quoting Cook et al. (1974):

An argument probably contains yielding cues and is likely to be sufficient for persuasion . . . ,
this approach is quite different from measuring units of message learning that reflect attention
to a message, but do not necessarily reflect comprehension of its crucial change-inducing
points (1976, p. 13).

Recipient-Generated Cognitive Responses.   Essentially, this hypothesis holds
that the underlying process linking learning and attitudes involves thoughts generated by the recipient during the communication. These "cognitive responses"
include counterarguments, supportive arguments, source derogation, and curiosity. The main proponent of this view advocates shifting attention from retention
of communication content per se to retention of these "cognitive reactions" to
the communication (Greenwald, 1968). These cognitive reactions may be related
to message content or they may be externally generated, i.e., not directly linked
to the communication.

Anderson and Hubert (1963) found that attitude change due to message exposure varied greatly from what recall of message content would logically indicate.
They decided that impression and verbal content memories are quite distinct.
Perhaps, as Waugh and Norman (1965) proposed, message content that is rehearsed, processed, or reacted to in some manner is placed in a secondary
memory that may be critical to long-term communication effects.

The idea that cognitive responses to persuasive messages are important determinants of attitude change is far from new (e.g., Hovland, Lumsdaine, and
Sheffield, 1949, p. 301; Hovland, Janis, and Kelley, 1953, p. 11; Kelman, 1953,
pp. 187, 211). However, the bold idea of actually measuring these responses is
quite new (see Wright, 1974b). Three studies (Greenwald, 1968; Calder, Insko,
and Yandell, 1974; Wright, 1974b) have directly measured cognitive responses
both immediately and after a delayed time interval and allowed some insight into
the temporal processing of cognitive responses. Other studies (Leavitt, Waddell,
and Wells, 1970; Ward and Ray, 1974; Gillig and Greenwald, 1974) have
explored the relationship of initial cognitive responses to delayed measures of
attitude and behavior.

Greenwald (1968) examined several measures, including his operationalization of cognitive responses. After a Likert-type opinion pretest, subjects wrote
down one-sentence reactions to the message's main points after each of the three
paragraphs. Immediately after the communication, subjects answered an opinion
posttest in which they listed all of their thoughts (positive and negative) relevant
to the issue and then indicated the source of these ideas (message-originated,
personal-reactions-oriented, or other). They then responded to unexpected questions concerning free recall of both the three main points and their written
responses. This entire posttest was then unexpectedly readministered one week
later.

The partial correlations (pretest partialed out) between both the immediate and one-week delayed posttest beliefs and (1) the content of cognitive reactions to the communications (number of positive reactions minus the number of negative ones), (2) the number of main arguments recalled, and (3) retention of the content of cognitive reactions (the number of positive reactions minus the number of negative ones) were analyzed.

The best predictor of beliefs was the content of the initial reactions written during the communication (average r = .52). The next best predictor (average r = .30) was the index of retained cognitive reactions content (especially in the delayed condition). There was virtually no relationship between retention of the communication content and belief. (In a separate study in which there were no delayed measures, Greenwald found that recipient-generated reactions correlated higher with beliefs than recipient modifications of message ideas or externally generated operations.

Since the number of reactions (mean number = 5.37) varied more than the content reaction measure (maximum = 3), the use of the thought-listing procedure as the opinion posttest probably favored its correlations with the cognitive reactions. Despite this possible statistical artifact, these results give strong support to the hypothesis that cognitive responses to persuasion and their retention are important functional dependent mediators of immediate and persisting persuasion, whereas mere retention of communication content is not.

Calder, Insko, and Yandell (1974) used Greenwald's measure of cognitive response in an experiment that varied the number of positive and negative arguments. After the message, there were both immediate and delayed (either one week or two weeks) measurements of cognitive response and rated opinion. The results indicated that increasing the number of arguments in either direction was effective in inducing the advocated opinion and that opinion did not decrease over the two weekly interims. Although the total number of all generated thoughts did not vary with the total number of message arguments, the number of positive and negative reactions did vary with the number of positive and negative message arguments. Generally, the number of cognitive responses declined over time, with most of the decrease in the first week.

When the sources of specific cognitive responses were measured, recipient-generated thoughts correlated less with opinion ratings than either recipient-modified or externally originated thoughts. The time patterns of these three types of thoughts closely resembled the patterns of opinions. The relationship was also reflected by a multiple correlation coefficient of .62 of all three sources of thought with opinion [compared to only .10 simple correlation with the content recall of the same messages in a previous experiment (Insko, 1964)]. Overall, a strong support was found for the hypothesis that the number and direction of message arguments influenced the types of cognitive responses, which, in turn, were highly related to both immediate and persisting attitude change.

Wright (1973) coded cognitive responses to an advertisement into one of four categories: counterarguments (noting discrepancies between message content and one's existing belief system), support arguments (noting congruencies), source derogation, and curiosity. The negative effects of counterarguing responses correlated higher with message acceptance than the positive and negative effects, respectively, of support arguments and source derogations. Furthermore, both recipient-modified and recipient-generated responses were more related to acceptance than advertisement-originated responses.

In further analysis, Wright (1974a) found that subjects who were cued to be more highly involved with the message content exhibited no differences in immediately measured responses compared to less involved subjects. However, two days after audio advertising exposure, highly involved subjects reported significantly more curious responses and fewer counterargument responses than before, whereas less involved subjects significantly increased the number of support arguments. In other words, the highly involved subjects appeared to substitute information-seeking thoughts for resistance thoughts over time (as the intervening activities hypothesis would predict), whereas the less involved subjects added supportive thoughts (as the discounting cues and delayed filtering hypotheses would predict). Wright (1975) also found very high overlap of reported responses for the two measurement periods and, as with immediate attitude change, found a strong lingering negative correlation between immediate counterarguing and delayed attitude measures.

Some advertising research has found that initial verbal responses—coded in fashions similar to those of Greenwald and Wright—appear to correlate with both immediate and delayed measures of affect. For example, Maloney (1962) found that responses of curious disbelief were more highly related to immediate ratings of readiness to use than nothing-hard-to-believe responses (a type of support arguing) which, in turn, were more correlated than responses of nonbelief (counterarguing).

Krugman (1975) argues that, the more cognitive responses solicited by advertising or the more involving advertising is, the more likely it is that the "easy in/hard out" model applies. Krugman's (1966, 1966–1967) proposition that a response measure of any "connections" of the *advertising content* to the exposed person's self-experience would be highly related to any successful influence attempt was somewhat supported in a field study by Bogart, Tolley and Orenstein (1970). Leavitt, Waddell, and Wells (1970) examined the relationship of recall responses coded for "Personal Product Response" and a measure taken six weeks later of brand-bought last. Among initial product users, recallers specifically relating the *product* to themselves in any way were more likely, six weeks later, to have last bought the advertised cereal or tuna. Ward and Ray (1974) found that one television antidrug-use commercial that induced more initial counterarguing than another commercial on the same topic seemed to produce more reports of subsequent drug discussions ten to fourteen days later. Viewers of another ad, which produced more personal connections, were more likely to report later that they had read a mailed antidrug booklet and had found it helpful.

To summarize, the sheer diversity of viewpoints and evidence regarding the relationship between learning and attitude persistence seems to suggest an equivocal empirical status. However, it is not so equivocal that one cannot make any statements regarding the relationship. Our interpretation of the literature suggests that retention is indeed a key mediator of attitudinal persistence. Much of the failure to find consistent and unequivocal results can be attributed to differences in research paradigms and their adequacy to test the retention-persistence relationship and to variations in the operationalization of dependent variables (Kapferer, 1976).

The key to clearer results may be to shift attention from learning of message content to cognitive responses generated by audience members. This focus views audience members as information processors, and, as such, may help to explain how message cues are selected and evaluated in terms of the receiver's own background and predispositions and how they are stored in memory.

FACTORS AFFECTING PERSISTENCE OF COMMUNICATION EFFECTS

The preceding section has reviewed research in an attempt to understand the processes underlying persistence or duration of communication effects. We have examined how learning decays over time and the varying processes which may influence the duration of attitude change. In the last subsection, we reviewed research pertaining to the relationship between persistence of learning and persistence of attitude change resulting from communication.

We turn now to evidence which may be of more practical value to advertisers—the factors which affect persistence. This section offers hypotheses from communication and advertising research about factors which interact with carryover, or persistence, effects. These factors include the media schedule, the advertising medium, the particular advertising appeal and format, the product-brand marketing situation, and the consumer segment. In terms of the pictorial model (Figure 1), the media schedule and advertising medium are situational factors which may influence consumer informtion processing; the advertising appeal and format variables are message factors; and the consumer segment refers to defined groups of consumers who may process advertising information in different ways.

Media Schedule

The media schedule is defined as the number and timing of advertising exposures. On the basis of past research, it appears that, along with intervening supportive activities, repetition is the most important factor affecting the persis-

tence of advertising effects. Although the efficiency of added advertising exposures in increasing effect is controversial (Simon, 1965, 1969), there is little
doubt that repetition is very effective in the important function of preventing
decay (Ostheimer, 1970; Stewart, 1964).

Some evidence for repetition effects is found in the communication research
literature. For example, Cromwell and Kunkel (1952) found that attitude change
following a single exposure of a speech had nearly completely regressed to the
premessage level one month later but that one additional exposure at that time
was able to return attitude change to the level after the first message. Cook and
Insko (1968) found that a simple conclusion reminder eleven days after exposure
facilitated persistence of attitude change.

Other evidence for the effectiveness of repetition is reported in the marketing
literature. Politz (1960) conducted a field experiment in which copies of the
Saturday Evening Post were hand-delivered to subjects two days apart with
instructions to read through the magazine and then return it by mail. Particular
ads were counted as being exposed to a subject only if a glue spot was broken.
Interviews were conducted three days after delivery of the second magazine.
Politz's results showed that, compared to a single ad exposure, two ad exposures
two days apart approximately doubled the familiarity of the brand and its claim
and the expressed willingness to buy, and tripled the belief in claim. However,
the lack of an interview after the first magazine delivery meant that the test ads
exposed only in the first magazine were more liable to be forgotten before
measurement—a fact that might help the reported relative effectiveness of repeated ads. A subsequent report of the same experiment (Lucas and Britt, 1963)
stated that increases from the second ad exposure were, on the average, twice as
great for established brands as for newer brands. Another magazine field study
(Hubbard, 1970) showed that repetition over a long time period can positively
affect sales as well as awareness, and attitudes.

Amount of Repetition.   Research has established that repetition is effective in
inducing persistence primarily through slowing the decay process. We now consider the effects of varying amounts of repetition on persistence. One particular
repetition condition that is especially conducive to persistence effects is that of
overlearning. Like Ebbinghaus, other researchers have found that practice (repetition) beyond the initial amount necessary to learn a task perfectly results in
substantial persistence of learning over long periods of time (Krueger, 1929,
1930; Postman, 1962). However, if the subject matter is meaningful prose,
overlearning appears to affect the absolute amount of learning and retention but
not the rate of decay (Gilbert, 1957).

Craig, Sternthal, and Olshan (1972) studied the effects of 100 percent learning
(7 exposures), 200 percent learning (14 exposures), and 300 percent learning (21
exposures) of 12 print advertisements. The 200 percent learning condition resulted in more retention after 28 days than did the 300 percent condition. Both

overlearning conditions produced consistently better retention after 1, 7, and 28 days than did the 100 percent learning condition. The authors speculated that, somewhat similar to the "boomerang" results discussed earlier, the inverted U-curve for the number of brand names recalled may have been due to an offsetting effect of increasing retention and increasing irritation, corresponding to decreasing motivation to retrieve the brand names. A subsequent experiment (Craig, Sternthal, and Leavitt, 1976) that controlled for inattention and reactance revealed that, as hypothesized, increasing repetition up to 400 percent learning monotonically increased recall after 14 and 28 days, but no differences were found between 100, 200, 300, and 400 percent learning for shorter time periods of 2 or 7 days. Of course, the simple brand recall measure overlooks differences in the quality of retained thoughts or responses (Bahrick, 1964). There is also the possibility that the constant repetition of an ad campaign can make even a perfectly retained advertising appeal, such as "I'd walk a mile for a Camel," rather meaningless with no retained responses to that slogan (Amster, 1964; Amster and Glassman, 1966). It would be very interesting to examine directly the effects of a high number of exposures on delayed cognitive response measures such as counterarguing and support arguing.

Only one line of research has studied the effects of high amounts of repetition on attitudes. Zajonc et al. (1971) found positive monotone effects from as many as 81 exposures of nonsense syllables. In another experiment Zajonc et al. (1972) found that the positive attitude change effects of 25 consecutive exposures of nonsense syllables remained one week later, even though a learning-type measure of latency of word associations decreased over the week delay.

Repetition Processes. In addition to research showing that repetition affects persistence by slowing decay of effects, some recent research has examined cognitive responses to repetitious communication, using methods similar to Greenwald's (1968) discussed earlier (see Sawyer, 1974, 1977).

Research has shown that inverted U-curve and monotonically negative effects of repetition may result if either the repeated stimuli or their presentation format is of low complexity. Explanation of these results is offered by Berlyne's (1970) two-factor theory, which says the negative effects of tedium from repeated exposures may offset or overwhelm the positive effects of habituation or reduced uncertainty of response to the stimuli. However, Crandall, Harrison, and Zajonc (1975) found the negative boredom effect may be only transitory, whereas the positive effect is permanent. Even repeated stimuli resulting in negative effects or an inverted U-curve when attitude was measured immediately showed monotonically increasing attitude when measures were delayed one week later. Stang (1974) also concluded that satiation effects were short-lived. He found that studies incorporating even as small a measurement delay as a few minutes were much more likely to show positive effects of exposure.

The effectiveness of repetition in changing attitudes in the long term might be explained by an experiment by McCullough and Ostrom (1974). They showed subjects five variations of one of two advertising campaigns—one ad immediately after another. While watching each of the five ads, subjects were asked to list their cognitive reactions in a procedure similar to Greenwald's The net positiveness of the cognitive responses steadily and significantly increased with repetition. The number of total responses remained quite constant, while the number of positive ones increased and the number of negative ones decreased. Furthermore, the public-service campaign, which was expected to generate more agreement, evoked significantly more favorable responses than a toiletries-product campaign. The findings suggest that, after initial negative, defensive responses have been elicited, the more positive responses to subsequent exposures lead to more favorable attitudes. Obviously, more research on repetition effects which would measure cognitive responses and delayed attitude change would be very useful.

Johnson and Watkins (1971) examined the effects of repetition of messages containing sources varying in credibility. Their results also bear on the question of the duration of repetitious messages. In their first experiment (1970) the investigators found that, while repetition was effective in increasing content recall and attitude change, there were no differences in the decay of attitude change for one, three, or five exposures when measured ten weeks later. However, they found different delayed effects for a shorter (four-week) period in a second experiment (1971) that manipulated source credibility (high or low), number of message exposures (one or five), and opinion measurement delay (none or four weeks). Although higher source credibility increased attitude change, repetition showed no main effects. However, significant interactions were obtained for repetition by source, repetition by delay, and repetition by source by delay. As can be seen in Figure 3, the high-credibility source message decayed significantly but no decay was found for the less credible source. Repetition led to less attitude decay than did a single exposure, primarily because there ws less attitude decay after five exposures than after one exposure in the high-source-credibility condition. The authors speculated that repetition positively affected initial learning and slowed the rate of forgetting (although the rate was not measured in the experiment). The greater decay for the high-source-credibility treatment was probably due to the greater initial increase for that source, hence, the greater absolute decay. Because the low-credibility source inhibited iniital attitude change to such a strong degree, repetition had little opportunity to increase persistence.

Krugman (1972) offers an extremely interesting theoretical explanation of the television advertising repetition process. His thesis is, "campaign effects based on, say, 20 or 30 exposures are only multiples or combinations of what happens in the first few exposures." The very *first exposure* (defined as actual attention by the consumer) is dominated by a "what *is* it?" response—an attempt to define

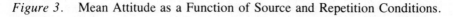

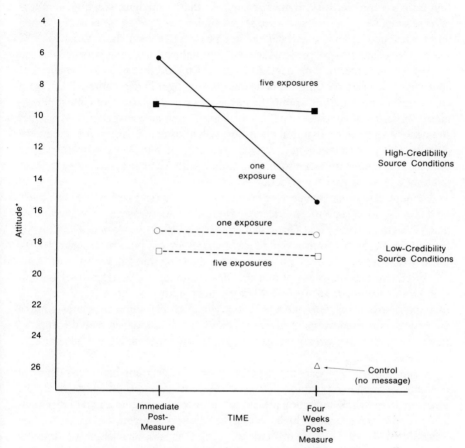

Figure 3. Mean Attitude as a Function of Source and Repetition Conditions.

*The lower the attitude score, the more agreement with the persuasive message.
Source: Johnson and Watkins (1971)

or understand the ad stimulus. He suggests that a totally novel stimulus requires some initial attention and classification response attempt—even if that response is to discard the object as of no further interest. The *second exposure* may result in further unfinished cognitive classification. However, due to the probable recognition, the cognitive response is, at least, vastly facilitated and shortened. Instead, the response is much more likely to be dominated by evaluative "what *of* it?" reactions in which the consumer judges the personal relevance of this now not totally unfamiliar advertisement. The *third exposure* then becomes a true reminder—if there is some consequence of the earlier evaluations yet to be fulfilled. But it is also the beginning of disengagement, of withdrawal of attention from a completed task. Krugman suggests that campaigns with high numbers of exposures work in the same manner. A majority of people selectively screen most television commercials and do not progress beyond the "What *is* it?" stage. The evaluative response is most likely delayed until the person is in the market for the advertised product. Multiples of the third reminder exposure will continue to be effective until the consumer is no longer in the market. Thus, for a convenience good, multiple reminder exposures could be effective almost indefinitely. In terms of persistence effects of "third" reminder exposures, Krugman stresses the value of recognition measures which, as noted earlier, are often very slow to decay. Also, as noted earlier, measures of initial cognitive responses such as "personal connections" may correlate with whether a reminder exposure is likely to have a positive effect.

Although Krugman's conjecture is mainly untested (and perhaps not testable), he does cite some supportive evidence. Both his work measuring eye movement data (Krugman, 1968) and Grass and Wallace's (1969) work with CONPAAD response indicate that from two to four exposures are optimal. McDonald (1970), in an extensive analysis of purchase diary data interrelated with media data, identified two exposures as optimal. Finally, Maloney's (1966) similar Continuous Survey Approach to Attitude Measurement study for Leo Burnett indicated that three exposures was most effective in affecting three measures—brand awareness, acceptance, and preference. However, Maloney stressed the impracticality of estimating average response, since effects of individual ads varied a great deal.

To summarize, it appears that repetition increases learning and slows decay of content learning and attitude effects. Recent research suggests that the mechanism by which repetition affects persistence might be understood by examining cognitive responses which occur over a period of repetitious exposure (see Sawyer, 1974, 1977). It is difficult to specify an absolute length of time for which effects persist after repetitious exposure is stopped, since the studies reviewed vary greatly in stimulus materials, measurements, and other aspects. However, we can observe from the available empirical evidence that few effects remain after about ten weeks, except in cases of extreme duration observed in overlearning experiments. Krugman's three exposure and uninvolved learning theses, however, may mean that it is easy to underestimate the duration of advertising effects—since one reminder exposure may surprisingly easily trigger a buying response.

Timing of Ad Exposure.   Besides frequency, another aspect of the media schedule that appears to affect the persistence of communication effects is the timing of the media exposures. Two relevant subfactors of timing are the spacing of repeated exposures and the degree of isolation of a brand's advertising exposures from those of competitors.

Concerning the spacing of repeated exposures, research on learning indicates that massed practice (short intervals) is more effective than distributed practice in producing initial learning (McCrary and Hunter, 1963). In advertising research, Strong (1916) varied the interval between four dummy magazine advertising exposures, and measured ad recognition one month after the last exposure. He reported that a weekly interval was superior to monthly or daily intervals which, in turn, were superior to immediate reviewing. Burt and Dobell (1925) investigated the effect of different schedules of various sets of visual and audio materials on a paired-associate type of recall and recognition. When measured sixteen days after the first exposure, recall was superior in a schedule of an initial presentation followed three days later by another, compared to a schedule with a ten-day interval between first and second exposures.

Two major field studies (Zielske, 1959; Strong, 1972) experimentally manipulated both the number of advertising direct-mail exposures and their timing. Zielske compared a schedule of one ad exposure per week for thirteen weeks to a schedule of one ad exposure every four weeks (monthly) for thirteen times. Recall was measured every week for the first thirteen weeks and then every two weeks until the end of the year in the weekly schedule condition and every two weeks for thirteen months in the monthly condition. Zielske's smoothed results (see Strong, 1972) are shown in Figure 4. It can be seen that, in both schedules, repetition was very effective at increasing ad recall. Soon after the thirteenth exposure, 63 percent of the people who had been mailed weekly ads recalled some of the ad content, as did 48 percent of those receiving monthly ads. Forgetting was quite rapid and decayed in an Ebbinghaus fashion. In the weekly condition, the percentage recalling the ads after thirteen exposures was cut in half four weeks later and decreased by two-thirds after six weeks.

Similar to past lab research results, the rate of forgetting decreased as the number of exposures increased. Three weeks after a single exposure, the percentage remembering the advertising dropped from 14 percent to 3 percent—a 79 percent rate of decrease, whereas four weeks after thirteen monthly exposures, there was only a 23 percent decrease, from 48 percent to 37 percent. In terms of persistence over the entire year, the monthly schedule was superior with an average weekly remembrance of 29 percent compared to 21 percent for the weekly schedule (Zielske and Pomerance, 1958).

Strong (1972) replicated part of Zielske's direct-mail experiment, comparing a weekly schedule of thirteen ads with a biweekly schedule of six ads and a monthly schedule of four ads. In addition to ad recall, Strong's study included measures of top-of-mind brand mention and acceptance of ad content. Although the time schedule and frequency variables were partly confounded, Strong's results were interesting. Repetition (coded into frequency quartiles) positively affected ad recall and brand mention, and the length of exposure interims was inversely related to these measures. Concerning acceptance of ad content, no direct relationship with the number of exposures was found. However, as with

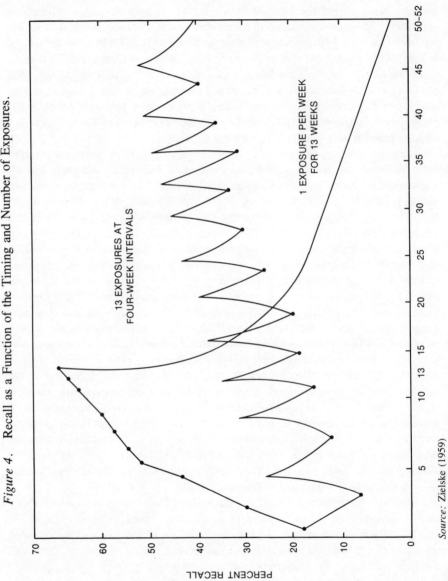

Figure 4. Recall as a Function of the Timing and Number of Exposures.

Source: Zielske (1959)

the cognitive measures, the weekly schedule was more effective than the biweekly or monthly schedules. Contrary to what was expected from Zielske's results, relatively little forgetting occurred over a three-week period and the previously discussed "boomerang" effect on belief was found.

Strong (1974) combined the recall data from both his and Zielske's study and ran simulations of various schedules based on the derived regression equations. The results suggest that quarterly flights of three to four biweekly exposures achieved higher average weekly recall (32.2 percent) over a year period than did thirteen consecutive monthly (30.1 percent), biweekly (29.7 percent), or weekly exposures (26.5 percent). Whether similar results might be obtained for effects on attitudes and behavior is debatable. Strong (1972) speculated that improved measurement of acceptance of content and brand evaluation might have produced results more affected by repetition and time and more consistent with the measures of learning. However, it does seem safe to conclude that (1) persistence of obtained communication effects is facilitated by repetition and (2) spaced individual exposures or spaced groups of exposures (bursts) are more effective schedules than massing of exposures when the objective is maximum average communication over the entire period in question.

Besides the timing of repeated exposures, another important aspect of timing is the sequencing of exposures relative to competitors' advertisements. Available research evidence from the order effects literature (Miller and Campbell, 1959; Insko, 1964) previously displayed indicates that there is usually a recency advantage; i.e., of two messages, the one heard most recently usually has a greater impact. If a marketer has a very strong argument or the ability to purchase a lot of exposures or if the goal is long-term effects, then it might be advantageous to get exposure before competitors. If the goal is immediate impact, the last exposure is probably a more attractive position (Gerhold and McGuire, 1966).

Of course, the managerial usefulness of such order effects research is not great since individual consumers are continually in the market. Also, since competitors generally use repetition, any action based on order effects calls for similar repetition schedules. A less conventional hypothesis proposes the advantage of isolating one's brand advertisements from competitors' both in terms of the times and media used. Although proactive and retroactive inhibitions can occur even when dissimilar or irrelevant stimuli ads of noncompetitors are presented (Burnstein, 1962), such interference is particularly great when similar stimuli (such as competitors' ads) closely precede or follow (Underwood and Ekstrand, 1967). Also, competing messages that occur close together may lead to more counterarguing and less positive attitude change (Gillig and Greenwald, 1974; McGuire, 1964). All of this research points to the advantage of exposure timing that is unique from competitors'. It would appear wise to consider media vehicles and times that trade off penetration of target segment for uniqueness from competition (Greyser, 1972).

Advertising Medium

The strongest direct evidence of a "medium" advantage is in the previously discussed research showing stronger persistence effects for audiences writing their own pro-arguments than for audiences passively reading a message (Watts, 1967) and in research on discussion (Janis and Hoffman, 1971) and role playing (Culbertson, 1957; Janis and Mann, 1965).

Evidence is scant regarding effects of different mass media on persistence of communication. Conventional wisdom suggests that the effects of print media—especially magazines—will be more enduring than those of broadcast media, since readers may have repeated exposure to magazine ads as they leaf through the publication several times (Coffin, 1975). Krugman (1967) also hypothesizes that print media are more involving than broadcast media. The former require relatively more purposive effort, while television watching can be characterized by what Krugman calls the "bleary-eyed" viewer. Although it may be that any differences are due to the fact that more involving and more differentiable products are more likely to appear in print than on television (Preston, 1970), some evidence of more immediate connections in cognitive responses to print messages compared to television has been found (Hsia, 1968; Bogart, Tolley, and Orenstein, 1970). Krugman (1966) quoted some evidence that might refute Preston's (1970) conjecture. A *Time* study showed that involvement with advertising tends to be higher for magazines than for television for high-involvement products but no different with low-involvement products. Krugman (1970) also found that one magazine ad produced a higher proportion of cognitive arousal, as measured by brain waves, than did three television commercials.

In a more controlled experiment, Wright (1974a) found significantly more total cognitive responses, less source derogation, and more support arguments for a print version of an advertisement than for a radio version. Cueing women that they would be asked to evaluate the product depicted in the ad ("high content involvement") increased counterarguing for the print message but not for the radio message. Although acceptance of the ad message was not affected by the medium, buying intention was higher for the print condition than for the radio. In addition to the immediately measured cognitive response activity, delayed responses were elicited two days later; among the.involved women supportive responses to the radio ad increased, but not to the print ad. Initially, the rapid transmission rate of broadcast media, compared to the more audience-controllable input of print, probably inhibits both the amount and variability of response activity. Over time, relatively more opportunity exists for increases in cognitive responses to broadcast media; these responses may, in turn, be related to different amounts of persistence of attitude change and behavior. If such hypothesized differences in cognitive response activity do exist, it may be even more important to assess delayed, as well as immediate, effects for broadcast media than for print because of the former's greater potential for increased cognitive response over time.

To summarize, little systematic evidence exists concerning the effects of advertising medium on persistence of communication effects. The existing evidence suggests that the audience-controlled input of print advertising may generate more immediate learning and cognitive responses than "low-involvement" broadcast exposures. Over time, however, increases in reactions to broadcast advertising may occur.

Advertising Format and Appeals

Some advertisements are more memorable than others due to their appeals—sex, humor, comparison ads, etc.—or to their formats, such as typography or visual techniques in commercials. Our review of research yielded various studies dealing with the relationship between persistence of advertising and format or appeals. The following areas will be examined in turn:

1. Refutational appeals
2. Fear appeals
3. "Soft-sell" appeals
4. Amount of information
5. Self-attribution appeals
6. Advertisements with incomplete copy

Refutational Appeals. A message employing refutational appeals presents and then refutes (counterargues) arguments that are contrary to the message's viewpoint—somewhat analogous to comparison advertising. Most advertising messages, of course, present only supportive points in favor of the viewpoint and do not mention any potential drawbacks or refute claims in the message. The study of refutational appeals has focused on their greater effectiveness compared to supportive appeals in inducing resistance to subsequent attacking or competitive claims (McGuire, 1964). In addition to McGuire's work with noncontroversial topics, refutational advertising appeals have been found effective in inducing resistance in general (Bither, Dolich, and Nell, 1971) and in changing attitudes of users of competing products (Faison, 1961; Sawyer, 1973) and attitudes of more educated consumers (Faison, 1961).

Some research has examined the effects of refutational appeals over time. McGuire hypothesized that refutational appeals would "inoculate" people against attacks on previously unquestioned ("germ-free") beliefs. Supportive appeals, on the other hand, would provide information but little or no motivation to resist subsequent persuasion. Following this reasoning, McGuire (1964) hypothesized that, compared to a refutational message, a supportive appeal is immediately more persuasive, but that later, after an attacking message is presented, the refutational appeal is superior.

McGuire also examined the effects of using the same arguments that appear in attacks as the arguments in the refutational appeal (refutational-same appeals) versus using different arguments (refutational-different appeals). The refutational-same appeal both informs people and provides a motivational basis to resist the attacks. Consequently, the effects should persist initially and then decay. The refutational-different message merely motivates people to resist; therefore, results should show some initial increases with time as bolstering information is gathered, and then decay. Finally, the effects of the supportive appeal, which contains information but little motivation, should simply decay with time.

McGuire (1962) tested these hypotheses in an experiment in which the subsequent attacking message was viewed either immediately or two to seven days later. The results nearly exactly matched the predictions based on the underlying motivation and information processes over time. Other experiments involving the delayed effects of active (self-written) defenses tended to produce similar results of the refutational-different appeal (McGuire, 1964; Rogers and Thistlethwaite, 1969).

Szybillo and Heslin (1973) attempted to replicate McGuire's results with advertisements about the effectiveness of safety air bags in automobiles. They presented either refutational-same, refutational-different, supportive, or no-defense ads and then varied the credibility of the source of a subsequent attacking message (government agency or auto manufacturer) and the time between defense and attack (thirty minutes or three days). The authors hypothesized that the refutational-same ad would be most effective in resisting the attacking message, followed by refutational-different, supportive, and no-defense ads. It was found that, when the attack was immediate, there were no significant differences in the delayed condition. The effects of the supportive appeal did not decay, whereas the effects of the refutational appeals decayed down to the level of the supportive appeals. Interestingly, there was somewhat less decay of the refutational appeals in the low-credibility-attack condition than for the high-credibility attack. The authors concluded that a time interval longer than three days might be necessary to find the hypothesized time advantage of refutational advertising appeals.

Support for this latter speculation by Szybillo and Heslin comes from a previous study by Faison (1961). Faison exposed three radio commercials for an automobile, a gas range, and a floor wax. Half the subjects viewed "conventional" one-sided positive ads, while the other half viewed two-sided commercials with both positive and negative points about the advertised brands. Unfortunately, no detailed data were reported. However, Faison concluded that the two-sided ads were significantly more effective than the one-sided ads for all three products. Most effective were the ads for the low-priced floor wax. Especially important were the results of a subsequent second measure four to six weeks after initial ad exposure. Faison reported that "neither the one-sided nor the two-sided arguments had shown diminishing effects." In fact, subjects who had listened to the two-sided commercials showed an *increase* in attitudes toward the brands. Although it is impossible from Faison's abstract to assess the quality of his research, his results do offer support to McGuire's contentions about the persistence of effects of two-sided messages.

One other recent experiment with refutational appeals gave additional insight into their persistence. Gillig and Greenwald (1974) presented either a refutational-same communication or an irrelevant one a few minutes before a persuasive message attacking widely-held beliefs about health practices. The source of the attacks was varied as either high or low in credibility. Some respondents were given both immediate and two-week-delayed opinion posttests and others gave cognitive responses immediately after exposure. Regarding cognitive responses, the two high-credibility conditions produced a majority of agreement responses. In the low-credibility conditions, the refutational defense led primarily to counterarguing when the attack was presented, whereas the irrelevant message led to source discounting. After two weeks, the irrelevant condition showed a sleeper-type effect, as would be predicted by the discounting cues hypothesis; moreover, there were no significant differences between the high- and low-credibility attacks after two weeks. When the attacks were preceded by the refutational defense, the highly credible attack was more effective than the low-credibility source in reversing the effects of the refutational defense, and these relative effects declined by about the same small amount over two weeks.

Positive reactions appeared to correspond with more positive opinions but these positive opinions were relatively less time resistant than the initially lower opinions which resulted from the message condition which caused source discounting and counterarguing. Furthermore, as Syzbillo and Heslin found, the refutational appeal was relatively more effective over time in the low-credibility-source condition. This may imply that the attitudes coinciding with counterarguing cognitive responses decay less rapidly than those associated with source discounting responses. Gillig and Greenwald suggest that sleeper effects may depend on conditions in which audiences are unprepared to counterargue.

Fear Appeals. One type of advertising appeal that is gaining increasing attention from marketing researchers is the use of fear (Ray and Wilkie, 1970; Sternthal and Craig, 1973). This upsurge of research interest reflects a parallel resurgence of advertising campaigns which use some variety of fear appeals, e.g., campaigns for life insurance firms and alarm systems. Research on the question of whether high levels of physical threat are more effective than low-fear appeals or messages using no fear has produced no simple answers. Both negative and positive relationships between fear level and changes in attitude and behavior have been reported, and models which allow for nonmonotonic relationships have been proposed (e.g., Janis, 1967; McGuire, 1968b; Levanthal, 1970).

The effects of fear appeals over time have been examined in a few studies. Although results are not totally conclusive, the overall finding seems to be that high-fear appeals are more effective over time.[3] Levanthal and Niles (1964) concluded that negative relationships between fear and persuasion seemed to result when measures were delayed following exposure (e.g., Janis and Fesh-bach, 1953), while opposite results were found with immediate measurement (e.g., Levanthal, Singer, and Jones, 1965). However, when Levanthal and Niles conducted an experiment to test this conclusion, they failed to find the expected results. Fear, manipulated by the length of exposure (8 to 32 minutes) to highway safety movies, was at first positively related to changes in auto-safety-related opinions and intentions; this attitude change dissipated back to pre-exposure levels over a one-week period. Although the difference was not significant, somewhat less decay was found for the high-fear conditions. This result was consistent with Haefner (1956), who found that high-fear messages about the dangers of atomic bomb testing were more effective than low-fear appeals both immediately and two weeks after message exposure.

Insko, Arkoff, and Insko (1965) tested the effects on seventh-graders of high- and low-fear messages about the health hazards of smoking. The high-fear message was more effective than the low-fear message in immediately changing intentions about smoking behavior. Although the high-fear message was still more effective after one week, the difference was much smaller due to a "sleeper-like" effect by which the effectiveness of the high-fear condition decreased and that of the low-fear message increased over time.

One study that was especially well conceived and helped to eliminate some of the problems of past fear research (Higbee, 1969) reported mixed results of fear messages over time. Evans et al. (1970) tested five message conditions in a program to improve the toothbrushing habits of junior high school students. The high-fear, low-fear, and positive-social approval messages were all followed by four specific recommendations about proper tooth care. The fourth message condition contained only those four recommendations, and the fifth condition contained a longer, more elaborate version of the same recommendations. Several measures were taken immediately, five days, and six weeks after message exposure.

Reported anxiety was increased more by high fear than low fear and the magnitude of these effects decreased over time. However, the high-fear appeal resulted in the least amount of *retained information,* followed by the low-fear appeal, and then by the simple and elaborate recommendations and social-approval messages. Over time, these differences in retention decreased to non-significant levels. For immediate *behavior intention*, both fear conditions were equally effective and were significantly more effective than the other three messages. However, as the effects of all the messages decreased over time, the effects of the high-fear message showed relatively greater persistence than any other message at the end of six weeks. Figure 5 shows the results for *reported toothbrushing behavior*. It can be seen that, somewhat similar to intended behavior, the high-fear appeal was most effective after five days and six

Figure 5. Reported Behavior Change Scores for Treatment Groups.

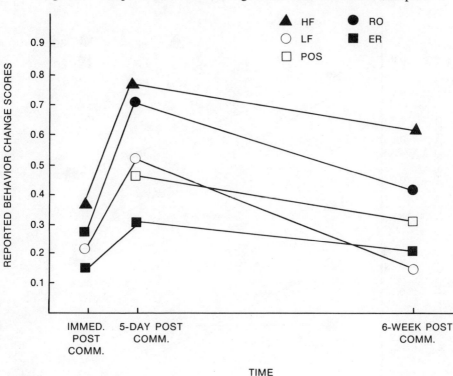

Source: Evans et al. (1970).

weeks. Interestingly, the short recommendation-only message was second most effective. Although the statistical significance was not reported, it appears that the low-fear appeal showed the largest decrease from five days to six weeks.

Figure 6 shows the changes in *actual dental hygiene behavior,* which was accurately measured after five days and six weeks by a disclosing wafer (see Evans et al., 1968). It can be seen that the actual behavior induced by the various messages differed drastically from the reported behavior. The elaborated recommendations and the positive support appeals—the two least effective on reported behavior—were the most effecting in changing actual behavior. The high-fear appeal was only third most effective. However, it was interesting to note that the high-fear message and the recommendations-only message—which were most effective for reported behavior—appeared to decrease relatively less in terms of actual behavior than other messages.

In addition to highlighting the effectiveness of alternatives to fear messages, Evans's field experiment serves to show the complexities of the multiple effects

Figure 6.   Actual Behavior Change Scores for Treatment Groups.

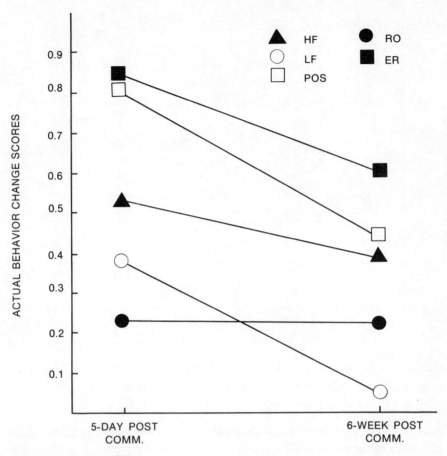

Source: Evans et al. (1970).

of fear appeals over time. Other research has shown that the effects of fear over time vary between intentions and behavior (e.g., Levanthal and Watts, 1966; Chu, 1966; Levanthal, Singer, and Jones, 1965). More fear research—especially in advertising contexts—is needed to clarify the conditions under which the effects of fear persist over time, relative to other appeals.

"Soft-Sell Appeals.   One controversy in advertising concerns the relative effectiveness of "soft-sell" and "hard-sell" appeals. The former are low-keyed, often humorous or relatively pleasant, and usually contain implicit or subtle claims that must be grasped by the audience. The latter tend to be forceful and factual with very explicit claims thrust upon the audience. Krugman (1962)

speculated that the subtleties of the typical soft-sell ad would not "wear out" from repetition as fast as would hard-sell ads in the high-repetition context of ads for consumer packaged goods. Some support for this hypothesis has been reported (Ray and Sawyer, 1971; Silk and Vavra, 1974). Although no direct tests of the persistence effects of soft-sell ads are available, several relevant areas of research offer some insight.

One aspect of soft-sell advertising appeals involves the pleasantness of the message. Pleasantness may be due to the general mood of the commercial, some contained entertainment, or even some direct humor. Some controversy exists over whether the effectiveness of an advertisement is a direct function of its pleasantness or whether unpleasant or irritating ads may also, like pleasant ones, be more effective than neutral ads. Most research indicates that a pleasant message environment facilitates immediate attitude change (Janis, Kaye, and Kirschner, 1965; Rosnow, 1965). In an extensive review, Silk and Vavra (1974) speculate about a discounting cues process in which negative ads lose any immediate negative effects and become more persuasive over time.

Pleasant messages—especially humorous ones—may facilitate opinion change through distraction (Festinger and Maccoby, 1964; Bither, 1972; Gardner, 1970; Haaland and Venkatesan, 1968). That is, cognitive defenses of audience members are distracted from the persuasive intent of the ad, which facilitates attitude change. Osterhouse and Brock (1970) found that distraction decreased counterarguing cognitive responses and increased attitudes, when measured immediately. Such reduced counterarguing seemed likely to result in prolonged persistence of attitude change. However, one study that measured both the immediate and three-weeks-delayed attitudinal effects of matched sets of humorous and serious messages failed to support the hypothesis of greater persistence effects for the humorous messages. Lull (1940) found that two serious messages were equally effective as two humorous ones in both the immediate and delayed conditions. Other research (see Sternthal and Craig, 1973) has failed to find humorous messages superior. Finally, there is some evidence that source credibility can be enhanced by the use of humor—especially for topics of low interest (Gruner, 1967; 1970). Perhaps advertisements with humor can facilitate persistence by moderating the negative effects of low credibility.

Other than pleasantness, soft-sell ads are usually characterized by the subtleness of their conclusions. Experiments which have compared messages containing explicitly drawn conclusions to messages with vague or no explicit conclusions have consistently found greater immediate attitude change for the explicit messages (e.g., Hovland and Mandell, 1952; Cooper and Dinerman, 1951). However, if subtle ads which do not contain explicit conclusions result in the audience's becoming more actively involved with the message, more persistence would be expected (e.g., Watts, 1967). Such reasoning receives some support from the work of Katz and his associates (Katz, Sarnoff, and McClintock, 1956; Stotland, Katz, and Patchen, 1959). "Self-insight" message conditions, which let the subject interpret a complex rationale against prejudice, tend to be more effective over time than purely informational messages. Also, as discussed earlier, some support for the delayed filtering of complex implications hypothesis has been reported (McGuire, 1960a, 1960c; Cohen, 1957).

The evidence that the effects of pleasant or humorous messages and of subtle messages with implicit conclusions have greater relative persistence leads to predictions of greater persistence of persuasion for soft-sell ads than for hard-sell ads. Again, advertising research is needed to test this hypothesis.

Amount of Information.   One advertising decision involves the optimal amount of information to include in an ad. From the standpoint of memory, it would seem that the use of a unique selling proposition—combined with repeated exposure—would be most effective (Reeves, 1961). It would also seem that the simpler and less cluttered the message, the more likely it would be easily perceived and retained and the less likely it would encounter retroactive interference. However, the results of one experiment offer evidence that several appeals in one message may be superior in both changing attitude and partially maintaining that change. Cook and Insko (1968) constructed public-policy messages of about 2,000 words which contained either six or two appeals or values. When attitude change was measured four, seven, and eleven days after the messages, the six-value messages produced significantly more positive attitudes than the two-value messages. Although such a difference might be explained by a hypothesis of delayed effects of the more complex six-value message, the authors advocated the position that an attitude is likely to become more internalized (see Kelman, 1961) and thus more time resistant as a greater number of appeals and/or more important appeals are linked to the new attitude.

The results of the Cook and Insko experiment might also be explained by the perceived repetition of the message's strong points and by the slightly longer length. Repetition within a message has proved effective in prolonging attitudes. Weber (1971) found that, over three to seven weeks, attitudes decayed significantly less than in other conditions when a high-credibility source was mentioned 22 times in a message. Repeating a message's conclusion seven times in a high-social-approval situation was much more effective than a one-conclusion-only message at maintaining changed attitude over six weeks (Cook and Wadsworth, 1972). Also, as reported earlier, longer messages result in more enduring attitude effects than shorter messages. (Levanthal and Niles, 1965; Calder, Insko, and Yandell, 1974). These data are somewhat disconcerting to marketers, in light of the trend to shorter television commercials, and resultant "clutter." This trend may be associated with one toward lower day-after recall (Starch, 1970). Clearly, a priority area for advertising research is the relationship between commercial length, amount of information in messages, repetition, and, ultimately, the duration of advertising effects.

Self-Attribution Appeals. Consumer researchers are beginning to focus on Kelley's (1967) attribution theory as a useful explanation for consumer attitudes and behaviors (e.g., Settle, 1972; Scott, 1973; Burnkrant, 1975). In this theory, people are hypothesized to infer attitudes regarding themselves and others from what they observe and see. One recent experiment suggested the effectiveness of a self-attribution appeal in producing persisting behavior change. Miller, Brinkman, and Bolen (1975) compared the effectiveness of varied repetitions of attribution appeals with normal persuasive appeals on the littering behavior of fifth-grade children. The self-attribution messages (e.g., "you are neat") were significantly more effective than the persuasive messages ("you should be neat") in inducing neatness and pickup behavior both immediately and after two weeks. A second experiment designed to improve mathematics performance showed a similar advantage for self-attribution messages after two weeks. The authors hypothesized that the self-attribution message, which presents the desired behavior as a present fact, results in reduced counterarguing (which was not measured). Perhaps advertisers could present evidence of superiority (e.g., "more of you people buy Brand X than any other brand") in a similar way to produce more enduring effects.

Advertisements with Incomplete Copy. Since Zeigarnik's (1927) classic study, it has been consistently found that incomplete tasks are better remembered than complete tasks (e.g., Butterfield, 1964). This may be true due to a created tension for completion which improves memory, active completion being reinforcing and thus increasing learning (Heller, 1956), or the fact that active participation is apt to produce longer memory than passive participation. Advertisers have sometimes employed copy that might lead to a Zeigarnik effect in ad-ending slogans like "Winston tastes good like a _____" or "To a smoker, it's a _____."

Heimback and Jacoby (1972) conducted a laboratory experiment which indicated that ads can produce a Zeigarnik effect on memory and that such memory may persist over time. Four test commercials were exposed within an audio version of a television program. Test conditions included two ad factors: completeness (complete, interrupted at beginning, interrupted at end) and pause after ad (no pause before resumption of program or a four-second delay). Subjects were pretested and classified according to their usage awareness of the product classes (cigarettes, chewing gum, mouthwash, and a headache remedy) and brands. Recall of the ad copy was measured both immediately and one week later.

The results indicated a Zeigarnik effect in both the immediate and delayed conditions. End-cut commercials produced the highest initial recall which decayed only very slightly; beginning-cut ads were more effective than complete ads but both latter effects decayed relatively rapidly. Thus, the commercials cut at the end produced 33.8 percent more immediate recall than complete versions and exhibited a 52.4 percent advantage one week later. Including a pause after the commercial had no main effect on recall, but there was a significant but complex interaction of pause, ad completeness, and initial brand awareness.

For familiar commercials that use incomplete endings, the Zeigarnik effect may lead to a persisting advantage in memory. Research that examines measures other than recall could ascertain whether the increased learning coincides with more positive beliefs, attitudes, and purchase intentions. Heimback and Jacoby (1972) did report that, in another experiment, no immediate change in general liking of the incomplete commercials was found.

The Product and the Brand

Presumably, an established brand name is a factor in gaining a share of the consumer's memory. Brand name and symbol repetition would seem to strengthen persistence effects on the basis of evidence reviewed to this point. It is also conceivable that persistence effects may vary depending on the number of brands within a product group. It might be, for example, that advertising for a brand in a product group containing relatively few competitors would persist more than advertising for a brand in a more dense product group, since fewer brands and messages would be competing for the consumer's attention and memory.

A primary question concerns what relative advantage, if any, is held by an "established" company or brand. The issue is comparable to that investigated in research concerned with whether an initial communication is likely to have a stronger effect (primacy) than a communication received closer to measurement (recency). Miller and Campbell (1959) hypothesize a net primacy effect resulting from an advantage of prior entry. That is, for two stimuli equal in impact at a given point, the stronger (e.g., a more familiar or more established brand) stimulus will decay less rapidly than the weaker stimulus. This prediction is based on Jost's Second Law of Learning (Jost, 1897). In terms of the marketing situation, this may suggest that the established advertiser should have an advantage in terms of persistence effects in communication relative to less established advertisers.

This notion raises implications for current "corrective advertising" practices of the Federal Trade Commission, which may require an advertiser to run advertising that first cites earlier advertising that has been deemed misleading and then "corrects" the particular misleading impression. Several studies have reported that a corrective advertising campaign of this type did indeed negate and somewhat reverse the effects of the previous campaign (Dyer and Kuehl, 1972; Hunt, 1973; Kassarjian, Carlson, and Rosin, 1975; Mazis and Adkinson, 1976). However, on the basis of Jost's law and notions from the sleeper effect research, one could speculate that, although the impact of the two ads appeared equal, the effects from the less established corrective advertising would decay more rapidly than the effects from the more established deceptive advertising. Sawyer (1976) concluded that studies indicating effectiveness of corrective advertising over heavily repeated, deceptive ad campaigns when the effects are measured immediately may be misleading. Due to the more rapid decay of the corrective advertising, the effects of the prior deceptive advertising are likely to predominate with time. However, two recent studies of the effects of corrective advertising (Dyer and Kuehl, 1978; Sawyer and Semenik, 1978) have not supported Sawyer's prediction.

The durability of the effects of an established company's reputation on evaluations of a new product was examined in a study of industrial buyer behavior by Levitt (1965). Company (source) reputation was varied by identifying a paint salesman as being from a highly regarded long-established chemical company (Monsanto) or from a lower-in-credibility fictitious company.

Of importance in the present paper are the changes occurring over the five weeks between the immediate and delayed measurements. The results showed some decay in the high-source-credibility condition but an increase in the low-credibility condition for the measure of willingness to recommend that the product be given serious consideration by others within the company. Although no tests of statistical significance were reported, Levitt's results lend support to the discounting cues hypothesis discussed earlier. As Levitt observed (1965, p. 511):

> A sleeper effect hurts the well-known company but helps the lesser known company. As the sales prospect forgets the well-known source his originally favorable attitude toward the product declines; as he forgets the lesser-known source, his originally less-favorable attitude toward the product becomes more favorable.

The "good" presentation was generally more effective than the "poor" presentation, and there were no interactions with source credibility over the five weeks.

The extent to which Levitt's findings can be generalized to media advertising for consumer or industrial products can be questioned. Weinberger (1961), for example, suggests that repetition of advertising is probably more likely to reinforce the original effect of the advertising message, thus inhibiting development of the sleeper effect.

Weinberger's reasoning appears to be supported by earlier communication research on effects of "reinstatement of the communicator." For example, Kelman and Hovland (1953) exposed subjects with similar attitudes toward juvenile delinquency to identical messages varying only in source credibility. Immediately following exposure, effects were greatest among subjects exposed to the high-credibility source. Three weeks later, subjects were reexposed to the communication and half were also reminded of the communicator's credibility. Among those reminded of the communicator, the original findings were maintained; however, among those not reminded of the communicator, there was a significant decrease in agreement with the high-credibility communicator, and a small near-significant increase in agreement with the low-credibility communicator. The sleeper effect did not operate when there was repetition of the communicator—a situation analogous to advertising, which is generally repetitious.

Familiarity of Advertising

There is no clear-cut evidence regarding whether or not the repetition characteristics of media advertising diminishes the opportunity for the product to be dissociated from its advertising—similar to the sleeper effect. "Low involvement" notions of television advertising exposure (Krugman, 1966–1967) seem to reinforce Weiss's suggestion (1953) that attention diminishes with repetition under conditions of "low motivation to buy or learn" (Krugman, 1966–1967). Moreover, Weiss (1953) and Berlyne (1966) suggest that repeated presentation of emotionally provocative stimuli leads to a kind of affective adaptation and reduction of arousal. Silk and Vavra (1974) argue that such affective adaptation might operate to offset the kinds of effects expected as a result of reinstating the source and thus might possibly negate the sleeper effect.

Again, empirical evidence is scant. However, contemporary advertising views suggest a "wear-out" model of persistence effects—i.e., advertising can greatly increase initial awareness and trial, but a satiation point is reached, followed by a decay phase. In the satiation phase there is no increased effectiveness with repeated exposures and in the decay phase there is a reverse effect of declining effectiveness with repeated exposures. The notion of wear-out thus denotes a negative carry-over effect of past advertising exposures.

Greenberg and Suttoni (1973) reflect this view in their review of studies conducted by several private advertising testing firms. For example, the authors cite a Marplan study (*TV Age,* 1967) in which matched groups of viewers were exposed to the same television commercials from ten to twenty-four times over the eight weeks. The dependent variable was "interest," measured by pupil dilation. Interest increased to a peak after fifteen exposures, and declined thereafter. However, Marplan cautions that interest varies by creative approaches and product category.

Although complete data are not presented, the authors conclude that wear-out of television commercials can be compared to verbal learning curves described by Jacobovitz (1956):

> First is the generation phase where knowledge increases because of repeated exposure to the stimuli. Knowledge then reaches a satiation point where a person having little intrinsic interest or involvement in the subject matter feels there is nothing else to learn from the information presented. At this point, a person begins to forget the information he has already learned in spite of continuing exposure to the stimuli because he has mentally tuned it out . . . This is the decay phase (Greenberg and Suttoni, 1973, p. 49).

Support for this assertion is provided by studies by Appel (1971), Grass (1968), Wallace (1970), and Grass and Wallace (1969). In Appel's study, recall of eighty-one 60-second commercials for thirty-one different brands was tested. While actual exposure could not be controlled, average level of recall resembled the inverted U-shaped curve: recall peaked when commercials were on the air about one month, and decayed linearly after that.

The studies by Grass (1968), Wallace (1970), and Grass and Wallace (1969) extended laboratory studies to actual field experiments with DuPont advertising. When the same commercial was repeated six times (AAAAAA), interest declined after the second or third exposure. Insertion of a different commercial in the next to the last position (AAAABA) "revived interest momentarily" but interest returned to the earlier point on the decay curve for the last exposure. When two commercials were alternated (ABABAB), interest declined but at a slower rate, and, when six different commercials were used, little interest was observed. The authors noted that only recall and interest follow this "generation-satiation-decay" pattern; attitudes maintain the level reached at the satiation stage, or even increase slightly with repeated exposure.

Consumer Segment

Investigators have long sought to classify groups of people in terms of susceptibility to persuasion (e.g., Janis and Field, 1959; Janis, 1963; McGuire, 1968a). The question can be raised as to whether it is possible to segment groups of consumers in terms of relative magnitude of carry-over effects of advertising.

It would seem that a general intelligence factor might be related to longer carry-over effects, since measures of carry-over usually include memorial processes. Intelligence should be negatively related to persuasibility and yielding, since more intelligent persons should have more bases for belief, better critical abilities, and higher self-esteem, all characteristics which would allow the person to defend himself against the impact of persuasive communications. One can add from more recent research (Greenwald, 1968; Wright, 1974b) that highly intelligent individuals might be more likely to counterargue than less intelligent individuals.

Early communication research found modest evidence for a negative relationship between intellectual ability and persuasibility; high-intelligence subjects were more influenced by two-sided than by one-sided presentation of issues, were more influenced by communications containing "impressive, logical arguments," and less influenced by messages based on generalities or illogical argumentation (Janis, 1963).

McGuire (1968a) suggests that intelligence is negatively related in tests of suggestibility, but not in tests of persuasibility. He argues in terms of his model's "compensation" principle that intelligence should be expected to be positively related to message reception—i.e., higher "scanning" and attention span abilities among higher intelligence individuals (the receptor mediator)—but negatively related to the yielding mediator. It may be that attitude change, although initially less for more intelligent individuals, is relatively persistent. High decay rates of learning and attitude change would be expected for individuals lower in intelligence.

Certain personality characteristics have been found to interact with time in affecting attitude change, although no research has explicitly attempted to examine their effects on advertising carry-over. Cohen (1957) investigated the message receiver's "need for cognition," and found a negative relationship with attitude change decay. McGuire (1964) and Watts (1967) found that opinion change is more persistent if the receiver actively participates in, rather than passively receives, persuasive communications. Such notions are generally consistent with "low-involvement" notions suggested by Krugman (1968).

Some evidence concerning attitudinal effects of cognitive responses to communication, and levels of audience involvement, are suggestive of kinds of consumer segment dimensions important in predicting carry-over effects. In Wright's (1974b) research discussed earlier, communications that generated support arguments also produced more positive attitudes, but were likely to decay more rapidly than communications that produced initial negative attitudes and counterarguments. Wright also found that self-confidence was positively related to counterargument production, suggesting a possibility for segmentation.

Ward and Ray (1974) reasoned that senior high school students would be more involved in topics relating to drug abuse, relative to junior high school students and parents, and would counterargue more in response to anti-drug-abuse advertisements. This finding was obtained, as were expectations regarding longer-range effects (i.e., interpersonal communication). These results suggest the utility of acute involvement as an individual characteristic mediating persistence effects.

Marketing applications of general personality tests, as well as more recent attempts at specifically designed instruments (e.g., "psychographics"), have been related to a variety of consumer behaviors, but not to questions of persistence of communications (Wells and Beard, 1973). However, earlier research on effects of general and situation-specific self-confidence on yielding suggests the importance of distinguishing between general factors which may affect patterns of persistence of communication across all communication situations and factors which may be related to relatively specific persistence effects (Cox, 1967; Bauer, 1967). That is, it may be more fruitful to search for specific interactions between audience segments and message characteristics than for segments of the population who are more likely to exhibit longer carry-over effects for all messages.

One experiment classified matched samples of individuals in terms of relative amount of exposure to television advertising (Grass, 1970). The "light-exposure" group saw from one to three commercials per month for a consumer product, the medium group four to six commercials, and the heavy-exposure group seven to twelve commercials. The heavy-exposure group peaked in brand awareness after one month of exposure, and then declined. The light- and medium-exposure groups required two months to reach a peak, consistent with previous repetition research. The important results, however, are that the heavy-exposure group reached a somewhat higher peak in brand awareness than the other two groups, and that decay in brand awareness for this group did not appear as severe as for the two less exposed groups after three months.

Another segmentation variable that may be useful in predicting persistence effects is multiple brand purchasing. Olson and Jacoby (1973) report that multi-brand purchasers (in a specific product category) could correctly recall, unaided, more specific product information about brands in the product category than could unibrand purchasers. Moreover, multibrand purchasers based choice decisions on a greater number of product dimensions. Contrary to prediction, unibrand purchasers were not able to recall more information about their preferred brand, compared to multibrand purchasers. The authors speculate that this may reflect a desire on the part of consumers to simplify choice decisions and avoid additional information. This intriguing suggestion may imply that, once a saturation point is reached in terms of product information, marketers may augment persistence effects by changing advertising appeals.

CONCLUSIONS

This paper has assessed theory and research pertinent to the question of the persistence of advertising effects. We have included research about persistence effects on learning, cognitive responses, attitudes and behavior, and the inter-relationships of these effects over time.

Rather than a tedious review and summary of the discussion to this point, we conclude with a series of propositions—or, more accurately, working hypotheses.

A first set of propositions deals with cognitive responses: both persistence effects of cognitive responses, and factors affecting them.

> Cognitive processes at the time of exposure and immediately following exposure are likely to be extremely important factors affecting persistence. These processes may include rehearsal of counterarguments, support arguments, source derogation, curiosity, and connections to personal life.
>
> Initial cognitive responses of counterarguing and source derogation generate less positive attitudes than do cognitive responses of support arguing. However, attitudes based on the former responses may decay less rapidly over time than the latter.
>
> Cognitive responses of "curiosity" may be the most resistant to decay.
>
> Advertising that produces counterarguing or source derogating cognitive responses at low levels of advertising exposure is likely to produce less negative cognitive response at higher exposure levels.

A second set of propositions pertains to attitude decay, a response variable frequently studied in research on persistence effects:

Unlike learning, attitudes may actually increase (i.e., become more salient or favorable) over time. Attitude decay rates are likely to differ in different communication situations.

There is little or no relationship between initial learning of advertising content and later attitudes.

Retention of advertising content is not related to persistence of attitude change.

Retention of initial cognitive reactions is directly related to persistence of attitudes.

A third set of propositions concerns the impact of marketing factors on the duration of responses to communication:

Advertising campaigns accompanied by much word-of-mouth activity are much more likely to produce persisting attitudinal effects than campaigns accompanied by little or no word-of-mouth activity.

Certainly the greatest aid in producing enduring communication effects is positive product experience before and/or after message exposure. In fact, the purchase opportunity may be necessary to "trigger" a delayed increase or change in conscious brand perception or attitude.

Advertising by brand leaders produces more persistence effects than advertising by less established brands, but this advantage decreases with time.

There is little current evidence that individual characteristics are related to persistence effects of advertising.

Finally, a fourth set of propositions focuses on messages and media scheduling factors which may be related to differential persistence effects:

Persistence of learning and attitudes is inversely related to amount of advertising or brand competition.

High levels of repetition are very effective in preventing decay of both initial learning and attitude change.

For a given number of advertising exposures, persistence in learning over a given time period is greater for a spread schedule of advertising exposures than for a concentrated schedule.

Because of the opportunity for reexposure and the potential for active audience involvement, print media are likely to produce greater persistence effects than broadcast media.

Qualified messages may exhibit relative persistence of persuasive effects as the qualifications are forgotten more quickly than the main message arguments.

Refutational appeals in advertising produce greater persistence effects than supportive appeals—especially in a message with a low-credibility source.

Advertising generating high level of fear produces greater persistence effects than a message generating low amounts of fear.

Soft-sell advertising appeals produce greater persistence effects than hard-sell advertising.

Advertising that includes several product benefits results in greater persistence of attitudes than advertising presenting fewer product benefits.

Sleeper effects are not likely to be found in advertising under conditions of message repetition.

Once consumers learn product information, persistence effects will be greater if advertising appeals are changed than if identical brand information advertising is continued.

It is our hope that these propositions might serve as stimuli for future research to test their validity and reliability.

FOOTNOTES

*The authors wish to thank Lawrence Light, BBD&O; Thomas Coffin, NBC; Thomas Cook, Northwestern University; and Alvin Silk, M.I.T., for their help.

[1]This discussion of PM and SM is taken primarily from Jung (1968), pp. 137–139.

[2]These distinctions were suggested in a slightly different form by Kapferer (1976).

[3]A notable exception to this generalization is the research about the effects of threat levels on attitudes and behavior in creating resistance to temptation (Aronson and Carlsmith, 1963; Freedman, 1965).

REFERENCES

Aaker, D. A., and Day, G. S. (1971), "A Recursive Model of Communication Processes," in D. A. Aaker (ed.), *Multivariate Analysis in Marketing: Theory and Application,* Belmont, Calif.: Wadsworth, pp. 90–114.

Amster, H. (1964), "Semantic Satiation and Generation: Learning? Adaption?" *Psychological Bulletin* 62: 272–286.

———, and Glasman, L. D. (1966), "Verbal Repetition and Connotative Change," *Journal of Experimental Psychology* 71: 389–395.

Anderson, N. H., and Hubert, S. (1963), "Effects of Concomitant Verbal Recall on Order Effects in Personality Impression Formation," *Journal of Verbal Learning and Verbal Behavior* 2: 379–391.

Appel, V. (1966), "The Reliability and Decay of Advertising Measurements," speech to the National Industrial Conference Board, October 28.

——— (1971), "On Advertising Wearout," *Journal of Advertising Research* 11: 11–13.

Aronson, E., and Carlsmith, J. M. (1963), "Effect of Severity of Threat on the Devaluation of Forbidden Behavior," *Journal of Abnormal and Social Psychology* 66: 584–588.

Bahrick, H. P. (1964), "Retention Curves: Facts or Artifacts?" *Psychological Bulletin* 61: pp. 188–194.

Barnard, N. (1955), *Advertising and Forgetting,* Cranfield, England: Cranfield School of Management.

Bartlett, F. C. (1952), *Remembering: A Study in Experimental and Social Psychology.* New York: Macmillan.

Bauer, R. A. (1967), "Consumer Behavior as Risk Taking," in D. F. Cox, ed., *Risk Taking and Information Handling in Consumer Behavior,* Division of Research, School of Business Administration, Harvard University, Boston, Mass.

Berlyne, D. E. (1966), "Curiosity and Exploration," *Science* 153: 25–33.

——— (1970), "Novelty, Complexity, and Hedonic Value," *Perception and Psychophysics* 8: 279–286.

Bither, S. W. (1972), "Effects of Distraction and Commitment on the Persuasiveness of Television Advertising," *Journal of Marketing Research* 9: 1–5.

Bither, S. W., Dolich, I. J., and Nell, E. B. (1971), "The Application of Attitude Immunization Techniques in Marketing," *Journal of Marketing Research* 8: 56–61.

Bogart, L., Tolley, S. B., and Orenstein, F. (1970), "What One Little Ad Can Do," *Journal of Advertising Research* 10: 3–15.

Burnkrant, R. E. (1975), "Attribution Theory in Marketing Research: Problems and Prospects," in M. J. Schlinger, ed., *Advances in Consumer Research* 2, Chicago: Association for Consumer Research: 465–469.

Burnstein, E. (1962), "Some Effects of Cognitive Selection Processes on Learning and Memory," *Psychological Monographs* 76.

Burtt, H. E., and Dobell, E. M. (1927), "The Curve of Forgetting for Advertising Material," *Journal of Applied Psychology*, 11: 5–21.

Butterfield, E. C. (1964), "The Interruption of Tasks: Methodological, Factual, and Theoretical Issues," *Psychological Bulletin* 62: 309–322.

Calder, B. J., and Insko, C. A., and Yandell, B. (1974), "The Relation of Cognitive and Memorial Processes to Persuasion in a Simulated Jury Trial," *Journal of Applied Social Psychology* 4: 62–93.

Capon, N., and Hulbert, J. (1973), "The Sleeper Effect: A Review and Evaluation," Research Paper No. 24, Graduate School of Business, Columbia University.

Carey, J. W. (1964), "Personality Correlates of Persuasibility," in S. A. Greyser, ed., *Proceedings, American Marketing Association,* Chicago: American Marketing Association: 30–43.

Chu, G. (1966), "Fear Arousal, Efficacy, and Imminency," *Journal of Personality and Social Psychology* 4: 517–524.

Clarke, D. G. (1975), "Econometric Measurement of the Duration of the Advertising Effect on Sales," unpublished Working Paper, Harvard Business School.

Coffin, T. (1975), "Some Notes Regarding the Design of an ARF Study of the Automated Checkstand as a Tool for Advertising Research," unpublished mimeo.

Cohen, A. R. (1957), "Need for Cognition and Order of Communication as Determinants of Opinion Change," in C. I. Hovland et al. eds., *The Order of Presentation in Persuasion,* New Haven: Yale University Press, pp. 79–97.

Colley, R. (1961), *Defining Advertising Goals for Measured Advertising Results,* New York: Association of National Advertisers.

Cook, T. D., and Flay, B. R. (1975), "The Temporal Persistence of Experimentally Induced Attitude Change: An Evaluative Review," unpublished mimeo, Northwestern University, Evanston, Ill.

———, Gruder, C. C., Hennigan, K. M., and Halanaj, J. (1974), "The Sleeper Effect in the Context of the Discounting Cue Hypothesis," unpublished mimeo, Northwestern University, Evanston, Ill.

———, and Insko, C. A. (1968), "Persistence of Induced Attitude Change as a Function of Conclusion Re-exposure: A Laboratory-Field Experiment," *Journal of Personality and Social Psychology* 9: 322–328.

———, and Wadsworth, A. (1972), "Persistence of Induced Attitude Change as a Function of Overlearned Conclusions and Supportive Attributions," *Journal of Personality* 40: 50–61.

Cooper, E., and Dinerman, H. (1951), "Analysis of the Film 'Don't Be a Sucker': A Study of Communication," *Public Opinion Quarterly* 15: pp. 243–264.

Cox, D. F. (1967), "Risk Taking and Information Handling in Consumer Behavior," Division of Research, School of Business Administration, Harvard University.

Craig, C. S., Sternthal, B. and Leavitt, C. (1976), "Advertising Wearout: An Experimental Analysis," *Journal of Advertising Research.*

————, ————, and Olshan, K. (1972). "The Effect of Overlearning on Retention," *Journal of General Psychology* 87: 85–94.

Crandall, R., Harrison, A. A., and Zajonc, R. B. (1975), "The Permanence of the Positive and Negative Effects of Stimulus Exposure: A Sleeper Effect?," unpublished manuscript.

Cromwell, H., and Kunkel, R. (1952), "An Experimental Study of the Effect on Attitude of Listeners of Repeating the Same Oral Propaganda," *Journal of Social Psychology* 35: 175–284.

Culbertson, F. M. (1957), "Modification of an Emotionally Held Attitude Through Role Playing," *Journal of Abnormal and Social Psychology* 54: 230–233.

Dillehay, R. C., Insko, C. A., and Smith, M. B. (1966), "Logical Consistency and Attitude Change," *Journal of Personality and Social Psychology* 3: 646–654.

Dyer, R. F., and Kuehl, P. G. (1972), "The 'Corrective Advertising' Remedy of the FTC: An Experimental Evaluation," *Journal of Marketing* 36: 27–33.

————, and ———— (1978), "A Longitudinal Study of Corrective Advertising," *Journal of Marketing Research*.

Ebbinghaus, H. (1964). *Grundzuge der Psychologie,* Leipzig, Germany: 1885, trans. by H. A. Ruger and C. E. Bussenius, *Memory,* New York: Dover.

Elms, A. C. (1966), "Influence of Fantasy Ability on Attitude Change Through Role-Playing," *Journal of Personality and Social Psychology* 4: 36–43.

Evans, R. I., Rozelle, R. M. Lasater, T. M., Dembroski, T. M., and Allen, B. P. (1968), "New Measure of Effects of Persuasive Communications: A Chemical Indicator of Toothbrushing Behavior," *Psychological Reports* 23: 731–736.

————, ————, Rozelle, R. M. Lasater, T. M., Dembroski, T. M., and Allen, B. P. (1970), "Fear Arousal, Persuasion, and Actual Versus Implied Behavioral Change: New Perspective Utilizing a Real-Life Dental Hygiene Program," *Journal of Personality and Social Psychology* 16: 220–227.

Faison, E. W. J. (1961), "Effectiveness of One-Sided and Two-Sided Mass Communications in Advertising," *Public Opinion Quarterly* 25: 468–469.

Festinger, L., and Maccoby, N. (1964), "On Resistance to Persuasive Communications," *Journal of Abnormal and Social Psychology* 68: 359–366.

Freedman, J. L. (1965), "Long-Term Behavioral Effects of Cognitive Dissonance," *Journal of Abnormal and Social Psychology,* 1: 145–155.

————, and Sears, D. (1965), "Selective Exposure," in L. Berkowitz, ed., *Advances in Experimental Social Psychology,* Vol. 2, New York: Academic Press, pp. 57–97.

Gardner, D. M. (1970), "The Distraction Hypothesis in Marketing," *Journal of Advertising Research* 10: 25–30.

Gerhold, P. E. J., and McGuire, W. J. (1966), "Basic Research and Advertising Practice: A Dialogue," in L. Bogart, ed., *Psychology in Media Strategy,* Chicago: American Marketing Association, pp. 66–88.

Gilbert, T. F. (1957), "Overlearning and the Retention of Meaningful Prose," *Journal of General Psychology* 56: 281–289.

Gillig, P. M., and Greenwald, A. G. (1974), "Is It Time to Lay the Sleeper Effect to Rest," *Journal of Personality and Social Psychology* 29: 132–139.

Grass, R. C. (1968), "Satiation Effects of Advertising," *Proceedings, 14th Annual Conference,* New York: Advertising Research Foundation.

————, and Wallace, W. H. (1969), "Satiation Effects of TV Commericals," *Journal of Advertising Research* 9: 3–9 (September).

Greenberg, A., and Garfinkle, N. (1962), "Delayed Recall of Magazine Articles," *Journal of Advertising Research* 2: 28–31.

————, and Suttoni, C. (1973), "Television Commerical Wearout," *Journal of Advertising Research* 13: 47–57 (October).

Greenwald, A. G. (1968), "Cognitive Learning, Cognitive Response to Persuasion, and Attitude Change," in A. G. Greenwald, T. C. Brock, and T. M. Ostrom, eds., *Psychological Foundations of Attitudes*, New York: Academic Press.

Greyser, S. A. (1972), "Shell's 1961 Media Strategy," in S. A. Greyser ed., *Cases in Advertising and Communications Management*, Englewood Cliffs, N.J.: Prentice-Hall, pp. 141-144.

Gruner, C. (1967), "Effects of Humor on Speaker Ethos and Audience Information Gain," *Journal of Communication* 17: 228-233.

———— (1970), "The Effect of Humor in Dull and Interesting Information Speeches," *Central States Speech Journal* 21: 160-166.

Haaland, G., and Venkatesan, M. (1968), "Resistance to Persuasive Communications: An Examination of the Distraction Hypothesis," *Journal of Personality and Social Psychology* 9: 167-170.

Haefner, D. (1956), "Some Effects of Guilt-Arousing and Fear-Arousing Persuasive Communications on Opinion Change," *American Psychologist:* 359.

Haskins, J. B. (1964), "Factual Recall as a Measure of Advertising Effectiveness," *Journal of Advertising Research* 4: 2-8.

Hebb, D. O. (1949), *The Organization of Behavior*, New York: John Wiley.

Heimback, J. T., and Jacoby, J. (1972), "The Zeigarnik Effect in Advertising," in M. Venkatesan, ed., *Proceedings, Third Annual Conference*, Chicago: Association for Consumer Research, pp. 746-757.

Heller, N. (1956), "An Application of Psychological Learning Theory to Advertising," *Journal of Marketing* 20: 249-254.

Higbee, K. L. (1969), "Fifteen Years of Fear Arousal: Research on Fear Appeals, 1953-1968," *Psychological Bulletin* 72: 426-444.

Holt, L. E., and Watts, W. A. (1973), "Immediate and Delayed Effects of Forewarning of Persuasive Intent," *Proceedings of the 81st Annual Convention*, American Psychological Association.

Hovland, C. I. (1951), "Human Learning and Retention," in S. S. Stevens, ed., *Handbook of Experimental Psychology*, New York: John Wiley, pp. 613-689.

————, Janis, I. L., and Kelley, H. H. (1953), *Communication and Persuasion*, New Haven: Yale University Press.

————, Lumsdaine, A. A., and Sheffield, F. D. (1949), *Experiments on Mass Communication*, Princeton, N.J.: Princeton University Press.

————, and Mandell, W. (1952), "An Experimental Comparison of Conclusion-Drawing by the Communicator and by the Audience," *Journal of Abnormal and Social Psychology* 47: 581-588.

————, and Weiss, W. (1951), "The Influence of Source Credibility on Communication Effectiveness," *Public Opinion Quarterly* 15: 635-650.

Hsia, H. (1968), "On Channel Effectiveness," *TV Communication Review*, 16: 245-267.

Hubbard, ba. W. (1970), "A Study of Advertising Effects," *in Modern Medicine,"* New York: Modern Medicine.

Hunt, H. K. (1973), "Effects of Corrective Advertising," *Journal of Advertising Research* 13: 15-22.

Hunter, I. M. L. (1964), *Memory*, London: Penguin.

Insko, C. A. (1964), "Primacy Versus Recency in Persuasion as a Function of the Timing of Arguments and Measures," *Journal of Personality and Social Psychology* 69: 381-391.

————, Arkoff, A., and Insko, U. M. (1965), "Effects of High and Low Fear-Arousing Communications upon Opinions Toward Smoking," *Journal of Experimental Social Psychology* 1: 256-266.

Jacobovitz, L. A. (1956), "Semantic Satiation in Concept Formation," *Psychological Reports* 17: 113-114.

Janis, I. L. (1963), "Personality as a Factor in Susceptibility to Communication," in W. Schramm, ed., *The Science of Human Communication*, New York: Basic Books, pp. 57-58.

—— (1967), "Effects of Fear Arousal on Attitude Change: Recent Developments in Theory and Experimental Research," in L. Berkowitz, ed., *Advances in Experimental Social Psychology,* Vol. 3, New York: Academic Press, pp. 167–225.

——, and Feshbach, S. (1953), "Effects of Fear-Arousing Communications," *Journal of Personality and Social Psychology* 48: 78–92.

——, and Field, P. B. (1959), "A Behavioral Assessment of Persuasibility: Consistency of Individual Differences," in I. L. Janis et al., eds., *Personality and Persuasibility,* New Haven: Yale University Press, pp. 29–54.

——, and Hoffman, D. (1971), "Facilitating Effects of Daily Contact Between Partners Who Make a Decision to Cut Down on Smoking," *Journal of Personality and Social Psychology* 17: 25–35.

——, Kaye, D., and Kirschner, P. (1965), "Facilitating Effects of 'Eating-While-Reading' on Responsiveness to Persuasive Communications," *Journal of Personality and Social Psychology* 1: 181–186.

——, and Mann, L. (1965), "Effectiveness of Emotional Role-Playing in Modifying Smoking Habits and Attitudes," *Journal of Experimental Research Personality* 1: 84–90.

Johnson, H. H., and Watkins, T. A. (1970), "The Effects of Message Repetition on Attitude Change," paper presented at the meeting of the Midwestern Psychological Association, Cincinnati, Ohio (May).

——, and —— (1971), "The Effects of Message Repetitions on Immediate and Delayed Attitude Change," *Psychonomic Science* 22: 101–103.

Jost, A. (1897), "Die Assoziationsfestigkeit in ihrer Abbangigkeit von der Verteilung der Wiederholungen," *Zeitschrift für Psychologie und Physiologie der Sinnesorgane:* 436–472.

Jung, J. (1968), *Verbal Learning,* New York: Holt, Rinehart and Winston.

Kapferer, J. N. (1976), "Memorization and Persistence of Attitude Change," paper read to the workshop on Cognitive Models of Consumer Decision Processes, Centre d'Enseignement Superieurs des Affaires, Jouy-en-Josas, France (January).

Kassarjian, H. H., Carlson, C. J., and Rosin, P. F. (1975), "A Corrective Advertising Study," in M. J. Schlinger, ed., *Advances in Consumer Research,* Vol. 2, Chicago: Association for Consumer Research, pp. 631–642.

Katz, D., Sarnoff, I., and McClintock, C. (1956), "Ego Defense and Attitude Change," *Human Relations* 9: 27–45.

Kelley, H. H. (1967), "Attribution Theory in Social Psychology, in D. Levin, ed., *Nebraska Symposium on Motivation* 14: 192–238.

Kelman, H. C. (1953), "Attitude Change as a Function of Response Restriction," *Human Relations* 6: 185–214.

—— (1961), "Processes of Opinion Change," *Public Opinion Quarterly* 25: 57–78.

——, and Hovland, C. I. (1953), " 'Reinstatement' of the Communicator in Delayed Measurement of Attitude Change," *Journal of Abnormal and Social Psychology* 48: 327–335.

Kreuger, W. L. (1929), "The Effects of Overlearning on Retention," *Journal of Experimental Psychology* 12: 71–78.

—— (1930), "Futher Studies in Overlearning," *Journal of Experimental Psychology* 13: 152–163.

Krugman, H. E. (1962), "An Application of Learning Theory to TV Copy Testing," *Public Opinion Quarterly* 26: 626–634.

—— (1965), "The Impact of Television Advertising: Learning Without Involvement," *Public Opinion Quarterly* 29: 349–356.

—— (1966), "Answering Some Unanswered Questions in Measuring Advertising Effectiveness," *Proceedings of the 12th Annual Meeting of the Advertising Research Foundation,* New York: ARF, pp. 18–23.

—— (1966–1967), "The Measurement of Advertising Involvement," *Public Opinion Quarterly* 30: 583–596.

_____ (1968), "Processes Underlying Exposure to Advertising," *American Psychologist* 23: 245–253.

_____ (1970), "Electroencephalographic Aspects of Low Involvement: Implications for the McLuhan Hypothesis," Report No. 70–113, Marketing Science Institute, Cambridge, Mass.

_____ (1972), "Why Three Exposures May Be Enough," *Journal of Advertising Research* 12: 11–14 (December).

_____ (1970), "Opportunities in Advertising Research of the Future," speech to American Marketing Association, New York Chapter, January 30.

Lavidge, R. J., and Steiner, G. A. (1961), "A Model for Predictive Measurement of Advertising Effectiveness," *Journal of Marketing* 25: 59–62.

Leavitt, C., Waddell, C., and Wells, W. (1970), "Improving Day-After Recall Techniques," *Journal of Advertising Research* 10: 13–17.

Levanthal, H. (1970), "Findings and Theory in the Study of Fear Communications," in L. Berkowitz, ed., *Advances in Experimental Social Psychology,* Vol. 5, New York: Academic Press, pp. 119–186.

_____, and Niles, P. (1964), "A Field Experiment on Fear-Arousal with Data on the Validity of Questionnaire Measures," *Journal of Personality* 32: 459–479.

_____, Singer, R. P., and Jones, S. (1965), "The Effects of Fear and Specificity of Recommendation upon Attitudes and Behavior," *Journal of Personality and Social Psychology* 2: 20–29.

_____, and Watts, J. C. (1966), "Sources of Resistance to Fear-Arousing Communications on Smoking and Lung Cancer," *Journal of Personality* 34: 155–175.

Levitt, T. (1965), *Industrial Purchasing Behavior,* Division of Research, Graduate School of Business Administration, Harvard University.

Lewin, K. (1958), "Group Decision and Social Change," in E. E. Maccoby, T. M. Newcomb, and E. L. Hartley, eds., *Readings in Social Psychology,* New York: Holt, Rinehart and Winston, pp. 197–211.

Lucas, D. B., and Britt, S. H. (1963), *Measuring Advertising Effectiveness,* New York: McGraw-Hill.

Luh, C. W. (1922), "The Conditions of Retention," *Psychological Monographs* 31.

Lull, P. (1940), "The Effectiveness of Humor in Persuasive Speech," *Speech Monographs* 7: 26–40.

Maccoby, E. E., Maccoby, N., Romney, A. K., and Adams, J. S. (1961), "Social Reinforcement in Attitude Change," *Journal of Abnormal and Social Psychology* 63: 109–115.

Maloney, J. C. (1966), "Attitude Measurement and Formation," paper presented to American Marketing Association Test Marketing Workshop, Chicago.

_____ (1962), "Curiosity vs. Disbelief in Advertising," *Journal of Advertising* 2: 2–8.

Marder Associates, Eric (1968), *A Study of the Decay of the Effects Produced by Twelve Ads in LIFE Magazine,* New York: Eric Marder Associates.

Mazis, M. B., and Adkinson, J. E. (1976), "An Experimental Evaluation of a Proposed Corrective Advertising Remedy," *Journal of Marketing Research* 13: 178–183.

McCrary, J. W., and Hunter, W. S. (1953), "Serial Position Curves in Verbal Learning," *Science* 117: 131–134.

McCullough, J. L., and Ostrom, T. M. (1974), "Repetition of Highly Similar Messages and Attitude Change," *Journal of Applied Psychology* 59: 395–97.

McDonald, C. (1970), "What Is the Short-Term Effect of Advertising?," *ESOMAR Congress Papers,* Barcelona, pp. 463–485.

McGraw-Hill (1964), "Memory for Advertising," *Laboratory of Advertising Performance,* Data Sheet No. 5260, New York: McGraw-Hill.

McGuire, W. J. (1957), "Order of Persuasion as a Factor in 'Conditioning' Persuasiveness," in C. I. Hovland et al., eds., *The Order of Presentation in Persuasion,* New Haven: Yale University Press, pp. 98–114.

———— (1960a), "Cognitive Consistency and Attitude Change," *Journal of Abnormal and Social Psychology* 60: 345–353.

———— (1960b), "Direct and Indirect Persuasive Effects of Dissonance-Producing Messages," *Journal of Abnormal and Social Psychology* 60: 354, 358.

———— (1960c), "A Syllogistic Analysis of Cognitive Relationships," in C. I. Hovland and Rosenberg, eds., *Attitude Organization and Change,* New Haven: Yale University Press, pp. 65–111.

———— (1962), "Persistence of the Resistance to Persuasion Induced by Various Types of Prior Belief Defenses," *Journal of Abnormal and Social Psychology* 64: 241–248.

———— (1964), "Inducing Resistance to Persuasion: Some Contemporary Approaches," in L. Berkowitz, ed., *Advances in Experimental Social Psychology,* Vol. 1, New York: Academic Press, pp. 191–229.

———— (1968a), "Personality and Attitude Change: An Information-Processing Theory," in A. G. Greenwald, T. C. Brock, and T. M. Ostrom, eds., *Psychological Foundations of Attitudes,* New York: Academic Press, pp. 171–196.

———— (1968b), "Personality and Susceptibility to Social Influence," in E. F. Borgatta and W. W. Lambert, eds., *Handbook of Personality Theory and Research,* Chicago: Rand McNally, pp. 1130–1187.

———— (1968c), "The Nature of Attitudes and Attitude Change," in G. Lindzey and E. Aronson, eds., *The Handbook of Social Psychology,* Vol. 2, 2nd edition, Reading, Mass.: Addison-Wesley, pp. 136–314.

———— (1972), "Attitude Change: An Information-Processing Paradigm," In G. G. McClintock, ed., *Experimental Social Psychology,* New York: Holt, Rinehart and Winston, pp. 108–141.

Melton, A. W. (1963), "Implications of Short-Term Memory for a General Theory of Memory," *Journal of Verbal Learning and Verbal Behavior* 3: 1–21.

Miller, N., and Campbell, D. T. (1959), "Recency and Primary in Persuasion as a Function of the Time of Speeches and Measurement," *Journal of Abnormal and Social Psychology* 59: 1–9.

Miller, R. L., Brickman, P., and Bolen, D. (1975), "Attribution Versus Persuasion as a Means for Modifying Behavior," *Journal of Personality and Social Psychology* 31: 430–441.

Mitnick, L. L., and McGinnies, E. (1958), "Influencing Ethnocentrisim in Small Discussion Groups Through a Film Communication," *Journal of Abnormal and Social Psychology* 56: 82–90.

Newcomb, T. M. (1963), "Persistence and Regression of Changed Attitudes: Long-Range Studies," *Journal of Social Issues* 4: 3–13.

Norman, D. A. (1969), *Memory and Attention: An Introduction to Human Information Processing,* New York: John Wiley.

Ogilvy, D. (1967), *Confessions of an Advertising Man,* New York: Dell.

Olson, J., and Jacoby, J. (1973), "Measuring Multi-Brand Loyalty," in S. Ward and P. Wright, eds., *Advances in Consumer Research* 1: 447–448.

Osterhouse, R., and Brock, T. (1970), "Distraction Increases Yielding to Propaganda by Inability Counterarguing," *Journal of Personality and Social Psychology* 15: 344–358.

Ostheimer, R. H. (1970), "Frequency Effects Over Time," *Journal of Advertising Research* 10: 19–22.

Papegeorgis, D. (1963), "Bartlett Effect and the Persistence of Induced Opinion Change," *Journal of Abnormal and Social Psychology* 67: 61–67.

Pelz, E. B. (1958), "Some Factors in 'Group Decision,' " in E. E. Maccoby, T. M. Newcomb, and E. L. Hartley, eds., *Readings in Social Psychology,* New York: Holt, Rinehart and Winston.

Peterson, R. C., and Thurstone, L. L. (1933), *The Effect of Motion Pictures on the Social Attitudes of High School Children,* Chicago: University of Chicago Press.

Politz Media Studies (1960), *The Rochester Study,* New York: Saturday Evening Post.

————, and Rau, L. (1957), "Retention as a Function of the Method of Measurement," *University of California Publications in Psychology* 8: 217–270.

Postman, L. (1962), "Retention as a Function of Overlearning," *Science* 135: 656–667.

Preston, I. L. (1970), "A Reinterpretation of the Meaning of Involvement in Krugman's Models of Advertising Communication" *Journalism Quarterly* 47: 287-295.

———— (1977), "Research on Consumer Perception of Puffery and Other Non-Explicit Selling Claims in a Context of FTC Examination of Implied Representation," in A. G. Woodside, J. N. Sheth, and P. D. Bennett, eds., *Foundations of Consumer and Industrial Buying Behavior,* New York: American Elsevier.

Ray, M. L. (1969), "Can Order Effect in Copy Tests Be Used as an Indicator of Long-Term Advertising Effect?," *Journal of Advertising Research* 9: 45-52.

———— (1969), "The Present and Potential Linkages Between the Microtheoretical Notions of Behavioral Science and the Problems of Advertising," paper presented to the TIMS/University of Chicago Symposium on Behavioral and Management Science in Marketing.

————, and Sawyer, A. G. (1971), "Repetition in Media Models: A Laboratory Technique," *Journal of Marketing Research* 8: 20-29.

————, ————, and Strong, E. C. (1971), "Frequency Effects Revisited," *Journal of Advertising Research* 11: 14-20.

————, ————, Rothschild, M. L., Heeler, R. M., Strong, E. C., and Reed, J. B. (1973), "Marketing Communication and the Hierarchy of Effects," *Sage Annual Reviews of Communication Research,* Vol. 2, Beverly Hills, Calif.: Sage.

————, and Wilkie, W. L. (1970), "Fear: The Potential of an Appeal Neglected by Marketing," *Journal of Marketing* 34: 54-62.

Reeves, R. (1961), *Reality in Advertising,* New York: Knopf.

Rogers, R. W., and Thistlethwaite, D. L. (1969), "An Analysis of Active and Passive Defenses in Inducing Resistance to Persuasion," *Journal of Personality and Social Psychology* 11: 301-308.

Rosnow, R. L. (1965), "A Delay-of-Reinforcement Effects in Persuasive Communication?" *Journal of Social Psychology* 67: 39-43.

Rothschild, M. L., and Ray, M. L. (1973), "Involvement and Political Advertising Effectiveness," paper presented to 1973 Conference of the American Association for Public Opinion Research, Asheville, N.C.

Sawyer, A. G. (1971), "A Laboratory Experimental Investigation of the Repetitive Effects of Advertising," unpublished Ph.D. dissertation, Stanford University.

———— (1973), "The Effects of Repetition of Refutational and Supportive Advertising Appeals," *Journal of Marketing Research* 10: 23-33.

———— (1974), "The Effects of Repetition: Conclusions and Suggestions About Laboratory Research," in G. D. Hughes and M. L. Ray, eds., *Buyer/Consumer Information Processing,* Chapel Hill: University of North Carolina Press, pp. 190-219.

———— (1976), "The Need to Measure Attitudes and Beliefs Over Time: The Case of Deceptive and Corrective Advertising," paper presented at the Annual Educators Meeting, American Marketing Association, Memphis (August).

———— (1977), "Repetition and Affect: Recent Empirical and Theoretical Development," in A. G. Woodside, J. N. Sheth, and P. D. Bennett, eds., *Foundations of Consumer and Industrial Buying Behavior,* New York: American Elsevier, pp. 229-42.

————, and Semenik, R. J. (1978), "Carry-Over Effects of Corrective Advertising," *Proceedings,* Association of Consumer Research.

Schulman, S. I., and Worrell, C. (1970), "Salience Patterns, Source Credibility, and the Sleeper Effect," *Public Opinion Quarterly* 34: 371-382.

Scott, C. A. (1973), "Attribution Theory: A Review," unpublished working paper, Ohio State University.

Sears, D. O. (1968), "Selective Exposure," in R. P. Abelson et al., eds. *Theories of Cognitive Consistency: A Sourcebook,* Chicago: Rand McNally.

Settle, R. B. (1972), "Attribution Theory and Acceptance of Information," *Journal of Marketing Research* 9: 85–88.

Silk, A. J., and Vavra, T. G. (1974), "The Influence of Advertising's Affective Qualities on Consumer Response," in G. D. Hughes and M. L. Ray, eds., *Buyer/Consumer Information Processing,* Chapel Hill: University of North Carolina Press, pp. 157–186.

Simmons, W. R. and Associates (1965), "A Study of Retention in Advertising in Five Magazines," New York: W. R. Simmons and Associates Research, Inc.

Simon, J. L. (1965), "Are There Economies of Scale in Advertising," *Journal of Advertising Research* 5: 15–20.

—— (1969), "New Evidence for No Effect of Scale in Advertising," *Journal of Advertising Research* 9: 38–41.

Stang, D. J. (1974), "Methodological Factors in Mere Exposure Studies," *Psychological Bulletin* 81: 1014–1025.

Starch, D., Inc. (1970), *30 Days in Atlanta,* New York: Daniel Starch, Inc.

Sternthal, B., and Craig, C. S. (1973), "Humor in Advertising," *Journal of Marketing* 37: 12–18.

——, and —— (1974), "Fear Appeals: Revisited and Revised," *Journal of Consumer Research* 1: 22–34.

Stewart, J. (1964), *RepeitiRepetitive Advertising in Newspapers: A Study of Two New Products,* Cambridge, Mass.: Harvard Bureau of Business Research.

Stotland, E., Katz, D., and Patchen, M. (1959), "The Reduction of Prejudice Through the Arousal of Self-Insight," *Journal of Personality* 27: 507–531.

Strong, E. K. (1914), "The Effect of the Size of Advertisements and the Frequency of Their Presenta-dissertation, Stanford University.

—— (1974), "The Use of Field Experimental Observations in Estimating Advertising Recall," *Journal of Marketing Research* 11: 369–378.

Strong, E. K. (1914), "The Effect of the Size of Advertisement and the Frequency of Their Presentation," *Psychological Review* 21: 136–152.

—— (1916), "The Factors Affecting a Permanent Impression Developed Through Repetition," *Journal of Experimental Psychology* 1: 319–338.

Szybillo, G. J., and Heslin, R. (1973), "Resistance to Persuasion: Innoculation Theory in a Marketing Context," *Journal of Marketing Research* 10: 369–403.

TV Age (1967), "Quest for Boredom" (December 18).

Underwood, B. J. (1957), "Interference and Forgetting," *Psychological Review* 64: 49–60.

—— (1964), "Degree of Learning and the Measurement of Forgetting," *Journal of Verbal Learning and Verbal Behavior* 3: 112–129.

——, and Ekstrand, B. R. (1967), "Studies of Distributed Practice XXIV: Differentiation and Proactive Inhibition," *Journal of Experimental Psychology* 74: 574–580.

——, and Schultz, R. W. (1960), *Meaningfulness and Verbal Learning,* Philadelphia: Lippincott.

Venkatesan, M. (1973), "Cognitive Consistency and Novelty Seeking," in S. Ward and T. S. Robertson, eds., *Consumer Behavior: Theoretical Sources,* Englewood Cliffs, N.J.: Prentice-Hall, pp. 354–385.

Wallace, W. H. (1970), "Predicting and Measuring the Wearout of Commercials," speech to the Kansas City American Marketing Association (April 1).

Ward, S., and Ray, M. L. (1974), "Cognitive Responses to Mass Communications: Results from Laboratory Studies and a Field Experiment," paper presented to Theory and Methodology Division, Association for Education in Journalism, San Diego (August).

Watts, W. A. (1967), "Relative Persistence of Opinion Change Induced by Active Compared to Passive Participation," *Journal of Personality and Social Psychology* 5: 4–15.

——, and McGuire, W. J. (1964), "Persistence of Induced Opinion Change and Retention of Inducing Message Content," *Journal of Abnormal and Social Psychology* 68: 233–241.

Waugh, N. C., and Norman, D. A. (1965), "Primary Memory," *Psychological Review* 12: 89–104.

Weber, S. J. (1971), "Source Primacy-Recency Effects and the Sleeper Effect," paper presented at the Annual Meeting of the American Psychological Association, Washington, D.C. (September).

Weinberger, M. (1961), "Does the 'Sleeper Effect' Apply to Advertising?" *Journal of Marketing* 25 (6): 65–68 (October).

Weiss, W. (1953), "A Sleeper Effect in Opinion Change," *Journal of Abnormal and Social Psychology* 48: 173–180.

Wells, W. D., and Beard, A. D. (1973), "Personality and Consumer Behavior," in S. Ward and T. S. Robertson, eds., *Consumer Behavior: Theoretical Sources,* Englewood Cliffs, N.J.: Prentice-Hall, pp. 354–395.

Wittaker, J. O., and Meade, R. D. (1968), "Retention of Opinion Change as a Function of Differential Sources Credibility: A Cross-Cultural Study," *International Journal of Psychology* 3: 103–108.

Wilson, W., and Miller, H. (1968), "Repetition, Order of Presentation, and Timing of Arguments and Measures as Determinants of Opinion Change," *Journal of Personality and Social Psychology* 9: 184–188.

Wood, J. P. (1961), *Advertising and the Soul's Belly,* Athens, Ga.: University of Georgia Press.

Wright, P. L. (1973), "The Cognitive Processes Mediating Acceptance of Advertising," *Journal of Marketing Research* 10: 53–62.

―――― (1974a), "Analyzing Media Effects on Advertising Responses," *Public Opinion Quarterly* 38: 192–205.

―――― (1974b), "On the Direct Monitoring of Cognitive Response to Advertising," in G. D. Hughes and M. L. Ray, eds., *Consumer/Buyer Information Processing,* Chapel Hill: University of North Carolina Press, pp. 220–248.

―――― (1975), "Factors Affecting Cognitive Resistance to Advertising," *Journal of Consumer Research* 2: 1–9.

Zajonc, R. B., Swap, W. C., Harrison, A. A., and Roberts, P. (1971), "Limiting Conditions of Relativity," *Journal of Personality and Social Psychology* 18: 384–391.

―――― , Shaver, P., Tavris, C., and Van Kreveld, D. (1972), "Exposure, Satiation, and Stimulus Discriminability," *Journal of Personality and Social Psychology* 21: 270–280.

Zeigarnik, B. (1927), "Über das Behalten von Erledigten und Unerledigten Handlungen," *Psychologische Forschungen* 9: 1–85.

Zielske, H. A. (1959), "The Remembering and Forgetting of Advertising," *Journal of Marketing* 23: 239–243.

―――― , and Pomerance, E. C. (1958), "A Controlled Experiment in Advertising Scheduling," unpublished mimeo, Foote, Cone, and Belding, Inc.

REDLINING IN MORTGAGE MARKETS: RESEARCH PERSPECTIVES IN MARKETING AND PUBLIC POLICY

Thaddeus H. Spratlen, UNIVERSITY OF WASHINGTON

I. INTRODUCTION

The term "redlining" refers to traditional insurance or lending practices in which biased decisions about insurability or credit availability are made on a categorical basis. The biases in the decisions are related primarily to the racial/ethnic identity of those seeking insurance or credit, and to the age and location of the property associated with the credit or insurance application. For the mortgage-lending case that is the subject of this chapter certain prospective borrowers, properties and residential locations have been selected and/or excluded on the basis of ethnic, racial, property-age or other neighborhood categories. Market areas or boundaries have been more or less arbitrarily established and decisions about lending have been made on categorical rather than individual criteria of credit-

Research in Marketing—Volume 2, 1979, pages 315–343.
Copyright © 1979 by JAI Press Inc.
All rights of reproduction in any form reserved.
ISBN 0-89232-059-1

worthiness. Hence, certain groups of prospective borrowers, types of properties and neighborhood locations have been defined as being high risk, less desirable and not creditworthy. They have been redlined in the pattern suggested in Figure 1.

Mortgage credit and investment funds have been denied or made available only on restrictive terms. Yet such lending decisions involving redlining have not been made in accordance with borrower-specific risks, costs, repayment capacity or quantifiable economic values associated with each individual loan or investment alternative. Although not reviewed in detail in this chapter, there is a developing body of literature in journals for law, real estate, urban economics and related fields which analyzes the various dimensions of this complex and discriminatory process.

In this chapter several relationships between redlining and marketing are identified. Redlining is also described as a socioeconomic problem with widespread, negative consequences. Although still very much in dispute and in the formative stages of development, research methods and research findings on redlining are reported and interpreted. In addition, the need for further research on redlining is discussed along with a proposed multivariate methodology. Finally, the marketing implications of redlining research and public policy issues are presented. Major sections of the chapter are devoted to each of these topics.

II. REDLINING AND MANAGERIAL MARKETING

There are several ways in which redlining and marketing are interrelated. In its most general form marketing seeks to enhance or facilitate customer needs and want satisfaction. Thus, mortgage lenders as marketers are expected to meet consumer, community and societal needs for mortgage credit, subject of course to the economic-financial requirements of profitability. But redlining blocks the satisfaction of a need on categorical and discriminatory grounds. Its practice means that prospective borrowers or sellers of property who are redlined cannot exchange their resources for the asset values or wealth represented by residential property. Economic, psychic or other forms of need satisfaction and fulfillment are blocked.[1]

A second connection can be made between redlining and marketing with respect to market demand. Marketing seeks to manage demand in a micro sense of adjusting offerings and responding to market opportunities. When redlining is practiced opportunities in certain portions of the inner-city market are neither evaluated nor recognized on their merits. Lenders simply define their acceptable market boundaries as excluding redlined areas.

At a macro-level redlining results in the mismanagement of demand for mortgage credit.[2] This occurs through the assignment of some groups of individuals or properties to a not-creditworthy category when, in fact, they could meet acceptable credit standards, if evaluated on an individual rather than a categorical basis. A closely related point is that market supply for real estate financing is also

Figure 1. Descriptions and Patterns of Redlining.

Description \ Pattern	Borrowers (Assuming comparable individual creditworthiness)	Types of Properties (Assuming individual marketability)	Locations/Neighborhoods (Assuming individual marketability)
1. Heavily Redlined	Nonwhites; members of ethnic minority groups	Older homes (40 years old or older); low-priced homes, e.g., under $15,000	Predominantly nonwhite areas presumed to be declining
2. Sometimes Redlined	Whites who prefer to live in racially mixed neighborhoods and/or older homes	Older homes in areas of mixed zoning and land use	Areas of changing ethnic composition, especially from white to nonwhite
3. Generally Not Redlined	Whites who live in entirely or nearly all-white neighborhoods	New homes in exclusively low density suburban neighborhoods	Homogeneous and stable areas, especially if they have predominantly white residents

directly and adversely affected by redlining. The reduced availability of adequate financing in redlined areas reflects disinvestment or the systematic shifting and preferred placement of funds in nonredlined areas by lenders. This practice in turn makes insurance more costly and difficult to obtain, and eventually depresses the market for real estate in redlined areas.

A third connection can be made in relation to market segmentation. Managerial marketing uses segmentation as a basic approach to delineating and targeting marketing programs and plans. More effective use of resources is expected to result from directing marketing effort toward customer groups in the marketplace which exhibit similar needs, interests or other demand-related characteristics. However, for redlining, segmentation takes on particularly negative stereotypes and associations. For example, invidious distinctions relating to race, property-age and neighborhood characteristics are used as a basis for avoiding marketing activities in areas where potential exists for mortgage lending activity. Thus, redlining takes on the character of demarketing.[3]

On the supply side of the market, redlining segments for purpose of credit allocation. It establishes a biased categorical preference rating regarding the availability of mortgage credit.

There are also several public policy-market performance issues which connect marketing and redlining. As consumerism issues, questions arise as to the rights of individuals who are subjected to redlining. Is it reasonable to expect that all prospective borrowers will get a fair hearing and evaluation on the individual merits of their financial capability? Additional questions include: Is adequate information provided on mortgage credit policies and terms? What are the choices available to those who are redlined? What forms of redress are available to those who have been redlined? Do they have a voice or a chance to be heard?

A more general market performance question arises in public policy regarding lenders' charter responsibilities to provide financial services to various communities. From a managerial point of view this concerns the expectations as well as the obligations to which mortgage lenders are subject as quasi-public institutions. Since they are entrusted with the means to meet a community's mortgage credit needs, should they categorically abandon a community in the absence of a clear and present danger of nonrecoverable losses? The answers to these and other questions regarding redlining represent some important tasks for marketing research. The results would be expected to show the extent to which certain areas of need have been neglected and underserved or the extent to which consumer rights and needs are served.

III. MACRO-MARKETING AND WELFARE ASPECTS OF REDLINING

One additional perspective of redlining is summarized before presenting research methods and findings in some detail. This pertains to the aggregate, external effects of system-wide economic and social consequences of redlining. In macro-marketing terms this includes various value issues and performance out-comes associated with the marketing practices of institutions in finance, insur-ance, and real estate industries. Two value judgments which bias lending as outlined in Figure 1 should be mentioned. One is that there is an implied unde-sirability of older, racially mixed neighborhoods. The second is that risk can be assigned categorically on the basis of the racial-ethnic identity of prospective borrowers. Available research does not support either of these judgments.

As to performance outcomes in mortgage markets, there are several external effects which should be recognized. One manifestation of the restricted flow of mortgage loans in redlined areas is the displacement effect of redlining. Since credit availability is at such a low level, displaced borrowers must seek credit from alternative sources and usually under adverse terms. They commonly turn to real estate contracts and purchases on assignment or assumption. Since various financial restrictions and legal limitations are associated with these "noninstitu-tional" forms of real estate financing, displaced borrowers are likely also to be disadvantaged borrowers.

A further reflection of disadvantaged status in mortgage markets is the discouraged-borrower effect. It produces a class of prospective borrowers who have become discouraged and have withdrawn from market search and related activities.[4] They also neither seek redress to known or expected discrimination nor appeal to potential sources of help through industry or non-industry organiza-tions. This includes federal, state, and local regulatory commissions and agencies as well as review boards to hear complaints of discrimination. Even community fair housing groups and coalitions against redlining are not properly utilized.

Economic and social welfare effects of redlining are defined and measured with respect to such outcomes as the maldistribution of credit and housing in-vestment funds, depressed and deprived conditions of home ownership for par-ticular groups and, ultimately, the waste of resources allocated to housing. Neither a developed theory of redlining nor reported research results amply trace these various interrelationships. Yet there are logical and observable conditions which indicate the extent to which those subjected to redlining are worse off with respect to housing resources than those not subject to redlining.

In a descriptive way, many of the influences on redlining in particular and residential mortgage lending in general are summarized in Figure 2. Their wel-fare dimensions can be described briefly. General influences are discussed for a particular type of influence such as borrower characteristics and then the welfare aspects of redlining are illustrated.

The need or desire for home ownership is defined by several factors. House-hold income is the single most important factor based on multiple regression analysis of home ownership (Carliner, 1974). Marital status, family size and age are also key variables. In addition, strong motivating influences are dictated by the status, stability, and related expectations associated with home ownership in the economy and society.

Segregation and discrimination in housing market raise costs, limit supplies

Figure 2. General and Redlining Influences on Residential Mortgage Lending.

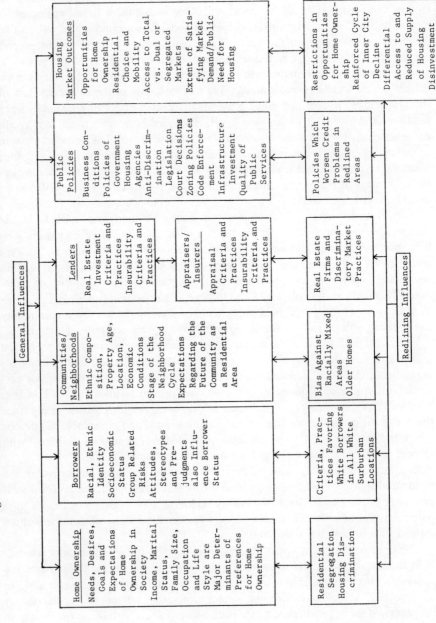

and further reduce demand by those subjected to redlining. For example financing is made available only in certain neighborhoods; and even then it may be under adverse terms. A closely related point is that redlining contributes to the maintenance of a dual housing market; one in which housing consumers are predominately white, the other in which they are predominately black. While this raises some basic questions that are well developed in the literature on housing discrimination, the adverse effects and relationships between redlining and housing market activity on a system-wide level should be noted.

Ability to repay the loan extended is a primary criterion in establishing the creditworthiness of borrowers. Income, assets, occupation, liabilities, payment history on previous loans, are some of the financially relevant criteria.

When redlining occurs, groups or categorical risk factors enter into consideration. Biases which lead to prejudging prospective borrowers influence credit decisions. Thus, race rather than re-payment capability per se may exert a strong influence on whether a loan is obtained. Obviously, then, the individual so prejudged receives less in housing value than his economic circumstances would provide in the absence of redlining.

To sum up the remainder of the illustration in Figure 2, it should be noted that residential mortgage lending practices include various financial, real estate, and related considerations of capital management. Traditional emphasis on community wide and neighborhood assessment, for example, may well arbitrarily restrict the flow of mortgage loan funds. Thus, older, less well-maintained schools, greater congestion, and vacant properties are likely to accompany an older housing stock in which a majority of the housing units may be 40–50 years old or older. Traditional investment practices may also be compounded by equally conservative appraisal and guaranteeing practices of government agencies (Miller, 1964). Clearly, residential segregation and strongly entrenched personal preferences of whites to exclude blacks and other minorities from open housing markets further compound the decision-making process of lending institutions. When the decisions made are discriminatory, the flow of capital in residential markets is adversely affected. Disinvestment occurs. Opportunities for home-ownership are restricted. The net effect of both outcomes is to reinforce the cycle of inner-city decline and urban decay. In welfare terms, the withdrawal of credit availability weakens the capital base of housing investment. Neighborhood decline is accelerated. Also potentially valuable housing stock is allowed to deteriorate as part of a "self-fulfilling prophecy"—that older, racially mixed neighborhoods and prospective borrowers who desire to live in them are high risks.

IV. REDLINING: THE RESEARCH FINDINGS

Most of the research which has been done on redlining has been presented in reports of community organizations and governmental agencies, legal briefs for court cases and law review articles. The findings are generally policy-reinforcement- or action-oriented. Except for some of the law review articles very little has appeared that has the technical, theoretical and methodological content of academic research. Virtually none of it has been developed from a marketing perspective.

For this discussion, four categories of analysis have been identified: legal, descriptive, correlation and regression, and other multivariate techniques. The legal research has been used to establish the basis for court and regulatory action. It is of particular interest to marketing since it often affects standards and practices of decisionmaking. Responsibilities or obligations to be assumed by lenders, appraisers and others involved in mortgage transactions as well as possible remedies which may be sought by those subjected to redlining are also identified in legal research.

Descriptive research helps to define patterns of lending in geographic, institutional or related financial terms, e.g., the types of instruments used to finance real estate transactions. Because data are limited primarily to property sales, descriptive research addresses mainly the supply side of mortgage lending. Very little is revealed about the nature of demand in mortgage markets. In terms of quantity and data availability most research on redlining falls into this category. For marketing and public policy purposes it reveals primarily the geographic areas included within mortgage markets. The racial/ethnic character of these areas can also be inferred. Included within this category would be most of the research using disclosure data required by the Home Mortgage Disclosure Act of 1975 (U.S. Senate, 1975). Most lending institutions are required to report loans made by postal Zip Code areas for 1976 and in subsequent years by census tracts.

Several studies have been issued in which correlation and regression analysis has been used. It becomes possible to statistically isolate some of the relationships and parameters of the redlining process. Such techniques provide strong evidence for more conclusively analyzing and interpreting mortgage lending activities and decisions. The standards, practices and results of mortgage lending can be more precisely evaluated using such techniques. Eventually, the speculation offered in earlier parts of the chapter can be replaced with more statistically precise and valid formulations using correlation and regression techniques.

Because of data limitations, other multivariate methods (e.g., cluster and discriminant analysis) are the least used to date in research on redlining. The private and sensitive nature of financial data on borrowers partly accounts for the lack of data. However, the unwillingness of lenders and others to subject the data to analysis on a confidential basis and costliness of survey research among borrowers are the primary reasons for the lack of data. However, as the proposed methodology developed below in Section V suggests, the best hopes for conclusive and definitive results are likely to be based on such multivariate techniques.

A. Legal Analysis and Research[5]

Legal analysis and research on redlining have used primarily anecdotal, situational or individual case and *prima facie* evidence to infer discriminatory practices. Circumstantial and descriptive data have been used as a basis for showing the effects of discrimination on the flow of residential mortgage credit. The results have been used to provide criteria, prohibitions and remedies for preventing discrimination by lenders according to race, color, sex, marital status or other categorical attributes of prospective borrowers which are not individually and specifically related to creditworthiness. From a marketing point of view, lenders have been required to broaden the market for mortgage loans by eliminating arbitrary and categorical exclusions of certain borrowers. This has also increased the supply of mortgage credit to some extent in older, central city neighborhoods.

1. Research of Statutes. Applicable statutes which prohibit racially discriminatory lending practices (racial redlining)[6] extend in time from the Civil Rights Act of 1866 to the Civil Rights Act of 1968 (the latter is known as the Fair Housing Act). For example, the 1968 statute directly prohibits discrimination in the financing of housing by stating in part that:

> It shall be unlawful for any [of an enumerated list of financial institutions] to deny a loan or other financial assistance to a person applying therefor for the purpose of purchasing . . . a dwelling, or to discriminate against him in the fixing of the amount, interest rate, duration, or other terms or conditions of such loan or other financial assistance, because of the race, color, religion, or natural origin of such person or of any person associated with him in connection with such loan or other financial assistance, or of the present or prospective owners, lessees, tenants, or occupants of the dwelling or dwellings in relation to which such loan or other financial assistance is to be given. . ." (U.S. Code, Vol. 42, Section 3605).

Generally, to be effective for court decisions, legal research must show racially disparate effects in lender practices in order to establish the existence of redlining.

Administrative rules of regulatory agencies also represent similar statutory prohibitions for applicable institutions. In the case of federal savings and loan associations, this is illustrated in (Federal Home Loan Bank Board, *Regulations* Section 528.2(d)). These were enacted as a basis for Board exercise of its authority in conjunction with the nondiscrimination requirements of Title VIII of the Civil Rights Act of 1968.

A more detailed presentation of the statutory as well as other legal analysis and research may be found in Flahive and Winokur (1976), pp. 73–88.

2. Research of Cases. In the earliest anti-redlining case at the U.S. District Court level (Southern District of Ohio, Western Division), racial redlining was at issue. It was alleged by the plaintiffs, a white couple who were denied financing in an older racially mixed neighborhood of Cincinnati, that the refusal was discriminatory. Moreover, it was contended that the appraisal used in the lending decision was itself a racially biased procedure. During the trial it was indicated that ethnic composition of the neighborhood and whether a neighborhood was changing from white to nonwhite were included as part of the Professional

Residential Appraisal used by the defendant, Oakley Building and Loan Company of Cincinnati. The clear implication of the use of such criteria is that blacks and other minorities have an adverse effect on property values. Moreover, they are used ostensibly by lenders to justify "writing off" or refusing to make loans in integrated, mixed or "declining" neighborhoods.

Through qualitative data, legal reasoning and circumstantial indications of the discriminatory effects of redlining, the court ruled in favor of the plaintiffs (*Laufman et al. v. Oakley Building and Loan Company,* 1976). Moreover, redlining was declared to be an illegal practice as cited under 42 United States Code Sections 3604, 3605, and 3617. Sections 804 and 805 of Title VIII of the Civil Rights Act of 1968 and Title VI of the Civil Rights Act of 1964 were also referenced as prohibiting redlining.

A subsequent U.S. Supreme Court ruling clearly imposed more stringent data support by including "racially discriminatory intent or purpose." Disparate or disproportionate impact or effects *alone* are not sufficient. They represent only part of legal proof. [See *Village of Arlington Heights v. Metropolitan Housing Development Corporation* (1977)]. By implication, future legal research will have to get at lender motives as well as the racially disparate effects associated with redlining.

3. *Legal Analysis: The Law Review Literature.*   From a research perspective a few additional ideas about legal analysis should be mentioned. Besides, statutory interpretation and case precedents, statistical analyses of disparate effects are also important in determining whether redlining exists in mortgage markets.

Statistics provide a supplementary way of establishing an inference of discrimination. They may even substitute for specific observed or circumstantial acts of discrimination. Yet no precise mathematical formula are required. They should at least support a *prima facie* case of discrimination, and thereby shift the burden of contrary proof to the defendant for explanation. Three criteria of using statistics have been identified by (Montlack, 1976). They are:
1. The degree of disparity of treatment shown by the statistics;
2. The relevance of the particular statistics to the discrimination in question; and,
3. The nature of possible explanation of the data.
Moreover, to refute statistical evidence, a compelling state interest must be shown. This is a very strict test, devised by the U.S. Supreme Court to place the largest possible burden upon those engaging in racial discrimination.

Percentages and proportions based on black or minority representation seem to be the most common measures of disparate patterns. However, the need for plaintiffs to use more sophisticated statistical analysis has been recognized. One example is the case of *Mabin v. Lear Siegler* (1972), where the court reversed the trial court ruling that the disproportionately low number of liquor licenses granted to blacks relative to their representation in the population raised an inference of unconstitutional discrimination by the licensing authority. Thus, data and analyses offered in the future will need to be more valid and reliable if it is to be accepted as legal proof of racial redlining.

From a market performance perspective, additional qualitative and speculative examples of discrimination through redlining have also been provided in the law review literature. Thus, Andrews and Shier (1976, p. 814) point out that (1) redlining may constitute "refusing to deal," (2) restraining trade, or (3) making tying arrangements as a result of denying loans on strictly racial or geographic considerations or imposing unwarranted terms on the loans which are made in redlined areas. In addition, they suggest that the practice may constitute a breach of the lender's duty (especially in thrift institutions) to its depositors to make funds available for local home finance (ibid., 1976, pp. 814–815).

Legal analysis and research seem to support that redlining has been practiced in some mortgage markets. Moreover, it is an unlawful practice which has materially adverse effects on mortgage supply and demand by groups, properties and neighborhoods in redlined areas. The material presented in the following section on descriptive research relating to redlining further amplifies the supply and market boundary dimensions of redlining. Of course, there still is only the inference of redlining based on statistically disparate patterns of lending.

B. Descriptive Analysis and Research

Through descriptive analysis and research redlining has been presented in terms of its racial-ethnic, geographic and mortgage-flow characteristics. Market boundaries and patterns have been described. Proportions, ratios, averages and mortgage volume comparisons (sometimes in relation to deposits) have been made between redlined and non-redlined areas. Descriptive inferences of discrimination have been based on disparities between lending in areas suspected of being redlined and those in which lending has not been affected by redlining. Thus, it is contended that risk-bearing, ability-to-pay and related lending criteria alone would not account for the disparities that have been identified. To bring about reported patterns lending decisions would have had to have been influenced by racial, geographic, age or other discounting and restrictive criteria which determine the flow of mortgage lending—and on discriminatory or biased categorical grounds unsupported by specific criteria of creditworthiness.

Both quantitative and qualitative relationships have been analyzed. The latter include a broad range of judgmental factors and underlying assumptions in mortgage lending decision-making.

1. Quantitative Relationships. Descriptive research has documented extreme disparity in levels of lending between redlined and nonredlined areas. Several such studies have been summarized in U.S. League of Savings Associations (1977). A few examples will suggest the extent of disparity. It generally exceeds by a wide margin actual income or related economic differences between areas.

A study of Los Angeles County mortgage lending showed that East Los

Angeles (comprising mostly Hispanic residents) received only $1 per capita, whereas those of Beverly Hills received $617 per capita (Andrews and Shier, 1976, p. 816). Those in Watts, a predominately black community, received substantially less than $1 per capita.

In the San Francisco Bay Area it was found that 12 percent of the total population received 0.6 percent of total mortgage financing. A Los Angeles-based group, Center for New Corporate Priorities, reported that for redlining areas of the city, over 14 percent of the population received less than 1 percent of the amount of single family residential loans (Andrews and Shier, 1976, p. 816).

In Washington, D.C., a city with almost three-fourths black residents, only 7.4 percent of all real estate loans closed by saving and loan associations between 1972 and 1974 went to residents in the city to buy single-family homes; and only 11.6 percent of all real estate loans were originated on inner-city properties (Congressional Budget Office, 1976, pp. 8–9). The District of Columbia Council reported that only 8 percent of the mortgage loan money from 13 institutions located in Washington went to home buyers in the District between 1972 and 1975 (Lippman, 1975). A 1973 Urban League study of Bronx County, New York showed similarly small fractions of inner city lending by banks and other financial institutions (Devine et al., 1973).

Based largely on experience in the Chicago area, Greenberg (1975) reported on studies supporting the practice of redlining. Based on a 1974 study by the Federal Home Loan Study Bank of Chicago, lenders in redlined areas reinvested only 4¢ to 8¢ for each $1 of deposits, whereas in suburban areas reinvestment reached as much as 31¢ per dollar of deposits. A Seattle comparison in 1975 showed less than 25¢ per dollar for the predominately black area and over $2.00 in the suburbs (Seattle Community Council Federation Report, 1975). Another Seattle study showed similar results. Lending was at or near zero in census tracts with predominately black residents. In predominately white and more affluent tracts loans were made at a rate as high as three times the average number of transactions per month (Washington State Human Rights Commission, 1977). Also, more transactions were made in some average-level tracts in one month than occurred in predominately black areas in three years.

An example of data for descriptive analysis is presented in Table 1. Data are for Seattle. There is some consistency between all indicators of economic and housing conditions. Mortgage lending is substantially at variance with supporting data. Lending was at zero in two tracts for eight sample months over a three year period. Interestingly, percentage levels were comparable for one of the tracts bordering on the predominately black community of Seattle. The highest level was reached in a tract which had a predominately black population in 1970 (50.2 percent). However, the location of sales in the tract were almost entirely in the area where white residents have remained in view-oriented properties near Lake Washington.

The evidence in these and other descriptive studies suggests that levels of

Table 1. Racial Composition and Housing-Related Characteristics for Selected Seattle Central Area Census Tracts in 1970; 1974 and 1974–1976

Tract Number	Black	White	Other	Central Area Sample Study Transactions	Index (Per Cent City Average)			Index of Housing Condition
					Mortgage Loans*	Income	House Value	
Core								
76	42.3	53.3	3.5	3	15	73	85	75
77	90.3	7.4	2.3	6	30	77	77	50
79	54.9	39.1	6.0	2	10	54	80	66
87	74.9	8.1	17.0	0	0	65	80	53
88	90.7	5.2	4.1	9	45	80	82	47
Border								
64	19.9	76.9	3.2	22	110	110	109	71
78	50.2	46.2	3.6	34	170	109	103	98
86	26.2	50.8	23.0	0	0	54	71	48
89	65.9	24.7	9.4	6	30	81	89	64
90	48.2	14.8	37.0	1	5	82	79	91

Note: Seattle City Average (Median) Income, 1970 = $11,037; Average Value of Single Family Dwelling, 1970 = $19,600; Index of Housing Condition (1974) City Average = 100; Sample Study of Average Number of Mortgage Loans per Tract (1974–76) = 20. (*Loan data are subject to exaggerated fluctuations because of the small number base.)

Source: U.S. Census data for racial composition, income and housing value; City of Seattle, Office of Policy Planning for housing condition index; mortgage loans from Washington State Human Rights Commission Report.

lending without redlining would not be as low as they are. It is to be expected that demand levels would be lower in older, minority areas. After all, demand for homes is largely a function of income, stable employment and some minimal assets (down payment, equity in property, etc.). These are typically lower in redlined areas. But they are far from being zero. Moreover, lenders and their supporters have not provided any evidence other than nonlending to support their position that the absence of lending is an absence of consumer demand or creditworthy borrowers. They may be discouraged borrowers, even high risk borrowers. But it has not been documented that there are so few creditworthy borrowers in such large parts of U.S. central cities.

2. Qualitative Relationships. Descriptive analysis is also based in part on qualitative and judgmental elements of the mortgage lending process. It is recognized that lenders have many subtle and elusive ways of redlining. Besides outright refusals or denials as implied in the descriptive evidence, the criteria employed may legitimize redlining. They may impose discriminatory payment terms, including substantially larger down payments and higher interest rates (Agelasto and Listokin, 1976). Properties may simply be underappraised. And this becomes increasingly easy as appraisers themselves become more captive of lenders as employees rather than as independent technicians. Lenders may also simply raise the requirements by emphasizing conventional loans over FHA or VA loans. This excludes a larger proportion of prospective borrowers from mortgage markets. Moreover, the predominant form of financing may be through noninstitutional credit—assignments, contracts, etc.

Other judgmental factors form part of the "conventional wisdom" of mortgage lending. The criteria may be regarded as racist, elitist and suburban-biased. Areas with high proportions of blacks and other minorities are considered less desirable than communities which are mainly white. Elitism enters into consideration of appraising which assigns higher value to homogeneity (meaning white) and a lower value to heterogeneity (meaning nonwhite, multi-ethnic, etc.). (Cf. Knowles, 1974.) The suburban bias comes about with the notion of neighborhood cycle theory and the inevitability of neighborhood decline. By implication and practice, then, old is bad, new is good. Lending is expected to be curtailed or assigned special high risk status when average ages extend into the over 40-year category, without specifying specific property conditions of marketability.

Thus, one of the most extensive studies made of New York City found that there has been and through the early 1970s continued to be redlining in communities which had recently changed or were in the process of changing in racial composition from white to black or to Spanish-speaking (Sternleib, 1972). Clearly such logic and reported experience set up a self-fulfilling prophecy. Lenders withdraw rehabilitation and mortgage funds. Areas begin to show evidence of disrepair and deterioration. Markets become depressed. Demand is discouraged and distorted. But, in the end, the victims—residents of these areas—are blamed.

Loans are denied, according to lenders, because demand does not exist, borrowers are not creditworthy, or properties are not bankable.

Of course, from a research perspective, descriptive analysis has numerous weaknesses and limitations. Precise measures and loan decision criteria cannot be provided. Only lenders or borrowers have these data. Such documentation becomes extremely costly and difficult to obtain. Thus, statistical evidence to date has been primarily sales and disclosure data obtained primarily by government requirements or indirectly through tax assessors, title companies or other nonlender sources.

Although public policies have had to be formulated to respond to the problems of redlining, more and better statistical analyses are needed. To date there are a few studies in which correlation and regression techniques have been used.

C. Correlation and Regression Analysis

Among the studies available in mid 1977, the use of correlation analysis was reported in Feins and Grothaus (1975). Of particular relevance is the finding that (in analyzing the number of associations making loans, the number of conventional loans made and the dollar volume of these loans in each of the study areas by Zip Code), conventional lending was negatively related to the percent of population that was nonwhite (ibid., p. 290). Positive relations were reported for median family income, percent of owner occupied houses built before 1940, and percent of white residents who had not moved in four years (ibid.). The value of coefficients was not indicated. But these authors did note the fact that postal zones comprised too large an area to permit the needed more precise examination of whether discrimination existed in mortgage loan extensions. Thus, from this and other correlation analysis presented to date on redlining, only general inferences are supported. Considerably more and better data are needed in order to obtain stronger and more precise relationships. It is only through such analyses that clearer and more definitive statements can be made. With the exception of work by Loury (1976) much the same could be said of reported applications of multiple regression techniques (Devine et al., 1973). The reasons that this is so can be explained principally by the lack of behavioral or borrower-lender and property-specific information.

The most extensive study of data on mortgage lending which have been subjected to multiple regression analysis is the one reported by Loury (1976). Using 1974 data compiled on an SMSA level by the Comptroller of the Currency in cooperation with the Federal Reserve Board, Federal Home Loan Bank Board and Federal Deposit Insurance Corporation, he had available the following variables: applicants' race, sex, marital status, income, tenure on the job, assets, indebtedness, cash flow for debt service, purchase price of property, disposition of the loan, loan requested (ibid., p. 7). A total of 12,086 observations were collected. But no property location or property age data were obtained.

Six separate regression equations were estimated. Multiple correlation coefficients on race for the regressions are consistently in the neighborhood of .7; indicating that a logit specification fit the cross section data reasonably well (ibid., p. 14).

Included among the findings were (ibid., p. 15 ff.)

1. The gross race dummy variable had a statistically significant negative coefficient at slightly above the 10 percent level of confidence.[7]

2. There appears to be lending discrimination against high income nonwhites; implying that the likely desegregation or "pioneering" into white neighborhoods is discouraged. The negative coefficient for income at upper levels and involving properties valued about $75,000 was significant at 5 percent.[8] For this group, race was the single most important determinant of the probability of being granted a loan.

3. Racial disparities can be identified in terms of their influence on mortgage credit availability (i.e., probability of getting a mortgage loan). Again with respect to Cleveland, "the pure effect of being nonwhite on the probability of receiving a loan is equivalent to the effect of having an illiquid financial position" (Loury, 1976, p. 17). At the national level, $8,045 of additional annual income is needed to offset the pure effects of race on probability of loan approval (ibid., p. 18).

The magnitude or extent of disparity cannot be rationalized as a result of necessary or sound business practices. Nonwhites who are best able to repay a loan suffered relatively the greatest amount of discrimination in the 1974 study.

Loury provided additional statistical tests of the racial effects on loan approval probability. They further confirmed the findings based on multiple regression analysis.

D. Other Multivariate Methods of Analysis

Data limitations and the recency of interest in redlining from a research perspective account for the absence of applications of factors, cluster or discriminant analysis in the literature. Some refinements of regression methods with simultaneous equations are in preparation, based on work being done in urban economics. However, the applications discussed in the following section interpret some key relationships which are likely to be highlighted in future multivariate analysis of redlining as more and better data become available.

V. A PROPOSED MULTIVARIATE METHODOLOGY[9]

In view of the controversies and criticisms surrounding mortgage lending decisions, there is a need for some systematic procedures which provide sound evaluative and classification criteria. Among the several possibilities, discriminant and cluster analysis seem best suited to the task. The former set of techniques provides an effective means of identifying and predicting the groups in which prospective borrowers belong, given clearly defined criteria of creditworthiness. When properly applied, this would remove the arbitrary categorical biases associated with redlining. From a lender perspective discriminant analysis offers the means of predicting or explaining good and bad mortgage credit behavior based on specified borrower, property, location or other relevant variables. Cluster analysis, on the other hand, facilitates the identification of homogeneous subgroups among similar borrowers, properties, locations or other relevant characteristics. Taken together these methods can be used to avoid as well as detect redlining. That is, they can help lenders avoid redlining by properly rather than arbitrarily classifying prospective borrowers. Yet they can also help detect redlining, if sufficient data are available to uncover misclassification of creditworthy borrowers along with marketable properties and locations.

Questions might well be asked why the reference to a proposed methodology when these techniques have been applied in various aspects of credit analysis. For example, Morton (1974) has presented an extensive application of discriminant analysis using data on foreclosure and delinquency experience. Mainly three different parameters are involved. In contrast to the prediction or explanation of delinquency and foreclosure relationships in mortgage lending, there are some conceptual and statistical difficulties which must be resolved in the application to redlining. Conceptually, there are built-in biases which are not explicitly a part of the credit application process. Statistically, there is a more serious missing data problem than is encountered in working with approved loans that go bad. Some elaboration of these points is provided in the remaining discussion of the application to redlining.

A. Discriminant and Cluster Analysis: The Redlining Case

The procedures used in a hypothetical case are described. The required data for a complete analysis are not available.[10]

Initially two types of areas were identified. They were:
1. Suspected redlined areas.
2. Control areas.

The first comprised census tracts with one third or more nonwhite residents in 1970. This was recognized as the "tipping point" from which a tract is expected to continue to change from white to nonwhite. These were defined as the most likely targets for redlining. The control group tracts were those which had comparable median income levels and house values, but differed in racial/ethnic composition.

In order to establish similarity among the tracts statistically the tract data for Seattle were analyzed using the UWBCL cluster analysis program.[11] In this way the choice of tracts for comparison was made objectively.

The output of the cluster analysis showed four statistically homogeneous groupings. The largest combination of comparable tracts using median income and house value as criterion variables were found in Cluster 4. This is shown in Table 2. The two types of areas included the following census tracts:

1. Suspected redlined—76, 77, 79, 87, 88, 89, 90, 100, and 101.
2. Control—29, 33, 34, 47, 48, 50, 52, and 54.

The relative positions of the four clusters are shown in Figure 3. Median incomes and house values are most uniformly lowest in Cluster 4.

The variables to be used in the discriminant analysis would be those selected from the standard mortgage loan application. In summary form they are illustrated in Table 3.

The next task of discriminant analysis is to predict proper group membership using "loan application decision" as the dependent variable—approved (accepted), not approved (rejected). The effectiveness of the analysis would be judged by its predictive power in designating the group into which each observation (application) should be assigned.

Using hypothetical data and a stepwise method (in which independent variables are entered in the order of their greatest contribution to explaining the loan application decision), a sample output is shown in Tables 4 and 5.

It should be noted that the differences between the groups in Table 4 are highly significant. That is the association between "area" and "application decision" is nearly significant at the .01 level. The Gamma value as a measure of the strength of the association is very strong.

It should be noted that had the data been real, one could infer that those applying for loans in the suspected redlined areas were far more likely to be rejected than those in the control areas. Here again, the Gamma and Chi-square statistics would provide a basis for supporting the inference.

The effect of area can be determined in other ways. It could be suppressed in a subsequent run and the predictive results could then be compared.

A more useful analysis in the redlining would be to focus on those observations which were *incorrectly* classified. Thus, redlining would be indicated, if all or most of the predicted for rejection were actually accepted from the control area. The reverse would be argued if most of those predicted for acceptance in the redlined area were actually rejected.

A real data analysis would need to provide evidence of redlining discriminators and creditworthiness discriminators. That is, using the variables list from Table 3, it is presumed that redlining discriminators would be census tract (1), year property built (8), and ethnic/racial identification (14) along with secondary information on the changing racial mix of the tract in which the property is located and perceived riskiness-decline of the area. Yet as reported in other research riskiness or creditworthiness are more significantly linked with borrower income, family size, existence of junior financing, and loan-to-value ratio along with such secondary factors as divorce, catastrophic injury, and related

Table 2.   Cluster Analysis Printout of Cluster 4 Using Median Income and House Value per Tract

Cluster 4 with Observations		Census Tract #	% Nonwhite	1970 Median Income $	Median House Value ($X100)
13	.147	CT13		9581	169
17	.271	CT17		9912	164
18	.118	CT18		9463	172
27	.125	CT28		9472	163
28	.250	CT29	2.4	9863	172
32	.307	CT33	2.5	9981	162
33	.173	CT34	3.2	9665	169
34	.486	CT35		10297	179
35	.155	CT36		9603	166
44	.099	CT45		9406	170
46	.046	CT47	3.2	9095	163
47	.202	CT48	1.9	9747	169
48	.081	CT49		9327	166
49	.465	CT50	5.2	10328	171
51	.083	CT52	6.4	9140	179
52	2.572	CT53		6266	238
53	.045	CT54	5.7	9115	164
70	2.122	CT73		5708	121
71	.309	CT74		8712	198
72	.244	CT75		7397	173
73	.056	CT76	46.7	8029	167
74	.108	CT77	92.6	8474	151
76	1.216	CT79	61.7	5908	156
78	4.173	CT85		5207	250
79	1.449	CT86		5924	139
80	.393	CT87	89.8	7135	157
81	.023	CT88	95.1	8793	161
82	.027	CT89	75.1	8929	174
83	.108	CT90	86.0	9098	154
84	3.808	CT91		3790	150
86	.211	CT94		9772	170
91	.371	CT99		10016	155
92	.324	CT100	47.0	9959	179
93	.290	CT101	34.1	9723	185
95	.118	CT103		9411	161
99	2.216	CT107		4889	162
100	.623	CT108		10587	163
101	.350	CT109		7864	141
102	.402	CT110		7700	196
104	.553	CT112		9644	135
105	.533	CT113		10450	166

Note: Census tracts in Cluster 4 not chosen for study had minority populations between 6.4% and 34.1%.

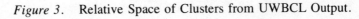

Figure 3.   Relative Space of Clusters from UWBCL Output.

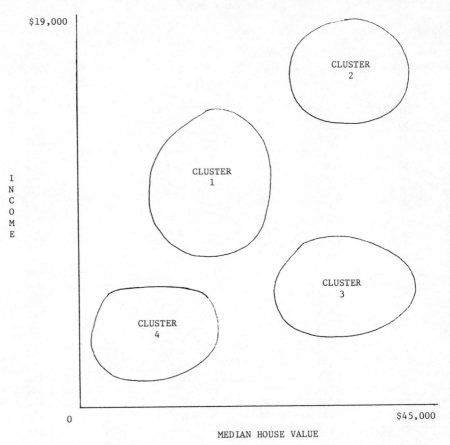

sources of severe economic reversals. For managerial and public policy purposes
we need to know which variables are the good discriminators for each category.

B. Problems of Data Availability and Bias

Ideally, mortgage credit data are needed for all loan applicants. Information
analyzed to date includes accepted credit risks. Yet a fundamental issue surrounding redlining is that creditworthy borrowers are being arbitrarily excluded.
Hence either lenders or borrowers are needed from whom rejection data can be
obtained. Lenders have been unwilling to provide such data and turned-down
borrowers are very difficult to identify and even less available and willing to
divulge their loan experiences. There would appear to be more serious limitations

Table 3.   Variables to Be Used in Discriminant
Analysis of Mortgage Loan Data

Variable

1.	Census Tract
2.	Appraisal Value
3.	Purchase Price
4.	Loan Amount Requested
5.	Length or Maturity of the Loan
6.	Interest Rate Charged
7a.	Conventional Financing
7b.	FHA Financing
7c.	VA Financing
7d.	Other Financing (including Junior Financing)
8.	Year Property Built
9.	Borrower's Occupancy Status in Subject Property
10.	Borrower's Household Income
11.	Monthly Mortgage Payment (principal and interest)
12.	Total Liabilities (Household)
13.	Total Assets (Household)
14.	Ethnic/Racial Identification
14a.	Caucasian/White
14b.	Black
14c.	Asian
14d.	Spanish-Origin
14e.	American Indian
14f.	Other
15.	Marital Status
16.	Sex
17.	Age
18.	Occupation
19.	Family Size
20.	Lender Decision
20a.	Approved
20b.	Not Approved
20c.	Other

than the built-in bias and technical limitations of discriminant analysis techniques. Money, time and effort in pursuit of the data will eventually lead to the needed availability. The technical limitations can be handled in a more straightforward way. Beyond the comments presented here, a more elaborate technical description can be found in Morton (1974), and Morrison (1974).

The most commonly expressed form of bias in the use of discriminant analysis occurs because the equation for the discriminant function is formed from the observations and is then applied to predict the form of those same observations. Therefore, the predictive level of the equation is somewhat inflated. With large sample sizes this problem should be negligible. However, there is a way to

Table 4.   Sample Crosstabulation of Area by Status of Loan Application*

		Area	
Status	Control	Suspected Redlined	Row Total
Rejected	10	19	29 (38.2%)
Accepted	31	16	47 (61.8%)
Column Total	41 (53.9%)	35 (46.1%)	

*Chi-square = 5.94045 with 1 degree of freedom
  (Significance = .0148)
*Gamma = −.57276

preclude this bias from setting in. One can run a ''hold-out'' or ''split-half'' sample, whereby the equation is derived from (a portion) or half of the observations and is then applied to the second (portion) half. This method is suggested as a precaution if enough observations are available.

Other variations might also be introduced into the computer runs. For instance, area might be dropped out of the analysis and ethnic identification might be substituted in its place. It would be interesting to see whether the prediction equation is enhanced by the change or not. Further possibilities would include separate analyses for each type of financial institution, or perhaps, for each individual institution.

Obviously, the techniques proposed in this chapter are not without limitations. A major assumption is that the data are accessible. Furthermore, it is assumed that the information is accurate and complete. Depending on the control methods in force during the data collection, these assumptions might not be reasonable. Furthermore, one might argue that the application of an equation to loan determination is unrealistic, since most bank officers do not perform their analyses with equations. However, it is precisely that point which prompted the decision to propose procedures in which the process could be quantified. A statistically

Table 5.   Sample Prediction Results from Discriminant Analysis
Using Hypothetical Data*

Actual Group	Number of Cases	Predicted Rejected	Predicted Accepted
Rejected	29	18	11
Accepted	47	6	41

*77.6 percent of cases correctly classified
*Chi-square = 23.211 with 1 degree of freedom
  (Significance = .000)

objective equation is merely a projection of observable consistencies that appear in the lending institutions' policies. The relative "goodness" of the derived equation would be the percentage of observations correctly classified. If a highly significant prediction equation is produced, then the major factors are apparently being weighed roughly in the same manner that the loan officers unconsciously do it in their minds. If this case develops, the results can then be declared "valid" and the conclusions can be considered useful.

A further consideration is that past history might seriously affect the number of loan applicants from an area. For instance, it is widely accepted that realtors often play a large part in the search and selection of lenders. Often they will tell the prospective applicant where he can and cannot expect to obtain a mortgage loan. Therefore, for instance, the number of rejected applicants might be artificially low, particularly from redlined areas.

Finally, it should be emphasized that the methods proposed here were limited in scope to home mortgage lending. Other vital issues of home-improvement loans and business development loans are also integral to the redlining issue. They are simply outside the scope of this chapter.

VI. IMPLICATIONS FOR MARKETING AND PUBLIC POLICY

The analysis and research discussed here suggest several implications for marketing and public policy. To marketing management they suggest that the technology is readily available for making decisions that are risk-averse and which also do not involve redlining. By more correctly classifying mortgage applicants both the private interests of lenders and the public interests of credit availability can be more adequately served.

For the makers of public policy there are indications that disclosure data on mortgage lending will lead to the clearer delineation of how market areas are being served. The analysis of the data can lead to closer scrutiny of the mortgage lending process. Lender accountability should be enhanced. The reasons supporting their decisions and the relationships associated with them can become better understood. Both should lead to the better overall management of mortgage credit and investment resources.

The discussion also would suggest that analysis and research on redlining are marketing-related. Useful insights can be provided for management as well as the makers of public policy.

There may be aspects of marketing as a technology for influencing attitudes and behavior which can address the biased content of the redlining process. As noted in the discussion sources of bias are traceable to assumptions and beliefs regarding property locations, ethnic compositions of neighborhoods and the risk-uncertainty aspects of group attributes in the older parts of cities. The biases involved mean that the rules of decision making for explicitly and individually determining borrower creditworthiness or property marketability are not strictly adhered to. Marketing might be used to effect changes in the organizational decision-making by lenders and others involved in mortgage lending decisions. Thus, loan committee members could be re-educated through the use of marketing techniques to manage risks through ways other than redlining. Risk-pooling and co-insurance arrangements among lenders could be made more attractive as alternatives, for example.

From the perspective of marketing and consumer behavior there is one other implication which should be noted. This pertains to the importance of demographic attributes in analysis and research of redlining in mortgage credit markets.

At a micro-level of brand choice, demographic factors may not be very sensitive and useful as correlates or discriminators for predicting behavior. However, for home ownership and housing choices or other behavior at the product class level as in mortgage credit markets this appears not to be so (Sheth, 1974, p. 4). Since housing is strongly tied to biogenic and sociogenic consumer needs and wants, demographic attributes appear to be very strong and sensitive elements for explaining and predicting consumer behavior. Moreover, public policy responses to redlining (say on the matter of racial bias and discrimination) are likely to be linked to demographic characteristics. Thus, one of the clear implications of the analysis and research presented is that a strong case can be made for a return to demographic attributes for the sensitive and substantive analysis of mortgage credit behavior and market relationships. Important discriminators as suggested by the proposed methodology would, indeed, be ethnic/racial identity, age, marital status, family size, occupation and geographical area of residence. In addition to the categorical biases of redlining associated with these demographic variables there may even be elements of mortgage credit risk and uncertainty which can be linked to them. This of course remains to be demonstrated in future analysis and research of data on redlining. But the analysis and the evidence does indicate that from a marketing perspective, we may have been too hasty in virtually abandoning socioeconomic-demographic factors in certain areas of consumer behavior (Sheth, 1974, pp. 3, 6, 8, 11).

VII. CONCLUSIONS

Analysis and research of redlining are still in a very early stage of development. Redlining as a concept is highly normative, judgmental and subject to conflicting interpretations (e.g., as risk-aversion and as racial discrimination). Data and methods of analysis are quite inadequate. Yet enough has been presented to suggest that redlining is a relevant and researchable topic for marketing.

As demonstrated in other forms of credit analysis as well as in the studies cited, discriminant analysis offers an effective approach to extending and operationalizing research on redlining.

More and better analysis and research of redlining are needed to guide managerial as well as public policy in mortgage credit markets. The future is at stake for real estate wealth and investments as well as the home environment of urban areas.

The data and relationships presented in the chapter have provided an overview of redlining from a marketing perspective. As more and better data become available for analysis and research, better use can be made of the explanatory and predictive power of multivariate techniques. As the data and relationships associated with redlining become better known, they will in turn lead to the identification of strategies and remedies for solving the urban problems which accompany the practice of redlining.

Reviewing the analysis and research of redlining should help to increase the awareness of the process as a marketing as well as an urban problem. Through efforts to provide better analysis and research results, marketing can be utilized to help solve the problems which accompany redlining in mortgage markets.

FOOTNOTES

1. Michael Mulhern expressed this in a paper prepared for a doctoral seminar in marketing, University of Washington, May 1977.

2. A widely disputed issue in the redlining controversy is whether effective demand really exists in redlined areas. Lenders claim that it does not. The opposing view is that demand does exist but is depressed or discouraged by past practices of lenders as well as by other economic and environmental factors. For a detailed background discussion, including considerations of risk, see United States League of Savings Associations (1977).

3. This term includes decisions to abandon a product or drop it from the market offering of a firm. A reduced supply of a product or service is the result. Also, only certain groups or classes of customers may be discouraged from consumption. For redlining this means refusing or restricting credit to certain groups or neighborhoods which could meet financial tests of creditworthiness, if considered on an individual basis.

4. This is similar to the discouraged-worker phenomenon in the labor force resulting from prolonged unemployment and rejection in the job-search process.

5. Appreciation is expressed to Mark Zerr, a student in the MBA-Law joint program at the University of Washington, for research completed for this section of the chapter during Spring Quarter 1977; and to the Departmental Research Committee for graduate student financial support.

6. Note that categorical exclusion and discrimination may be on property-age, value of the subject property, and the like, as well as ethnic composition of the neighborhood and related racial factors.

7. As Loury (1976) notes: "What this means is that if lenders in Cleveland were not practicing discrimination, then the odds are nearly one in ten that a sample such as ours would generate a coefficient on R as large in absolute value as the one shown in the table (-0.29846, with a standard error of 0.18886).

8. Small sample and cell sizes with these individuals limits their overall impact on the total population or study results. Loury states further: "It is clear from the magnitude of these coefficients that, among those buying high priced properties, race is the most important single determinant of the probability of being granted a loan" (p. 16).

9. The examples and data comparisons used in this section are based primarily on the work by Arima (1976). The study was prepared under the present author's supervision.

10. This would include specific and statistically relevant borrower, property and location characteristics.

11. This is a canned cluster analysis program for use on the CDC 6400 system at the University of Washington, School of Business Administration.

REFERENCES

Agelasto, Michael, and Listokin, David (1976), "Redlining in Perspective: An Evaluation of Strategies to Deal With the Urban Financing Dilemma," paper presented to the American Real Estate and Urban Economics Association, Washington, D.C., May 21. Manuscript 22 pages.
—— (1975), *The Urban Financing Dilemma: Disinvestment-Redlining,* Exchange Bibliograhy # 890, Monticello, Ill.: Council of Planning Librarians (October).
Andrews, Elaine M., and Shier, Matthew J. (1976), "Redlining: Why Make a Federal Case Out of It," *Golden Gate University Law Review,* Vol. 6, No. 3: 813–850 (Spring).
Arima, John S. (1976), "Redlining: Issues, Research, and Analysis in Relation to Social and Political Marketing," Seattle: School of Business Administration, University of Washington.
Bailey, Martin J. (1966), "Effects of Race and Other Demographic Factors on the Values of Single Family Houses," *Land Economics* 42: 215–220 (May).
Becker, Gary (1971), *The Economics of Discrimination,* 2nd edition, Chicago: University of Chicago Press.
Boyer, Bryan (1973), *Cities Destroyed for Cash,* Chicago: Follett Publishing Company.
Carliner, Geoffrey (1974), "Determinants of Home Ownership," *Land Economics* 50: 109–119 (May).
Case, Fred E. (1972), *Inner City Housing and Private Enterprise,* New York: Praeger.
Congressional Budget Office (1976), *Housing Finance: Federal Programs and Issues,* Staff Working Paper, Washington D.C.: Government Printing Office (September 23).
"Court Says Redlining is Illegal," *Equal Opportunity in Housing,* Report Bulletin 18, March 8, 1976, Englewood Cliffs, N.J.: Prentice-Hall, pp. 1–2.
Denton, John H., (1964), *Race and Property,* Berkeley, Calif.: Diablo Press.
Devine, Richard J., et al. (1973), *Where the Lender Looks First: A Case Study of Mortgage Disinvestment in Bronx County, 1960–1970,* New York: National Urban League.
Federal Home Loan Bank Board (1974), *Regulations 1974,* Section 528.2(d). Washington, D.C.: The Board.
Feins, Judith, and Grothaus, Darel E. (1975), "An Analysis of the Federal Home Loan Bank of Chicago's Survey of Urban Lending and Savings Patterns by Cook County Insured Associations," in Calvin P. Bradford, et al., *The Role of Mortgage Lending Practices in Older Urban Neighborhoods: Institutional Lenders, Regulatory Agencies and Their Community Impacts,* Evanston, Ill.: Center for Urban Affairs, Northwestern University, pp. 260–297.
Flahive, Marty, and Winokur, James L. (1977), "Some Legal Aspects of Residential Mortgage Lending," City of Denver, Department of Community Development, *Study of Redlining and Disinvestment,* pp. 73–88 (April).
Furstenberg, George M. von, and Green, R. Jeffrey (1974), "Estimation of Delinquency Risk for Home Mortgage Portfolios," *American Real Estate and Urban Economics Journal,* Vol. 2, pp. 5–37 (Spring).
—— (1974), "The Effect of Income and Race on the Quality of Home Mortgages: A Case for Pittsburgh," in G. M. von Furstenberg, B. Harrison and A. R. Horowitz, eds., *Patterns of Racial Discrimination,* Vol. 1, Housing, Lexington, Mass.: D.C. Heath.
——, Harrison, Bennett, and Horowitz, Ann R., eds. (1974), *Patterns of Racial Discrimination,* Vol. I, Housing, Lexington, Mass.: D.C. Heath.

Greenberg, Freddi L. (1975), "Redlining—The Fight Against Discrimination in Mortgage Lending," *Loyola University (Chicago) Law Journal* 6 (1): 71–89 (Winter).

Haar, Charles M. (1960), *Federal Credit and Private Housing: The Mass Financing Dilemma,* New York: McGraw-Hill.

Harrison, Bennett (1974), "Discrimination in Space: Suburbanization and Black Unemployment in Cities," in G. von Furstenberg, et al., *Patterns of Discrimination,* Lexington, Mass.: D.C. Heath, pp. 21-53.

Haugen, R. A., and Heins, A. J. (1969), "A Market Separation Theory of Rent Differentials in Metropolitan Areas," *Quarterly Journal of Economics* 83: 660-672 (November).

Johnson, D. A., Porter, R. J., and Mateljan, P. L. (1971), "Racial Discrimination in Apartment Rentals," *Journal of Applied Social Psychology* 1: 364-377.

Kain, John F., and Quigley, John M. (1972), "Housing Market Discrimination, Home Ownership, and Savings Behavior," *American Economic Review* 62: 263-277 (June).

——— (1974), "Mortgages and Home Ownership Among Black Households: Reply," *American Economic Review* 63 (June).

King, Thomas, and Mieszkowski, Peter (1973), "An Estimate of Racial Discrimination in Rental Housing," *Journal of Political Economy* 81: 590-606 (May/June).

Knowles, Louis L., and Prewitt, Kenneth, eds. (1969), *Institutional Racism in America,* Englewood Cliffs, N.J.: Prentice-Hall.

Lapham, Victoria (1971), "Do Blacks Pay More for Housing?" *Journal of Political Economy* 79: 1244-1257 (November-December).

Laufman, et al., v. Oakley Building and Loan Company (1976), 408 Federal Supplement, pp. 489.

Laurenti, Luigi (1960), *Property Values and Race: Studies in Seven Cities,* Berkeley, University of California Press.

Lippman, Thomas W. (1975), "Savings-Loan Firms Lend Suburbs Most," *The Washington Post* (April 25).

Loury, Glenn C. (1976), "An Analysis of Discrimination in Mortgage Lending," report prepared for The Center for National Policy Review, Washington, D.C., nd., 1976 references. Manuscript, 29 pages.

McEntire, David (1960), *Residence and Race.* Berkeley: University of California Press.

Mabin v. Lear Siegler, Inc. (1972), 457 Federal Second District Court, pp. 806.

Mao, James C. T. (1960), *Residential Mortgage Financing,* Michigan Business Reports, No. 34, Ann Arbor: Bureau of Business Research, University of Michigan.

Miller, Loren (1964), "Government's Responsibility for Residential Segregation," in John P. Denton, ed., *Race and Property,* Berkeley, Calif.: Diablo Press, pp. 58-76.

Montlack, Kenneth (1976), "Using Statistical Evidence to Enforce the Laws Against Discrimination," *Cleveland State Law Review* 22: 259-280.

Morrison, Donald G. (1974), "Discriminant Analayis," in Robert Ferber, ed., *Handbook of Marketing Research.* New York: McGraw-Hill, Ch. 8, pp. 2-442-2-457.

Morton, T. Gregory (1974), *A Discriminant Function Analysis of Residential Mortgage Delinquency and Foreclosure,* Storrs: University of Connecticut, Center for Real Estate and Urban Economic Studies (August).

Muth, Richard F. (1974), "Residential Segregation and Discrimination," in George M. von Furstenberg, B. Harrison and A. R. Horowitz, eds., *Patterns of Racial Discrimination,* Vol. I, Housing, Lexington, Mass.: D.C. Heath, pp. 107-119.

Olsen, Edgar O. (1969), "A Competitive Theory of the Housing Market," *American Economic Review* 59: 612-622 (September).

——— (1974), "Do Blacks Pay More for Housing," in G. von Furstenberg, B. Harrison, and A. R. Horowitz, *Patterns of Discrimination,* Lexington, Mass.: D.C. Heath, pp. 205-211.

Pascal, Anthony, ed. (1972), *Racial Discrimination in Economic Life,* Lexington, Mass.: D.C. Heath.

———— (1970), "The Analysis of Residential Segregation," in John P. Crecine, ed., *Financing the Metropolis,* Beverly Hills, Calif.: Sage Publications, pp. 401–434.

———— (1967), *The Economics of Housing Segregation,* Santa Monica, Calif.: The Rand Corporation.

Pettigrew, Thomas F., ed. (1975), *Racial Discrimination in the United States,* New York: Harper & Row.

"Pilot Survey on Possible Housing Discrimination," *Federal Reserve Bulletin* May (1975), pp. 336–339.

Pitts, Robert (1964), "Mortgage Financing and Race," in John H. Denton, ed., *Race and Property,* Berkeley, Calif.: Diablo Press.

Pritchard, Allen E. (1975), "Urban Conservation Policy Needed to Stop Abandonment of Central Cities," *The Mortgage Banker:* 41, 43–46 (July).

Quigley, John M. (1974), "Racial Discrimination and the Housing Consumption of Black Households," in G. von Furstenberg, Bennett Harrison and Ann R. Horowitz, eds., *Patterns of Discrimination,* Lexington, Mass.: D.C. Heath, pp. 121–137.

Rapkin, Chester (1969), "Price Discrimination Against Negroes in the Rental Housing Market," in J. F. Kain, ed., *Race and Poverty—The Economics of Discrimination,* Englewood Cliffs, N.J.: Prentice-Hall, pp. 112–121.

————, and Grigsby, William (1960), *The Demand for Housing in Racially Mixed Areas,* Berkeley: University of California Press.

Searing, Daniel A. (1973), "Discrimination in Home Finance," *Notre Dame Lawyer:* 1113–1144 (June).

Seattle Community Council Federation (1975), *Redlining and Disinvestment in Central Seattle: How the Banks Are Destroying Our Neighborhoods,* Seattle, Wash.: The Federation (July).

Sheth, Jagdish N. (1974), "Role of Demographics in Consumer Behavior," unpublished paper, n.d., 1974 references, 13 pages.

Spratlen, Thaddeus H. (1976), "Redlining in Residential Mortgage Lending: A Case of Racial and Location Discrimination in Mortgage Markets?" Working Paper, Social Science Research Center, Howard University, Washington, D.C. (July). Manuscript 22 pages.

Sternlieb, George (1972), *The Housing Dilemma: The Dynamics of New York City's Rent Controlled Housing,* New York: New York City Housing and Development Administration.

Straszheim, Mahlon R. (1974), "Racial Discrimination in the Urban Housing Market and Its Effects on Black Housing Consumption," in G. von Furstenberg, B. Harrison, and A. R. Horowitz, eds., *Patterns of Racial Discrimination,* Vol. I, Lexington, Mass.: D.C. Heath, pp. 139–164.

Struyk, Raymond J. (1975), "Determinants of the Rate of Home Ownership of Black Relative to White Households," *Journal of Urban Economics* 2: 291–306 (October).

U.S. Code, 42 U.S.C. Section 3605 (U.S. Civil Rights Act of 1968, Title VIII).

U.S. League of Savings Associations (1977), *Risk vs. Discrimination in the Expansion of Urban Mortgage Lending,* Chicago, Ill.: The League (April).

U.S. Senate, 94th Congress, 1st Session, Report No. 94–187, *Home Mortgage Disclosure Act of 1975,* pp. 1, 4.

Village of Arlington Heights v. Metropolitan Housing Development Corporation 45 (1977), *U.S. Law Weekly,* 4073, U.S. Missouri, District.

Vitarello, James (1975), "The Redlining Route to Urban Decay," *Focus* 3: 4–5, Washington, D.C.: Joint Center for Political Studies (August).

Walzer, Norman, and Singer, Dan (1974), "Housing Expenditures in Urban Low Income Areas," *Land Economics* 50: 224–231 (August).

Washington State Human Rights Commission (1977), *Patterns of Residential Mortgage Lending and Property Sales in Seattle, 1974, 1975 and 1975,* Seattle, Wash.: The Commission. (Preliminary Report of the Redlining Task Force.)

Wells, William O., and Sheth, Jagdish N. (1974), "Factor Analysis," in Robert Ferber, ed., *Handbook of Marketing Research,* New York: McGraw-Hill, Ch. 9, pp. 2-458-2-471.

White, Anthony G. (1976), *Discrimination in Housing Loans—Redlining. A Selected Bibliography,* Monticello, Ill.: Council of Planning Librarians (February) 5 pages.

Winger, Alan R. (1973), "Some Internal Determinants of Upkeep Spending by Urban Home Owners," *Land Economics* XLIX: 474-479 (November).

PSYCHOLOGICAL GEOGRAPHY

William D. Wells, NEEDHAM, HARPER & STEERS

ADVERTISING, INC.

Fred D. Reynolds, UNIVERSITY OF GEORGIA

INTRODUCTION

Weather, climate and terrain have a great many direct and obvious effects upon consumer behavior. The cold winters of the North require warm clothing, central heating and antifreeze. Snow provides the base for snowmobiles, snow tires, sleds and skis. And the hot sun of the Southwest encourages sunglasses, wide-brimmed hats and air-conditioned cars.

But some regional differences in consumer behavior are not so easily explained by physical geography alone. Iced tea and homemade biscuits are more common in the Southeast than in other parts of the country. Brandy consumption is unusually high in certain Midwestern states. Big cars are relatively popular in Texas, relatively unpopular in California.

Research in Marketing—Volume 2, 1979, pages 345–357.
Copyright © 1979 by JAI Press Inc.
All rights of reproduction in any form reserved.
ISBN 0-89232-059-1

345

Differences of the latter kind reflect a complex interplay of physical geography, local culture, and marketing history. And although they account for a significant portion of consumer behavior, they have received very little attention in the marketing literature.

This article is a preliminary exploration of the psychology of geography. It shows regional differences in consumers' life-styles, and the associations between these differences and regional differences in the use of products, services and media.

PERSPECTIVE

Writers describing consumer behavior frequently acknowledge that regional differences exist, but they pay relatively little attention to these differences, and many apparently believe that regionalism is vanishing in the United States (Engel et al., 1973; Kotler, 1976; Tucker, 1964). For instance, Engel et al. state that while geographic differences are still important, mobility is contributing to their decline.

> Geographic areas in a nation develop their own culture... the Southwest appears to have a characteristic style of life that emphasizes the casual form of dress, outdoor entertaining, and unique forms of recreation. Decision making in the Southwest is presumably less rigid and perhaps more innovative than the conservative, inhibitied attitudes toward new products that are supposedly characteristic of the Midwest. A fair assessment would seem to be that even though these geographic differences are still important, mobility is contributing to their decline (1973).

The nonmarketing literature also conveys the assumption that regional differences in attitudes and behavior are on the wane. This position, which has been advocated for over twenty years, is attributed to the homogenizing effects of interregional migration and the common influences of the mass media (Mayo, 1964; Merrill, 1957; Zelinsky, 1973).

Like many widely held beliefs, the homogenization hypothesis is not based upon conclusive empirical evidence. Census data do indicate regions of the United States have converged with respect to several demographic characteristics including fertility, sex ratio, and marital status of females (Labovitz, 1962). However, no published data indicate that regional variations in basic values, beliefs, attitudes and interests are diminishing.

Even the arguments supporting the homogenization hypothesis can be seen to work both ways. Consider the common-influences argument: there is ample evidence that the mass media do not have mass effects; rather, they have differing effects according to the predispositions of the audiences (Klapper, 1960). Perhaps we should expect a reinforcement of existing values and beliefs among regions, instead of a convergence.

The interregional migration argument may be equally tenuous. To produce convergence, migration must include vast numbers of widely dispersed movers who are *not* influenced by the prevailing social structures of their destinations, either before or after the physical move is completed. Yet, acculturation is as real as enculturation, especially among the young. Ecology affects life-style (Adams, 1977) and some movers are attracted to new locations because of their perception of and preference for the beliefs and values held by persons at these locations (Zelinsky, 1973). Moreover, mobility, in the sense of interregional migration, is not as substantial as popularly assumed. While it is true that two out of every five American families changed their place of residence between 1970 and 1975, of all the families that moved, three out of every five relocated in the same community, and one out of every five relocated in the same state. Only one out of every five relocated to a different state, and many of those who did move out of state moved to another state in the same region (Linden, 1976).

Existing empirical evidence raises doubts concerning the assumption that the United States is losing its geographic differences and becoming a mass, homogeneous society. For instance, Glenn and Simmons (1967) examined ten national polls covering a period 1950 to 1961. These polls included questions on religion, morals, social and ethnic, work, political issues and other values and beliefs. The conclusion was that regions have actually *diverged* in a large number of attitudes because of differing rates of change among regions.

If, then, regionalism is persistent, the substantive question is the nature of regions. How do regions differ in life-styles, in consumption-related variables? How are they similar?

The literature characterizes the South as traditional and conservative, as a region that emphasizes the values of a rural, small-town kind of social system—values associated with an inward-looking, native-born population with few connections to the external world (Cash, 1941; Glenn and Simmons, 1967; Prunty, 1976; Wirth, 1964). Further, persons residing outside the South are said to hold strong, negative views of the South as a place to live (Gould and White, 1975; Hart, 1967). In contrast, the West frequently is characterized as a liberal, open and outward-looking society noted for its willingness to initiate new ideas (Glenn and Simmons, 1967; McWilliams, 1973). The East is viewed as liberal and cosmopolitan (Gould and White, 1967). As we have seen, Engel, Kollat and Blackwell (1973) characterized the Southwestern life-style as innovative, emphasizing casual dress, outdoor entertaining and unique forms of recreation; and they characterized the Midwest as conservative and holding inhibited attitudes toward new products.

Like the belief about U.S. homogenization, however, these characterizations often are impressionistic, nondata-based assumptions. Empirical evidence on the nature of regions clearly is needed to justify, replace or modify impressions. In this article we provide some of this evidence, and we also venture some conjecture about the relationships presented. We are aware of the dangers of making causal inferences from survey data—they are always tenuous. Nevertheless, we believe it is important to *think about* survey data, and we believe that it is worthwhile to speculate about sets of relationships as a source of hypotheses for further investigation.

THE STUDY

Self-administered questionnaires were sent to 2,000 men who were members of Market Facts' Consumer Mail Panel. As an incentive, respondents were promised a "nice gift." Completed questionnaires were returned by 1,491 of the men (75 percent). The mail-out sample had been balanced on major demographic variables; a demographic check of the returns showed that the responding group was a good quota sample of male household heads.

The questionnaire, intended to measure consumers' life-styles, contained approximately 150 attitude, interest and opinion items answered on a six-point agree–disagree scale. It also contained questions about frequency of participation in 100 activities, and frequency or amount of purchase of more than 100 products and services. Finally, it contained questions about possession of major durables, magazine and newspaper reading, radio listening, and TV viewing.

The activity, attitude, interest and opinion items were factor analyzed (principal components, varimax rotation). Items with loadings of at least .45 were selected to represent each of the 42 factors. And these items, along with all the purchasing and appliance ownership items, plus all the media items, were cross-tabulated by groups of states selected to represent five regions of the country.

The regions, and the states selected to typify them, were:

East: New York, New Jersey, Rhode Island, Massachusetts, and Connecticut (201 respondents)

South: Alabama, Georgia, Mississippi, and Louisiana (94 respondents)

Midwest: Ohio, Indiana, Illinois, Missouri, and Iowa (287 respondents)

Southwest: Arizona, New Mexico, Texas, Colorado, and Oklahoma (127 respondents)

West: Washington, Oregon, and California (207 respondents)

REGIONAL DIFFERENCES

East

The states selected to represent "The East" are all in the urbanized northeastern quadrant. Southeastern seaboard states were excluded, as were the more rural states of northern New England.

As might be expected, men from this metropolitan, cosmopolitan part of the country scored relatively high on a factor that represents interest in foreign travel (Table 1). As might also be expected, in view of the population density of this

Table 1. Interest in Foreign Travel, Guns and Hunting

Factor Name:	Percent Agree				
Foreign Travel	East	West	South	Southwest	Midwest
I would like to take a trip around the world (.71)*	70	66	61	62	71
I would like to spend a year in London or Paris (.61)	40	38	36	24	29
I like to visit places that are totally different from my home (.55)	79	75	63	65	73
Guns and Hunting					
There should be a gun in every home (.55)	30	41	71	56	41
Went hunting (at least once last year) (.46)	18	32	43	40	29

*Numbers in parentheses are factor loadings.

region, they scored relatively low on a factor that indicates strong interest in guns and hunting (also Table 1).

The guns and hunting data in Table 1 suggest some hypotheses about the complexities of the relationships between the geography of a region and the attitudes and behavior of the people who live there. Much of the Northeast is so urbanized that hunting in local fields is out of the question. Hunting is therefore a less common activity among Easterners, and one would expect that possession of firearms would be less common in the East as well. One might further expect that a lower rate of gun ownership would lead to a lower level of agreement with "There should be a gun in every home." Note that this statement is a general statement of social policy. It refers to possession of guns in general and makes no specific reference to hunting.

Men in the Northeast also differed from men in other parts of the country in consumption of products and use of media. These differences will be noted in descriptions of the psychological geography of other regions.

West

In view of the climate and terrain of the West Coast, it is not surprising that men who live in Washington, Oregon, or California are more likely than men who live in other regions to have gone camping, hiking, or backpacking within the past year (Table 2). While regional propensity to fresh air is of course well known to manufacturers of camping equipment, it is perhaps less obvious to marketers of products that might be tied to outdoor themes.

It is possible that the emphasis on nature indicated by the camping, hiking, backpacking data is at some level related to the relative de-emphasis on mouthwash and deodorant, and the relative emphasis on certain health-related foods (also Table 2). And it is possible that the relatively low penetration of instant coffee in the West is due in part to a perception that this product is artificial, not natural or real.

We do not advance these speculations with any great confidence, but we believe that this set of relationships at least raises the possibility that there is more to these consumption patterns than historical accident or local marketing events.

South

Table 3 shows that men in the South, as represented by Alabama, Georgia, Mississippi, and Louisiana, are by far the most enthusiastic proponents of traditional male-female roles. More than in any other region, the men there believe that a woman's place is in the home.

Men in the South have other very traditional attitudes as well. They place great emphasis on law and order, on community and family life, and on suppression of overt sex (Table 3).

The contrast between the attitudes of men in the South, on one hand, and attitudes of men in the East and the West, on the other, is particularly important. While absolute levels of agreement are high in all regions (a fact worth noting in itself), the contrast between the coasts and the South suggests that mass media material acceptable in the region of origin may be unacceptable in other regions of the country. This conclusion applies to television program content; to the content of books, films and magazines; and of course to advertising.

Table 2. Western Pattern

Outdoor Activities			Percent Agree		
(At least once last year)	West	East	South	Southwest	Midwest
Camping (.69)	49	28	31	42	37
Hiking (.64)	59	49	47	45	43
Backpacking (.59)	16	8	7	5	4
Picnic (.49)	79	78	65	73	79
Mouthwash & Deodorant					
Everyone should use a deodorant (.65)	78	78	85	88	81
Everyone should use a mouthwash to help control bad breath (.51)	56	64	80	64	67
Use Once a Week or More					
Mouthwash	40	48	62	54	47
Men's Cologne	55	58	72	71	61
Yogurt	11	9	2	3	4
Cottage Cheese	40	27	17	30	41
Vitamin Tablets	44	36	21	35	30
Instant Coffee	31	40	33	24	36
Regular Coffee	72	59	63	66	58

Table 3.   Traditional Attitudes Characteristic of the South

Percent Agree

Traditional Family Ideology	South	East	West	Southwest	Midwest
A woman's place is in the home (.70)	66	43	45	59	56
The working world is no place for a woman (.68)	32	16	18	26	28
Men are smarter than women (.57)	46	31	32	42	38
The father should be the boss in the house (.56)	85	71	77	83	77
Law and Order					
Police should use whatever force is necessary to maintain law and order (.64)	83	74	74	79	73
I am in favor of very strict enforcement of all laws (.64)	95	87	85	85	88
Communism is the greatest peril in the world today (.50)	69	53	48	57	56
Community Activities (At least once last year)					
Worked on a community project (.71)	50	39	31	34	34
Did volunteer work (.71)	51	44	41	49	47
Went to a club meeting (.67)	63	67	55	50	61
Influential					
I am influential in my neighborhood (.66)	52	39	38	42	42
My friends and neighbors often come to me for advice (.63)	67	60	63	61	54
Children					
When making important family decisions, consideration of the children should come first (.66)	62	49	48	50	51
Children are the most important thing in a marriage (.58)	64	52	42	46	53
Sex					
TV commercials place too much emphasis on sex (.68)	76	67	64	74	70
There is too much emphasis on sex today (.66)	81	72	68	72	79

Southwest

When compared with men in other parts of the country, men in the Southwest (as here defined) are low in interest in foreign travel (Table 1); and, along with men in the Southeast, they are high in interest in guns and hunting (Table 1); and low in interest in booze (Table 4).

Men in the Southwest are relatively heavy readers of the Sunday paper, the daily morning paper and *National Geographic;* relatively light readers of the

Table 4.   Do-It-Yourself Activities, Alcohol Consumption and
Newspaper Reading in the Southwest

			Percent Agree		
Do-It-Yourself	Southwest	East	West	South	Midwest
Worked on a do-it-yourself project at least once last year (.61)	82	77	83	70	81
I am good at fixing mechanical things (.61)	78	77	73	63	71
Alcohol					
A drink at the end of the day is a perfect way to unwind (.79)	29	40	37	30	38
Had a cocktail before dinner (at least once last year) (.78)	53	79	77	59	75
Had wine with dinner (at least once last year) (.51)	49	70	72	38	62
Drink (once a week or more often)					
Domestic wine	8	15	28	5	16
Blended Whiskey	7	16	13	4	13
Scotch	2	12	8	5	7
Newspaper Reading					
Sunday paper (4+ issues in past 4 weeks)	74	73	65	63	69
Morning paper (9+ issues in past 10 days)	37	34	30	31	30
Evening paper (9+ issues in past 10 days)	39	54	35	48	52

daily evening paper (also Table 4). Whether any of this constitutes "unique forms of recreation" suggested in Engel et al. (1973) is a very difficult question to answer indeed.

What about the characterization that decision making in the Southwest is less rigid and more innovative than the "conservative, inhibited" attitude toward new products characteristic of the Midwest? (Engel et al., 1973). The Life-Style questionnaire contained some items that bear upon innovativeness in decision making. The data (Table 5) show no indication that men in the Southwest are more innovative than men in other parts of the country, and they show no indication that men in the Midwest are more conservative or inhibited. With the exception of one item specific to food, the highest innovativeness scores come from the East.

We make this point, not to belittle Engel, Kollat and Blackwell's fine text, but rather to illustrate how vague our models of consumer behavior really are. Engel, Kollat and Blackwell's description of regional differences in life-style is intuitively appealing, yet, according to all available evidence, it is substantially incorrect. We know so little about consumer behavior that a very wide range of findings can have intuitive appeal, whether they are correct or not.

Table 5.   Regional Differences in Innovativeness

Percent Agree

	Southwest	Midwest	South	East	West
I like to try new foods that (have not tasted before)	61	66	64	69	73
I like to buy new and different things	60	68	63	70	66
I am usually among the first to try new products	22	30	23	38	37
I am the kind of person who will try anything once	39	53	56	65	56

Midwest

Men in the Midwest differed from men in other parts of the country on only one life-style dimension: They indicated unusually high levels of visiting relatives, and of entertaining in the home (Table 6). Note that the practice of visiting relatives, and of entertaining at home, is surprisingly rare in the South.

The Midwest is also distinguished by relatively high levels of ownership of water softeners and of color TV sets, but not of other appliances (Table 6). It is hypothesized that the appliance ownership pattern reflects a complex combination of need (water softeners in the Midwest), tradition (freezers in the South) and age of existing housing (automatic dishwashers and garbage disposals in the West and Southwest).

REPLICATION

One must always beware of relationships obtained by ransacking a computer full of data. Even when the relationship is intuitively appealing, there is always the possibility that it was obtained by chance.

The regional differences reported above were found in a survey conducted in 1975. Essentially the same questionnaire was administered one year later to a demographically matched but entirely independent sample. How many of the regional differences found in the 1975 survey would reappear in a second survey one year later?

First the good news. Although some absolute levels of agreement changed between 1975 and 1976, *all* of the relationships cited above reappeared in the second study.

This is not to say that all of the regional differences discovered in the 1975 survey reappeared when the study was repeated. The 1975 survey indicated that Eastern men are less interested in sports than are men in other parts of the country, that Western men are more interested in cooking and baking, that Southern men are unusually concerned about how much salt and how much

Table 6. Visiting and Entertaining; Appliance Ownership

Percent Agree

	Midwest	East	West	South	Southwest
Visiting and Entertaining					
(Nine or more times last year. . . .)					
Visited relatives (.58)	79	71	63	69	67
Entertain people in my home (.51)	61	56	61	45	47
Product			*Percent Owning*		
Water Softener	21	6	14	1	9
Color TV Set	83	79	83	65	77
Freezer	62	48	58	68	60
Automatic Dishwasher	42	44	56	42	56
Garbage Disposal	35	11	50	8	44
Room Air Conditioner	42	45	28	45	39

cholesterol they eat, that Southwestern men are most likely to be do-it-yourselfers, and that Midwestern men are unusually concerned about dirt and germs. All of these relationships evaporated in 1976.

CROSS-VALIDATION

Even replication does not fully prove a point. The two surveys described above had a lot in common—questionnaire design, sampling procedure, question wording, even the specific states used to define the regions. It is always possible that a replicated finding might disappear with a different questionnaire, a different sample of respondents, or a different definition of the independent variable.

Target Group Index, a large-scale syndicated survey, contains many questions that touch upon the topics covered by the Life Style study. However, the questions are all worded differently, the questionnaire format is entirely different, responses are obtained via personal interview with a large probability sample, and the TGI definition of geographic regions is different from the definition employed in the Life Style research.

The availability of the TGI data makes possible a cross-validation of the Life Style findings on those topics in which the two studies overlap. The overlap is far from complete; otherwise the Life Style study would be superfluous. But a look at the overlap that does exist is informative. We are indebted to Axion Market Research, the owners of the TGI data, for permission to publish the comparisons presented here.

The TGI study confirms that men in the East are more interested in foreign travel than are men in other parts of the country. It shows that more of them have taken a trip outside the United States within the past three years, that more of them have a valid passport, and that more of them read the travel section of the Sunday newspaper.

TGI affirms that men in the East do relatively little hunting. It also corroborates the inference that fewer of them possess guns. It says nothing, one way or the other, about attitudes toward guns in general.

TGI shows that Western men are particularly apt to engage in rugged outdoor activities—more camping and more backpacking, as in the Life Style study. It also shows lower use of mouthwash and deodorant in the West, and higher use of yogurt, cottage cheese, and regular coffee. As in the Life Style findings, Western use of instant coffee was found to be relatively low.

According to TGI, men in the Southeast are more likely to belong to a church board, but they are *less* likely to belong to a fraternal order or a veterans' club, to have addressed a public meeting or to be active in local and civic issues than are men in other parts of the country. This finding helps to refine and focus, rather than totally cross-validate, the Life Style conclusion about high participation in community activities.

The TGI data reveal that men in the Southeast are more likely to have purchased children's toys and are more likely to be regular watchers of *The Waltons* and *The Wonderful World of Disney*. Both these findings support the Life Style conclusions with respect to Southern men's orientation toward children. And, according to TGI, Southeastern men are relatively infrequent readers of *Playboy*, *Penthouse*, and *Oui*, supporting the Life Style finding with respect to Southern attitudes toward expression of overt interest in sex. Nothing could be found in the TGI data that would either support or deny the idea that Southern men are the staunchest advocates of the notion that a woman's place is in the home.

TGI also shows that Southwestern men, along with Southeastern men, are relatively low consumers of most forms of alcohol, and it validates the appliance ownership pattern shown in Table 6.

In sum, *all* of the regional differences that replicated also cross-validated wherever overlapping data could be found to test them.

UNIFORMITIES

The focus so far has been on regional *differences*. Quite a number of the Life Style factors showed no regional differences, or showed mixed differences—variation on some items but not on others. Items which showed little regional variation are presented in Table 7.

Consumers, both during a recession and when the economy was moving upward, differed little on matters dealing with finances. They said they were concerned with dependability and prices and that they were not spendthrifts. A majority appeared optimistic about future income.

A majority in all regions reported working under pressure. Even so, they

Table 7.   Uniformities

			Percent Agree		
Item	East	West	South	Southwest	Midwest
I find myself checking prices even on small items	77	76	79	76	78
I will probably have more money to spend next year than I have now	55	57	56	51	57
I pretty much spend for today and let tomorrow bring what it will	25	30	27	24	23
When buying appliances I am more concerned with dependability than price	94	93	94	89	90
I work under a great deal of pressure most of the time	61	63	60	58	58
I get more headaches than most people	18	17	18	17	14
I wish I could leave my present life and do something entirely different	30	29	31	30	31
I stay home most evenings	77	80	80	83	79
Our home is furnished for comfort, not style	91	93	93	89	94
Many companies are taking advantage of the energy crisis to increase their profits unfairly	90	87	86	89	86

seemed satisfied with life and willing to stay home in the evenings. Finally, almost everyone in all regions agreed that companies were taking advantage of the energy crisis.

These basic similarities are important because they represent the thoughts and behaviors Americans have in common, and because they form the perspective against which regional differences can be addressed.

SUMMARY AND CONCLUSIONS

This article demonstrates the existence and nature of regional differences in activities, attitudes, interests and opinions—life-styles—that appear to be directly related, in complex ways, to consumer behavior. The differences are not large in absolute terms, but when one considers the fact that each of the regional samples contained individuals from all parts of the adult age spectrum; from virtually every education, occupation and income level; and from cities, suburbs, small towns and farms—it is remarkable that regional differences persisted.

As expected, the South can be characterized as traditional, the West as relatively liberal, and the East as cosmopolitan and innovative. However, expected characterizations of the Southwest and Midwest did not appear.

We do not defend these particular regional differences as being overwhelmingly important in setting marketing policy. But we do contend that differences of this kind are real, and are important enough to warrant serious, detailed empirical investigation.

REFERENCES

Adams, Ronald J. (1977), "Degree of Urbanization and Its Impact on Consumer Behavior," unpublished Ph.D. dissertation, University of Georgia.

Cash, W. J. (1941), *The Mind of the South,* New York: Knopf.

Engel, James F., Kollat, David T., and Blackwell, Roger D. (1973), *Consumer Behavior,* 2nd ed. New York: Holt, Rinehart and Winston.

Gillin, John (1955), "National and Regional Cultural Values in the United States," *Social Forces* 34: 107–113 (December).

Glenn, Norval D., and Simmons, J. L. (1967), "Are Regional Cultural Differences Diminishing?" *Public Opinion Quarterly* 31: 176–193 (Summer).

Gould, Peter R., and White, Rodney (1975), *Mental Maps,* Baltimore, Md.: Penguin.

Hart, John Fraser (1967), *The Southeastern United States,* Princeton, N.J.: Van Nostrand.

Klapper, Joseph T. (1960), *The Effects of Mass Communication,* New York: Free Press.

Kotler, Philip (1976), *Marketing Management,* 3rd ed., Englewood Cliffs, N.J.: Prentice-Hall.

Labovitz, Sanford I. (1962), "Regional Analysis of the United States," unpublished M.A. thesis, University of Texas, Austin.

Linden, Fabian (1976), "The Geography of Demand, 1975," *Conference Board Record* 13 (August).

Mayo, Selz C. (1964), "Social Change, Social Movements and the Disappearing Sectional South," *Social Forces* 43: 1–10 (October).

McWilliams, Carey (1973), *Southern California, an Island on the Land,* Santa Barbara, Calif.: Peregrine Books.

Merrill, Francis E. (1957), *Society and Culture,* Englewood Cliffs, N.J.: Prentice-Hall.

Prunty, Merle C. (1976), "Two American Souths: The Past and the Future," keynote address, 31st Annual Meeting, Southeastern and Middle Atlantic Division of the Association of American Geographers in Fredericksburg, Va. (November 21).

Tucker, W. T. (1964), *The Social Context of Economic Behavior,* New York: Holt, Rinehart and Winston.

Wirth, Louis (1964), "Urbanism as a Way of Life," in Louis Wirth, ed., *On Cities and Social Life,* Chicago: University of Chicago Press.

Zelinsky, Wilbur (1973), *The Cultural Geography of the United States,* Englewood Cliffs, N.J.: Prentice-Hall.

OTHER SERIES OF INTEREST FROM JAI PRESS INC.

Consulting Editor for Economics: Paul Uselding, University of Illinois

ADVANCES IN ACCOUNTING
Series Editor: George H. Sorter, New York University

ADVANCES IN APPLIED MICRO-ECONOMICS
Series Editor: V. Kerry Smith, Resources for the Future, Washington, D.C.

ADVANCES IN DOMESTIC AND INTERNATIONAL AGRIBUSINESS MANAGEMENT
Series Editor: Ray A. Goldberg, Graduate School of Business Administration, Harvard University

ADVANCES IN ECONOMETRICS
Series Editors: R. L. Basmann, Texas A & M University, and George F. Rhodes, Jr., Colorado State University

ADVANCES IN THE ECONOMICS OF ENERGY AND RESOURCES
Series Editor: John R. Moroney, Tulane University

APPLICATIONS OF MANAGEMENT SCIENCE
Series Editor: Randall L. Schultz, Krannert Graduate School of Management, Purdue University

RESEARCH IN CORPORATE SOCIAL PERFORMANCE AND POLICY
Series Editor: Lee E. Preston, School of Management and Center for Policy Studies, State University of New York - Buffalo

RESEARCH IN ECONOMIC ANTHROPOLOGY
Series Editor: George Dalton, Northwestern University

RESEARCH IN ECONOMIC HISTORY
Series Editor: Paul Uselding, University of Illinois

RESEARCH IN EXPERIMENTAL ECONOMICS
Series Editor: Vernon L. Smith, College of Business and Public Administration, University of Arizona

RESEARCH IN FINANCE
Series Editor: Haim Levy, School of Business, The Hebrew University

RESEARCH IN HEALTH ECONOMICS
Series Editor: Richard M. Scheffler, George Washington University

RESEARCH IN HUMAN CAPITAL AND DEVELOPMENT
Series Editor: Ismail Sirageldin, The Johns Hopkins University

RESEARCH IN INTERNATIONAL BUSINESS AND FINANCE
Series Editor: Robert G. Hawkins, Graduate School of Business Administration, New York University

RESEARCH IN LABOR ECONOMICS
Series Editor: Ronald G. Ehrenberg, School of Industrial and Labor Relations, Cornell University

RESEARCH IN LAW AND ECONOMICS
Series Editor: Richard O. Zerbe, Jr., SMT Program, University of Washington

RESEARCH IN MARKETING
Series Editor: Jagdish N. Sheth, University of Illinois

RESEARCH IN ORGANIZATIONAL BEHAVIOR
Series Editors: Barry M. Staw, Graduate School of Management, Northwestern
   University, and L. L. Cummings, Graduate School of Business, University of
   Wisconsin

RESEARCH IN PHILOSOPHY AND TECHNOLOGY
Series Editor: Paul T. Durbin, Center for Science and Culture, University of
   Delaware

RESEARCH IN POLITICAL ECONOMY
Series Editor: Paul Zarembka, State University of New York - Buffalo

RESEARCH IN POPULATION ECONOMICS
Series Editors: Julian L. Simon, University of Illinois, and Julie DaVanzo,
   The Rand Corporation

RESEARCH IN PUBLIC POLICY AND MANAGEMENT
Series Editor: Colin Blaydon, Institute of Policy Studies and Public Affairs,
   Duke University

RESEARCH IN URBAN ECONOMICS
Series Editor: J. Vernon Henderson, Brown University

*ALL VOLUMES IN THESE ANNUAL SERIES ARE AVAILABLE AT
INSTITUTIONAL AND INDIVIDUAL RATES.
PLEASE ASK FOR DETAILED BROCHURE ON EACH SERIES*

A 10 percent discount will be granted on all institutional standing orders placed
directly with the publisher. Standing Orders will be filled automatically upon
publication and will continue until cancelled. Please indicate with which volume
Standing Order is to begin.

 **JAI PRESS INC.**
P.O. Box 1678
165 West Putnam Avenue
Greenwich, Connecticut 06830

(203) 661-7602   Cable Address: JAIPUBL

Research in Marketing

A Research Annual

Series Editor: **Jagdish N. Sheth, Department of Business Administration, University of Illinois.**

Volume 1. **Published 1978 Cloth** **333 pages** **Institutions: $ 27.50**
ISBN 0-89232-041-9 **Individuals: $ 14.00**

CONTENTS: **Research in Productivity Measurement for Marketing Decisions,** Louis P. Bucklin, University of California - Berkeley. **Simulation of Risk Attitudes in Joint Decision Making by Marketing Firms in Competitive Markets,** Ralph L. Day, Indiana University and Jehoshua Eliashberg, University of Missouri. **Interpretative Versus Descriptive Research,** Ernest Dichter, Ernest Dichter Associates International, Ltd. **The Household as a Production Unit,** Michael Etgar, State University of New York - Buffalo. **Some New Types of Fractional Factorial Designs for Marketing Experiements,** Paul E. Green, University of Pennsylvania, J. Douglas Carroll, Bell Laboratories and Frank J. Carmone, Drexel University. **Optimizing Research Budgets: A Theoretical Approach,** Flemming Hansen, A.I.M., Copenhagen. **Choosing the Best Advertising Appropriation When Appropriations Interact Over Time,** Haim Levy, The Hebrew University and Julian L. Simon, University of Illinois, **Advertising and Socialization,** John G. Myers, University of California - Berkeley. **Multi-Product Growth Models,** Robert A. Peterson, University of Texas - Austin and Vijay Mahajan, Ohio State University. **Advocacy Advertising: Corporate External Communications and Public Policy,** S. Prakash Sethi, University of Texas - Dallas. **An Empirical-Simulation Approach to Competition,** Randall L. Schultz, Purdue University and Joe A. Dodson, Jr., Northwestern University. **Field Theory Applied to Consumer Behavior,** Arch G. Woodside, University of South Carolina and William O. Bearden, University of Alabama.

Volume 3. **October 1979** **Cloth** **425 pages** **Institutions: $ 32.50**
ISBN 0-89232-060-5 **Individuals: $ 16.50**

CONTENTS: **Paradigms for Marketing Theory,** James M. Carman, University of California - Berkeley. **A Model-Based Methodology for Assessing Market Response for New Industrial Products,** Jean-Marie Choffray and Gary L. Lilien, Massachusetts Institute of Technology. **A Typology of Consumer Needs,** Janice G. Hanna, University of Calgary. **On Construction of Mathematical Models in Marketing,** Vithala R. Rao, Cornell University. **Consumption of Mass Communication,** Preben Sepstrup, Aarhus School of Economics and Business. **How to Ask Questions About Drinkers and Sex: Response Effects to Threatening Questions,** Seymore Sudman, University of Illinois, Norman Bradburn, NORC, Edward Blair and William Locander, University of Houston. **What Can Be Done About Interviewer Bias?,** Donald S. Tull and Larry E. Richards, University of Oregon. **Temporal Dimension of Consumer Behavior: An Exploration with Time-Budget,** M. Venkatesan, University of Oregon and John Arndt, Norwegian School of Business and Economics. **Marketing Mix Decision Rules for Nonprofit Organizations,** Charles B. Weinberg, Stanford University. **Testing Stochastic Models of Consumer Choice Behavior: A Methodology for Attacking the Many-to-One Mapping Problems,** R. Dale Wilson, Pennsylvania State University. **A Multivariate Stochastic Model of Brand Choice and Market Behavior,** Fred Zufryden, University of Southern California.

JAI PRESS INC., P.O. Box 1678, 165 West Putnam Avenue, Greenwich, Connecticut 06830.

Telephone: 203-661-7602 **Cable Address: JAIPUBL**

Research in Law and Economics

A Research Annual

Series Editor: **Richard O. Zerbe, Jr., SMT Program, University of Washington.**

The contributions to be included in this series represent original research by scholars internationally known in their fields. A few articles generally based on outstanding dissertations by younger scholars will also be included. The contributions will include theoretical, empirical and legal studies considered to belong to the law-economics genre.

Volume 1.   April 1979   Cloth   285 pages   Institutions: $ 27.50
ISBN 0-89232-028-1   Individuals: $ 14.00

CONTENTS: State Occupational Licensing Provisions and Quality of Service: The Real Estate Business, Sidney L. Carroll and Robert J. Gaston, University of Tennessee, Knoxville. **Dynamic Elements of Regulation: The Case of Occupational Licensure,** William D. White, University of Illinois, Chicago Circle. **Airline Performance Under Regulation: Canada vs. the United States,** William A. Jordon, York University. **Airline Market Shares vs. Capacity Shares and the Possibility of Short-Run Loss Equilibria,** James C. Miller, III, American Enterprise Institute flr Public Policy Research. **The Political Rationality of Federal Transportation Policy,** Ann F. Friedlaender and Richard de Neufville, Massachusetts Institute of Technology. **A New Remedy for the Free Rider Problem? Flies in the Ointment,** Roger C. Kormendi, University of Chicago. **Toward a Theory of Government Advertising,** Kenneth W. Clarkson, University of Miami School of Law, and Robert Tollison, Virginia Polytechnic Institute and State University. **Protecting the Right to Be Served by Public Utilities,** Victor P. Goldberg, University of California, Davis. **The Role and Resolution of the Compensation Principle in Society: Part One - The Role,** Warren J. Samuels, Michigan State University, and Nicholas Mercuro, University of New Orleans. **The Dynamics of Traditional Rate Regulation,** Patrick C. Mann, Regional Research Institute, West Virginia University. **Price Discrimination and Peak-Load Pricing Subject to Rate of Return Constraint,** David L. McNichol, U.S. Treasury Department. **Index.**

Supplement 1 to Research in Law and Economics

Economics of Nonproprietary Organizations

Editor: **Kenneth W. Clarkson and Donald L. Martin, Law and Economics Center, University of Miami.**

September 1979 Cloth   Ca. 330 pages   Institutions: $ 28.50
ISBN 0-89232-132-6   Individuals: $ 14.50

CONTENTS: Series Editor's Preface. Editor's Introduction.

MANAGERIAL CONSTRAINTS. **Managerial Behavior in Nonproprietary Organizations,** Kenneth W. Clarkson, University of Miami. **The Economics of Seat Pricing: Rose Bowl vs. Hong Kong,** Steven Cheung, University of Washington. **Delivered Comments,** Ross D. Eckert, University of Southern California and H.E. Frech, University of California - Santa Barbara. **Discussion.** MUTUAL ORGANIZATIONS. **Health Insurance: Private, Mutuals or Government,** H.E. Frech, University of California - Santa Barbara. **The Union as a Nonproprietary Firm,** Donald Martin, University of Miami. **Delivered Comments,** Louis DeAlessi, University of Miami and Walter Oi, University of Rochester. **Discussion.** CHARITABLE ORGANIZATIONS. **Charity and Nonproprietary Organizations,** Earl Thompson, University of California - Los Angeles. **Private Goods, Collective Goods: The Role of the Non-Profit Sector,** Burton Weisbrod, University of Wisconsin. **Delivered Comments,** Mark Pauly, Northwestern University and Armen A. Alchian, University of California - Los Angeles. **Discussion.**

GOVERNMENTAL ORGANIZATIONS. **Is There a Theory of Public Organizations?**, *C. M. Lindsay*. **Producing Knowledge in Nonproprietary Organizations**, *Roland McKean*. **Delivered Comments**, *Andrew Whinston and James Buchanan*. **Discussion**. **General Discussion**. **Index**.

Volume 2.	Spring 1980	Cloth	Ca. 250 pages	Institutions:	$ 27.50
ISBN 0-89232-131-8				Individuals:	$ 14.00

CONTENTS: **Economic Analysis of Federal Election Campaign Regulation.** *Burton A. Abrams and Russel F. Settle, University of Delaware.* **The Quality of Legal Services: Peer Review, Insurance and Disciplinary Evidence,** *Sidney L. Carrol and Robert J. Gaston, University of Tennessee.* **Price Discrimination in the Municipal Electric Industry,** *Daniel R. Hollas, University of Michigan and Thomas S. Friedland, University of Illinois.* **The Resolution of the Compensation Problem in Society,** *Warren J. Samuels and Nicholas Mercuro, Michigan State University.* **Monopoly Profits and Social Losses,** *Levis A. Kochin, University of Washington.* **The Evaluation of Rules for Making Collective Decisions: A Reply to Kormendi,** *T. Nicholas Tideman, Virginia Polytechnic Institute and State University.* **Tort Liability for Negligent Inspection by Insurers,** *Victor P. Goldberg, University of California - Davis.* **The Economics of Property Rights: A Review of the Evidence,** *Louis De Alessi, University of Miami.* **The Problem of Social Cost in Retrospect,** *Richard O. Zerbe, University of Washington.*

A 10 percent discount will be granted on all institutional standing orders placed directly with the publisher. Standing orders will be filled automatically upon publication and will continue until cancelled. Please indicate with which volume Standing Order is to begin.

▰Ai JAI PRESS INC., P.O. Box 1678, 165 West Putnam Avenue, Greenwich, Connecticut 06830.

Telephone: 203-661-7602   Cable Address: JAIPUBL

Research in Corporate Social Performance and Policy

A Research Annual

Series Editor: **Lee E. Preston, School of Management and Center for Policy Studies, State University of New York – Buffalo**

Volume 1.   Published 1978   Cloth   306 pages   Institutions: $ 27.50
ISBN 0-89232-069-9   Individuals: $ 14.00

CONTENTS: Introduction, *Lee E. Preston.* **Corporate Social Performance and Policy: A Synthetic Framework for Research and Analysis,** *Lee E. Preston, State University of New York - Buffalo.* **An Analytical Framework for Making Cross-Cultural Comparisons of Business Responses to Social Pressures: The Case of the United States and Japan,** *S. Prakash Sethi, University of Texas - Austin.* **Research on Patterns of Corporate Response to Social Change,** *James E. Post, Boston University.* **Organizational Goals and Control Systems: Internal and External Considerations,** *Kenneth J. Arrow, Harvard University.* **The Corporate Response Process,** *Raymond A. Bauer, Harvard University.* **Auditing Corporate Social Performance: The Anatomy of a Social Research Project,** *William C. Frederick, University of Pittsburgh.* **Managerial Motivation and Ideology,** *Joseph W. McGuire, University of California - Irvine.* **Empirical Studies of Corporate Social Performance and Policy: A Survey of Problems and Results,** *Ramon J. Aldag, University of Wisconsin and Kathryn M. Bartol, Syracuse University.* **Social Policy as Business Policy,** *George A. Steiner and John F. Steiner, University of California - Los Angeles.* **Government Regulation: Process and Substantive Impacts,** *Robert Chatov, State University of New York - Buffalo.* **Managerial Theory vs. Class Theory of Corporate Capitalism,** *Maurice Zeitlin, University of California - Los Angeles.* **Appendix A: The Management Process Audit Manual,** *Raymond A. Bauer, Harvard University, L. Terry Cauthorn and Ranne P. Warner.* **Appendix B: Canadian Corporate Social Responsibility Survey,** *Donald W. Kelly, Public Affairs International Ltd.* **Appendix C: Guidline for Social Performance Case Studies,** *Donald W. Kelly, Public Affairs International Ltd., R. Terrence McTaggant, Niagara Institute.*

Volume 2.   September 1979   Cloth   Ca. 320 pages   Institutions: $ 27.50
ISBN 0-89232-133-4   Individuals: $ 14.00

TENTATIVE CONTENTS: **The Corporation in the Political Arena,** *Edwin M. Epstein, University of California - Berkeley.* **Social Responsibility in Large Electric Utility Firms: The Case For Philanthropy,** *Ferdinand K. Levy, Georgia Institute of Technology and Gloria M. Shatto, Trinity University.* **The Political Character of Business in an Organizational Regime,** *Malcolm D. Schlusberg, Syracuse University.* **Corporate Political Influence on Regulatory Performance,** *Steven N. Brenner, Portland State University.* **The Strength of the American Business Creed,** *David Vogel, University of California - Berkeley.* **Social Performance of the Multinational Corporation,** *David H. Blake, University of Pittsburgh.* **Social Performance of International Infant Formula Industry,** *James E. Post, Boston University.* **Corporate Social Performance in Germany,** *Meinolf Dierkes, International Institute for Environment and Society, Berlin.* **Corporate Social Performance in Reporting in France,** *Francoise Rey, ESSEC, Cergy, France.* **Corporate Response to Unemployment: A British Perspective,** *Keith MacMillan, Henley, Oxon, England.* **A Theory of the State-Owned Firm in a Democracy,** *R. Joseph Monsen and Kenneth D. Walters, University of Washington.*

Research In Organizational Behavior

An Annual Series of Analytical Essays and Critical Reviews

Series Editor: **Barry M. Staw, Graduate School of Management Northwestern University.**

Volume 1. Published 1979 Cloth 478 pages Institutions: $ 32.50
ISBN 0-89232-045-1 Individuals: $ 16.50

CONTENTS: **Editorial Statement,** Barry M. Staw, Northwestern University. **Beyond Open System Models of Organization,** Louis R. Pondy, University of Illinois and Ian I. Mitroff, University of Pittsburgh. **Cognitive Processes in Organizations,** Karl E. Weick, Cornell University. **Organizational Learning: Implications for Organizational Design,** Robert Duncan and Andrew Weiss, Northwestern University. **Organizational Design and Adult Learning,** Douglas T. Hall and Cynthia V. Fukami, Northwestern University. **Organizational Structure, Attitudes and Behaviors,** Chris J. Berger, Purdue University and L. L. Cummings, University of Wisconsin - Madison. **Toward a Theory of Organizational Socialization,** John Van Maanen and Edgar H. Schein, Massachusetts Institute of Technology. **Participation in Decision-Making: One More Look,** Edwin A. Locke and David M. Schweiger, University of Maryland. **Leadership: Some Empirical Generalizations and New Research Directions,** Robert J. House and Mary L. Baetz, University of Toronto. **Performance Appraisal Effectiveness: Its Assessment and Determinants,** Jeffery S. Kane, Western Electric Company and Edward E. Lawler, III, University of Michigan. **Bibliography. Index.**

Series Editors: **Barry M. Staw, Graduate School of Management, Northwestern University, and Larry L. Cummings, Graduate School of Business, University of Wisconsin.**

Volume 2. Fall 1979 Cloth 450 pages Institutions: $ 32.50
ISBN 0-89232-099-0 Individuals: $ 16.50

CONTENTS: **Construct Validity in Organizational Behavior,** Donald P. Schwab, University of Wisconsin. **Rationality and Justification in Organizational Life,** Barry M. Staw, Northwestern University. **Time and Work: Towards an Integrative Perspective,** Ralph Katz, Massachusetts Institute of Technology. **Collective Bargaining and Organizational Behavior Research,** Thomas A. Kochan, Cornell University. **Behavioral Research on Unions and Union Management Systems,** Jeanne Brett, Northern University. **Institutionalization of Planned Organizational Change,** Paul S. Goodman and Max Bazerman, Carnegie-Mellon University and Edward Conlon, Georgia Institute of Technology. **Work Design in the Organizational Context,** Greg R. Oldham, University of Illinois and J. Richard Hackman, Yale University. **Organizational Growth Types: Lessons from Small Institutions,** A. C. Filley and R. J. Aldag, University of Wisconsin. **Interorganizational Processes and Organizational Boundary Activities,** J. Stacy Adams, University of North Carolina.

JAI PRESS INC., P.O. Box 1678, 165 West Putnam Avenue, Greenwich, Connecticut 06830.

Telephone: 203-661-7602 Cable Address: JAIPUBL